MERTON &
CONFUCIANISM

MERTON &
CONFUCIANISM

RITES, RIGHTEOUSNESS AND
INTEGRAL HUMANITY

Edited by Patrick F. O'Connell

FONS VITAE

The Fons Vitae Thomas Merton Series
Merton & Sufism: The Untold Story, 1999
Merton & Hesychasm: The Prayer of the Heart, 2003
Merton & Judaism: Holiness in Words, 2003
Merton & Buddhism: Wisdom, Emptiness,
and Everyday Mind, 2007
Merton & The Tao: Dialogues with John C. H. Wu
and the Ancient Sages, 2013
Merton & The Protestant Tradition, 2016
Merton & Indigenous Wisdom, 2019
Merton & Confucianism: Rites, Righteousness
and Integral Humanity, 2021

First published in 2021 by
Fons Vitae
49 Mockingbird Valley Drive
Louisville, KY 40207
http://www.fonsvitae.com

Copyright Fons Vitae 2021

Library of Congress Control Number: 2021932291

ISBN 978-1941610-848

Grateful acknowledgment is due to: the trustees of the Thomas Merton
Legacy Trust for permission to include previously unpublished material
by Thomas Merton (Copyright © 2021 by The Trustees of the Thomas
Merton Legacy Trust); Learn 25 for permission to publish transcrip-
tions of audio recordings of Merton conferences; John Charles Sih
for permission to publish the letters of Paul Sih to Thomas Merton;
Columbia University Press for permission to reprint the essay "Thomas
Merton, Matteo Ricci and Confucianism" by Wm. Theodore de Bary.

This book was typeset by Neville Blakemore, Jr.

Printed in Canada

"If a man be really bent on human-heartedness, there is no wickedness in him . . . . A human-hearted ruler wants security for himself, and so he makes others secure. He wishes to get a wider sphere of influence, and so he extends other people's spheres of influence. The ability to draw parallels from matters very near to oneself may be called the art of human-heartedness. . . . The man bent on public service, if he be human-hearted, will under no circumstances seek to live at the expense of his human-heartedness. There are occasions when he will lay down his life to preserve his human-heartedness."

Confucius, *Analects*

"It is only the man who is entirely real in this world who has the capacity to give full development to his human nature. If he has that capacity, it follows that he has the capacity to give full development to other men's human nature. If he has that capacity, it follows that he has the capacity to give full development to the natures of all species of things. Thus it is possible for him to be assisting the transforming and nourishing work of Heaven-and-Earth. That being so, it is possible for him to be part of a trinity of Heaven, Earth and himself. . . . It is only the man who is completely real in the world, who can weave the fabric of the great basic strands in human society, who can establish the great foundations of this world, and who can understand the transforming and nourishing work of Heaven-and-Earth."

Confucius, *Doctrine of the Mean*

"The classic *Ju* philosophy of Confucius and his followers can be called a traditional personalism built on the basic social relationships and obligations that are essential to a humane life and that, when carried out as they should be, develop the human potentialities of each person in his relation to others. In fulfilling the commands of nature as manifested by tradition, which are essentially commands of love, man develops his own inner potential for love, understanding, reverence, and wisdom."

Thomas Merton, *The Way of Chuang Tzu*

"The whole philosophy of Kung is much more than a philosophy: it is a *wisdom*, that is to say, it is not a doctrine, but a *way of life* impregnated with truth. One only comes to know the doctrine by living the truth which it contains, and that truth is not a partial truth but the whole meaning of existence, both for the person and for the society to which he belongs. One can only fully live the Confucian doctrine by living in a religious society governed by a sacred ritual, which is a practical 'acting out' of the wisdom immanent in nature."

Thomas Merton, "Classic Chinese Thought"

"The Ox Mountain parable of Mencius: Note the importance of the 'night spirit' and the 'dawn breath' in restoring to life the forest that has been cut down. Even though the Ox Mountain forest has been cut to the ground, if the mountain is left to rest and recuperate in the night and the dawn, the trees will return. But men cut them down, cattle browse on the new shoots: no night spirit, no dawn breath – no rest, no renewal – and finally one is convinced that there never were any woods on the Ox Mountain. So, Mencius concludes, with human nature. Without the night spirit, the dawn breath, silence, passivity, rest, man's nature cannot be itself."

Thomas Merton, *Conjectures of a Guilty Bystander*

"In its original purity, the Confucian ideal is basically *personalistic*. The fundamental justification for filial piety is that our person is received as a gift from our parents and is to be fully developed out of gratitude toward them. Hence, the astounding fact that this filial piety is not simply a cult of the parent as such, but a development of one's own gifts in honor of the parents who gave them to us. . . . This basic attitude is said to be 'the foundation of virtue and the root of civilization.'"

Thomas Merton, "Christian Culture Needs Oriental Wisdom"

CONTENTS

THE FONS VITAE THOMAS MERTON SERIES   IX

THOMAS MERTON'S PRAYER   XI

INTRODUCTION
    Patrick F. O'Connell   XIII

ACKNOWLEDGEMENTS   XXX

PART I – SOURCES

THE THOMAS MERTON/PAUL SIH CORRESPONDENCE   3

MERTON'S READING NOTES ON CONFUCIANISM
    AND RELATED MATERIAL   81

CONFUCIANISM IN MERTON'S NOVITIATE CONFERENCES
    The Confucian *Analects* in Conferences on the Vows   161
    Novitiate Conferences on Confucianism
    and Chinese Culture   165

PART II – STUDIES

THOMAS MERTON AND CONFUCIAN RITES: "THE FIG LEAF
    FOR THE PARADISE CONDITION"
    John Wu, Jr.   215

"WISDOM CRIES THE DAWN DEACON": THOMAS MERTON
    AND "THE OX MOUNTAIN PARABLE"
    Paul M. Pearson   237

THOMAS MERTON, MATTEO RICCI, AND CONFUCIANISM
    Wm. Theodore de Bary   251

"A WAY OF LIFE IMPREGNATED WITH TRUTH":
    DID THOMAS MERTON UNDERVALUE CONFUCIANISM?
    Patrick F. O'Connell   267

MO TZU AND THOMAS MERTON
    Robert E. Daggy   291

INDEX   305

ABOUT THE EDITOR   336

This book is dedicated to Charles P. Farnsley who as mayor of Louisville governed during the life of Thomas Merton. He was deeply inspired by Confucian ideals and used them openly as a guiding orientation towards his dream of an enlightened society and harmonious world.

Owsley Brown III

THE FONS VITAE
THOMAS MERTON SERIES

Scholars, lay readers, and spiritual seekers in a broad spectrum of
religious theories and practices regard the Cistercian monk Thomas
Merton (1915-1968) as one of the most important spiritual writers
of the last half of the twentieth century. The late Ewert Cousins,
a Professor of Religion and the General Editor of the Crossroad
World Spirituality Series distinguished Merton as an "axial figure"
who bridged estrangements between religious and secular perspectives. Dr. Cousins opined that Merton is more important today than
in his lifetime. He is an iconic figure who modeled inter-religious
dialogue for those who seek a common ground of respect and
understanding for the varied ways in which human beings realize
the sacred as a foundation for their lives. Merton's life and writing remain a bridge for others to cross and engage one another in
the pursuit of common moral values that acknowledge the dignity
of all earth's inhabitants. Merton's inclusive intellect, expansive
religious imagination, and his heart's zeal for unity among peoples
were the fruit of his monastic inner work. In his personal journal
for April 28, 1957 he highlighted these dimensions of his vocation
as a monastic writer:

> If I can unite in myself, in my own spiritual life, the thought
> of the East and the West, of the Greek and Latin Fathers, I
> will create in myself a reunion of the divided Church, and
> from that unity in myself can come the exterior and vis-
> ible unity of the church. For, if we want to bring together
> East and West, we cannot do it by imposing one upon the
> other. We must contain both in ourselves and transcend
> them both in Christ.

The Fons Vitae publishing project for the study of world religions
through the lens of Thomas Merton's life and writing brings Merton's timeless vision of all persons united in a "hidden ground of
Love" to a contemporary audience. The previous seven volumes
in our series – *Merton & Sufism, Merton & Hesychasm, Merton &
Judaism, Merton & Buddhism, Merton & The Tao, Merton & The*

Protestant Tradition, and *Merton & Indigenous Wisdom* – feature essays by international scholars that assess the value of Merton's contributions to inter-religious dialogue. In addition to these volumes, Fons Vitae celebrated Merton's centenary (1915-2015) with a special volume, *We Are Already One: Thomas Merton's Message of Hope*, in which over one hundred contributors reflected on their first encounters with Merton's writing and the continued pressure that the Christian monk's life and witness has exerted on their spiritual engagements for world peace.

This eighth volume in our series, *Merton & Confucianism*, presents three major resources for investigating Merton's engagement with Confucianism in the context of his wider studies of East Asian spiritual traditions, and gathers five previously published articles on Merton's interest in Chinese traditions.

The forthcoming ninth volume, *Merton & Hinduism*, will complete our Thomas Merton and the World's Religions project that seeks to promote the study and practice of contemplative traditions north and south, east and west.

Jonathan Montaldo and V. Gray Henry
General Editors for the Fons Vitae Thomas Merton Series

THOMAS MERTON'S PRAYER

The following prayer was offered by Thomas Merton at the First Spiritual Summit Conference in Calcutta. It appears as part of Appendix V in *The Asian Journal of Thomas Merton*. We offer it again here as the context from which this book arose and in which it has been prepared for publication.

> Oh God, we are one with You. You have made us one with You. You have taught us that if we are open to one another, You dwell in us. Help us to preserve this openness and to fight for it with all our hearts. Help us to realize that there can be no understanding where there is mutual rejection. Oh God, in accepting one another wholeheartedly, fully, completely, we accept You, and we thank You, and we adore You, and we love You with our whole being, because our being is in Your being, our spirit is rooted in Your spirit. Fill us then with love, and let us be bound together with love as we go our diverse ways, united in this one spirit which makes You present in the world, and which makes You witness to the ultimate reality that is love. Love has overcome. Love is victorious. Amen.

INTRODUCTION

Patrick F. O'Connell

Confucianism may sometimes appear to resemble an easily over-looked step-child among the world's religions. When W. W. Norton instituted its new series of Anthologies of World Religions in 2015, no volume on Confucianism appeared alongside those on Christianity, Judaism, Islam, Hinduism, Buddhism and Daoism.[1] The reason for this omission certainly could not be a lack of influence on the part of Confucianism, since in the course of history it has actually touched more people than almost any other way of life, but is due to its ambiguous status as to whether it should be classified as a religion at all.[2]

It may seem that this relative neglect also applies to the role of Confucianism in the interreligious activity of Thomas Merton. Although Confucianism in fact drew Merton's attention quite early in his study of Asian traditions and featured quite prominently in the earliest articles he wrote on what he described as "Oriental wisdom" at the beginning of the 1960s, his growing interest in and enthusiasm for Buddhist and Taoist thought seemed to indicate a relative lack of engagement with Confucianism, and scholars have paid considerably less attention to Merton's reflections on Confucianism than to his writings on other traditions. But to assume that Merton's interest in Confucianism was transient or inconsiderable would be to underestimate numerous indications to the contrary. While neither as extensive nor as developed as his explorations of Zen, or his versions of the writings associated with the Taoist sage Chuang Tzu, his discussions of Confucian ideas and texts are an integral part of his overall interaction with Eastern thought. Indeed the very fact that Merton explicitly considered the question

---

1. *The Norton Anthology of World Religions*, Jack Miles, general editor, 6 vols. (New York: W. W. Norton, 2015).

2. See Miles' Preface, included in each volume, in which he raises the issue of Confucianism as a religion and states, "We choose to leave that question in abeyance" (xxxi), while noting that the chief reason for excluding this tradition from the anthology is that its canon is "widely translated and . . . relatively accessible" (xxxii).

of whether Confucianism could or should be considered a religion, and what the implications of this question might be for the issue of whether and in what sense "Christian Culture Needs Oriental Wisdom," to borrow the title of one of Merton's earliest essays on Asian spiritual teachings, in which Confucianism is a central focus, suggests that a consideration of Confucianism must not be overlooked in any comprehensive presentation of Merton's inter-religious – or inter-spiritual – thought.

When it appeared that the relative paucity of available primary and secondary material might result in the omission of a volume on Confucianism in the Fons Vitae Thomas Merton Series, which otherwise includes books encompassing the entire range of Merton's remarkable interactions with the world's principal spiritual traditions, I hesitantly volunteered to assemble a collection of texts that could fill this potential lacuna. While I certainly cannot claim to be a scholar of Confucianism, or of world religions generally, the invitation of the late Msgr. William Shannon to join with himself and Christine Bochen in co-authoring *The Thomas Merton Encyclopedia* provided an opportunity to write the entry on Confucianism,[3] as well as on the other East Asian traditions; and for the past two decades I have regularly taught courses on Christianity and World Religions, including Confucianism, in which Merton has served as a model and guide for a Christian response to other religions as found in *Nostra Aetate*, the 1965 Declaration on the Relationship of Christianity to Non-Christian Religions issued by the Second Vatican Council. This in many ways prophetic document has served as a kind of Magna Carta for developing positive and creative relationships with other religions, rooted in the remarkable assertion that "Christianity rejects nothing true or holy in these traditions, and that often they reflect a ray of that light that enlightens every person"[4] – a clear reference to the Word who becomes fully enfleshed in the person of Jesus, as expressed in the Prologue to the Gospel of John. The proposal to include a volume on Confucianism as an integral, indeed essential, part of the Fons

---

3. Patrick F. O'Connell, "Confucianism," in William H. Shannon, Christine M. Bochen and Patrick F. O'Connell, *The Thomas Merton Encyclopedia* (Maryknoll, NY: Orbis, 2002) 74-75.

4. Walter Abbott, SJ, ed., *The Documents of Vatican II* (New York: America Press, 1966) 662-63; Merton quotes these words in his Preface to Thomas Merton, *Mystics and Zen Masters* (New York: Farrar, Straus and Giroux, 1967) ix; subsequent references will be cited as "*MZM.*"

Vitae series was enthusiastically welcomed by series co-editors Virginia Gray Henry and Jonathan Montaldo, resulting in the collection of materials gathered in the present volume, of substantial length, and, one hopes, breadth and depth as well.

One of the attractive features of the Fons Vitae Merton series is its flexibility, the variety of forms the different volumes have taken, allowing the contents of each to be determined by the specific appropriateness to the tradition being considered. *Merton & Sufism* collects virtually all previously published work on Merton and Islam, along with newly transcribed excerpts from Merton's own conferences on Sufism;[5] *Merton & Hesychasm* includes an impressive amount of published as well as unpublished primary and secondary texts on Merton and Orthodox Christianity;[6] *Merton & Buddhism*[7] and *Merton & Indigenous Wisdom*[8] consist mainly of studies by recognized scholars specifically commissioned for these volumes; *Merton & Judaism* is largely made up of presentations delivered at a conference on this topic;[9] *Merton & the Protestant Tradition*[10] includes a series of personal testimonies to Merton's influence by Protestant pastors and scholars, along with an extensive survey of Merton's growing interaction with figures and writings of other Christian denominations; *Merton & the Tao*[11] has a twin focus on *The Way of Chuang Tzu*,[12] Merton's volume of poetic renderings of the Chinese sage, and on his fruitful relationship with the Chinese scholar and Catholic convert John Wu that contributed specifically to this and other collaborative projects and to deepening his appreciation of Eastern wisdom. Some of the volumes include helpful general articles providing background information or a

---

5. Rob Baker and Gray Henry, eds., *Merton & Sufism: The Untold Story* (Louisville, KY: Fons Vitae, 1999).

6. Bernadette Dieker and Jonathan Montaldo, eds., *Merton & Hesychasm: The Prayer of the Heart* (Louisville, KY: Fons Vitae, 2003).

7. Bonnie Thurston, ed., *Merton & Buddhism: Wisdom, Emptiness, & Everyday Mind* (Louisville, KY: Fons Vitae, 2007).

8. Peter Savastano, ed., *Merton & Indigenous Wisdom* (Louisville, KY: Fons Vitae, 2019).

9. Beatrice Bruteau, ed., *Merton & Judaism: Holiness in Words – Recognition, Repentance, and Renewal* (Louisville, KY: Fons Vitae, 2003).

10. William Oliver Paulsell, ed., *Merton & the Protestant Tradition* (Louisville, KY: Fons Vitae, 2016).

11. Cristóbal Serrán-Pagán, ed., *Merton & the Tao: Dialogues with John Wu and the Ancient Sages* (Louisville, KY: Fons Vitae, 2013).

12. Thomas Merton, *The Way of Chuang Tzu* (New York: New Directions, 1965).

gathering of relevant ancillary materials on the religion, situating Merton's own work in a broader context. *Merton & Hinduism*, the final volume of the series still to come, is a rich compilation of previously published and newly commissioned articles.

The contents of *Merton & Confucianism*, then, are not required to conform to any pre-existing template, and consequently exhibit both a family resemblance to previous volumes in the series and some elements unique to this collection. It consists of two sections, Sources and Studies, the former including three distinct resources for investigating Merton's engagement with Confucianism in the context of his wider studies of East Asian spiritual traditions, the latter bringing together five previously published articles on Merton's interest in Confucian and (in one case) related Chinese traditions. It is to be hoped that making the extensive materials in Part I much more readily accessible will stimulate and encourage further research and publication on the hitherto somewhat neglected topic of Merton and "Classic Chinese Thought."

This first section begins with the complete extant correspondence between Merton and Paul K. T. Sih, Catholic convert and the founding director of the Institute for Asian Studies at St. John's University in New York.[13] It includes 47 letters exchanged between the two from April 10, 1961 to October 3, 1967, 29 from Sih and 18 from Merton (with indications of at least three other Merton letters that have apparently not survived). Though ranging beyond

---

13. Paul Kwang Tsien Sih (1910-1978) graduated from Soochow University in Shanghai in 1933, and two years later earned a doctoral degree at the University of Rome while serving as attaché at the Chinese Embassy there from 1933 through 1936. After his return to China in the latter year, he served successively as Deputy Director, Director and Director-General of the Ministry of Railways and Ministry of Communications for the Chinese government through 1943, then as technical counselor for the Chinese Ministry of Foreign Affairs until the conclusion of the Second World War. Between 1945 and 1949 he returned to Rome as the Minister Plenipotentiary at the Chinese Embassy in Italy. After the Communist takeover in mainland China, he relocated to the United States and in 1951 became Professor and Director of the Institute for Far Eastern Studies at Seton Hall University in New Jersey, where he remained until 1959, when he became Professor of History at St. John's University and founded the Center for Asian Studies there, for which he served as director until his death. He relates the story of his conversion to Catholicism in his autobiography, *From Confucius to Christ* (1952). He was also the author of *Democracy in East Asia* (1957), *Chinese Culture and Christianity* (1957) and *Decision for China* (1959), as well as editing numerous volumes on religious and political topics and writing more than 100 articles and reviews for popular and scholarly journals.

the subject of Confucianism to discussion of the other major East Asian traditions, as well as many other topics related to their shared faith and common interests, it was initiated by Sih to express his appreciation of Merton's first published article on Asian religious teachings, "Classic Chinese Thought,"[14] in which Confucianism is a major focus, and traces Sih's role both in providing the texts for and facilitating the publication of Merton's next major piece of writing on Confucian and Taoist materials, variously titled "Two Chinese Classics," "Christian Culture Needs Oriental Wisdom" and "Love and Tao."[15] The 34 letters that survive from the years 1961 through 1963 testify to the warm relationship that developed between the two men, marked by Merton's supportive efforts on behalf of the St. John's Institute, Sih's encouragement of Merton's desire, never fulfilled, to learn Chinese; frequent exchange of publications, including Sih's generous gift of the full 8-volume set of Chinese classic texts, recently republished, by the late nineteenth-century translator James Legge; frequent exchange of news about mutual friends, particularly John Wu, Sih's baptismal sponsor; and preparations for and reflections on Sih's March 1962 visit to Gethsemani. Though the frequency of correspondence decreases in subsequent years, particularly after Merton's move into his hermitage in August 1965, there is no diminishment of the shared respect and affection between the two men, and the correspondence reveals Sih's ongoing support for Merton's deepening engagement with Chinese wisdom, Buddhist as well as Confucian and Taoist, throughout the 1960s, along with Merton's enthusiastic appreciation for Sih's efforts, through the work of the Asian Studies Center and his own writing and editing, to make that wisdom more readily accessible not only to Merton himself but to a broader American audience. While most of Merton's letters to Sih have already been published, usually in somewhat abridged form, in the first volume

14. Thomas Merton, "Classic Chinese Thought," *Jubilee* 8.9 (January 1961) 26-32; *MZM* 45-68.

15. Thomas Merton, "Christian Culture Needs Oriental Wisdom," *Catholic World* 195 (May 1962) 72-79, reprinted in *A Thomas Merton Reader*, ed. Thomas P. McDonnell (New York: Harcourt, Brace, 1962) 319-26; rev. ed. (Garden City, NY: Doubleday Image, 1974) 295-303; Thomas Merton, "Two Chinese Classics," *Chinese Culture Quarterly* 4 (June 1962) 34-41, reprinted in *Mystics and Zen Masters* as "Love and Tao" (69-80); a version of the essay incorporating all the material from both versions, retaining the more evocative title from the *Catholic World* article, is included in *Thomas Merton, Selected Essays*, ed. Patrick F. O'Connell (Maryknoll, NY: Orbis, 2013) 102-12.

of his collected letters, *The Hidden Ground of Love*,[16] none of Sih's side of the correspondence has previously appeared in print. The complete correspondence made available here, with extensive annotation, now serves to complement that between Merton and John Wu that has been collected in *Merton & the Tao*.

The second section of Part I is drawn from a rich trove of primary source material not previously represented in print,[17] extensive annotated transcriptions from three of the more than sixty reading notebooks Merton kept throughout his monastic life, consisting of summaries, quotations and comments on an astonishing range of books and articles that attracted his attention, and sometimes serving as a repository for outlines or rough drafts of various poems and essays. While it is impossible to determine with certainty the chronological order of the undated entries found in the three notebooks that contain material on Confucianism and other East Asian traditions, the briefer notes found in the two copybooks numbered 52 and 56 may predate the much more extensive survey of Chinese thought included in the notebook numbered 58A, judging both from the type of material found in the respective notebooks and on the fact that there would seem to be little reason to record quotations and summaries in separate volumes if the larger book were already available. In any case, the order of the transcriptions of relevant material from the three notebooks corresponds to the numerical listings assigned to these notebooks.

Notebook 52, smaller in size than the others, is dated 1961-1962 on the basis of excerpts included on later pages from books published in these years, but the three pages of excerpts from the Confucian *Analects* (preceded by a pair of Zen koans) that occupy the opening pages are possibly somewhat earlier.[18] A couple of

---

16. Thomas Merton, *The Hidden Ground of Love: Letters on Religious Experience and Social Concerns*, ed. William H. Shannon (New York: Farrar, Straus, Giroux, 1985) 548-56.

17. The only comparable published material is found in "Part Two: Complementary Reading" in Thomas Merton, *The Asian Journal*, ed. Naomi Burton Stone, Brother Patrick Hart and James Laughlin (New York: New Directions, 1973) 261-92.

18. If the dates 1961-1962 assigned to Notebook 52 are accurate, then Notebook 58A clearly predates it, at least in part, as some of the material comes from as early as 1960 if not before. Some of the material in Notebook 52, such as Hans Küng's *The Council, Reform and Reunion* (New York: Sheed & Ward, 1961), definitely come from this period, and if in his opening pages of the notebook Merton was using the most popular edition of Paul Reps' book *Zen Flesh,*

later pages provide a brief introductory summary of Confucian writings based on the anthology *Sources of Chinese Tradition*[19] that will be the principal resource for Merton's more extensive notes and comments in the latter notebook, followed by a page of brief notes on the *I Ching*,[20] which Merton was reading in the spring of 1959.[21] Notebook 56 contains a couple of pages from an early twentieth-century source summarizing the various periods of Japanese history,[22] followed by a page providing a similar outline of Chinese history; while not highlighting Confucianism in particular these outlines do situate Confucian elements in the context of the wider sweep of Japanese and Chinese cultural and political development and so are included in the transcriptions.

By far the most significant of these notebooks in providing indications of Merton's acquaintance with and appreciation for Confucianism, along with other influential streams of traditional Chinese thought, is that numbered 58A, with its more than 40 pages of notes, beginning with historical and geographical outlines and summarizing the findings of a French Catholic theologian[23] and a German art historian[24] before moving on to a more detailed consideration of classical Chinese texts. As already mentioned, Merton relies principally on *Sources of Chinese Tradition*, following its arrangement, relying on its headnotes and quoting

---

Zen Bones, published by Doubleday Anchor at the very outset of 1961, then the archivist's dates would apply to the entire notebook. But the cloth edition of Reps' book (Rutland, VT: Charles Tuttle) appeared in 1957, and the actual translation of the relevant material used by Merton goes back to 1934 (*The Gateless Gate*, transcribed by Nyogen Senzaki and Paul Reps [Los Angeles: John Murray, 1934]), so Merton could easily have encountered the two passages he quotes, either from a primary or secondary source, before early 1961. It seems more likely, based on the material found in the respective volumes, that Notebook 52 (as well as Notebook 56) preceded Notebook 58A, but this is not certain.

19. *Sources of Chinese Tradition*, compiled by Wm. Theodore de Bary, Wing-tsit Chan and Burton Watson (New York: Columbia University Press, 1960).

20. *The I Ching or Book of Changes*, trans. Richard Wilhelm and Cary Baynes, 2 vols. (New York: Pantheon, 1950).

21. See Thomas Merton, *A Search for Solitude: Pursuing the Monk's True Life. Journals, vol. 3: 1952-1960*, ed. Lawrence S. Cunningham (San Francisco: HarperCollins, 1996) 266-67 [3/3/1959]; 267 [3/10/1959]; 279-81 [5/12/1959].

22. Kakuzo Okakura, *The Ideals of the East with Special Reference to the Art of Japan*, 2nd ed. (New York: Dutton, 1904).

23. François Huang, *Ame Chinoise et Christianisme* (Paris: Casterman, 1957).

24. Helmut Wilhelm, "Confucianism," *Encyclopedia of World Art*, ed. Bernard Myers, 17 vols. (New York: McGraw-Hill, 1959-83) 3.775-82.

liberally from its selections not only of Confucian but also of Taoist and Mohist writings, but he also includes extensive quotations from the translations by Legge of both Confucius[25] and Chuang Tzu,[26] as well as material on the latter from Lin Yutang,[27] and comments in detail on Ezra Pound's versions of significant Confucian works.[28] There are even whole pages of lists of Chinese terms accompanied by Merton's own renditions of the corresponding Chinese characters. For Mencius, the "Realists" (Legalists) and Chuang Tzu he supplements his *Sources* excerpts with others from Arthur Waley's *Three Ways of Thought in Ancient China*.[29] In later sections on medieval and earlier modern periods he incorporates information found in the analytical surveys of Liu Wu-Chi[30] and H. G. Creel.[31] An early draft of his adaptation of *The Ox Mountain Parable of Meng Tzu*[32] follows comments on its major source, *Mencius on the Mind* by I. A. Richards,[33] and a preliminary outline of his review essay "Two Chinese Classics" is followed by a detailed chapter-by-chapter outline of one of these works, the *Hsiao Ching*,[34] sent by Paul Sih along with John Wu's translation of the *Tao Te Ching*.[35] In all Merton consults more than a dozen different sources in compiling this mainly chronological survey of Chinese thought, principally Confucian but incorporating Taoist, Mohist and Legalist material

25. *The Chinese Classics*. A Translation by James Legge, D.D. Part I Confucius (New York: John B. Alden, Publisher, 1891).

26. *The Texts of Taoism: The Tao Te Ching and the Writings of Chuang-Tzu*, trans. James Legge, Introduction by D. T. Suzuki (New York: Julian Press, 1959).

27. *The Wisdom of Laotse*, translated and edited by Lin Yutang (New York: Modern Library, 1948).

28. *Confucius: The Great Digest & Unwobbling Pivot*, translation and commentary by Ezra Pound (New York: New Directions, 1951).

29. Arthur Waley, *Three Ways of Thought in Ancient China* ([1939] Garden City, NY: Doubleday Anchor, 1956).

30. Liu Wu-Chi, *A Short History of Confucian Philosophy* (Baltimore: Penguin, 1955).

31. H. G. Creel, *Chinese Thought from Confucius to Mao Tse-tung* (London: Eyre & Spottiswoode, 1954).

32. *The Ox Mountain Parable of Meng Tzu*, translated with an introduction by Thomas Merton (Lexington, KY: Stamperia del Santuccio, 1960); subsequently included as an appendix to Merton's essay "Classic Chinese Thought" (*MZM* 65-68).

33. I. A. Richards, *Mencius on the Mind: Experiments in Multiple Definition* (New York: Harcourt, Brace, 1932).

34. *The Hsiao Ching*, ed. Paul K. T. Sih, trans. Mary Lelia Makra, MM, Asian Institute Translations 2 (New York: St. John's University Press, 1961).

35. *Tao Teh Ching*, trans. John C. H. Wu, Asian Institute Translations 1 (New York: St. John's University Press, 1961).

as well. These notebooks provide the clearest evidence of just how intensive and extensive Merton's study of Confucian and related systems of thought was during the early 1960s.

Merton's earliest and latest discussions of Confucianism are found in conferences presented to the Gethsemani novices, the third and final bloc of material included in the Sources section of the present volume. As part of his explanation of natural law, probably dating from 1957, in his series of conferences on the Benedictine vows,[36] Merton includes a brief consideration of the Confucian virtue of "human-heartedness," illustrated by ten brief excerpts from the *Analects*, and compared quite positively to the teaching of St. Bernard, even to words of Christ in John's Gospel, and implicitly in this context to the Benedictine *Rule*. He emphasizes that such "maxims should be to us a revelation of the depth and wonder of the natural law" that prepares and points the way to its fulfillment in the Christian proclamation of the good news, and that to ignore or disparage such wisdom is to risk impeding one's own journey toward genuine sanctity.

Beginning in August 1964 and extending through an entire year until just before his retirement as novice master upon moving into his hermitage on August 20, 1965, Merton presented to the novices a series of weekly conferences on the spiritual implications of beauty, art and poetry. After discussing various individual poets, most recently T. S. Eliot and Gerard Manley Hopkins, two particular favorites, Merton announced his intention on June 3, 1965 to focus on classical Greek tragedy, but in fact he decides first to situate this discussion in the context of contemporaneous developments in the Far East, and devotes most of this and the four subsequent conferences in the series, through July 15, to Asian thought and art, particularly to Confucianism, before returning to the Greeks for the final four sessions of the series, concluding the day before his resignation of his mastership. In these five conferences, transcribed and published here for the first time, Merton's intention is not so much to provide a detailed explication of Confucian thought, or of the Chinese landscape painting to which he turns his attention in the course of his discussion, as to consider what insights can be gained from this material by the particular audience of aspiring monks he is

---

36. Thomas Merton, *The Life of the Vows: Initiation into the Monastic Tradition 6*, ed. Patrick F. O'Connell, Monastic Wisdom vol. 30 (Collegeville, MN: Cistercian Publications, 2012) 45-47.

addressing, almost certainly in the awareness that these are among the last occasions he will have for instructing them as novice master. Paralleling some of the material that is included in the Introduction to *The Way of Chuang Tzu*, being written at about the same time, he outlines key Confucian concepts (drawn principally from his reading of Fung Yu-lan's *Spirit of Chinese Philosophy*[37]) and correlates them explicitly with the virtues of authentic Benedictine monastic life and even with the central qualities of Christ's own earthly mission. As in his lectures on the vows almost a decade earlier, he presents the wisdom of Confucian thought as a kind of *preparatio evangelii*, a pattern that parallels and prepares for the good news of the gospel. He goes on to compare the Chinese character of *chung*, central to the teaching of the Confucian *Doctrine of the Mean*, the *Chung Yung*, both to the cross and to the "still point" of Eliot's *Four Quartets*, before getting into some rather esoteric discussion of Chinese logic that eventually points beyond the principle of contradiction to an experience of the center of reality that transcends all binaries and points toward the revelation of the divine name in Exodus 3 and toward an existential participation in wholeness that cannot be fully experienced or expressed by abstract concepts. Such a perception, Merton maintains, is characteristic of the best Oriental art, which arises out of and draws the viewer into silence and stillness and emptiness, an expression of and a participation in the *tao*. This attitude, Merton tells the novices as he prepares to return to his topic of Greek tragedy, prompts the free exercise of human energy and creativity in forming and shaping culture and so completing the Confucian triad of heaven, earth and humanity. This admirable model, Merton concludes, is at the heart of Confucian education, and of monastic formation as well, a clear endorsement of the pertinence of the Confucian vision for the way of life his students have chosen, and for the solitary modality of that life that he himself is about to begin in "the climate of this silent corner of woods . . . in which there is no need for explanations," where Kung Tzu and Meng Tzu, Confucius and Mencius, take their place amidst "the reassuring companionship of many silent Tzu's and Fu's."[38]

The earliest substantial article on Merton and Confucianism,

---

37. Fung Yu-lan, *The Spirit of Chinese Philosophy*, trans. E. R. Hughes (Boston: Beacon Press, 1962).

38. Thomas Merton, *Day of a Stranger* (Salt Lake City: Gibbs M. Smith, 1981) 35.

and thus the first of the five studies in Part II of the present volume, was written by John Wu, Jr., youngest son of Merton's friend and himself a Merton correspondent and visitor to Gethsemani, where he and his wife met Merton while on their honeymoon in the summer of 1968. A noted scholar of Merton and Eastern thought in his own right,[39] Wu writes in "Thomas Merton and Confucian Rites: 'The Fig Leaf for the Paradise Condition'"[40] about Merton's deep awareness (shared with the elder Wu) of "Confucianism as an exceptional philosophy of the person aimed at social and political harmony and anchored solidly on an idea of ritual whose function is to disclose the dimension of the sacred in human society." He calls attention to the contemplative aspects of Confucianism with which Merton resonated, a vision and project of restoration of primordial wholeness, as the deepest and most significant level of "Ju" thought, transcending the ethical and social dimensions that could, and sometimes did, degenerate into sterile ritualism rather than vibrant and dynamic participation in sacred order. Drawing on his own studies of Confucian thought and the work of such scholars as Julia Ching, Wu finds important points of contact between the Confucian ideal of the superior person, the fully integrated human being, and Merton's Christian personalism, his teaching on the true self. In his concluding reflections, he suggests that the insights of Merton and other Western or Western-influenced commentators might even have the potential of reviving the true image of the Confucian sage that had become ossified or conventionalized over the course of Chinese history, "reminding Easterners of a priceless treasure that a good number of us, anxious not to be left off the irrepressible express freight of modernization, have already

39. John Wu, Jr., Professor Emeritus of English Language and Literature at the Chinese Culture University, Taiwan, ROC, earned his BA degree from Seton Hall University and an MA from Chinese Culture University, with a thesis on "Eternal Values as Found in Lao Tzu's Tao Teh Ching" (in Chinese). He has published articles on Thomas Merton and Asia in *Asia Quarterly*, *Chinese Culture Quarterly*, *Cistercian Studies Quarterly*, *Cross Currents*, *Inter-Religious Quarterly*, *The Merton Annual* and *The Merton Seasonal*. He served as keynote speaker for the Third General Meeting of the International Thomas Merton Society in Colorado Springs, CO in 1993, and was a major contributor to the volume *Merton & the Tao* in the Fons Vitae Merton Series. He is the author of the bilingual volume *You Know My Soul: Reflections on Merton Prayers*, published in 2012. Since his return to America in 2017 after his retirement, he has been living in Virginia.

40. John Wu, Jr., "Thomas Merton and Confucian Rites: 'The Fig Leaf for the Paradise Condition,'" *The Merton Annual* 9 (1996) 118-41.

abandoned." As Merton saw Eastern wisdom as a challenge and gift to Western culture, so Wu, an Asian American who has spent most of his adult life living and teaching in Taiwan, sees a recip-rocal dynamism operative as well, with Western recognition and appreciation of the vitality of Confucian and Taoist thought as a resource for restoring to the East an awareness of its own most authentic insights, sowing "the seeds of a future renaissance" that will not mistake the fig leaf for the paradise within.

Paul M. Pearson, since 2002 Director of the Thomas Merton Center at Bellarmine University in Louisville, KY,[41] the major repository of Merton's archives, has repeatedly written about Merton's version of the *Ox Mountain Parable of Meng Tzu*, the fourth-century BCE Confucian thinker and the second great teacher in the Confucian tradition, whose writings constitute one of the "Four Books" that form the foundation of Confucian education. Written for three quite different audiences, his three articles on this brief meditation on human goodness suppressed by social and political pressures have considerable overlap, but each contains unique insights that complement and reinforce one another. The composite version presented here is based primarily on the most recent essay, "'Wisdom Cries the Dawn Deacon': Thomas Merton and 'The Ox Mountain Parable,'"[42] but incorporates material found only in the two earlier essays[43] as well in order to provide a

---

41. Paul M. Pearson is Director and Archivist of the Thomas Merton Center at Bellarmine University, Louisville, KY and Chief of Research for the Thomas Merton Legacy Trust. He serves as Resident Secretary of the International Thomas Merton Society, and was the ITMS president for 2005-2007. He completed a Ph.D. on Thomas Merton at Heythrop College, University of London, and also holds a Master's Degree in Library Science. He was a founding member and the first secretary of the Thomas Merton Society of Great Britain and Ireland, and has spoken on Merton throughout the world. He received the "International" Louie award from the ITMS in 1999 for his contributions to Merton studies and promo-tion of his legacy, and was awarded the 2010 and 2017 John Brubaker Memorial Award from the Catholic Library Association, as well as the Hidden Wholeness Award for International Unity and Diversity from Bellarmine University in 2011. He is author of *Seeking Paradise: Thomas Merton and the Shakers* (2003) and editor of *A Meeting of Angels: The Correspondence of Thomas Merton with Edward Deming and Faith Andrews* (2008) and of *Thomas Merton on Christian Contemplation* (2012) and most recently of *Beholding Paradise: The Photographs of Thomas Merton* (2020).

42. Paul M. Pearson, "'Wisdom Cries the Dawn Deacon': Thomas Merton and 'The Ox Mountain Parable'" *CEA Critic* 75.3 (November 2013) 278-84.

43. Paul M. Pearson, "The Ox Mountain Parable: An Introduction," *The*

comprehensive synthesis of Pearson's research on the importance of this brief work in evaluating Merton's response to Confucianism. In addition to providing information on Merton's sources and the process of composition and publication, he examines not only Merton's introduction and translation of the text of Mencius itself, but also the use Merton makes of it in the third, central section of his 1966 journal volume *Conjectures of a Guilty Bystander*,[44] which takes its title, "The Night Spirit and the Dawn Air," and much of its tone and perspective from the meditation of Mencius on the necessity for "the night spirit, the dawn breath, silence, passivity, rest" without which "our nature cannot be itself" (*CGB* 123). This material is considered in the context of the contents of *Conjectures* as a whole, with attention to the major themes of each of its five parts; it is also related to Merton's essay "Rain and the Rhinoceros"[45] and to other important writings of the 1960s such as "Is the World a Problem?"[46] and "The Climate of Mercy"[47] as well as Merton's writings on peace and social justice. Consequently "The Ox Mountain Parable" can be seen not as a marginal or peripheral project on Merton's part but as thoroughly integrated into his overall perception and expression of his vocation as monk and writer during the final decade of his life.

Certainly the highest profile piece included here is that by Wm. Theodore de Bary, arguably the premier American scholar of Confucianism in the twentieth century, a younger contemporary of Thomas Merton at Columbia, who died in July 2017,[48] less than

Merton Annual 15 (2002) 14-19; Paul M. Pearson, "Let Mercy Fall like Rain: Thomas Merton and the Ox Mountain Parable," *The Merton Journal* 18.1 (Eastertide 2011) 42-49.

44. Thomas Merton, *Conjectures of a Guilty Bystander* (Garden City, NY: Doubleday, 1966) 115-94; subsequent references will be cited as "*CGB*" parenthetically in the text.

45. Thomas Merton, *Raids on the Unspeakable* (New York: New Directions, 1966) 9-23.

46. Thomas Merton, *Contemplation in a World of Action* (Garden City, NY: Doubleday, 1971) 143-56.

47. Thomas Merton, *Love and Living*, ed. Naomi Burton Stone and Brother Patrick Hart (New York: Farrar, Straus, Giroux, 1979) 203-19.

48. Wm. Theodore de Bary (1919-2017), John Mitchell Mason Professor at Columbia University, was an early and influential leader in the study of Asian humanities in the United States. He received his undergraduate degree from Columbia in 1941 and returned there to complete his Ph.D. after service as an intelligence officer during World War II. He taught at the university from 1949 through the spring semester of 2017, continuing to teach *pro bono* after formally

a month short of his ninety-eighth birthday (and had continued to teach through the spring semester of that year!). His article, which began as the 2010 presentation for the prestigious Merton lecture series sponsored annually by the Columbia Catholic campus ministry, was first published in the Catholic journal *First Things* the following year,[49] and then in definitive form under the title "Thomas Merton, Matteo Ricci, and Confucianism" as part of the "Tributes and Memoirs" section of *The Great Civilized Conversation*, the final collection of de Bary's shorter writings, published in 2013.[50] It opens with an affectionate portrait filled with autobiographical reminiscences, then moves into a predominantly critical evaluation of Merton's treatment of Confucianism, which he finds considerably less cogent than his engagement with Buddhism or Taoism, a defect that he attributes principally to what he regards as Merton's failure to include Confucianism among the "world's great religions," and his supposed distinction between an idealized, unhistorical "pure" Confucianism as found in the canonical texts, and the way Confucianism actually functioned in Chinese culture through the centuries. He faults Merton for neglecting the key transformative contributions of the neo-Confucian movement of the twelfth century which was responsible for making the Confucian "Four Books," by which Merton himself was so deeply impressed, the central texts for Chinese education from that time into the modern era. As the title of the final version indicates, in the latter part of his presentation de Bary is particularly interested in Merton's laudatory portrait of the seventeenth-century Jesuit missionary Matteo Ricci, whose

retiring in 1989. He served the university as Provost from 1970 to 1978 and established the university's Heyman Center for the Humanities. In 2014, he was awarded the National Humanities Medal by President Barack Obama for fostering a global conversation based on the common values and experiences shared by all cultures. He was author or editor of more than twenty books on East Asian thought and culture, including *The Unfolding of Neo-Confucianism* (1975), *Principle and Practicality: Neo-Confucianism and Practical Learning* (1981), *The Rise of Neo-Confucianism in Korea* (1985), *The Message of the Mind in Neo-Confucianism* (1988), *Neo-Confucian Education* (1989) and *The Great Civilized Conversation: Education for a World Community* (2013), as well as editing influential source-books on Chinese, Japanese, Indian and Korean traditions for the Columbia Records of Civilization series.

49. Wm. Theodore de Bary, "Thomas Merton and Confucianism: Why the Contemplative Never Got the Religion Quite Right," *First Things* 211 (March 2011) 41-46.

50. Wm. Theodore de Bary, *The Great Civilized Conversation: Education for a World Community* (New York: Columbia University Press, 2013) 351-66.

remarkable accomplishments in presenting the gospel inculturated in a Chinese framework Merton highlights, an evaluation that de Bary endorses while lamenting that Merton "does not himself go as far into the issues (especially the Neo-Confucian ones) as we might like" in discussing the response of Ricci's Chinese dialogue partners, who "were eager to learn from Ricci whatever he could bring from the West that would help them remain true to their principles of civility." In concluding de Bary presents Merton as "from the start, more of a poet than a historian" and therefore as someone who "could resonate with nature – earthly, human, and divine" but who "would have had to be more of a historian and perhaps somewhat less of a pure contemplative in order to be brought truly 'down to earth' in a Confucian sense" – though he graciously notes in his closing remarks that few Confucians, much less himself, were able to combine successfully poetic and historical perspectives, and that perhaps if Merton's own life were not tragically cut short he might have caught up with, or have been caught up by, the historical dimension in a more substantive way.

This is followed by "A Way of Life Impregnated with Truth," my own response to de Bary,[51] first presented at the International Thomas Merton Society conference in June 2015, in which I suggest (perhaps somewhat more emphatically at some points that was strictly necessary) that further attention to the specific purpose and audience of Merton's writings on Confucianism, a consideration of Merton's references in his essays to works consulted (most important among them de Bary's own *Sources of Chinese Tradition*) and an opportunity to consult unpublished materials that were not available to him at the time, might have led to a more positive evaluation of Merton's response to Confucianism. I will not summarize the contents of this essay here, other than to point out that to the question raised in its subtitle – "Did Thomas Merton Undervalue Confucianism?" – the presentation gives an unreservedly (and one hopes, convincingly) negative response.

The final study included here is not, strictly speaking, on Confucianism at all, but on the rival system of Mo Tzu, disparaged particularly by Mencius, but thereby certainly pertinent to the overall focus of the present volume. "Mo Tzu and Thomas

---

51. "'A Way of Life Impregnated with Truth': Did Thomas Merton Undervalue Confucianism?" *The Merton Annual* 28 (2015) 112-33.

Merton"[52] originated as a presentation given by the late Robert E. Daggy[53] at a conference on Mohism at Shandong University in August 1994. Daggy begins by providing an introductory overview of Merton's life and work for a Chinese audience presumably unfamiliar with him, then goes on to summarize his engagement with Chinese thought in general, followed by laudatory comments from Chinese-American scholars including John Wu, Paul Sih, Richard Chi and Cyrus Lee. He then turns to examine Merton's relatively infrequent and largely negative comments on Mohism, influenced by the contemporary Confucian critiques of Mencius and others, as well as by the generally negative modern evaluation of Arthur Waley, who calls Mo Tzu's writings "feeble, repetitive," without "wit, beauty or force," expounding "on the whole rather sympathetic doctrines with a singular lack of aesthetic power." But he goes on to suggest that had Merton lived longer he might have recognized a deeper sense of affinity for Mo Tzu, whose asceticism, commitment to peacemaking and advocacy of a universal love modeled on the love of God for humanity show striking similarities to Merton's own core values. He marshals evidence to support his introductory claim that the two thinkers, widely separated in place and time, can profitably be considered together because "both came to the conclusion that universal love – a benign, benevolent, non-discriminating love – might be the governing principle, indeed the

---

52. Robert E. Daggy, "Mo Tzu and Thomas Merton," Afterword in Cyrus Lee, *Thomas Merton and Chinese Wisdom* (Erie, PA: Sino-American Institute, 1995) 117-30.

53. Robert E. Daggy (1940-1997) was the longtime director of Thomas Merton Center at Bellarmine University, Louisville, KY, the major repository of the Merton archives. His involvement with Merton studies began in 1974, when he was appointed consultant to the Merton Legacy Trust and associate director of the Bellarmine Merton Center; in 1980 he was promoted to the post of Center Director, a position he held until his resignation due to illness in spring, 1997, shortly before his death in December of that year. He edited *The Merton Seasonal* for twenty years and was a founding member and second president of the International Thomas Merton Society, which he served as resident secretary from its founding in 1987 until shortly before his death. He graduated from Yale University in 1962, studied oriental cultures at Columbia University, and received an M.A. and Ph.D. in history from the University of Wisconsin in 1968 and 1971, respectively. He lectured and wrote extensively on Merton and edited numerous works, including *Day of a Stranger*, *"Honorable Reader"*, *The Alaskan Journal*, *Encounter: Thomas Merton and D. T. Suzuki*, *Monks Pond*, *The Road to Joy*, the second volume of Merton's collected letters, and *Dancing in the Water of Life*, volume five of Merton's complete journals.

remedy, which would allow the world and all humans (not just an individual culture) to live in peace and harmony – and this love might be the world's salvation."

While the compendium of primary and secondary materials assembled in this volume certainly does not provide a definitive answer as to whether Confucianism can or should be classified as a "religion" in a sense that would make it eligible for inclusion in a series like that of the *Norton Anthology of World Religions*, it does justify its presence as an integral component of the Fons Vitae Merton Series. While Merton declares that Confucianism is "certainly not a religion in the same sense as Christianity," that it "is less a 'faith' than a sacred philosophy, a way of life based on archaic religious wisdom" (*MZM* 46), he recognizes and affirms "the profound Catholicity of Confucian philosophy" (*MZM* 46) as perceived by the early Jesuit missionaries to China, its compatibility with Christian revelation, its four-fold "mandala" of basic virtues – love, justice, ritual and wisdom – finding its perfect fulfillment in the person and work of Christ, who can be recognized in the early Christian–Confucian dialogue as "a kind of brief epiphany of the Son of Man as a Chinese scholar" (*MZM* 90). Confucianism was for Merton not a neglected step-child but in some ways an older brother to be treated with due respect, as in the Confucian five constant relationships (though this did not prohibit constructive criticism when appropriate). Merton's profoundly "catholic," holistic Catholicity, not an either/or but a both/and spirituality, open to the broadest and deepest sources of authentic human insight, explicitly embraces Confucianism along with the other major streams of Chinese wisdom: "the tone and value of my own interior world . . . . is open also to China, to Confucianism and to Zen, to the great Taoists" (*CGB* 167); this "openness to other cultures and spiritualities, especially I think the Chinese. . . . is not only relevant to my life and salvation but has crucial significance in my whole vocation."[54] It is the editor's hope that the material found in this present collection can assist us in understanding and appreciating why this is so.

---

54. Thomas Merton, *Turning Toward the World: The Pivotal Years. Journals, vol. 4:* 1960-1963, ed. Victor A. Kramer (San Francisco: HarperCollins, 1996) 147-48.

ACKNOWLEDGEMENTS

In conclusion I would like to express my gratitude to all those who have made this volume possible:

- to the Trustees of the Merton Legacy Trust, Peggy Fox, Anne McCormick and Mary Somerville, for permission to publish primary source materials by Thomas Merton and their consistent support in this and other projects;

- to Paul M. Pearson, director and archivist of the Thomas Merton Center at Bellarmine University, for providing access to the major primary sources for this volume, and for his own valuable contribution to the "Studies" section;

- to John Wu, Jr. for graciously allowing the re-publication of his pioneering essay on Merton and Confucianism;

- to Columbia University Press for permission to reprint the essay by the late Wm. Theodore de Bary, dean of American Confucian scholars;

- to Dr. John C. Sih for permission to publish the correspondence of his late father, Chinese-American Sinologist Paul K. T. Sih, with Thomas Merton;

- to Fons Vitae Merton Series co-editors Virginia Gray Henry and Jonathan Montaldo for their encouragement and support in bringing *Merton & Confucianism* to publication;

- to typesetter Neville Blakemore for his usual superb work with what has proved to be a particularly challenging text;

- to Owsley Brown III for his ongoing support of the Fons Vitae Merton Series and of the present volume in particular;

- to proofreader Anne Ogden and designer Steve Stivers for their important contributions in bringing this volume to completion with grace and efficiency;

- to Betsy Garloch of the interlibrary loan department of the Nash Library, Gannon University, for providing invaluable assistance in procuring needed materials during a particularly difficult period;

- to Violet Hurst, archivist of the Archdiocese of Boston, and Kevin Saffo of the interlibrary loan department of Boston College, for their assistance in locating and providing access to a previously unknown review by Thomas Merton;

- again and always to my wife Suzanne and our children for their continual love, support and encouragement in this and other projects.

Patrick F. O'Connell

PART I
SOURCES

THE THOMAS MERTON/PAUL SIH
CORRESPONDENCE

1. TLS[1]

St. John's University

GRAND CENTRAL AND UTOPIA PARKWAYS

JAMAICA 32, NEW YORK

INSTITUTE OF ASIAN STUDIES

OFFICE OF THE DIRECTOR[2]

April 10, 1961

Reverend Father Louis Merton
The Trappist Monastery
Gethsemane, Kentucky

Dear and Reverend Father Louis:

It was with a deep sense of admiration that I read your excellent article "Classic Chinese Thought"[3] published in the January 1961 issue of the Jubilee. Your profound, yet lucid, description of Confucian and Taoist traditions is both inspiring and thought-provoking. It reveals that in this twentieth century we can also see a St. Thomas in the effective use of a Chinese Aristotle.[4] As a

---

1. The following abbreviations are used for the letters: HLS: handwritten letter signed; HNS: handwritten note signed; TLS: typed letter signed; TALS: typed annotated letter signed; TLS[c]: typed letter signed [carbon]; TL[c]: typed letter [carbon]. All transcriptions have been made from the correspondence housed in the archives of the Thomas Merton Center (TMC), Bellarmine University, Louisville, KY.

2. Printed letterhead.

3. Thomas Merton, "Classic Chinese Thought," *Jubilee* 8.9 (Jan. 1961) 26-32; reprinted in Thomas Merton, *Mystics and Zen Masters* (New York: Farrar, Straus and Giroux, 1967) 45-68 (subsequent references will be cited as "*MZM*"). On August 14, 1960, Merton had written in his journal, "Finished article on Chinese Classic Thought last week. Enjoyed writing it" (Thomas Merton, *Turning Toward the World: The Pivotal Years. Journals, vol. 4: 1960-1963*, ed. Victor A. Kramer [San Francisco: HarperCollins, 1996] 31; subsequent references will be cited as "*TTW*").

4. In his article Merton makes essentially the same point, without of course

3

Chinese, I feel particularly grateful for your presenting the Oriental cultures to the West in such a forceful way.

Yesterday I visited Dr. John Wu,[5] my godfather. I was particularly happy to know that he will cooperate with you in translating some selected sayings of Chuang Tzu.[6] Incidentally, his new translation of Lao Tzu's *Tao Teh Ching*[7] is just completed. It is

presenting himself in the role of Aquinas: "At such a time it is vitally necessary for the West to understand the traditional thought of the great Asian cultures: China, India, and Japan. This is necessary not only for specialists, but for every educated person in the West. The cultural heritage of Asia has as much right to be studied in our colleges as the cultural heritage of Greece and Rome. Asian cultural traditions have, like our own ancient cultures, been profoundly spiritual. . . . If the West can recognize that contact with Eastern thought can renew our appreciation for our own cultural heritage, a product of the fusion of the Judeo-Christian religion with Greco-Roman culture, then it will be easier to defend that heritage, not only in Asia but in the West as well" (*MZM* 45-46). "The Christian scholar is obligated by his sacred vocation to understand and even preserve the heritage of all the great traditions insofar as they contain truths that cannot be neglected and that offer precious insights into Christianity itself. As the monks of the Middle Ages and the scholastics of the thirteenth century preserved the cultural traditions of Greece and Rome and adapted what they found in Arabic philosophy and science, so we too have a far greater task before us. It is time that we begin to consider something of our responsibility" (*MZM* 65).

5. John C. H. Wu (1899-1986), lawyer, judge, diplomat, author, educator, Catholic convert, and friend, advisor, correspondent and collaborator of Thomas Merton. He taught at Seton Hall University in New Jersey from 1951 until his retirement in 1968, thereafter moving to Taiwan and continuing to teach and write there until his death. For an extensive presentation of this relationship, see Cristóbal Serrán-Pagán, ed., *Merton & the Tao: Dialogues with John Wu and the Ancient Sages* (Louisville, KY: Fons Vitae, 2013) (subsequent references will be cited as "*Merton & the Tao*"), Part III: "The Spiritual Friendship between Thomas Merton and John Wu," which includes: John Wu, Jr., "God-Inebriated: An Introduction to the John C. H. Wu – Thomas Merton Correspondence" (127-49) and Lucien Miller, "The Thomas Merton – John C. H. Wu Letters: The Lord as Postman" (150-70); Part IV: "The Collected Letters of Thomas Merton and John Wu (1961-1968)," edited and annotated by John Wu, Jr. and Cristóbal Serrán-Pagán" (171-346); Part V: "The Collected Letters of Thomas Merton and John Wu, Jr. (1967-1968)" (347-63); Part VI: "*In Memoriam* of John C. H. Wu": John Wu, Jr., "Centennial Vignettes: Life with Father" (367-97).

6. Thomas Merton, *The Way of Chuang Tzu* (New York: New Directions, 1965); for the development and results of this project see *Merton & the Tao*, Part II: "Merton and Chuang Tzu," which includes: Lucien Miller, "Merton's *Chuang Tzu*" (47-83); Bede Bidlack, "Merton's Way of *Zhuangzi*: A Critique" (84-102) and Donald P. St. John, "Ecological Wisdom in Merton's *Chuang Tzu*" (103-23).

7. Lao Tzu, *Tao Teh Ching*, translated by John C. H. Wu, edited by Paul K. T. Sih, Asian Institute Translations 1 (New York: St. John's University Press, 1961).

edited by myself and published by St. John's University Press. I am presenting a copy with filial and grateful homage.

The Asian Institute at St. John's is now devoted to a translation series of Chinese tradition thought. In addition to the *Tao Teh Ching*, the *Hsiao Ching* (Confucian Classic of Filiality) has also been made and will be ready soon.[8] The third issue is a translation of a Zen Buddhist classic.[9] All these, like the *Tao Teh Ching*, will be published along with the Chinese text.

If in the future you should work on a Chinese classic which should be published and accompanied with a Chinese text, I shall be only too honored to offer my cooperation. St. John's University Press has the facilities to provide this special need.

May I beg for your blessing, I am

Father's devoted son in Christ,

PS:md[10]   Paul K. T. Sih
Enc.   Director

---

8. *The Hsiao Ching*, translated by Mary Lelia Makra, edited by Paul K. T. Sih, Asian Institute Translations 2 (New York: St. John's University Press, 1961).

9. Hui Neng, *The Platform Scripture: The Basic Classic of Zen Buddhism*, translated by Wing-tsit Chan, edited by Paul K. T. Sih, Asian Institute Translations 3 (New York: St. John's University Press, 1963).

10. Marjorie Dahm served as Dr. Sih's secretary during most of the period of this correspondence. Her August 18, 1961 letter, responding to Merton's letter dated two days earlier, to inform him that Dr. Sih was at a conference in Taiwan is included in the Sih file of the TMC archives.

2. TLS

St. John's University

GRAND CENTRAL AND UTOPIA PARKWAYS
JAMAICA 32, NEW YORK

INSTITUTE OF ASIAN STUDIES
OFFICE OF THE DIRECTOR

May 3, 1961

Reverend Father Louis T. Merton
Abbey of Gethsemane
Trappist, Kentucky

Dear Reverend Father Louis:

It was with a deep sense of gratitude that I received your gracious letter[11] this morning. Words are not enough to express my sincere appreciation for what you have said of Dr. Wu's work, the *Tao Teh Ching*.

Under separate cover, I am sending a copy of the *Hsiao Ching*, a Confucian Classic of Filiality, translated by Sister Lelia Makra of the Maryknoll Sisters who spent 30 years in China. I hope that this work will also invite your interest.

The third classic will be on Zen, as you kindly suggested. It is a new translation of the *Liu-tsu T'an-ching* (Platform Sutra of the Sixth Patriarch) by Prof. Wing-tsit Chan. The existing translations of this Zen Buddhist classic are either not adequately treated or based on unauthentic Chinese texts. The new translation will, I hope, make up for these deficiencies. It will be printed with the Chinese text on facing pages, as in the case of the *Tao Teh Ching* and the *Hsiao Ching*.

This Institute is fairly new.[12] At the present, it carries a limited program of instruction, research and publication. In addition to the translation series, it plans to publish another two series of monographs, one on Chinese philosophical studies and the other on

---

11. This letter, the first from Merton to Sih, is not extant.

12. Paul Sih (1910-78) was the founding director of the Institute of Asian Studies at St. John's University, which began in 1959, and he remained in this post until his death. It continues to operate up to the present.

Chinese social studies. "A Study of Wang Yang-ming" has already been completed by Carsun Chang.[13] It will go to the printer soon.

In developing this Institute which aims primarily at an intellectual and spiritual unification, I have realized more than ever that there can be no real antipathy between the higher spiritual traditions of the East and the West, but only a profound unity which we instinctively feel to be present but which we cannot yet bring to full expression. So far as the East is concerned, the spiritual tradition of China is of central importance. Chinese spirituality not only has much to receive from the Christian Faith, it also has much to give. Christianity will find a new development in this Asian context, while Chinese spirituality will find a new and spiritual elevation.

Strictly speaking, John the Baptist was the only Precuror [sic] of Christ. However, as Msgr. Guardini[14] once put it, Christ may have other precurors in Socrates from the heart of antiquity and in Buddha, who spoke the ultimate word in Eastern religious cognition. How about Confucius, Loo [sic] Tze, Mo Ti, Mencius, Chang [sic] Tzu and others? Were they not the heralds who sowed the "seeds of the Logos"[15] in the hearts of men before "the Word was

---

13. Carsun Chang, *Wang Yang-ming: Idealist Philosopher of Sixteenth-Century China* (New York: St. John's University Press, 1962). Wang Yang-ming (1474-1524) was a prominent figure in the "idealist" wing of the neo-Confucian movement, focusing on the development of interior wisdom: see "Moral Intuition and Action in Wang Yang-ming," in *Sources of Chinese Tradition*, compiled by Wm. Theodore de Bary, Wing-tsit Chan and Burton Watson (New York: Columbia University Press, 1960) 569-81.

14. See Romano Guardini, *The Lord* (Chicago: Henry Regnery, 1954) 305: "Perhaps Christ had not only one precursor, John, last of the prophets, but three: John the Baptist for the Chosen People, Socrates from the heart of antiquity, and Buddha, who spoke the ultimate word in Eastern religious cognition." Guardini (1885-1968) was a German theologian highly regarded by Thomas Merton, who called him "one of the most important and articulate Catholic authors of the moment" (Thomas Merton, *The School of Charity: Letters on Religious Renewal and Spiritual Direction*, ed. Patrick Hart [New York: Farrar, Straus, Giroux, 1990]) 145 (July 4, 1962 letter to Elaine M. Bane, OSF) (subsequent references will be cited as "*SC*"); see also his February 28, 1959 letter to Czeslaw Milosz (Thomas Merton, *The Courage for Truth: Letters to Writers*, ed. Christine M. Bochen [New York: Farrar, Straus, Giroux, 1993] 56) (subsequent references will be cited as "*CT*") and his April 15, 1959 letter to Mark Weidner, OCSO (*SC* 119).

15. This term (*logos spermatikos*), of Stoic origin, is particularly associated with St. Justin Martyr (d. 165). See J. N. D. Kelly, *Early Christian Doctrines*, rev. ed. (San Francisco: Harper & Row, 1978) 96: "His starting point was the current maxim that reason (the 'germinal logos' = λόγος σπερματικός) was what united

made flesh"?[16] We know that their knowledge was inadequate, yet this very inadequacy underlined the necessity of the Revelation. Your excellent article in the *Jubilee* has already pointed the way. I sincerely hope that you will continue this effort in bringing about a synthesis really possible between the East and West.

I am exceedingly happy to know that you may consider reviewing the *Tao Teh Ching* and the *Hsiao Ching* for the *Jubilee*. I have asked our University Press to send review copies to the *Jubilee* with the hope that it may contact you directly.

In the meantime I hope that you will allow me to quote two lines in your letter concerning Dr. Wu's work as a testimonial statement in our promotion sale pamphlets. The lines read: "It seems to me that it is certainly the best English translation of this great Classic which I so love. I can think of no other better qualified to communicate its spirit than John Wu." Your consent would be profoundly appreciated.

With filial gratitude and homage, I am

> Your devoted son in Christ,
> Paul K. T. Sih
> Director

PS: md

---

men to God and gave them knowledge of Him. Before Christ's coming men had possessed, as it were, seeds of the Logos and had thus been enabled to arrive at fragmentary facets of truth. Hence such pagans as 'lived with reason' were, in a sense, Christians before Christianity" (citing *First Apology* 32.8 and 46.3; *Second Apology* 8.1, 10.2 and 13.3).

    16. John 1:14.

3. HLS[17]

ABBEY OF GETHSEMANI
TRAPPIST, KENTUCKY[18]

May 23, 1961

Dear Dr Sih.

It has been a little while since I received your kind letter and later on the copy of the *Hsiao Ching* for which I am deeply grateful. I have also heard from Jubilee + they are willing to have me review the two books so I intend in due time to do an article on them.[19] I enjoy the *Hsiao Ching* very much indeed. In its simplicity it has roots in the highest wisdom + one is surprised at the "modern" sound of some of its basic intuitions. I hope to study these two books carefully + in trying to write of them worthily I hope I will myself grow in wisdom.

I would be perfectly glad to give you permission to quote the lines you desire in connection with Dr Wu's translation of the *Tao Te Ching* – I would just ask you as a favor to suppress four words "which I so love" as it seems to me better if I do not obtrude too much of my own personality into the picture.

However I am very glad if I can do anything to help with your important publishing project. I look forward to seeing the *Liu-tsu T'an Ching* when it appears.

With cordial good wishes + with the assurance of my prayers for the work of the Asian Institute, in which I shall remain keenly interested at all hours,

Very faithfully yours in Christ
f m Louis

---

17. An abridged version of this letter is published in Thomas Merton, *The Hidden Ground of Love: Letters on Religious Experience and Social Concerns*, ed. William H. Shannon (New York: Farrar, Straus, Giroux, 1985) 549 (subsequent references will be cited as "*HGL*").

18. Printed letterhead, which also included a chalice with a cross above it.

19. On June 16, 1961, Merton wrote in his journal, "Since it rained I stayed in and wrote the review of the 'Two Chinese Classics' sent by Paul Sih (*Tao Te Ching* and *Hsiao Ching*)" (*TTW* 128).

4. TLS

St. John's University

GRAND CENTRAL AND UTOPIA PARKWAYS
JAMAICA 32, NEW YORK

INSTITUTE OF ASIAN STUDIES
OFFICE OF THE DIRECTOR

June 8, 1961

Reverend Father Louis
Abbey of Gethsemani
Trappist, Kentucky

Dear Reverend Father Louis:

It was a special blessing to receive your most gracious letter of May 23rd. Words are not adequate to express my deep appreciation of your generous words on the *Hsiao Ching*. I look forward to seeing your article on the *Tao Teh Ching* and the *Hsiao Ching* in *Jubilee*. This will be a high honor for the Asian Institute.

Our third book in the Translation Series is the *Liu-tsu T'an-ching*. It will be printed in the same format of the *Tao Teh Ching* and the *Hsiao Ching* with English and Chinese texts on facing pages. The reason why I insist in printing the Chinese text along with the English text is due to the fact that Chinese classical works, as Western classics, have variant readings. Without an accompanying Chinese version it is difficult for the reader to trace the validity and originality of the translated text. In the *Tao Teh Ching* and the *Hsiao Ching* we have already see [*sic*] the advantage of printing both text and translation. We hope that a more serious scholarly effort in Oriental Studies will be fostered by such an approach.

In this respect, I am thinking very seriously about your forthcoming project concerning the *Chuang Tzu*. For reasons given above, it would be most helpful if the Chinese text were printed along with the translation. I have discussed this point with Dr. John Wu. He seems to be very much in favor of my suggestion. After publication of the *Tao Teh Ching* and the *Hsiao Ching* the Institute has obtained considerable experience in the printing and circulating of books made in this special format. I would be most appreciative if you would give some thought to this humble suggestion of mine.

On my part, I firmly believe that your work on the *Chuang Tsu*, with the cooperation of Dr. Wu, will be received with enthusiasm by both Western and Eastern scholars.

May I beg for your continued blessing, I remain

Yours most devotedly in Our Lord,

Paul K. T. Sih

5. TLS

St. John's University

GRAND CENTRAL AND UTOPIA PARKWAYS
JAMAICA 32, NEW YORK

INSTITUTE OF ASIAN STUDIES
OFFICE OF THE DIRECTOR

July 26, 1961

Rev. Father Louis Merton
Abbey of Gethsemani
Trappist, Kentucky

Dear Father Louis:

Please forgive me for not replying to your letter of July 12th[20] earlier than today. I also received a letter from Father Robert MacGregor of the *New Directions*,[21] a copy of which is herewith enclosed. He seemed not too familiar with your plan concerning Chuang Tzu. After I explained my position and my readiness for any cooperative project, he felt more relieved and promised to further discuss this matter later on. To me, a facing bi-lingual edition is a *must* for such a creative undertaking. Dr. Wu agrees completely with me on this view.

Dr. Wu is still in this country. His plan of going to Formosa seems to be in suspense. I understand that he will come up to see you sometime in August or September whether he goes to Formosa or not.

My book *From Confucius to Christ*[22] is out of print. Fortunately,

---

20. This letter is not extant.

21. Robert M. MacGregor was an editor working with James Laughlin at New Directions, one of Merton's main publishers. In an unpublished July 11, 1961 letter to Paul Sih (TMC archives), he wrote that Merton had contacted them about Sih's interest in a joint publishing venture of a bilingual text of Chuang Tzu, which he calls "an interesting idea," but which he notes might result in disinterest or even arouse animosity among "Sinologues," since Merton would not be translating from the original but working from already existing translations. He suggests that further discussion is needed to clarify the project. In the event, of course, the book was published by New Directions alone, with no corresponding Chinese text.

22. Paul K. T. Sih, *From Confucius to Christ* (New York: Sheed & Ward, 1952).

I have secured a copy for you. Under separate cover I am sending it together with a copy of my recent book *Decision for China: Communism or Christianity.*[23]

I consider it a special honor to be able to visit with you at a time most suitable to you. Either October or November in midweek is good for me. I shall be delighted to give a lecture to the Sisters of Loretto[24] on my visit. Please let me know if and when any plans materialize.

It is a special blessing to read your poem.[25] The world has a place for humility, yielding, gentleness and serenity. But to enjoy these benefits one must "Learn to unlearn one's learning," – A Taoist axiom so well expressed in your *Wisdom.*

Yours ever in Christ,

Paul K. T. Sih

PKTS:md
Enc.

---

23. Paul K. T. Sih, *Decision for China: Communism or Christianity* (Chicago: Henry Regnery, 1959).

24. The motherhouse of the Sisters of Loretto was located in Nerinx, KY, not far from the Abbey of Gethsemani, and was the home of Merton's friend Mary Luke Tobin, SL, an official observer at the Second Vatican Council and a leader among American women religious. Merton often arranged for visitors to Gethsemani to speak to the community, and particularly the novices, at Loretto as well. See Bonnie Thurston, ed., *Hidden in the Same Mystery: Thomas Merton and Loretto* (Louisville, KY: Fons Vitae, 2010).

25. The poem is evidently "Wisdom," referred to by title below, which begins: "I studied it and it taught me nothing. / I learned it and soon forgot everything else" (ll. 1-2) (Thomas Merton, *The Strange Islands* [New York: New Directions, 1957] 85; Thomas Merton, *The Collected Poems of Thomas Merton* [New York: New Directions, 1977] 279).

6. TLS[26]

jhs

ABBEY OF GETHSEMANI
TRAPPIST, KENTUCKY

Aug. 16, 1961

Dear Paul:

It is already a long time since your letter of July 26th and the arrival of the two books, which I was so happy to receive. I began your Autobiography, and then one of the novices needed a book of this type as a change so I lent it to him, (he enjoyed it very much) while I myself proceded with your DECISION FOR CHINA. The latter is clear and illuminating. I have not yet quite finished it but it is a very meaningful book to me, and I thank you both for having written it and for having sent it to me. I will go back to the auto-biography next, and expect to enjoy very much getting to know you, like John Wu.

It is a pity that John is not coming after all, as he is now on his way to Formosa. He urges me to try my own hand at Chuang Tzu, and although I was scared to even think of it, I did a couple of short passages the other day and found they came out all right. At least I thought they did, but probably I have no real way of knowing. Of course it is just a matter of putting together three or four transla-tions and then following hunches, which is what John advised me to do, saying he would go over the finished product and make all the corrections. But it is hardly a work of scholarship, and honestly if *this* is going to be the procedure, I wonder if there is any point in your publishing the book.

Can you recommend any collection of basic ideograms? I feel I ought to know about two or three hundred, in order to orient myself in the original text. It might give some semblance of point to my doing a version in English.

I am so glad you can plan to come down in the fall. I don't know if John would be able to come with you, since he has not come this summer. By that time we might have some material to talk about, anyway, if I make any more headway with the versions. My aunt from New Zealand[27] is probably coming through here in October,

---

26. An abridged and lightly edited version of this letter is published in *HGL* 549-50.

27. Merton's Aunt Kit, Agnes Gertrude Stonehewer Merton (1889-1968),

and I am not yet sure of the date. Hence November would be better for us. I suggest the week of November 6th. Could we plan on your coming down say on the Tuesday of that week for two or three days? I can make tentative arrangements with the nuns at Loretto. Of course Father Abbot would surely want you to talk here, and John also if he comes.

We can discuss the details later.

Meanwhile, I am so happy with your books. I feel it is essential to know as much as possible about the situation in China today. The future of the world is being decided in Asia. Of this there can be no doubt whatever.

I am sending you a couple of my own books, which you probably have not read. One of them, the *Behavior of Titans*[28] is composed mostly of parables and myths which you might enjoy. In any case they come to you as a pledge of sincere friendship.

You are right in saying that a facing Chinese-English edition of selections from Chuang Tzu is needed, and I am sure New Directions would cooperate with you in this matter if I am to be the "translator". But I think we will have to wait and see how it goes first.

With cordial good wishes and all blessings,

Faithfully in Christ

Tom Merton

---

visited him at Gethsemani in November 1961; see his journal entries for November 4 and 5 (*TTW* 176-78).

28. Thomas Merton, *The Behavior of Titans* (New York: New Directions, 1961).

7. TLS

St. John's University

GRAND CENTRAL AND UTOPIA PARKWAYS

JAMAICA 32, NEW YORK

INSTITUTE OF ASIAN STUDIES

OFFICE OF THE DIRECTOR

October 17, 1961

Reverend Father Thomas Merton
Abbey of Gethsemani
Trappist, Kentucky

My beloved Reverend Father Louis:

Please forgive me for not writing you earlier than today. I returned from Formosa a couple of weeks ago. This is the earliest opportunity for me to deal with my much-belated correspondence.

I appreciate greatly your letter of August 16th and the two books together with a copy of *Wisdom in Emptiness*[29] which arrived this morning. Like all other works of yours, these provide me with a spiritual inspiration which I cannot get elsewhere.

While in Formosa I discussed with Dr. Wu the way of translating the *Chang Tzu* [*sic*]. It seems to me that Dr. Wu's suggestion is very sound. You make the draft and let Dr. Wu check with the Chinese text. In this way you will have the maximum freedom of interpretation and Dr. Wu will give the greatest attention to its *faithfulness*. This teamwork, I believe, will provide the best chance of achieving an excellent version leading to the meeting of Eastern and Western minds. This is going to be a "super translation" as an ideal translation should be.

I am now working on the English translation of *The Platform*

---

29. "Wisdom in Emptiness, A Dialogue: D. T. Suzuki and Thomas Merton," *New Directions in Prose and Poetry* 17 (1961) 65-101; this was an interchange originally intended to serve as an introduction to Merton's selected translations of the early desert fathers, published as Thomas Merton, *The Wisdom of the Desert: Sayings from the Desert Fathers of the Fourth Century* (New York: New Directions, 1960). When its inclusion was blocked by Merton's Cistercian religious superiors, it was published separately in the New Directions annual anthology, and it eventually appeared as Part II of Thomas Merton, *Zen and the Birds of Appetite* (New York: New Directions, 1968) 99-138 (subsequent references will be cited as "*ZBA*").

Scripture of the Sixth Patriarch, a Zen Buddhist classic. It has been translated by Prof. Wing-tsit Chan of the Dartmouth College. A facing Chinese-English format will be used. It is being edited by myself. As soon as I finish the editing, I will submit it to you for your reading and correction. If I am not indulged in your charity, I would beg you to write a brief introduction so that it may be able to invite greater attention from the reading public.

I am not too sure whether I am able to leave here in November. If you have not yet made up any plans for my trip, I suggest that it be better postponed to a subsequent date. Otherwise I am willing to do whatever you may advise.

As to a book on Elementary Chinese, I feel it is difficult to suggest one. There are several books in this category yet none is useful to the reader without the assistance of a tutor. In your case, it may be helpful to have a Chinese-English dictionary. However, before one can use it, he has to acquaint himself with the 214 radicals which are the keys to the structure of Chinese. This, again, has to be learned through instruction. If you can obtain some kind of help from a Chinese, I will send some Chinese books for your use.

I have with me two Sisters of Charity from St. Louis. They are learning Chinese with great efficiency and plan to go to Formosa for missionary work.

May I beg for your continued blessing, I am

Yours devotedly in Christ,

Paul K. T. Sih

PKTS:md

8. TLS[30]

jhs

ABBEY OF GETHSEMANI
TRAPPIST, KENTUCKY

Oct 24 1961

Dear Paul:

Very many thanks for your good letter of a week ago. I am glad to hear you have returned safely from Formosa, and are back at work at St John's. As for the Chuang Tzu suggestion, since both you and John agree, I must say I resign myself to it, and will attempt to do the work, in fact will enjoy it shamelessly: but it will certainly take time. We have here Matthews Chinese English dictionary[31] but I cannot make head or tail of it. However I plan to go through it and learn a hundred or so ideograms that may prove essential for this kind of text. I wish there was some sensible way of learning the 214 radicals but perhaps that doesn't make sense either without help from a Chinese. I will look around. A professor in the Baptist Seminary in Louisville might be able to give me some leads. But I will stay with Chuang Tzu and will try to do the work in the late winter.

In November I am going to be taken up with a writing job[32] that has been put off too long already and since you will probably not be able to get away I think it is best to put off the visit of you and John until next spring. Do you think it best for you to come together? I have not heard from him about this. I wrote to him tentatively putting off the visit.

I am especially happy to hear the *Platform Scripture* is coming along and I want very much to write a preface. I have not yet asked permission but I think there ought to be no special difficulty as this is a particular situation. I will let you know, but meanwhile

---

30. An abridged version of this letter is published in *HGL* 550.

31. *A Chinese–English Dictionary: Compiled for the China Inland Mission by R. H. Mathews* (Shanghai: China Inland Mission Press, 1931); revised edition: *Mathews' Chinese–English Dictionary* (Cambridge, MA: Harvard University Press, 1943), edited by Australian Congregationalist missionary Robert Henry Mathews (1877-1970).

32. This is possibly Thomas Merton, *Clement of Alexandria: Selections from* The Protreptikos (New York: New Directions, 1962), mentioned in journal entries of November 14, 19, 21 (*TTW* 179, 181, 182).

do please send the text as soon as convenient as I am anxious to read it. This can be a very important little publication and I think there is every hope that it will receive attention.

With every cordial good wish, and in union of prayers,

Devotedly yours in Christ

Tom Merton

9. TL[c]

November 15, 1961

Reverend Father Thomas Merton
Abbey of Gethsemani
Trappist, Kentucky

Dear Reverend Father Louis:

Please forgive me for not replying to your letter of October 24 earlier than today. I was glad to know that you have been getting along exceedingly well with the work on Chuang Tzu. It seems to me that the Matthews Chinese-English Dictionary is a good book for a beginner in the study of Chinese. As I said before, you would enjoy the study more if you had the assistance of a Chinese, even for a few lessons.

I talked with Dr. Wu about our possible trip to Gethsemani this coming spring. So far we have not foreseen anything which would prevent us from doing so. Of course, there might be a difficulty for us to travel together. We can see to it as things develop.

The *Platform Scripture* is still in composition. As soon as it is completed I shall forward a copy for your reading.

Last week I had the pleasure of meeting Mrs. Robert Hoguet[33] in her residence at New York. Although she is suffering from her crippled hip, she seems very healthy in view of her advanced age. I showed her the *Tao Teh Ching*. After reading a few lines, she immediately showed me your book on the Sayings of the Desert Fathers.[34] Indeed, there is a special kinship between the Eastern Sage and Western Wisdom.

Enclosed please find a reprint of my article on "The Mind of Asia in the Modern World" recently published in *World Justice*[35]

---

33. Louise Robbins Lynch Hoguet (1882-1965) was the widow of prominent New York lawyer and business leader Robert L. Hoguet (d. 1961), who had been active in many civic and religious groups. Presumably he and his wife had been supporters of the St. John's Institute of Asian Studies. The family's interest in China is evident from the involvement of their son, banker and civic leader Robert L. Hoguet, Jr., in the work of the China Institute, which promoted educational and cultural exchanges with China, becoming its chairman in 1980.

34. I.e. *The Wisdom of the Desert*.

35. Paul K. T. Sih, "The Mind of Asia in the Modern World," *World Justice*

by the Louvain University, Bruxelles, Belgium. I hope that you may like to have it.

May I beg for your continued blessing, I am

Father's filial son in Christ,

PKTS:md
Enc.

10. TLS[36]

jhs

ABBEY OF GETHSEMANI
TRAPPIST, KENTUCKY

Jan. 2, 1962

My Dear Paul:

Please forgive me for my very long silence. I hope that the sending of the WISDOM OF THE DESERT as soon as you referred to it was, temporarily, a sufficient sign of life and of friendship.

Naturally at Christmas more than at any other time I tend to be swamped with letters, like everyone else. So if I have been silent it does not mean that I have not prayed for you, and now I wish you all the best of new years and every grace.

John Wu says he wants to come down some time in the spring.[37] As I say, you should feel free to arrange to come down with him, or come at some other time that would be more convenient to you. February looks as if it were going to be rather crowded, now. I don't remember if I suggested that as a feasible time when I last wrote to John. In January we are on retreat after the 19th and that knocks out most of the month. March is Lent but that makes no special difference. Easter is not the best time, at least not Holy Week, as then too we are absorbed completely in liturgical offices. But anyway, I wanted to remind you.

Jubilee has said nothing whatever about publishing the article I sent them on the two Classics, the Lao Tse and the Filial Piety Classic. I do not really know whether they have given up the idea or what. I will finally push them again, for the third or fourth time, and try to find out. If they do not use it, I want of course to try it elsewhere.

---

36. An abridged version of this letter is published in *HGL* 550-51.

37. In his October 21, 1961 letter to Merton, Wu writes: "Early part of 1962 will suit me perfectly. I will write you further about the date" (*Merton & the Tao* 215). In his December 12 letter to Wu, Merton asks: "when would it be convenient for you to come down this next spring?" and inquires about the possibility of January, between semesters, or possibly later (*Merton & the Tao* 220). There is no further mention of a possible visit around this time, which did not take place, in the extant Merton–Wu correspondence.

I will look forward to receiving the Zen Sutra one of these days. I am in a mood for some Zen, with the complications of Christmas, Cold War, and the Lord knows what behind me. There are times when one has to cut right through all the knots, and the Zen view of things is a good clean blade.

All blessings in the New Year,

Ever cordially yours in Christ

Tom Merton.

11. TL[c]

January 4, 1962

Reverend Father Thomas Merton
Abbey of Gethsemani
Trappist, Kentucky

Dear Reverend Father Louis:

In one of your letters to me you indicated that you had written a review article on the *Tao Teh Ching* and the *Hsiao Ching* to be published sometime around the autumn of 1961 in the *Jubilee*. I have been most anxious to read it and, I am sure, it must be most inspiring.

Up to the present, it has not yet appeared in the *Jubilee*. Incidentally, Dr. Vincent Smith,[38] editor of the *New Scholasticism*, is looking for such an article. In case the *Jubilee* decides not to use it, Dr. Smith will be very happy to publish it in the *New Scholasticism*. I respectfully submit this suggestion for your kind consideration.

May I take this opportunity to wish you a joyous Christmastide and a very Happy New Year.

Gratefully yours in Christ,

Paul K. T. Sih
Director

PKTS:md

---

38. Vincent E. Smith (1915-72) was editor of *The New Scholasticism*, quarterly journal of the American Catholic Philosophical Association, from 1948 to 1966. He had become director of the Philosophy of Science Institute at St. John's University in 1959, after teaching at Catholic University, the University of Notre Dame and elsewhere.

12. TLS[39]

jhs

ABBEY OF GETHSEMANI
TRAPPIST, KENTUCKY

Jan 28, 1962

Dear Paul

After much delay I have finally got the copy of the article on the two Chinese Classics back from Jubilee, and I am sending it right along to you. It is all ready for publication in the "New Scholasticism" or any other magazine you see fit. Of course you must feel free to make changes and corrections as I am no scholar in this field and I would not want to say anything that would be incorrect or misleading.

We have just come out of a week's retreat and this has increased the delay. I am very sorry.

With very best wishes to you and also to John Wu, whose Christmas letter I much enjoyed.[40] I will reply to him when I get a chance.

Cordial blessings to you both,
Sincerely in Christ

Thomas Merton

---

39. An abridged version of this letter is published in *HGL* 551.

40. December 19, 1961 letter to Merton (*Merton & the Tao* 222), in which Wu mentions "The gift of your friendship" as a particular reason for being thankful at Christmas that year. The next extant communication from Merton to Wu is a postcard at Eastertime (April 18, 1962) (*Merton & the Tao* 225) in which he mentions his enjoyment of Paul Sih's visit and his hope that Wu might be able to visit in the summer.

13. TLS

St. John's University

GRAND CENTRAL AND UTOPIA PARKWAYS

JAMAICA 32, NEW YORK

INSTITUTE OF ASIAN STUDIES

OFFICE OF THE DIRECTOR

January 29, 1962

Reverend Father Thomas Merton
Abbey of Gethsemani
Trappist, Kentucky

Dear Reverend Father Louis:

Please forgive me for not replying to your letter of January 2nd earlier than today. I was exceedingly happy to know that you will ask *Jubilee* to publish your article on the two classics, the *Tao Teh Ching* and the *Hsiao Ching*. These two book [*sic*] have been receiving increasing attention from the American reading public. However, your evaluation will further promote the circulation on a widespread scale.

Today I received the mimeographed articles on "Christian Action in World Crisis"[41] and "Father Max Josef Metzger"[42] written by you. I read it with deep gratitude and appreciation. In this balance of terror we Catholics are still in need of a Christian principle with regard to war and peace. We are in the Cold War, but we have to work for peace, even a cold peace. The signs are that this cold peace is in the making. Both Russia and the United States are looking forward to it. We must exert every effort to sustain the tensions

---

41. Subsequently published as Thomas Merton, "Christian Action in World Crisis," *Blackfriars* 43 (June 1962) 256-68; Thomas Merton, *The Nonviolent Alternative*, ed. Gordon C. Zahn (New York: Farrar, Straus & Giroux, 1980) 219-26 (subsequent references will be cited as "*NA*"); Thomas Merton, *Passion for Peace: The Social Essays*, ed. William H. Shannon (New York: Crossroad, 1995) 80-91 (subsequent references will be cited as "*PP*").

42. Subsequently published (anonymously) as "Testament to Peace: Fr. Metzger's Thoughts about the Duty of the Christian," *Jubilee* 9.11 (March 1962) 22-25; *PP* 53-55 (two brief selections from Metzger with all of Merton's commentary); "A Martyr for Peace and Unity: Father Max Josef Metzger (1887-1944)," *NA* 139-43 (Merton's commentary followed by all fifteen excerpts from Metzger).

and negotiate for a possible "truce" if not a true peace. During the "truce" many things could happen including the disintegration of totalitarian structure on the other side of the world.

I am going to Winona, Minnesota, in the first of March for lectures at St. Teresa College.[43] On my way to New York, I plan to come to Gethsemani with the view of paying you my personal tribute. I shall be in Louisville on March 7 and will come to your Abbey on March 8th. I would appreciate your informing me of the most convenient way to reach your place from Louisville. I am planning to come back to Louisville on the same day.

Ever gratefully yours in Christ,

Paul Sih

PKTS:md

---

43. The College of Saint Teresa was a Catholic women's college in Winona, MN, founded and operated by the Franciscan Sisters of Rochester, MN from 1907 until its closing in 1989.

14. TL[c]

February 21, 1962

Reverend Father Thomas Merton
Abbey of Gethsemani
Trappist, Kentucky

Dear Reverend Father Louis:

I appreciate greatly your letter and the article. Words are not enough to express my deep gratitude for your generous thought and care. I recommend also the copy of your "Ascetical and Mystical Theology"[44] which must be of real value to my study of Christian spirituality.

I am pleased to come to Louisville from Chicago around midnight of March 7. If possible, please make hotel reservations at the Hotel Brown for the night of March 7. I understand that there is a bus connection between Louisville and Gethsemani. Then I will take an early bus as I am planning to leave Louisville for New York at 5:15 p.m. of March 8th.[45]

I will bring with me some teaching materials on Chinese, and hope that you may enjoy having them.

Yours ever in Christ,

PKTS:md

---

44. Mimeographed copy of Merton's notes for a series of conferences given in the spring and summer of 1961 to newly ordained monks, now published as Thomas Merton, *An Introduction to Christian Mysticism*, ed. Patrick F. O'Connell (Kalamazoo, MI: Cistercian Publications, 2008).

45. See Merton's journal entry for March 12, 1962: "Paul Sih was here the other day, and we got going on Confucius. I learned from him the rather complex skill of reading the Chinese Dictionary, and I will keep at the classics in the original (with a translation handy of course!). Even if I only learn one or two characters, and look long at them in their context, something worth while has been done" (*TTW* 210).

15. TLS

St. John's University

GRAND CENTRAL AND UTOPIA PARKWAYS

JAMAICA 32, NEW YORK

INSTITUTE OF ASIAN STUDIES

OFFICE OF THE DIRECTOR

March 27, 1962

Rev. Father Thomas Merton
Abbey of Gethsemani
Trappist, Kentucky

Dear Reverend Father Louis:

Please forgive me for not writing you earlier than now. Since my return to New York, I have busied myself with lectures and all the miscellaneous things.

When I lectured at Nazareth College[46] in the evening of March 8, I interviewed the two Chinese students there. I felt that their knowledge of Chinese is rather limited and that they might be of little help to your study, particularly in the classical language. My humble advice is to secure a Chinese Trappist and let him stay with you for one year or at least six months. With this arrangement, I am confident that you will be able to attain your intended goal.

I am enclosing some mimeographed sheets which are being used for the instruction of the classical language. If you find them useful, I will mail the succeeding materials from time to time.

I am very happy to inform you that St. John's has decided to publish the Zen classic. The author has also agreed to cooperate. I will meet the author in the first week of April. After this meeting, I may be able to send the manuscript for your private reading.

Your article on "Two Chinese Classics" has been sent to the *Chinese Culture Quarterly*[47] in Taipei, Taiwan. The Editor promised

---

46. Nazareth College in Louisville, KY was founded in 1920 by the Sisters of Charity of Nazareth, the first four-year Catholic college for women in the state. In 1969 it was renamed Spalding University after the foundress of the order, Mother Catherine Spalding, and is now a co-educational university.

47. Thomas Merton, "Two Chinese Classics," *Chinese Culture Quarterly* 4

to publish it in the June 1962 issue. As to the *Catholic World*,[48] I understand that Father Sheerin,[49] the Editor, will make direct contact with you.

In the current issue of *America* (March 31, 1962), Father Norris Clarke, S.J., wrote a very significant article "Is the West 'God's Civilization'?"[50] He quoted with admiration your article from *Commonweal* (Feb. 9, 1962).[51] I feel that this article has pointed out very forcefully the basic need of the re-Christianization of the West.

Before I conclude this, I must express my profound gratitude for your courtesy and paternal hospitality extended me during my visit with Gethsemani. Words actually cannot express this sentiment which can only be felt in the depth of my heart. I told Father Berry[52] and Dr. Wu of our pleasant meeting. They are very grateful

(June 1962) 32-41; *MZM* 69-80 (as "Love and Tao").

48. Thomas Merton, "Christian Culture Needs Oriental Wisdom," *Catholic World* 195 (May 1962) 72-79; Thomas Merton, *A Thomas Merton Reader*, ed. Thomas P. McDonnell (New York: Harcourt, Brace, 1962) 319-26; rev. ed. (Garden City, NY: Doubleday Image, 1974) 295-303. This version lacks seven substantial paragraphs found in the "Two Chinese Classics" version near the beginning of the article but adds an extensive conclusion commenting on the implications of this new title. A "complete" version with this title that includes all material found in each of the published articles, with an extensive headnote providing background information, is found in Thomas Merton, *Selected Essays*, ed. Patrick F. O'Connell (Maryknoll, NY: Orbis, 2013) 102-12.

49. John B. Sheerin, CSP (1906-1992) was editor of *The Catholic World*, published by the Paulist Fathers, from 1948 to 1972, an early leader in ecumenical dialogue and a theological advisor at the fourth and final session of the Second Vatican Council (1965). In an unpublished March 12, 1962 letter, Fr. Sheerin wrote to Merton about his interest in publishing "Christian Culture Needs Oriental Wisdom" in *The Catholic World* (TMC arvhives).

50. W. Norris Clarke, SJ, "Is the West 'God's Civilization'?"*America* 106.25 (March 31, 1962) 853. Fr. Clarke (1915-2008) was a Jesuit philosopher who taught at Fordham University for more than fifty years.

51. Thomas Merton, "Nuclear War and Christian Responsibility," *Commonweal* 75 (Feb. 9, 1962) 509-13; *PP* 37-47.

52. Thomas Berry (1914-2009) was a Passionist priest well-known for his advocacy of the integration of evolutionary science and spiritual consciousness, strongly influenced by the work of Pierre Teilhard de Chardin, and an outspoken advocate for protecting the environment. After completing a doctorate at the Catholic University of America, he spent a year in China in 1948-49 and later wrote two books on Asian religious traditions, *Buddhism* (New York: Hawthorne Books, 1966) and *Religions of India* (New York: Bruce-Macmillan, 1971). After teaching at Seton Hall University from 1957 to 1961 he joined the faculty at St. John's University from 1961 to 1965, moving to Fordham University in 1966,

for your kind remembrance of them.

With filial gratitude and homage, I remain

Yours filially in Christ,
Paul Sih

PKTS:nd
Encs.

where he founded and directed the History of Religions program until his retirement in 1979. From 1970 to 1995, he served as director of the Riverdale Center of Religious Research in New York.

16. TALS

St. John's University

GRAND CENTRAL AND UTOPIA PARKWAYS

JAMAICA 32, NEW YORK

INSTITUTE OF ASIAN STUDIES

OFFICE OF THE DIRECTOR

May 3, 1962

Reverend Father Thomas Merton
Abbey of Gethsemani
Trappist, Kentucky

Dear Reverend Father Louis:

Since I wrote you last, I have been busying myself with reviewing a number of books for various magazines. I was happy to be told by Dr. Wu that you have recently written him[53] of your continued interest in Chinese language study.

Sister Virginia Teresa, a Maryknoll Sister from Hongkong, is doing advanced work in Chinese at the Institute. She informed me that Rev. Dom Paulinus Lee, O.C.S.O., (Monastery of Our Lady of Liese, Lantao, Hongkong) commands good knowledge of Chinese language and culture. If your Monastery could secure him as a visitor, he would be an ideal and most competent tutor in Chinese. It seems to me that for effective learning, a Chinese tutor is really indispensable. I am enclosing a newspaper clipping from Hongkong showing the recent pictures of this Dom Lee.[54]

---

53. No extant letter from Merton to Wu at this period mentions this; in his March 9, 1962 letter to Merton, Wu had written, "By this time, Paul must have seen you, Father. I imagine that you are making strides with your Chinese" (*Merton & the Tao* 224), so presumably Merton had responded in the missing letter to this remark. However in his June 7 letter to Wu, Merton writes, "I must admit I have done absolutely no work at all on Chinese, because I find that I simply waste too much time fumbling around in the dictionary and so little is done that it does not make sense to continue until some time in the future when I can get some instruction. So it will all have to wait a bit" (*Merton & the Tao* 227).

54. The clipping, from the February 2, 1962 issue of the *Hongkong Sunday Examiner*, includes three photos, the first of Abbot Eusebius Wagner, OCSO of the Abbey of New Clairvaux in Vina, CA, the founding monastery of the Monastery of Our Lady of Joy, Lantao Island, Hong Kong, with the abbey prior, Paulinus Lee, OCSO; the second is a photo of Dom Paulinus, in Hong Kong for the annual

As I told you in person, James Legge's *Chinese Classics* (8 volumes)[55] has been recently reprinted in Formosa. I have secured a set which, with Chinese and English texts, is really beautiful. The reprinted edition is even better than the original as all the misprints in the original are corrected in the reprinted text. I have ordered a set to be presented to you as a little gift in token of my filial admiration and homage. It left Formosa by surface mail on April 21 and will be due in Gethsemani sometime by the end of May or the beginning of June. I hope that it will reach you in good condition.

The Institute is editing a textbook of *Selected Works of Chinese Literature*[56] for the instruction of Chinese on the advanced level. It will be completed soon. I will send a copy as soon as available.

I am exceedingly happy to see that the *Catholic World* has published your article in its condensed form. I understand that already several Catholic colleges are beginning to consider very seriously introducing some non-Western cultural courses in their regular curriculum. The influence of your pen (I mean your typewriter) is indeed phenomenal!

I am still waiting for the final version of the Zen classic from the author. I shall send you a copy of the manuscript as soon as possible.

With renewed expressions of filial gratitude, and in union of

---

"visitation" of the Trappist Father Immediate at his abbey's daughter house, with five members of the Lantao community; the third, headed "Trappist Refectory," pictures the refectory of the abbey with Dom Eusebius and Dom Paulinus seated at the head table and other members of the community at tables set up along the walls perpendicular to the head table.

55. James Legge (1815-97), *The Chinese Classics: with a Translation, Critical and Exegetical Notes, Prolegomena, and Copious Indexes*, 5 vols. in 8 (Hong Kong: Legge/London: Trubner, 1861–1872; Hong Kong: Hong Kong University Press, 1960): vol.1: *Confucian Analects*, the *Great Learning*, and the *Doctrine of the Mean* (1861); vol. 2: *The Works of Mencius* ; vol. 3, parts 1 and 2: *Book of Historical Documents* (*Shoo King*); vol. 4, parts 1 and 2: *Classic of Poetry* (*She King*); vol. 5, parts 1 and 2: *Spring and Autumn Annals* (*Ch'un ts'ew*). This collection consists of the Confucian Four Books and three of the five so-called Confucian Classics, traditionally believed to be edited by Confucius; the other two, the *I Ching* and the *Book of Rites*, were originally intended to be included in this edition but instead appeared as part of the 50-volume *Sacred Books of the East* series, edited by Max Muller (Oxford: Clarendon Press, 1879-1910).

56. *Selected Works of Chinese Literature* (*Zhongguo wen xue xuan du*), 3 vols. (New York: American Association of Teachers of Chinese Language and Culture, 1963-1969).

prayers, I remain

Father's filially in Christ,

Paul K.T. Sih[57]

PKTS:md

P.S. I believe that you have already received the copy of WANG YANG-MING by Carsun Chang recently published by the Institute.[58]

---

57. Sih's signature is followed here and in his July 10, 1962 letter by what is evidently an ink-stamp reproduction of his name in Chinese characters.

58. Handwritten addition.

17. TLS[59]

jhs

ABBEY OF GETHSEMANI
TRAPPIST, KENTUCKY

May 9, 1962

Dear Paul:

Your letter of the 3rd reached me this morning. Thank you very much for it. The Wang Yang Ming has *not* reached me however. I do not want to miss it. I hope it was not lost.

Above all I am happy about the Zen Scripture. I look forward to seeing it, and pray that I may be worthy to write a suitable intro- duction. I see more and more the awful complexity of the western mind which is my mind also, for better or for worse. I have been meditating here and there on Buddhist classics, in a small way, and find there an admirable therapy and simplification, wonderfully adapted to clear the way for grace, provided one does not become obsessed with a pride in one's own skill in meditating (not neces- sarily an urgent danger for me) or one's interior purity (still less, I am afraid.) If Buddhism is humble, then it can be wonderfully and admirably humble and can offer for the humility of Christ a beautiful and appropriate dwelling.

In a word, I look forward to seeing the Zen Classic, and perhaps the Lord is just waiting for me to be simple enough to receive it.

Above all I appreciate your brotherly generosity in procuring for me the magnificent set of Legge which is on its way from Tai- wan. This I certainly look forward to with keen anticipation and I will make room for plenty of time in which to study it. This is a wonderful gift, I can think of few that have been greater or more significant to me. I will let you know when it arrives safely.

And also the *Selected Works*, of which you spoke when you were here. This I will not yet be able to read. Your suggestion about Dom Paulinus was a wise and welcome one. I know him well, he turned up quite by surprise on the day I was ordained and I remem- ber having lunch with him and the bishop after the ordination Mass. He is an old friend. But he seldom comes to Gethsemani, I don't know why. He would be an excellent helper. But of course I don't suppose he could afford that much time away from his community.

---

59. An abridged version of this letter is published in *HGL* 551-52.

The picture was a joy to me because one of the American monks had been a student of mine and the Hawaiian brother was one of my novices formerly.[60]

I got a very entertaining letter from John Wu lately,[61] which I will answer when I can. Meanwhile I want to get this off to you, with a copy of a prayer of mine which was read in Congress.[62] By the way, I was glad to be able to write a different ending for the version of the article in the Catholic World, but sorry that in their introductory note they insisted on calling the Tao te Ching a book of Confucian ethics.

With best wishes to you always and all blessings for your work at the Institute,

Very cordially yours in Christ,

Tom Merton

---

60. This is evidently the novice mentioned in Merton's journal entry of August 24, 1956: "Fr. Pedro, getting around to want to leave, wrote to his people in Hawaii to say that he might want to leave but . . . What can one do about the sea-change that goes on inexorably below the surface of a soul without consulting anybody? Only the surface of his soul consults me, since he doesn't even consult himself" (Thomas Merton, *A Search for Solitude: Pursuing the Monk's True Life. Journals, vol. 3: 1952-1960*, ed. Lawrence S. Cunningham [San Francisco: HarperCollins, 1996] 72; subsequent references will be cited as "*SS*").

61. A reference to Wu's May 1, 1962 letter to Merton, in which he relates a humorous story at his own expense: in his April 18 Easter note Merton had referred to a Miss Brenda Hsu and told Wu that if she urged him to visit Gethsemani he should take it as a message of an angel and come; when Wu subsequently telephoned Miss Hsu he began the conversation by saying, "Is this my angel?" only to discover he was speaking to her sister, who was evidently not Christian and was in any case not amused, and was mollified only when Wu mentioned the name of Merton, which she recognized. Later Wu spoke to Brenda herself about the incident, "and we had a good laugh over it" (*Merton & the Tao* 226). Merton replied to Wu in a letter of June 7 (*Merton & the Tao* 227-28).

62. This was a prayer for peace requested by Congressman Frank Kowalski of Connecticut and read by him in the House of Representatives on April 18, 1962, during Holy Week, just before Congress recessed for Easter, which was subsequently published in *The Congressional Record* 108.5.6937-6938 (*NA* 268-70; *PP* 327-29). The prayer and the circumstances surrounding its composition and delivery are discussed in James G. R. Cronin, "A Nation under Judgment: Thomas Merton, Frank Kowalski and the Congressional Peace Prayer," *The Merton Annual* 28 (2015) 30-39, and Thomas T. Spencer, "'And God's Forgiveness': Frank Kowalski and Merton's Prayer for Peace," *The Merton Seasonal* 31.4 (Winter 2006) 9-13.

18. TL[c]

June 14, 1962

Reverend Father Thomas Merton
Abbey of Gethsemani
Trappist, Kentucky

Dear Reverend Father Louis:

Please forgive me for not acknowledging your letter of May 9th sooner than now. I am enclosing a copy of St. John's Alumni News[63] in which your article on Oriental Wisdom was reproduced. (I note with satisfaction that they have not insisted, at this time, to label the *Hsiao* as a Taoist classic!)

Dr. John Wu told me that after his lecture in Indiana, he will come to meet you at Gethsemani.[64] I am confident that this happy occasion will result in something beyond our ordinary expectations.

The Zen classic has taken its final shape. I will send the entire manuscript within a week or so. The author himself has written a very long introduction. This makes it unnecessary for you to write another one. I feel that it would do a great deal of good to the prestige of the Institute if you would make an independent study of Zen and let us have this work published in the *Asian Philosophical Series.* I earnestly hope that you will consider this suggestion of mine after you receive the Zen manuscript.

Have you received the book on *Wang Yang-ming*? Do you like it? The author is a good friend of Dr. Wu and myself.[65] He is

63. Thomas Merton, "Oriental Wisdom," *St. John's University Alumni News* 3.7 (May 1962) 1-3.
64. See Wu's June 19, 1962 letter to Merton announcing his plans to come to Gethsemani on Saturday, June 23, after delivering a paper at the Conference on Oriental–Western Literacy and Cultural Relations at Indiana University, Bloomington, and to stay for two or three days (*Merton & the Tao* 229). For Merton's enthusiastic report on this visit see his journal entry of June 26, 1962 (*TTW* 228-29); see also Wu's equally enthusiastic comments on the visit in his June 30 letter to Merton (*Merton & the Tao* 230-32).
65. Carsun Chang (Chang Chun-mai) (1886-1969) was a prominent Chinese philosopher, public intellectual and political figure, founder of a Chinese social democratic party intended as an alternative to both the Chinese Communist and Nationalist parties. After the Communist victory he fled to Taiwan but was dissatisfied with the Nationalist regime there and spent most of his later years in the United States, where he continued to lecture and write.

about 80 years old, but still very active and energetic. He is now lecturing in Germany.

May I beg for your continued blessing, I am

Father's ever in Christ,

PKTS:md
Enc.

19. TLS[66]

jhs

ABBEY OF GETHSEMANI
TRAPPIST, KENTUCKY

June 28th, 1962

Dear Paul:

John Wu left us the other day after a most pleasant visit. It was really good to see him face to face and talk with him at leisure, or more or less at leisure. He will have told you already of his visit, I suppose. It was a grace for me.

Yes, I have received *Wang Yang Ming* and I find him very interesting. The combination of Confucianism with, as John points out, a latent Buddhism, has considerable possibilities, it would seem.[67]

Sorry I cannot write that preface for the Zen book, but I hope I will be able to look it over one of these days. Probably you will want to get it into print first. If you could fit in a couple of pages from me, perhaps you could let me know and something could be done.

As I told John I do not think I am ready to write a whole book on Zen. I do not yet have the capacity, and I must study much more. Also meditate much more. I do not know, either, whether a scholarly attempt is what is required of me now, or any other time, on this subject. It seems others might do a better job in that line. I hope to see a translation of a German Jesuit's book on Zen,[68] that is announced.

---

66. An abridged version of this letter is published in *HGL* 552.

67. In a November 28, 1961 letter to Merton about his book *The New Man*, Wu had compared Wang Yang-ming with the earlier neo-Confucian thinker Chu Hsi (1130-1200): "Chu Hsi is theoretically more transcendent. Wang Yang Ming, more immanentist. But I feel that Wang is more spiritual than Chu. My conclusion was that if one is thorough-goingly immanentist, one is bound to arrive at a transcendence more authentic than a rationalist could conceive of" (*Merton & the Tao* 217).

68. Heinrich Dumoulin, SJ, *A History of Zen Buddhism*, trans. Paul Peachey (New York: Pantheon, 1963). Dumoulin (1905-95), along with his Jesuit colleagues William Johnston and Hugo Enomiya-Lassalle at Sophia University in Tokyo, was a pioneer in interreligious dialogue with Zen Buddhists. Two of Merton's letters to him from 1964 respond to his invitation to come to Japan and experience Zen first-hand, an invitation he was unable to accept (see *HGL* 170-74).

Finally, the big volumes of the Classics have arrived and I am most pleased with them. They are a wonderful and treasured acquisition and I will strive to make the very best use of them as time goes on, if God wills.

With the most cordial good wishes,

Ever yours in Christ,
Tom Merton.

20. TLS

St. John's University

GRAND CENTRAL AND UTOPIA PARKWAYS

JAMAICA 32, NEW YORK

INSTITUTE OF ASIAN STUDIES

OFFICE OF THE DIRECTOR

July 10, 1962

Reverend Father Thomas Merton
Abbey of Gethsemani
Trappist, Kentucky

Dear Reverend Father Louis:

I was most grateful for your letter of June 28th and was happy to know that you have received the five volumes of the Classics.

Dr. Wu told me of his most pleasant visit with you at Gethsemani. I hope that I shall be able to renew my experience which has been so dear to my heart.

I hope that you have finished reading the book on *Wang Yang-ming*. The University Press is preparing a promotion piece for this book. We would appreciate it very much if you would care to write a few words so that we may be able to include them as testimonials.

As to the Zen classic, the manuscript has come into its final shape. It is ready for print. I am enclosing a copy for your reading. There are several changes in the text. It is not very clear. A clear copy will be made. I shall send you a copy as soon as it is available.

I quite understand the reason why you do not wish to write a whole book on Zen at the present time. However, I do earnestly hope that you will write an article on Zen as you did on the two books, *Tao* and *Hsiao*. Of course, there is no hurry. You may do it after the book on Zen is ready. In making this humble request, I am absolutely sure that anything coming from your pen is an inspiration to my present endeavor and future projects. The translation series is still in the infant stage. There leaves much to be done. What my Institute needs most now and in the future is moral support, and I could get no stronger support than from whatever you may care to say.

May I beg for your continued blessing, dear Father Louis, and I remain

Yours ever in Christ,
Paul Sih

PKTS:md
Enc.

21. TLS[69]

ABBEY OF GETHSEMANI
TRAPPIST, KENTUCKY

Aug 24, 1962

Dear Paul:

It is a long time since I received the remarkably interesting translation of the "Platform Sutra" and I ought to have acknowledged it long ago. The translation and the introduction by Wing Tsit Chan are both extremely interesting. It is an invaluable document, and will mean much to everyone who is interested in Zen Buddhism. I have not written about it as I wanted time to comment fully. I have not had time for that yet, and also I would like to keep the manuscript a little longer and go over it again. I expect to be in the hospital for a check up in a few days[70] and I will meditate on the text there, I hope. In any case it will get a second and more serious reading.

Certainly your suggestion for an article on Zen is a good one and I will keep it in mind. I certainly want to do this, and this would be an excellent occasion. That is why I want to keep the manuscript a little longer. Perhaps I can get to this around the end of Fall. At present I have several other jobs to do. Also I am supposed to get down to work on a book that I have been putting off.[71]

---

69. An abridged version of this letter is published in *HGL* 552.

70. Merton was in the hospital on Sunday, September 2 (presumably having come on Friday, August 31, since he is already able to note on Sunday that "Nothing has showed up in tests") and returned to Gethsemani on September 5; see the journal entries for September 2, 3 and 6 (*TTW* 241-44).

71. This is evidently the never-published *Prayer as Worship and Experience*, the manuscript of which Merton mentions correcting in his September 2 journal entry (*TTW* 242). Merton contracted to publish this book with Macmillan, not realizing that this would be in violation of his contract with his regular publisher, Farrar, Straus and Giroux; eventually the contract was voided and the book remained unpublished (though portions of it were later used in Merton's late book *The Climate of Monastic Prayer* [Washington, DC: Cistercian Publications, 1969], also published as *Contemplative Prayer* [New York: Herder & Herder, 1969]). For an overview of the problem see the introduction to Thomas Merton and Robert Giroux, *The Letters of Robert Giroux and Thomas Merton*, ed. Patrick Samway, SJ (Notre Dame, IN: University of Notre Dame Press, 2015) 16-17; the letters between Merton and Giroux between December 12, 1962 and September 6, 1963 (293-311) provide details; see also chapter VII of William H. Shannon, *Thomas Merton's Dark Path: The Inner Experience of a Contemplative* (New

This is not an adequate letter but it is at least an acknowledgement of the manuscript and an indication that I intend to do something about it, though I am not yet quite sure what.

Keep me posted with regard to all your interesting projects at the Institute for Asian Studies. Fr Dan Berigan[72] [*sic*] brought me messages from Fr Beer[73] [*sic*] and John Wu. I was glad to hear from them. The Chinese books are there but . . . . I think that perhaps I will have to put off serious work in this field until I am replaced as novice master by somebody else and can devote more time to study. This too may be a vain hope. But our prayers may be heard that some how I may get down to this work in an efficacious way. But I do not think it would be a wise economy of effort to spend a great deal of time trying to piece together riddles which a regular study course under a teacher would dispose of in a few minutes. And this too will have to wait until a really propitious situation arises. However, I am sure that somewhere along the line we will find a way to do this.

Father Abbot is going away to the General Chapter in a few days, in fact tomorrow. When he returns and as the year nears its end I will perhaps know more about all this. If he were to replace me in the novitiate I might perhaps ask permission to go somewhere and study though this would be extraordinary and perhaps impossible.

With the very best of wishes always

Cordially yours in Christ,
Tom Merton

York: Farrar, Straus, Giroux, 1982) 164-88 for a discussion of Merton's use of material from the 1962 manuscript in the later book.

72. Poet and peace activist Daniel Berrigan, SJ, who had been corresponding with Merton since November 1961 (see *HGL* 70-101 for Merton's letters to him) visited Gethsemani for the first time in mid-August 1962; see Merton's journal entry for August 21 (*TTW* 238).

73. I.e. Thomas Berry (see letter 15).

22. TL[c]

September 5, 1962

Reverend Father Thomas Merton
Abbey of Gethsemani
Trappist, Kentucky

My much-beloved Father Louis:

I appreciate greatly your kind letter of August 24th and am glad to know that you are interested in the reading of the Zen translation. You may keep the text as long as you like. The book is entering into the process of production. I will send a copy of page proof as soon as it is available. As it contains a Chinese text and Chinese characters in the introduction and notes, the printing work is rather complicated. I hope and pray that everything will turn out perfectly well. (The Chinese text is being type-set in Hongkong.)

As to the specialized study of Chinese language and literature, I must confess that it can be limited only to those who can give their full energy to the study in a professional manner. However, the capacity of the human mind is much greater than we thought in past generations. In the linguistic study of the Chinese language, I find that we can, with effective method and technological devices, achieve in one year what in previous days required two or even three years. I firmly believe that if you can spare one year's time and devote it entirely to the study of the *classical* Chinese (*wen-yen*, not *pai-hwa*[74]) much can be accomplished.

This fall we have a Dr. Chou with us. He will work as a research associate in cooperation with Father Berry. Dr. Chou is a fine scholar and an accomplished historian of the classical period of China. I hope that he will accomplish something during his stay here at St. John's.

I met Dr. Wu several times recently. He is now very much interested in Chinese ancient history. He joins me in sending you our best wishes and warmest respects.

Yours ever in Christ,

PKTS:md

---

74. *Wen-yen* is classical Chinese, written in the complex style used in classical literature, whereas *pai-hwa* (or *pai-hua*) is a form of written Chinese based on modern colloquial usage.

23. TLS

St. John's University

GRAND CENTRAL AND UTOPIA PARKWAYS

JAMAICA 32, NEW YORK

INSTITUTE OF ASIAN STUDIES

OFFICE OF THE DIRECTOR

September 25, 1962

Reverend Father Thomas Merton
Abbey of Gethsemani
Trappist, Kentucky

Dear Father Louis:

Today I received the September issue of *Jubilee* and am exceedingly delighted to read your excellent article on the Chinese rites and the vernacular.[75] It is most inspiring and thought-provoking.

Indeed, if missionaries are to be really successful, they must become one with the natives in their mission territory; and that means embracing the traditions, language, and customs of the people. The all-important thing is the Real Presence of Our Lord and our union with Him in offering the Supreme Homage to Our Father. But given a genuine spirit of worship and love, I cannot help thinking that the people assisting at the Holy Sacrifice would feel an even more intimate participation in it if they could hear the words in their own mother tongue, as happened in the Cenacle on the first Pentecost in the presence of our Blessed Mother. You have expressed so well the common sentiment and desire of the Chinese faithful who will say with St. Paul, "I will pray with the spirit, I will pray also with the understanding; I will sing with the spirit, I will sing also with the understanding."[76]

Incidentally, the Editor of the *Redman*, St. John's University Alumni Magazine, wishes to have a leading article on Sterilization and Abortion, a problem so important, yet so confusing at the

---

75. Thomas Merton, "The Jesuits in China," *Jubilee* 10.5 (September 1962) 35-38; *MZM* 81-90; in his September 2 journal entry he had remarked, "I hear censors have now stopped my article on the *Jesuit Missions in China!* What next?" (*TTW* 242) but this was evidently an erroneous rumor.

76. 1 Cor. 14:15.

present. We both think that it would be most ideal if you would write something on it. I fully understand that the burden of work already imposed on you does not allow further imposition on your time and energy. Yet this problem is so important to the future of mankind, I would appreciate it very much if you would consider writing something about it. Of course, if you cannot do this, I will fully understand your situation. Kindly favor me with a few words so that I shall be able to communicate with the Editor of the *Redman*.

With renewed assurance of filial devotion and homage, I am

Father's ever in Christ,
Paul K. T. Sih

PKTS:mdp

24. TLS[77]

jhs

ABBEY OF GETHSEMANI
TRAPPIST, KENTUCKY

Oct 16, 1962

Dear Paul:

The usual complaint of those who have too many occupations: I did not have time to get to your letter yet. But I am doing so finally. I am certainly very glad you liked the Jubilee article. I enjoyed writing it.

It is just not possible, though, for me to tackle the problem of Sterilization and Abortion for the *Redman*. That takes professional handling, and I am completely incompetent. I have no real grasp of the complexities of the thing, and it would be disastrous simply to grind out a repetition of the hackneyed responses that are usually given. Respect for the depths of human tragedy compel me not to approach such a subject without being fully qualified to treat it.

I hope soon to send you a copy of the new READER,[78] a collection of my work that is just out. I think you will like it, and perhaps they would want to review it in *Redman*. I know that is no compensation for failure to produce an article. . . .

And so, I send you all my best wishes, hope you are well and flourishing, and wish I could get back to Chinese studies. Alas, I am trying to finish a small book,[79] and can just about keep my head above water. And we have monastic problems on the horizon, with some important new changes to be made.[80] I will probably be concerned with the mechanics of these, and this means more work

---

77. An abridged version of this letter is published in *HGL* 553.

78. See above, n. 48.

79. This is probably a reference to Thomas Merton, *Life and Holiness* (New York: Herder & Herder, 1963), for which the official permission to publish is dated November 29, 1962 (iv).

80. Merton is referring to the merger of the choir novitiate with that of the lay brothers, and the establishment of a new monastic formation program for newly professed monks before they begin formal studies leading to ordination, both scheduled to begin on January 1, 1963. For details see the introduction to Thomas Merton, *Pre-Benedictine Monasticism: Initiation into the Monastic Tradition* 2, ed. Patrick F. O'Connell (Kalamazoo, MI: Cistercian Publications, 2006) xi-xvi.

and less time.

But the Lord holds all our affairs in the grasp of His loving peace, and we need not be too concerned.

With all cordial good wishes,
Faithfully in Christ,
Tom Merton

25. TALS

St. John's University

GRAND CENTRAL AND UTOPIA PARKWAYS

JAMAICA 32, NEW YORK

INSTITUTE OF ASIAN STUDIES

OFFICE OF THE DIRECTOR

January 31, 1963

Reverend Father Thomas Merton
Abbey of Gethsemani
Trappist, Kentucky

My much-beloved Father Louis:

Please forgive me for this much-belated acknowledgment of receipt of your booklet on "Clement of Alexandria." I read it with great interest and enthusiasm. As a matter of fact, Clement of Alexandria has always been my favorite model for Christian living in the modern world.

Even further he should be considered as the model for the intellectual apostolate in the mission lands of Asia. St. Paul was the first to adapt Christian thought to a new people. Later Justin and the apologists used Greek thought in defense of the Church. Clement, however, did much more. He took, for the first time, a positive approach to Greek learning and showed how well it could be united with Christian revelation to form one complete pattern of Christian wisdom, one integral Christian humanism, in which reason and revelation sustained, defended, and, each in its own way, perfected the other.

If Clement succeeded in giving a new vigor to the faith and adding richness to Christian culture by reference to Greek thought in the second century, why can not Christians now use the same program of the Catechetical School of Alexandria to integrate Christian teaching with the native traditions of Asia? Clement has done it before us. We need only to follow his path.

The difference between our work and his is that he worked in a corner of the eastern Mediterranean while we work in full view and in intimate contact with all the world. Clement worked with a philosophical and literary tradition. We must work with a[81] greater complex of philosophical and literary traditions and at the same time adapt ourselves to new social structures, new political forms, and an entirely new machine age. Thus our task is thousand-fold greater, and our Clement must be an entire body of Christian scholars working in various centers throughout the West and the East.

Our work needs unity. At present it is a haphazard, inconsistent disorganized thing. It is far too scattered. What we need most urgently is an overall direction by men with superlative talent in comprehending the whole problem in its entirety and in all its complexity. This is something which I feel should be seriously considered by the Ecumenical Council in Rome.[82]

Your inspiring work motivates me in saying something which might seem to be too idealistic. But I realize that without following the example set up by Clement, we could hardly face the situation which is often opposed to Christianity, but which is nevertheless in a state of expectancy, looking for better things.

Respectfully and gratefully,
Paul K. T. Sih

PKTS:mdp

P.S. The Zen Buddhist classic is now in print. It is expected to be available after a couple of months or so.[83]

---

81. "philosophical . . . with a" added by hand in lower margin and marked for insertion.

82. The first session of the Second Vatican Council had taken place in the fall of 1962.

83. Handwritten addition.

26. TALS

St. John's University

GRAND CENTRAL AND UTOPIA PARKWAYS
JAMAICA 32, NEW YORK

INSTITUTE OF ASIAN STUDIES
OFFICE OF THE DIRECTOR

April 9, 1963

Reverend Father Thomas Merton
Abbey of Gethsemani
Trappist, Kentucky

Dear Father Louis:

I appreciate greatly your letter of March 28 in sending a copy of your book review[84] of Father Dumoulin's *A History of Zen Buddhism*. Your critical comment on the difference between the Northern School of Shen-hsiu (神 秀) and the Southern School of Hui Neng (惠 能) is most thorough and thought-provoking. I believe that Father Dumoulin will feel appreciative of your constructive study.[85]

Our *Platform Scripture* is now in the final process of production. It will be available before the end of this month. I am most grateful that you put a plug in the article. Kindly insert the following in the footnote:

(12) *The Platform Scripture, The Basic Classic of Zen Buddhism*, translated and with an introduction and notes by Wing-tsit Chan, St. John's University Press, 1963.

I notice that on page 20, line 14, you referred the location of the Asian Institute of St. John's University to be in Brooklyn. Actually, it is situated in Jamaica. Will you please change the word

---

84. This was a mimeographed draft copy of what would be published as Thomas Merton, "The Zen Revival," *Continuum* 1 (Winter 1964) 523-28 and in expanded form as "Mystics and Zen Masters" (*MZM* 3-44).

85. Merton is critical of what he sees as Dumoulin's insufficient distinction between the "mirror-wiping" Zen of the Northern school and the more radical emptiness of Hui Neng (see *MZM* 29-34), relying particularly on D. T. Suzuki, *The Zen Doctrine of No Mind: The Significance of the Sutra of Hui-neng* (London: Rider & Company for the Buddhist Society, 1949, 1958).

"Brooklyn" into "Jamaica, New York"?

I am enclosing a set of galley-proofs of this work which you may like to see before the book comes out. There are a few changes in the galley but of minor importance. I shall send a copy as soon as available.

As this book is most important for a real understanding of Zen Buddhism, I earnestly hope that you, dear Father, will be good enough to write a review article so that it will receive greater attention from the reading public.

Last week I was in Dr. Wu's home and enjoyed the pleasure of reading your letter addressed to him.[86]

By the way I also enjoyed reading your foreword to Ernesto Cardenal's poems.[87] His works remind me of a Chinese poem by Chang Chien.[88] Entitled "The Temple Hill," it echoes his thought in a very beautiful manner. Permit me to reproduce it here:

THE TEMPLE HILL

The sun sets aflame the giant forest,
When I darken at dawn the ancient temple door.
A winding path leads me to the gloom sweet
The temple hall is almost chequered into night
By rioting shadows of trees and flowers;
While mountain-light is instinct with
Rejoicing bird-spirit all all round.
In the hush peace comes dropping
Into a mind stirless as a deep pool.

---

86. Merton's letter of March 28, 1963 (*Merton & the Tao* 247-48) which was also accompanied by his draft of the Dumoulin review.

87. The introductory note to Merton's translation of a selection of poems by the Nicaraguan poet (and future revolutionary) Cardenal, who had been a novice at Gethsemani under Merton's direction from 1957 to 1959 (see Thomas Merton, *Emblems of a Season of Fury* [New York: New Directions, 1963] 114-24). For their correspondence, see *From the Monastery to the World: The Letters of Thomas Merton and Ernesto Cardenal*, ed. and trans. Jessie Sandoval (Berkeley, CA: Counterpoint, 2017).

88. An early eighth-century poet of the T'ang Dynasty; the poem, also known as "Behind a Buddhist Retreat," is #98 in the celebrated anthology *T'ang-shih san-pai-shou*, or *Three Hundred Poems of the T'ang*, assembled in 1763 by the Chinese scholar Sun Chu. The translation is apparently unpublished, and may perhaps by Paul Sih himself.

The dust and din now turns silent as ashes
Save the breathing of the temple bell
Still lingers on and on.

May I wish you a very joyous Easter.

Yours ever in Him,
Paul K. T. Sih

PKTS:mdp
Encs.

27. TL[c]

May 13, 1963

Rev. Father Thomas Merton
Abbey of Gethsemani
Trappist, Kentucky

Dear Reverend Father Louis:

Enclosed please find a check of $24.00 for the honorarium of your article "Two Chinese Classics" published by the *China Culture Quarterly*. I would be most appreciative if you would sign and return the enclosed receipt to me at your earliest convenience.

The Zen book has already been completed. Due to a few misprints, we need a little more time for adjustments. I hope that it will be ready for distribution around the end of May.

With warmest regards, I am

Yours ever in Christ,

PKTS:mdp
Encs.

28. TLS

St. John's University

GRAND CENTRAL AND UTOPIA PARKWAYS

JAMAICA 32, NEW YORK

INSTITUTE OF ASIAN STUDIES

OFFICE OF THE DIRECTOR

June 3, 1963

Reverend Father Thomas Merton
The Trappists
Gethsemani, Kentucky

Dear Reverend Father Louis:

I appreciate greatly your two studies on Francois Fenelon.[89] I am positive that I shall enjoy reading them very much as I often did with previous works of yours.

Allow me to present a copy of *The Platform Scripture*, the basic Zen Buddhist classic. The production was delayed, as we have to reprint a few pages in which there are several serious misprints. Now it is ready. I hope that you will like it, at least, the format.

As the study of Zen has become a center of interest in the West I shall be most grateful if you will consider reviewing it or writing a special article, possibly for the *Jubilee*.

Considering our limited financial resources we have made a substantial investment in this book. It is hoped that this Buddhist classic will draw adequate attention from the American public. A

---

89. Two mimeographs on François de Salignac de la Mothe-Fénelon (1651-1715), Archbishop of Cambrai during the reign of Louis XIV and celebrated spiritual writer in the era of the French quietist controversy: one was published as Thomas Merton, "Reflections on the Character and Genius of Fénelon," a prefatory essay in *Fénelon: Letters of Love and Counsel*, trans. John McEwen (New York: Harcourt, Brace & World, 1964) 9-30; the other is an unpublished 14-page collection of passages from Fénelon on peace, entitled "A Ruler's Examination of Conscience: Some Texts from François Fénelon"; see his May 13, 1963 letter to Helen Wolff, the Harcourt, Brace publisher who had invited him to write the preface: "In writing about Fénelon I decided to mimeograph some texts from him on peace, and made use of a couple of passages that were in the ms. of the letters. I am not planning to publish this, though it may perhaps be printed somewhere like *The Catholic Worker*. So I hope I have your permission to do this" (*CT* 104).

word from your pen will, I am absolutely sure, greatly increase the prestige of this publication. Therefore, anything you may do for this modest book will be profoundly appreciated.

I have also sent a copy to Mr. Rice of the *Jubilee*.

I am going to St. Louis next week for a series of three lectures on Contemporary China at the University of St. Louis. I hope that I shall be able to come to Kentucky in the not too distant future.

With warmest and filial respects, I remain

Father's ever in Him

Paul K. T. Sih

29. TLS[90]

jhs

ABBEY OF GETHSEMANI
TRAPPIST, KENTUCKY

June 26, 1963

Dear Paul:

I deeply appreciated your letter of April 9th, though I did not get around to answering it. The Temple Hill poem was very attractive. I have written a brief review of the *Platform Scripture* for the Boston Pilot.[91] I haven't heard anything from Ed Rice, and from the way he dallied with the review of the other two texts, finally not publishing them, I think there would be small hope of his taking a review article of this. Perhaps I am wrong.

In any case I think it is a most handsome book, and I compliment you on it. I wish I had been able to do at least enough work on Chinese to take advantage of the Chinese text with translation. Unfortunately it is just not possible for me, with my heavy schedule, to advance with Chinese. Perhaps if I get out of the job of novice master it may become possible. That does not seem likely for a while at least.

It is always good to hear from you, and if you are going to be down this way please drop me a line and I will alert the Guest House to be ready in case you drop in. It would be a great pleasure to see you again.

With the most cordial good wishes, in Christ,
Tom Merton

---

90. An abridged version of this letter is published in *HGL* 553.

91. *The Pilot* was the newspaper of the Archdiocese of Boston; Merton's contact there was Thomas P. McDonnell, who edited the *Merton Reader*. *The Pilot* had previously published Merton's review of Heinrich Dumoulin's *The History of Zen Buddhism* and *The Development of Chinese Zen*, which was incorporated into the essay "Mystics and Zen Masters": Thomas Merton, "Monastic Christianity Encounters the Spirit of Zen," *The Pilot* 134.15 (April 13, 1963) 10.

30. TL[c]

July 15, 1963

Reverend Father Thomas Merton
Abbey of Gethsemani
Trappist, Kentucky

My much-beloved Father Louis:

I appreciate greatly your letter of June 26th and am grateful to know that you have written a review on the *Platform Scripture* for the Boston *Pilot*. I am sure that with your endorsement, the book will receive greater attention from the reading public.

At the present, Dr. Wu is doing an anthology of Chinese poems (with special emphasis on the T'ang period) which will be published by the Institute.[92] In the meantime I am in dire need of some studies on Oriental philosophy and culture. I would be most grateful if you, dear Father, will favor me and the Institute with something in this field for our publication in the *Asian Philosophical Series*. If you wish to put some of your published articles or papers together in a book form, we will be glad to undertake the publication also. We are trying to do our best so far as the printing and art work are concerned. You may notice this in the publications of the *Tao*, the *Hsiao* and the *Platform Scripture*.

Although we may not remunerate the author as adequately as the commercial firms, we are ready to pay loyalties [*sic*] not less than the ordinary standard. In the case of the Platform Scripture, we pay the author a loyalty of 10%. I know that you will not consider this seriously. But your institution may regard your writings as a help to its financial resources for community development. Therefore, I shall seek to extend the compensation as adequately as possible. In saying this I may seem to be too materialistic. However, I must be realistic when we are dealing with practical problems.

I am teaching two courses on modern China this summer. I have no definite plan to travel in the near future. In case you have any plan on publication which might need my presence, I shall be only too glad to make a trip to Gethsemani.

---

92. John C. H. Wu, *Four Seasons of T'ang Poetry* (Rutland, VT: Tuttle, 1972).

Wishing you an enjoyable summer and begging for your continued blessings, I am

Yours ever in Christ,

PKTS:mdp

31. TLS[93]

jhs

ABBEY OF GETHSEMANI
TRAPPIST, KENTUCKY

Aug. 18, 1963

Dear Paul:

I have been waiting to find out exactly what was going to be done with that review I wrote of the *Platform Scripture*. It still does not appear to have been printed in the *Pilot*. Maybe the editor thought it was too far out for a Catholic diocesan paper. I have written to inquire and if they have not printed it, I want it back to send to Jubilee. I will let you know.

It would be great to do a small book for you on Zen, but whichever way I look at it now, the project is just impossible. The main reason for this is that I have been in a great tangle with Farrar Straus and Co, which has resulted from my inadvertently violating a contract by offering a book to another publisher without the proper clearance.[94] This has caused untold trouble and at the moment I do not think it would be wise in any way for me to propose doing a book for you or for any other publisher, at least until I have worked out my contract with them. Besides, I have really been spreading my work out all over the place too much, and it is necessary at the present moment to get back within certain limits. So therefore I simply must avoid branching out again. I cannot undertake to do a book for you at the moment. It is a pity, but perhaps later.

This does not mean that you could not come down without this pretext. We do not need to be working on a book for you to visit here. September however is almost all taken up by the Louisville priests on retreat, but the rest of the fall, after the first week in October, is free as far as I know now. Do not hesitate to take a trip down if you feel like a couple of days of peace in the monastery! You will always be most welcome.

With all best wishes and blessings, always,
Most cordially yours in Christ,
Tom Merton

---

93. An abridged version of this letter is published in *HGL* 553-54.
94. See note 71 above.

32. TL[c]

August 22, 1963

Rev. Father Thomas Merton
Abbey of Gethsemani
Trappist, Kentucky

My much-beloved Father Louis:

I appreciate greatly your letter of August 18 and fully understand the situation which has made it difficult for you to do a book for me at the present. It is hoped that this project will materialize at a time when you feel more propitious and convenient.

It is most gratifying to know that you will send your review to *Jubilee*. This is even better than the *Pilot*. Kindly keep me informed of its development.

It is always a special blessing to be able to be with you in the monastery. I shall try to see in my schedule whether it is not possible to make a trip sometime in the latter part of November.

Sometime ago, you indicated your desire of re-translating some of Chuang-tzu's works. I may be able to contribute a small share of interpreting the Chinese text. This is only one instance. There are many other ways which, I am sure, would provide me with good chances of serving you, even in a very modest manner.

Most gratefully in Christ,

PKTS:dc

33. HLS[95]

ABBEY OF GETHSEMANI
TRAPPIST, KENTUCKY

October 2.

Dear Paul.

Please forgive my failure to answer your letter sooner. I have been in the hospital, and am still not able to type effectively.[96]

If you should be here over the Thanksgiving weekend I would be happy to see you + perhaps you could participate in a discussion on mysticism with some Baptists.[97]

I have not done much with Chuang Tzu but I might have a few pieces to discuss by then.

How is John Wu? I have not heard from him for a long time.[98]

With very best wishes in Christ

Tom Merton

The review appeared in the *Pilot* after all.[99] Did they send you a copy?

---

95. A lightly edited version of this letter is published in *HGL* 554.

96. See Merton's journal entries of September 19 and 20, 1963 concerning his time in the hospital due to cervical disc and other back problems (Thomas Merton, *Dancing in the Water of Life: Seeking Peace in the Hermitage. Journals, vol. 5: 1963-1965*, ed. Robert E. Daggy [San Francisco: HarperCollins, 1997] 16-18; subsequent references will be cited as "*DWL*").

97. See Merton's November 30, 1963 journal entry concerning discussions with visiting Baptist and Presbyterian seminary professors (*DWL* 40).

98. In *Merton & the Tao* (255), a letter to Merton from Wu is dated Aug 9, 1963, but this is evidently an error for June 9, 1965, as it refers to Merton's hospital stay as concluding on "the 6th" which corresponds to his June 4-6, 1965 stay in the hospital at Lexington (*DWL* 253); it also mentions his working on *The Way of Chuang Tzu*, and in Merton's journal entry for June 3 he writes: "Finished the introduction to *Chuang Tzu* this morning" (*DWL* 253). The most recent letter from Wu is dated March 31, 1963 (*Merton & the Tao* 249), and Merton's reply is dated June 23, 1963 (*Merton & the Tao* 252).

99. The review was published as Thomas Merton, "Gloss on Chinese Text," *The Pilot* 134.33 (August 17, 1963) 20. It is substantially identical to Part VIII of the final version of "Mystics and Zen Masters" (*MZM* 42-44).

34. TL[c]

October 28, 1963

Rev. Father Thomas Merton
Abbey of Gethsemani
Trappist, Kentucky

Dear Father Louis:

Please forgive me for this much-belated reply to your letter of October 2. The delay was caused by considering a possible plan for my visit to Gethsemani over the Thanksgiving weekend. As things turn out now, this becomes rather difficult. I have to attend several social engagements including a wedding ceremony. I feel that sometime in the Spring may be more opportune for this visit. By that time, you may have something more to be discussed on Chuang Tzu.

Dr. Wu is fine. He is working on a book relating to a study of Chinese thought.[100]

I received the *Pilot* and am deeply appreciative of what you have written.

With warmest regards and sincere gratitude,

Yours ever in Him,

Paul K. T. Sih
Director

PKTS:dc

---

100. This is probably a reference to what became John Wu, *The Golden Age of Zen* (Taipei: National War College/Committee on the Compilation of the Chinese Library, 1967; Garden City, NY: Doubleday Image, 1996), for which Merton wrote the introductory essay, "A Christian Looks at Zen" (*ZBA* 33-58).

35. TLS

St. John's University

GRAND CENTRAL AND UTOPIA PARKWAYS

JAMAICA, NEW YORK 11432

CENTER OF ASIAN STUDIES

OFFICE OF THE DIRECTOR

November 5, 1964

Reverend Father Thomas Merton
Abbey of Gethsemani
Trappist, Kentucky

Dear Father Louis:

I appreciate greatly your generous thought in sending a copy of your "Mystics and Zen Masters." I enjoyed reading this immensely and am particularly gratified for your remarks on my work at St. John's. I only hope that I can do a little more and a little better than what I have done in the past.

Your comments on Professor Chan's work[101] are most pertinent. I believe that he will realize these inadequacies and revise the text in the second edition, if any.

Enclosed please find a copy of a reprint on "Ch'an Teachings of Yun-men School" by Dr. Chang.[102] He is presently a research associate at the Center (this is our new designation) and is doing a special research on "The Transmission of the Lamp."[103] He is a close

---

101. Merton mentions that the terminology found in Wing-tsit Chan's translation differs from that used by Suzuki and other commentators on the Platform Scripture, and encourages the bracketed inclusion of the original Chinese terms as a way of indentifying words translated differently in English (see *MZM* 43-44).

102. Chang Chung-yuan (1907-1988) was a leading scholar of Taoism and other Chinese religious traditions who was professor of Philosophy at the University of Hawaii, Manoa. The 39-page offprint of his article "Ch'an Teachings of Yun-men School," reprinted from *Chinese Culture Quarterly* 5.4 (June 1964) 14-39, is now in the TMC archives.

103. *Original Teachings of Ch'an Buddhism Selected from The Transmission of the Lamp*, trans. Chang Chung-yuan (New York: Pantheon/Random House, 1969); this volume is made up of selections from a classic collection of Ch'an writings assembled in the early eleventh century. Apparently there was some discussion of Merton writing a preface for this work, mentioned by John Wu in

friend of Suzuki and spent two and a half years with him in Japan.

I am enclosing also a copy of Ambassador Tsian's talk[104] at St. John's. He is not a Christian. His view on China represents the general thinking of the Chinese people at large. I believe that you may like to have it.

With deep gratitude, I am

Yours ever in Him,

Paul K. T. Sih
Director

PKTS:dc
Enclosure

P.S. In case you wish to publish your "Mystics and Zen Masters" in the *Chinese Culture Quarterly* I am quite willing to submit it for you and believe that it will be published in the next issue.[105]

---

his December 2, 1965 letter to Merton (*Merton & the Tao* 306).

104. Dr. T. F. Tsian was the longtime ambassador of the Republic of China (Taiwan) to the United Nations.

105. Thomas Merton, "Mystics and Zen Masters," *Chinese Culture Quarterly* 6 (1965) 1-18.

36. TLS[106]

ABBEY OF GETHSEMANI
TRAPPIST, KENTUCKY

Nov 11, 1964

Dear Paul:

It was fine to hear from you again. I am glad that the Center has developed and that so much good work is coming out of it. I am really delighted to have the essay of Dr Chang and I will read it with great interest. The edition of the "Transmission of the Lamp" is important. I am glad we can look forward to it.

Thanks also for the talk of Ambassador Tsiang, which I will also read today.

You may certainly transmit the article on "Mystics and Zen Masters" to the CHINESE CULTURE QUARTERLY, but first I must make a few slight changes. I will send you another copy when I have done this.

May I please have John Wu's address? I have not heard from him for a long time.[107] Perhaps a letter went astray somewhere. Is he now in Taiwan? I suppose he must be very busy, but I hope he has not forgotten his old friends on this side of the world.

Best wishes to you always,

Most cordially yours in Christ,
T. Merton

---

106. An abridged version of this letter is published in *HGL* 554.

107. A card arrives from John Wu in December 1964 (*Merton & the Tao* 256-57), the first correspondence since the March 31, 1963 letter and is followed by a letter dated December 27, 1964 (*Merton & the Tao* 260-62) in response to Merton's letter of December 23, 1964 (*Merton & the Tao* 258-59).

37. HNS[108]

OUR LADY OF GETHSEMANI TRAPPIST, KENTUCKY[109]

Dear Paul,

Here is the revised text of *Mystics + Zen Masters*. As you see it has been published in a little known magazine[110] I don't suppose that will make any difference to the *Chinese Culture Quarterly*. So it is theirs if they will have it. Again, many thanks in Xt

Tom Merton

---

108. A lightly edited version of this letter is published in *HGL* 554-55, with a bracketed annotation: "[Probably November 1964]"; the note in the Sih correspondence file on the TMC website dates it November 11, the same day as the preceding letter.

109. Printed letterhead which includes a chalice with a cross above it centered between the name and address of the abbey.

110. See note 84 above.

38. TLS

St. John's University

GRAND CENTRAL AND UTOPIA PARKWAYS
JAMAICA, NEW YORK 11432

CENTER OF ASIAN STUDIES
OFFICE OF THE DIRECTOR

November 16, 1964

Reverend Father Thomas Merton
Abbey of Gethsemani
Trappist, Kentucky

Dear Father Louis:

Thank you very much for your letter of November 11 and the revised text of "Mystics and Zen Masters." I believe that the *Chinese Culture Quarterly* will be only too happy to publish it.

Dr. Wu is still in New Jersey. His address is: 3 Reynolds Place, Newark 6, New Jersey. I have selected and edited his essays into a book entitled "Chinese Humanism and Christian Spirituality." It will be published first in French by Casterman in Paris and Bruxelles in the early part of 1965.[111] The English edition[112] will be published by St. John's under my editorship. He is presently doing some translation and interpretation of Tu Fu's works.[113] I have also told him of your concern about his recent condition.

With warmest respects, I am

Yours ever in Christ,

Paul K. T. Sih
Director

PKTS:dc

---

111. John C. H. Wu, *Humanisme Chinois, Spiritualité Chrétienne*, ed. Paul K. T. Sih (Paris: Casterman, 1965).

112. Paul K. T. Sih, ed., *Chinese Humanism and Christian Spirituality: Essays of John C. H. Wu* (Jamaica, NY: St. John's University Press, 1965).

113. See note 92 above. Tu Fu (712-70) is one of the most celebrated T'ang Dynasty poets.

39. TLS

St. John's University

GRAND CENTRAL AND UTOPIA PARKWAYS
JAMAICA, NEW YORK 11432

CENTER OF ASIAN STUDIES
OFFICE OF THE DIRECTOR

April 20, 1965

Reverend Father Thomas Merton
Abbey of Gethsemani
Trappist, Kentucky

Dear Father Louis:

Allow me to inform you that your article "Mystics and Zen Masters" has been published by the *Chinese Culture Quarterly* in its Volume 6, No. 2, issue. The issue and the reprints will be forwarded to you as soon as they arrive.

Enclosed please find a check of $45 as a token honorarium. I would appreciate your acceptance of it.

Recently I have written several articles relating to the mind of Asia in the modern world. I am planning to put them together in book form.[114] A publisher seems interested in this work. However, I would feel very much encouraged if you would read the manuscript over and would, if you think it worthwhile, write a few lines as an introduction. I understand that you are very busy and should not impose anything on you, but since you have been so kind to me, I still venture to indulge myself to your generosity and charity.

With warmest regards, I am

Yours ever in Christ,

Paul K. T. Sih
Director

PKTS: dc

---

114. Evidently this collection of essays was never published.

40. TLS[115]

jhs

ABBEY OF GETHSEMANI
TRAPPIST, KENTUCKY

April 23, 1965

Dear Paul:

It was a pleasure to get your letter. I had been thinking of you lately. Thanks also for the check, and I will anticipate reception of the *Quarterly* in due course.

The news of your book is interesting and auspicious. It is true that I am quite busy, but I would certainly be interested in what you have to say. So if you are not in too much of a hurry for a reaction on my part, do not hesitate to send the ms. As to an introduction, let me leave that open for the time being. Rather than bind myself by a promise, when I already have so many commitments, let me just say that I will keep the possibility in mind, and that it will depend on how I am able to negotiate the other jobs I have on hand at the moment. I am afraid I am quite crowded, but we shall see.

Spring seems to have come down here, and everything is opening up. The birds sing and the trees blossom. One would want to have the talent of a Tu Fu to praise it all. How are the publications of the Center of Asian Studies coming along? Anything new? I think John told me you might be doing his translations of Chinese poets. I look forward eagerly to such a book. Please give my regards to John, to whom I owe a letter and I will write him soon.[116]

Cordial good wishes always, in the Lord,

Tom Merton

---

115. An abridged version of this letter is published in *HGL* 555.
116. Merton writes to Wu on June 9, 1965 (*Merton & the Tao* 272-74).

41. TLS

St. John's University

GRAND CENTRAL AND UTOPIA PARKWAYS

JAMAICA, NEW YORK 11432

CENTER OF ASIAN STUDIES

OFFICE OF THE DIRECTOR

April 26, 1965

Reverend Father Thomas Merton
Abbey of Gethsemani
Trappist, Kentucky

Dear Father Louis:

I appreciate greatly your letter of April 23. I am most happy that you will read my manuscript even in the midst of your busiest time. It will still take some time before the manuscript comes to its final shape. There is no hurry. I will present it to you when it is ready.

John is still working on his translations of Chinese poets. However, he spent most of his time on the study of Zen. He seems to be immersed in it as a sponge in the water!

I have edited some of his papers and published it first in French by Casterman. A copy is being sent to you under separate cover. The English edition is in the process of production. It will be published by St. John's University Press also under my editorship. I hope you will like to read it.

Yours ever in Him,

Paul K. T. Sih
Director

PKTS:dc

42. TL[c]

jhs

July 4, 1965

Dear Paul:

I was delighted to get your letter and to hear the translation of LIFE AND HOLINESS is coming along. It took me a little time to get around to writing the Foreword,[117] but I hope you were not inconvenienced by the delay. I hope the Foreword is satisfactory, if not we can discuss changes.

Let us be especially united in prayer for peace in the world. True peace cannot be attained by force, but only by reason and mutual understanding. Since the political situation is so complicated, we cannot rely just on human ingenuity, we must indeed trust completely in God, and pray that innocent people may not have to suffer for the sins of the rich and powerful.

I am always glad to hear from you and I am delighted to know that you are now in the seminary.[118] I am writing a book which includes studies of Oriental religion, particularly Zen, in relation to Christianity.[119] Do please pray for me that I may see the truth in these matters and write about it clearly, so that men may come to know and love God better.

With my cordial good wishes and prayers,

Fraternally yours in Christ,

---

117. This is evidently a reference to a Korean translation of *Life and Holiness*, for which Merton wrote a Preface in July 1965: see "Preface to the Korean edition of *Life and Holiness*" in Thomas Merton, *"Honorable Reader": Reflections on My Work*, ed. Robert E. Daggy (New York: Crossroad, 1989) 93-100. Sih's involvement in this project is not clear since the letter Merton refers to here has not survived.

118. Another piece of information included in the missing letter. Sih's seminary studies evidently did not last long and did not lead to ordination.

119. A reference to *Mystics and Zen Masters*.

43. TALS

St. John's University

GRAND CENTRAL AND UTOPIA PARKWAYS

JAMAICA, NEW YORK 11432

CENTER OF ASIAN STUDIES

OFFICE OF THE DIRECTOR

May 24, 1967

Reverend Father Louis
Gethsemani Trappist Monastery
Trappist, Kentucky

Dear Father Louis:

It has been a long time since we last corresponded. I understand that you are in complete seclusion and do not wish to have any contact with the outside world. However, for an extremely important project, I have to bother you at this time.

To further develop an effective dialogue between Chinese philosophy and Christian thought, I am preparing to edit a book entitled *The Legacy of Confucius* to be published by St. John's University Press under the auspices of the Center of Asian Studies.[120]

It would include significant writings relevant to the theme written principally by Dr. John C. H. Wu, myself, and you. Of your eminent writings, I am particularly interested in "Classical Chinese Thought" which appeared in January 1961 issue of *Jubilee*. When I consulted Mr. Edward Rice, Jr. on the project, he directed me to request your permission for including it in our volume.

As this would be entirely an educational enterprise for the benefit of the ecumenical movement, I would be grateful if you would grant us the permission free.

Dr. John Wu is now in Taipei. He is writing an official biography of Dr. Sun Yat-sen in English.[121] I don't think that he will come back to the States in the near future.

---

120. This projected collection was apparently never published.

121. John C. H. Wu, *Sun Yat-sen: The Man and His Ideas* (Taipei: Commercial Press, 1971). Sun Yat-sen (1866-1925) was the principal founding figure of the Chinese Republic in the early twentieth century.

Yours ever in Christ,

Paul K. T. Sih
Director

PKTS:dc

P.S. Under separate cover I am sending a complimentary copy of *Mencius: The Man and His Ideas* by Father Albert F. Verwilghen under my editorship.[122] I hope you will like it.[123]

---

122. Albert Felix Verwilghen, *Mencius: The Man and His Ideas* (Jamaica, NY: St. John's University Press, 1967).

123. Handwritten postscript.

44. TLS[124]

<u>ABBEY OF GETHSEMANI   TRAPPIST KENTUCKY 40073</u>[125]

May 27, 1967

Dear Paul:

It is so good to hear from you again. I often think about you and your work at the Center there. I haven't seen any books from there recently so I am happy to hear that *Mencius* is on the way. I want to get back into reading Chinese philosophy anyhow.

I am glad too that the *Legacy of Confucius* is on the horizon. The essay of mine on Classic Chinese Thought has now appeared in a book, however. I am perfectly willing for you to have it if you like, but it will be nothing more than a reprint. Evidently you have not seen the book, *Mystics and Zen Masters*, though I thought a copy had been sent by the publisher. I will see that you get one.

As I say, if you still want to use the essay, that is perfectly all right with me.

Recently I heard from John Wu, Jr.,[126] but not from John Sr. I must write to him. I wish he could get a publisher for his book on Zen. Can't St John's do something about that? I must write to him, anyway.

With my very best wishes,

Cordially yours in Christ,

Thomas Merton

---

124. A slightly abridged version of this letter is published in *HGL* 555.

125. Printed letterhead with horizontal rule below.

126. See his May 16, 1967 letter thanking Merton for a letter of support for his application for conscientious objector status (*Merton & the Tao* 349-50).

45. TLS

St. John's University

GRAND CENTRAL AND UTOPIA PARKWAYS

JAMAICA, NEW YORK 11432

CENTER OF ASIAN STUDIES

OFFICE OF THE DIRECTOR

June 16, 1967

Reverend Father Louis
Abbey of Gethsemani
Trappist, Kentucky 40075

My beloved Father Louis:

I appreciate greatly your letter of May 27 in allowing me to include your article on Classic Chinese Thought in the forthcoming book, *The Legacy of Confucius*.

A couple of days ago I received your autographed copy of *Mystics and Zen Masters*. I have read the first part and it is really inspiring. I hope that I shall be able to finish reading it during the Summer.

Dr. John Wu was recently betrothed to a Chinese girl.[127] After they are married in Taipei this Summer, they will come to this country. I hope that the marital union will provide new vitality and a new dimension to John's intellectual life.

Yours ever in Christ,

Paul K. T. Sih
Director

PKTS:dc

---

127. Wu first mentions "*In confidence*" being "in love with a Chinese lady in the forties" in his February 5, 1965 letter to Merton (*Merton & the Tao* 266) and in his January 26, 1968 letter to Merton provides some details about his wife (Agnes) and her impending move to America (*Merton & the Tao* 344).

46. TLS[128]

ABBEY OF GETHSEMANI TRAPPIST KENTUCKY 40073

July 18, 1967

Dear Paul:

Many thanks for the book on Mencius, in fact thanks for two copies. I was glad to get the extra one, and passed it on to our library. If I get a chance I may review it briefly for the magazine of our Order.[129]

I was happy to hear of John Wu's engagement. I know he easily gets lonely and I hope the new marriage will bring him companionship and joy – I am also glad to learn he will be back in this country. Really, I agree that the new marriage is probably what he needs to get him working again with greater enthusiasm. Did his book on Zen ever get into print? I hope it will, because it is very worth while.

With my warmest regards, as ever

Cordially yours in Christ,

Tom Merton.

---

128. A lightly edited version of this letter is published in *HGL* 555-56.
129. Merton did not in fact write a review of Verwilghen's book on Mencius.

47. TL[c]

October 3, 1967

Reverend Father Louis
Abbey of Gethsemani
Trappist, Kentucky 40073

Dear Father Louis:

Please forgive me for not replying to your letter of July 18 earlier than now. I went to Ann Arbor, Michigan, to attend an International Conference of Orientalists. Then I and my family went to Madison, Wisconsin, for a week with my second boy's family.[130] He is teaching at the University of Wisconsin as Profes-sor of Pharmaceutical Science.

Father Devine showed me his latest correspondence with you.[131] I am pleased that he has developed such a high admiration and respect for your Oriental scholarship and genuine friendship for St. John's.

Yesterday I spoke with Archbishop Yu-pin.[132] He is involved in convening an International Conference of Sinologists to be held in Taipei sometime in August-September, 1968. He plans to invite you as a speaker at the Conference. I believe that he may contact you about the program.

Dr. John Wu has come back to the United States. He plans

---

130. Charles J. Sih (b. 1933) received a doctorate in Bacteriology from the University of Wisconsin in 1958, and taught pharmaceutical chemistry at the university from 1960 until his retirement, serving as the Frederick B. Power Professor from 1978 and the Hildare Professor from 1987; he was the recipient of numerous awards, including the American Pharmaceutical Associate Award in 1987. He married Catherine E. Hsu in 1959 and is the father of three children.

131. In an unpublished letter of September 29, 1967 to Fr. Richard J. Devine, CM, dean of the graduate school at St. John's University (TMC archives), Merton expresses his admiration for the Center of Asian Studies and his regrets that it would be impossible for him to accept Fr. Devine's invitation to come to speak at St. John's.

132. Archbishop (later Cardinal) Paul Yu Pin (1901-78) had met Merton during the centenary celebrations at the Abbey of Gethsemani in 1949; see Merton's journal entry for June 4, 1949, in which Merton calls the Archbishop of Nanking "One of the most impressive people I have ever seen" (Thomas Merton, *Entering the Silence: Becoming a Monk and Writer. Journals, vol. 2: 1941-1952*, ed. Jonathan Montaldo [San Francisco: HarperCollins, 1996] 321).

to stay here for one year. Then he will go back to Taipei for a permanent stay. His new wife will arrive here in a few weeks. His book on Zen is being published in Taipei. I will send you a copy as soon as ready.

How about your review of Mencius? I would appreciate your sending a copy of the review whenever available.

With warmest respects and sincere gratitude, I am

Yours ever in Christ,

Paul K. T. Sih
Director

PKTS:dc

MERTON'S READING NOTES ON CONFUCIANISM AND RELATED MATERIAL

Reading Notebook 52 (1961-62)

2

Koans.

Where do you go from the top of a hundred foot pole?[1]

The past + future Buddhas are his servants. Who is he?[2]

3

Confucius.

The superior man thinks of virtue; the small man thinks of comfort. The superior man thinks of the sanctions of the Law, the small man thinks of favors he may receive.

Analects IV.xi.[3]

"The mind of the Superior man is conversant with righteousness. The mind of the mean man is conversant with gain.

An. IV.xvi.[4]

The reason why the ancients did not readily give utterance to their words was that they feared lest their actions should not come up to them.

An. IV.xxii[5]

What is the good of being ready with the tongue? They who meet men with smartness of speech for the most part procure

---

1. Ekai, called Mu-Mon, *The Gateless Gate: Comments on the Mumonkan*, trans. Nyogen Senzaki and Paul Reps, case 46, which reads: "How can you proceed on from the top of a hundred-foot pole?" in Paul Reps, *Zen Flesh, Zen Bones: A Collection of Zen and Pre-Zen Writings* (1957; Garden City, NY: Doubleday Anchor, 1961) 125 (subsequent references will be cited as "Reps").

2. The *Gateless Gate: Zen Comments on the Mumonkan*, case 45, which reads: "The past and future Buddhas, both are his servants. Who is he?" (Reps 125).

3. *The Chinese Classics*. A Translation by James Legge, D.D. Part I Confucius (New York: John B. Alden, Publisher, 1891) 25, which reads: "The Master, said, 'The superior . . . sanctions of law; . . . favours *which he may receive*'" (subsequent references will be cited as "Legge, *Classics* 1).

4. Legge, *Classics* 1.26, which reads: "The Master said, 'The mind of superior . . . righteousness; the mind . . . .'"

5. Legge, *Classics* 1.27, which reads: "The Master said, '. . . words, was . . . .'"

themselves hatred.

An. V.ɪv.[6]

I have heard that a Superior man helps the distressed but does not add to the wealth of the rich.

An. VI.ɪɪɪ 2[7]

Who can go out but by the door? How is it that men will not walk according to these ways?

An. VI.xv[8]

They who know the truth are not equal to those who love it + those who love it are not equal to those who find pleasure in it.

An. VI.xvɪɪɪ[9]

The man of virtue makes the difficulty to be overcome his first business, + success only a subsequent consideration. This may be called perfect virtue.

An. VI.xx.[10]

4

The wise find pleasure in water (alias the sea) the virtuous find pleasure in the hills. (alias Mountains) The wise are active, the virtuous are tranquil. The wise are joyful, the virtuous are long-lived.

An. VI.xxɪ.[11]

The man of perfect virtue, wishing to be established himself seeks also to establish others; wishing to be enlarged himself he seeks also to enlarge others.

An. VI.xxvɪɪɪ.2.[12]

---

6. Legge, *Classics* 1.28, which reads: "The Master said, '. . . with smartnesses of . . . .'" (V.ɪv.2).

7. Legge, *Classics* 1.33, which reads: "The Master said, 'When Ch'ih was proceeding to Ts'e, he had fat horses to his carriage, and wore light furs. I have heard that a superior . . . distressed, but . . . .'"

8. Legge, *Classics* 1.35, which reads: "The Master said, 'Who . . . .'"

9. Legge, *Classics* 1.35, which reads: "The Master said, 'They who know *the truth* . . . love it, and . . . .'"

10. Legge, *Classics* 1.35, which reads: "Fan Ch'e asked what constituted wisdom. The Master said, 'To give one's-self earnestly to the duties due to men, and, while respecting spiritual beings, to keep aloof from them, may be called wisdom.' He asked about perfect virtue. The Master said, 'The man . . . difficulty *to be overcome* his . . . and success . . . consideration; – this . . . .'"

11. Legge, *Classics* 1.35, which reads: "The Master said, '. . . water; the virtuous . . . hills. The . . . active; the . . .'"

12. Legge, *Classics* 1.36, which reads: "Now the man . . . himself, seeks . . . himself, he . . . ."

I have never refused my instruction to anyone.

An. VII.vii.[13]

I do not open up the truth to one who is not eager to get knowledge nor help out anyone who is not anxious to explain himself. When I have presented one corner of a subject to any one + he cannot learn from it the other three, I do not repeat my lesson.

An. VII.viii[14]

He did not sing on the same day in which he had been weeping.

An. VII.ix.2.[15]

I am not one who was born in the possession of knowledge; I am one who is fond of antiquity + earnest in seeking it there.

An. VII.xix.[16]

There were four things which the Master taught – letters, ethics, devotion of soul, and truthfulness.

An. VII.xxiv.[17]

There may be those who act without knowing why. I do not do so. Hearing much and selecting what is good + following it, seeing much + keeping it in memory; this is the second style of knowledge.

An. VII.xxvii.[18]

5

Confucius in his village looked simple + sincere + as if not able to speak.

An. X.i.[19]

The man of perfect virtue is cautious + slow in his speech. . . . When a man feels the difficulty of doing, can he be other than cautious + slow in speaking?"

An. XII.iii.[20]

---

13. Legge, *Classics* 1.37, which reads: "The Master said, 'From the man bringing his bundle of dried flesh *for my teaching* upwards, I have never refused instruction to any one.'"

14. Legge, *Classics* 1.37-38, which reads: "The Master said, 'I . . . *to get knowledge*, nor . . . any one . . . any one, and . . . .'"

15. Legge, *Classics* 1.38.

16. Legge, *Classics* 1.39, which reads: "The Master said, '. . . antiquity, and . . . it *there*.'"

17. Legge, *Classics* 1.40, which reads: ". . . taught, – letters . . ."

18. Legge, *Classics* 1.40, which reads: "The Master said, '. . . good and . . . much and . . . '"

19. Legge, *Classics* 1.51, which reads: "Confucius, in his village, looked simple and sincere, and as if he were not . . ." (X.i.1).

20. Legge, *Classics* 1.63, which reads: "1. Sze-ma New asked about perfect

The superior man has neither anxiety nor fear. . . When internal examination discovers nothing wrong what is there to be anxious about, what is there to fear?

An. XII.ɪᴠ.[21]

Hold faithfulness + sincerity as first principles + be moving constantly to what is right.

An. XII.x.[22]

If doing what is to be done be made the first business + success a secondary consideration – is not this the way to exalt virtue? To assail one's own wickedness + not to assail that of others, – is not this the way to correct cherished evil? For a morning's anger to disregard one's own life + to involve that of his parents, – is not this a case of delusion?

An. XII.xxɪ.[23]

28

551 BC. – birth of Confucius.[24] [6th to 3rd cent. BC. The Hundred
    Philosophers]
3rd c. The Great Wall was building.[25]
1 *The Great Learning* – cultivation of the Person (superior
    man)[26] is the "root."[27]

---

virtue. 2. The Master said, 'The man . . . cautious and slow . . . speech.' 3. 'Cautious and slow in his speech!' said New; – 'is this what is meant by perfect virtue?' The Master said, 'When . . . cautious and slow . . . ?'"

21. Legge, *Classics* 1.63, which reads: "1. Sze-ma New asked about the superior man. The Master said, 'The superior . . . fear.' 2. 'Being without anxiety or fear!' said New; – 'does this constitute what we call the superior man?' 3. The Master said, 'When . . . wrong, what . . . fear?'"

22. Legge, *Classics* 1.65, which reads: "Tsze-chang having asked how virtue was to be exalted, and delusions to be discovered, the Master said, 'Hold faithfulness and . . . principles, and . . . moving continually . . . right; – this is the way to exalt one's virtue'" (XII.x.1).

23. Legge, *Classics* 1.67, which reads: "1. Fan Ch'e rambling with the Master under *the trees* about the rain altars, said, 'I venture to ask how to exalt virtue, to correct cherished evil, and to discover delusions.' 2. The Master said, 'Truly a good question! 3. 'If doing . . . business, and . . . consideration; – is . . . others; – is . . . life, and . . . parents; – is . . . ?'"

24. See *Sources of Chinese Tradition*, compiled by Wm. Theodore de Bary, Wing-tsit Chan and Burton Watson (New York: Columbia University Press, 1960) 17 (in the introduction to Chapter II: Confucius [17-22]) (subsequent references will be cited as "*Sources*").

25. See the *Outline of Early Chinese History* (*Sources* 2).

26. Interlined above "Person".

27. See *Selections from The Great Learning*: "From the emperor down to the common people, all, without exception, must consider cultivation of the individual

cf S. 32.[28]

2 *Read Odes*.[29] – in light of commentary on Great Learning.[30]

3 *Analects* etc.

    a) *Jen* (humanity.) S. 28[31]

    b) *Li* – (rites) S. 31.[32]

29

+ *I Ching*[33]

    Yang = 3

    Yin = 2

3 Yang = old yang = 9

2 Yin = old yin = -x- 6.

2 yin 1 yang = 7 = young yang = –

2 yang 1 yin = 8 = young yin = - -

character as the root" (*Sources* 129).

    28. Selections from the *Analects* on "*The Gentleman*" (*Sources* 32-34).

    29. *Sources* 14-16.

    30. The reference is to the commentary attributed to Tseng Tsze (Tseng Tze; Tseng Tzu), a disciple of Confucius who is sometimes credited with composing *The Great Learning* (see *Sources* 128); this commentary on the text found in the edition of the neo-Confucian scholar Chu Hsi (1130-1200), which includes many references to the *Book of Odes*, is included in *Confucius: The Great Digest & Unwobbling Pivot*, translation and commentary by Ezra Pound (New York: New Directions, 1951) 35-89.

    31. Selections from the *Analects* on "*Humanity (jen)*" (*Sources* 28-29).

    32. Selections from the *Analects* on "*Rites and Music*" (*Sources* 30-31).

    33. See Merton's references to the *I Ching*, or *Book of Changes*, one of the five "Confucian Classics" and to C. G. Jung's Foreword to that work (*The I Ching or Book of Changes*, trans. Richard Wilhelm and Cary Baynes, 2 vols. [New York: Pantheon, 1950]), in Thomas Merton, *A Search for Solitude: Pursuing the Monk's True Life. Journals, vol. 3: 1952-1960*, ed. Lawrence S. Cunningham (San Francisco: HarperCollins, 1996) 266-67 [3/3/1959]; 267 [3/10/1959]; 279-81 [5/12/1959].

Reading Notebook 56
32
Kakuzo Okakura. *The Ideals of the East.* 1903.[1]
Comparing Shu vases to Greek.
"Like the calm and delicate jade compared with the flashing individualistic diamond, – the antithesis of ideals, the two poles of the decorative impulse of East and West . . . Among the
31 workers in metal and jade we find the *same passionate effort to realize the ideal of harmony* that absorbs the singers and painters of the period."[2]
40 Confucian ideal – symmetry born of dualism.
"The Chinese art consciousness must always have tended to the decorative – as shown in its extraordinary development of textiles and ceramics – had the Taoist mind not imparted to it its playful individualism + had Buddhism not come later to lift it up to the expression of commanding ideals. But even
41 if it had remained at the decorative it could never have sunk to the Bourgeois level . . ."[3]
Kutsugen – great individualist nature poet.[4]
51 *Kogaishi* – poet-painter, latter part of 4th cent. – Taoist.
"First in poetry, first in painting, first in foolishness."[5]
"His is the earliest voice to speak of the necessity of concentration on the dominant note in an art composition. "The

---

1. Kakuzo Okakura, *The Ideals of the East with Special Reference to the Art of Japan*, 2nd ed. (New York: Dutton, 1904). Okakura (1863-1913) was the founder of the Japan Art Institute and later the head of the Asian division of the Boston Museum of Fine Arts; he was a student and close associate of the American art historian Ernest Fenollosa (1853-1908), in whom Merton was also interested during this period: see the July 30, 1960 journal entry in Thomas Merton, *Turning Toward the World: The Pivotal Years. Journals, vol. 4: 1960-1963*, ed. Victor A. Kramer (San Francisco: HarperCollins, 1996) 25, and his July 27, 1960 letter to Victor Hammer in Thomas Merton and Victor and Carolyn Hammer, *The Letters of Thomas Merton and Victor and Carolyn Hammer: Ad Majorem Dei Gloriam*, ed. F. Douglas Scutchfield and Paul Evans Holbrook Jr. (Lexington: University Press of Kentucky, 2014) 111. Fenollosa's controversial theory of the pictographic origins of Chinese characters was very influential for the work of Ezra Pound on Confucianism, which Merton also read during this period: see below, pages 101, 104-105, 110-12.
2. Text reads: "like . . . jade, compared . . . diamond, the . . . poles, of . . . impulse in East . . . . amongst the . . . jade, we find . . ." (emphasis added).
3. Text reads: "the Chinese art-consciousness . . . towards . . . individualism, and . . . later, to . . . . decorative, it . . . bourgeois level."
4. See 44-45.
5. Text reads: ". . . painting, and . . ."

52 secret of portraiture" he said, "lies in *that*, revealed in the eye
of the subject."[6]
Shakaku – 5th cent. Six canons.
   1 Art seeks the "Life movement of the Spirit through the
   rhythm of things"[7]
   2 "The Law of Bones + Brushwork"[8]
53.   "The creative spirit in descending into a pictorial conception[9] must take upon itself organic structure. This great imagi-
native scheme forms the bony system of the work; lines take
the place of nerves + arteries, + the whole is covered with the
skin of color."[10]
3 Representation of nature . . .[11]
                    (other 3 ?[12])
54 *Calligraphy* – "Each stroke of the brush contains in itself the
principle of life and death interrelated with the other lines to
form the beauty of an ideogram"[13]
Dragon – symbol of change + power –[14]
   Dragon + Tiger – conflict of material forces with the
   infinite.[15]
184 Nō-play "The Nō dance is a direct appeal from mind to
mind, a mode by which unspoken thought is borne from
behind the actor to the unhearing + unheard intelligence that
broods within the heart of him who listens."[16]
33
Buddhism in Japan.
Introduced from Korea. 552 ad. (Asuka Period)
   (It had come to China in

---

6. Text reads: ". . . note, in . . . art-composition . . ." (51-52).
7. Text reads: ". . . Life-movement . . . Rhythm of Things" (52).
8. Text reads: "Brush-work" (52).
9. *Interlined above cancelled* composition
10. Text reads: "spirit, according to this, in . . . colour" (52-53).
11. "the idea of the depicting of Nature falls into a third place, subservient
to two other main principles" (52).
12. These are not mentioned in the text.
13. Text reads: ". . . itself its principle . . . death, inter-related . . . ideograph."
14. See 55.
15. See 55-56.
16. Text reads: "the Nō . . . to that unhearing and unheard . . ."

Hist Periods[17]

    Asuka period. 552 to 667. Influence of Tang Buddhism.[18]

    Nara Period.[19] – 710 – Nara (capital) founded. Gensho
(Shōgun – hereditary comm. in chief of Army virtual ruler of
Japan)[20] – colossal statues

    Heian period. 9th cent.[21]

        Mikkio or Esoteric Buddhism.

        True word or *Shingon* sect.[22]

    Fujiwara period – 898-1186.[23] National development of
Buddhism

        Women writers. (Murasaki – Genji) – Pure Land (gods)
        insular period rel. with China cut off.[24]

    Kamakura period. 1186-1394.[25] – *Feudal* – individual – *Samurai*
        Zen adopted here

    Ashikaga per. 1394-1587.[26] Nature in art (landscape esp.)
(Zen infl.) Nō-plays

    Toyotomi – Early Tokugawa[27] – from supremacy of
Hideyoshin, 1587 – constant civil war.

        Hideyoshi invades Corea: self-made man
        art = conspic. display stone castles (Portuguese influence
        Ukioye – "popular" art – age of revelry[28]
        Pageantry – splendor
        to accession of Yoshimune 1711.

    Later Tokugawa. 1711-1867[29]

        Kano – *Conventionalism* in art + life. Xenophobia –
        Popular art + writing celebrate pleasure.
        Kyoto – center of more living art at this time – but realism
        develops here[30]

---

17. See the outline of these periods (106-107).
18. See 83-107.
19. See 108-27.
20. (Shōgun . . . Japan) *added in right margin.*
21. See 128-40.
22. Heian . . . sect. *added in right margin and marked for insertion.*
23. See 141-52.
24. Insular . . . off. *added in left margin and marked for insertion.*
25. See 153-62.
26. See 163-84.
27. See 185-94.
28. *Ukioye* . . . revelry *interlined and marked for insertion.*
29. See 195-204.
30. Popular . . . here *added in left margin and marked for insertion.*

1867 – fall of the Shogunate – rise of Middle classes.
"Realistic art" – European influence – degeneration
Meiji – 1867 – struggle of East + West in Japanese culture.[31]
revival of Shintoism (centered on Emperor) – decline of
Buddhism.
Patriotism + nationalism. Flood of Western ideas.
Women Writers of Fujiwara. – Murasaki – Sheishonagon – Aka-
zome – Komachi[32]

144   Fujiwara period – "Confined to their island home with no
questions of state to trouble them the Court aristocracy found
their serious occupation in art and poetry. The lesser duties of
statecraft were left to inferiors . . . the handling of money +
the use of arms were fit only for the menial classes. Even the
administration of justice was relegated to the lower orders . . .[33]

145-6 *Jodo* (Pure Land)[34] – dominates in Buddhism "The prayer
which dissolves the self into union with the ocean of infinite
mercy takes the place of the proud assertion of the privilege
of manhood in self-realisation. . . .
Intoxicated with frantic love, men + women deserted the
cities + villages in crowds to follow Kuya or Ipen, dancing +
singing the name of Amida as they went

Art of Ashikaga Period – Highly *spiritual* art "Spirituality conceived as the essence or life of a thing, the characterisation of
the soul of things, a burning fire within"[35] 169

172   "The Ashikaga ideal owes its origin to the Zen sect[36] – a
"school of individualism" –

172   "The idea of conquest was completely orientalised, in
passing from that which is without to that which is within a

---

31. See 205-35.

32. See 143, which reads: "Seishonagon". Murasaki Shikibu (978-1014)
is best known as the author of the novel *The Tale of Genji*, written around the
beginning of the eleventh century; Seishonagon (c. 966-c. 1017) wrote *The
Pillow Book*, a book of disparate observations on her life at court, during the
same period; Akazome Emon (956-1041) was a court poet who later became a
nun after her husband's death; Ono no Komachi (c. 825-c. 900) was a poet and
a legendary beauty.

33. Text reads: "Confined in . . . home, with . . . trouble their sweet reveries,
the court . . . were functions fit . . ."

34. (Pure Land) *added in left margin and marked for insertion.*

35. Text reads: "Spirituality was conceived . . ."

36. Text reads: "The Ashikaga ideal owes its origin to the Zen sect of
Buddhism, which became predominant during the Kamakura period" (171).

man himself. Not to *use* the sword but to *be* the sword – pure, serene, etc. . . . .

177   "Not to display but to suggest, is the secret of infinity."[37]

179   "Ink painting, an innovation begun at the close of the Kamakura period, now supersedes color in importance."[38]

180   art – "not a depicting of nature but an essay on nature – Each stroke has its moment of life + death; all together assist in interpreting an idea which is life within life"[39]

34

China – History + Religion[40]

Main Periods.

Shu 1122 to 221 BC. – Confucius. BC. 551-479.[41]

in Yellow River Valley – communal life.

Shin 221-202 BC. brief, sweeping bid for power. (mongolian herdsmen).

First "Emperors" – censorship – hated by scholars – Great Wall.

Hang – 202 BC-220 AD.

Popular revolt leads to Empire + autocracy.

Civil Service exams in Confucianism – rigidity sets in. – Formal culture

Coming of Buddhism – 67 a.d.

The 3 Kingdoms 220-268 ad. Division of China

Taoism on top – Informality – love of nature –

Amidism flourishes[42]

The 6 Dynasties – 268-618 ad. division persists.

Culture centered in South.

Buddhism + Taoism flourish in north – Religious conflicts.

Tang. 618-907 ad. – Reunion of China under Taiso – Religious tolerance – Nestorianism comes

Center – Hoang Ho Valley – B. sects = Hosso – Kegon – colossal sculptures (B.)

"Classic" art.

Sung. 960-1280 ad. – center in Yang Tze.

---

37. Text reads: ". . . display, but . . ."

38. Text reads: "Ink-painting . . . colour . . ."

39. Text reads: "not a depictment of nature, but . . . nature; . . . Each stroke . . . assist to interpret an idea, which . . ."

40. Merton follows here the outline of Chinese history that concludes Okakura's introductory chapter (11-13).

41. Confucius . . . 479. *interlined and marked for insertion*

42. *Followed by cancelled* Nestorians enter China

Zen.

Neo-Confucianism (scholastic).

Gen – (Mongol). 1280-1368 ad. – Mongols take over under
Kubla Khan

Center. Pekin.

Ming – 1368-1662. – result of pop. uprising agst Mongols
center Nankin –

Capital Pekin –

Manchu – 1662-20th cent. Tartars – center Pekin.

Reading Notebook 58A
1

POETRY + WISDOM of the Ancients.

Introd. – SUMER.
1 The Tomb civilizations. Egypt. Etruria. Minoan, Cretan civ.
2 India Vedas etc.
   Upanishads.
   Yoga.
3 China. Confucius. The 4 books
   Lao Tse. Chuang Tzu
   Legalists + Mo Tsu.
      Neo-Confucians.
4 Israel. Old Test. esp. Sapiential bks
   Assyria + Babylonia
   Phoenicia
5 *Greece.*
6 *Buddhism* – India, China, Japan.
7 *Pre-Columbian* cultures of America.
      Wm F. Otto. Dionysios.[1]

2A
Geog.
   Names Ancient + Modern
   Ancient Mod
   Chin   Shansi[2]
   Ch'in   Shensi[3] – Ch'ang An = Hsian Fu.[4]
   Ch'u   Hunan[5]

---

1. Walter F. Otto, *Dionysos: Mythos und Cultus* (Frankfurt am Main: Klostermann, 1933); Merton's misspelling of the title and misnaming of the author suggests he has no first-hand acquaintance with this book and has just jotted down this information, perhaps mentioned in his source for the preceding summary, for future reference; a translation of a later edition (1960) appeared in 1965, which there is no evidence Merton would have seen: Walter F. Otto, *Dionysus: Myth and Cult*, trans. Robert B. Palmer (Bloomington: Indiana University Press, 1965). Under the author's name are two crossed-out illegible words, the second apparently fragmentary, which may have been the beginning of a note on another book.
2. Now Shanxi, located in northeast China.
3. Now Shaanxi, located in northwest China.
4. This is the location of a stele memorializing Nestorian Christian missionaries of the seventh century, erected in 781, subsequently hidden and rediscovered in 1625 – presumably Merton's reason for including mention of it.
5. Located in south central China.

Shu	Szechwan[6]
Wei	Honan[7]
Wu	Kiangsu[8]
You	Hupeh[9]
Yüeh	Chekiang[10]

2

CHINA

Pre Confucian.

BC

I Ching

Odes.   (King Wen + Wu[11])

Book of History. – (Chou – "chosen by heaven.")

The Hundred Philosophers.

VI Cent BC.

551. Confucius born in Lu (K'ung Chiu) 孔丘

V 479. Confucius Dies.   "Great Learning" written by Tzu Ssu. (?)[12]

470. *Mo Tzu* born[13]

IV cent *CHOU* – Chuang Tzu[14] – Wars among states. Ch'in
gradually emerging as leader of all.

III cent. Hsün Tzu[15]

Chin – build Empire with *Legalists*.[16]

BC II cent. *Han* – Wen[17] – Benevolent – Confucian

C. Culture   Wu (140 BC.)[18] – Legalist. "patronizes"

jells here.   Confucians.

Eclecticism – commentaries on Classics –

Yang-yin. – Magic. –

Syncretistic confusion of Taoism, Legalism,

---

6. Now Sichuan, located in southwestern China.

7. Now Henan, in central China.

8. Now Jiangsu, located in coastal China.

9. Now Hubei, located in central China.

10. Now Zhejiang, located in eastern coastal China.

11. Legendary founders of the Chou dynasty (twelfth century BCE), frequently referred to by Confucius and others.

12. See below, pages 103-105, 107-108.

13. See below, pages 120-24.

14. See below, pages 140-52; see also Thomas Merton, *The Way of Chuang Tzu* (New York: New Directions, 1965) (subsequent references will be cited as "*WCT*").

15. See below, pages 124-27.

16. See below, pages 127-30.

17. Reigned 179-157.

18. Reigned 140-87.

Magic – *called* Confucianism.

3

      CHINA

AD. –

I Cent. Han – continues

HAN   Buddhism enters China.

II Cent. Neo. Taoism – magico-religious Chang-Ling.[19]

III Cent. – Spread + power of Buddhism. *Liang* dyn. – Emperor
    Buddhist Neo Taoism (speculation)

LIANG 220-280 – 3 Kingdoms   Monastic refuge from
                          troubled world.
                          Kwan Yin – Amida –[20]

IV Cent   Zen (B. + Taoism. Personalists)

CHIN

VI Cent. Beginning of T'ang. *Taoism* in highest favor.
    Capital Ch'ang An

VII-X C. The 3000 T'ang poets, Wang Wei,
              Tu Fu, Po Chü-i[21]   Spring.   620-700

TANG   Widest expanse of empire
           (to Samarkand + Tashkent)   Summer. 700-780
           Nestorians accepted by Emperors. Autumn. 780-850
                                  Winter 850-900.

Tang. 3 Emperors die of drugs in search for elixir of life
      Mu Tsung (821-824) "died from an overdose of the
      medicine of immortality."[22]

X-XIII – Neo-Confucianism – strong influence of *Mencius*.[23]

SUNG   Canonization of the 4 Books. + of the *I Ching*.
        2 schools of NC. – Chu Hsi[24] + Lu Hsiang-shan.[25]
        Taoism becomes popular religion – superstition + magic.

XIV-XVII

MING   Neo-conf. of Wang Yang-Ming[26]

---

19. Second-century CE founder of religious Taoism, given the title Heavenly Teacher.

20. Names for the bodhisattva of compassion in Mahayana Buddhism.

21. Three of the most celebrated T'ang poets, whose lifetimes were 699-761, 712-70 and 772-846, respectively.

22. Tang . . . immortality." *written on opposite page*

23. See below, pages 112-20.

24. See below, pages 131-32.

25. See below, pages 132.

26. See below, pages 132.

XVII

MANCHU. Reaction of dissident philosophers – to Conf himself
 agst neo-C. – Ku Yen-wu[27] Huang Tsung Hsi[28]
> Agst buddhism – for practical morality + social justice.

4

François Huang. Ame Chinoise et Christianisme.[29]

Introd. Chinese mentality – for harmony, unity
> the language – concrete, musical
> thought – alien to systematisation – oriented to wisdom.

Confucius – for order + harmony – by right relationships
> degenerates into formalism, artificiality,
> favoritism, false optimism
> individual – seeks refuge from
> Confucianism in Taoism + Buddhism.

Tendency to skepticism + indifferentism in religion.
After national humiliations – seeking outlet in mystique
 of Marxism.
Pleroma of Xt is the true answer.

C I.   Rather than speak of the religions of China, more accurate
17   to deal with concrete religious spirit of the Chinese people.[30]

Archaic Religion – sources of information: excavations in
Honan.
> Bk of Odes, Bk of History. (VI Cent BC.)
> Animism – House-genii – Earth Mother.
> Cult of Heaven. (with divination).
> Cult of Ancestors

Classic Chinese Thought – V cent BC.

3 movements. Confucius
> Lao Tzu   all point to ancient wise kings –

---

27. Celebrated scholar (1613-82).

28. See below, page 132.

29. François Huang, *Ame Chinoise et Christianisme* (Paris: Casterman, 1957).

30. See Huang 17: "J'ai bien dit 'la religion' et non 'les religions.' Car, c'est l'esprit religieux du people chinois plutôt que le détail de chaque religion qu'il importe de mettre en lumière, d'autant plus que l'âme chinoise, répugnant à la distinction cartésienne, noie souvent les diverses doctrines religieuses dans une unité plus organique qu'organisée, plus vécue que systématique" ("I have specifically said 'religion' and not 'religions,' for it is the religious spirit of the Chinese people rather than the detail of each religion that it is important to bring to light, since the Chinese soul, repudiating the Cartesian distinction, often links diverse religious doctrines in a unity more organic than organized, more lived out than systematic").

to help restore harmony in
troubled times.
Mo Tzu

Mo Tzu. Theocentric – Personal God of Heaven
believed in real existence of spirits.
good works, heroic asceticism
emphasis on rewards + punishments
Love one another.
Lao Tzu. Cosmocentric Heaven = Tao – Not interested in
spirits – or in rites. – HUMILITY
Confucius – emphasis on man's moral conscience. Heaven –
Divine regulation of conscience.
Mystique of ritual.
Jen = benevolent love. based on golden rule.
Jen – works like rings going out from spot where stone has
fallen in water – to family – to village – to state – to
mankind.
Official Confucianism (under Han Dynasty. 206 BC. 220 AD.)
Confucianism established in reaction to T'sin Che HuangTi[31]
– builder of the Great Wall. (legalist?)
Book burning etc. to unite China by destroying traditions
Prepared way for uniform Confucianism.
Cult of Heaven (Emperor is priest)
Confucius (for the Scholars)
Ancestors   (Filial piety . . .

5

Han Taoism   revival of ancient animism + magic
(Chang Tao Ling)   spirits + angels. (hierarchies)
gods of Heaven – Earth, – Water.
quest for elixir of immortality
Buddhism (came under Han dynasty)
Mahayana – comes to China through central Asia.
Amidism – most popular form – introd. by Huei Yan –
former Taoist d. 416 AD.
Faith in Amida – personal salvation in pure land.
Kwan Yin.
Zen. "une revolte de la conscience interieure contre le
savoir livresque et contre les pratiques exterieures."[32]

31. First emperor of China (259-210).
32. "a revolt of the interior conscience against bookish knowledge and

Hui Neng (637-713)[33]
Effect on Taoism – Taoists form a monastic order
" " Confucians – metaphysics on Buddhist pattern
   Neo-Confucianism of 12th Cent. Synthesis of
   positivism + mysticism in metaphysics Chu-hi[34]
    Ascent to moral perfection + illumination beyond
     discursive knowledge, by virtues + meditation on
     Classics
   Popular Syncretism – divinisation of heroes + saints.
   Myths, magic etc.
His attitude – Regrets "quietism" of Taoists + Buddhists –
       though admires religion of faith in mercy –
       Amidism.
    " that the active theism of Mo Ti was suppressed
   Blames stagnation of Chinese religion since 12th
   Cent on this Passivity of Chinese – lack of fight
   or "sense of adventure."
What is the "fundamental religious attitude" of China?
  1 Fundamental concord between human + supra-human
   order – depends on order in world, to be effected by man.
  2 Consequences [danger of syncretism.
  a) Aspiration to universalism.
  b) Tolerance (practical harmony between the 3 religions)
 [Christianity – rather than be submerged – tended to close
   in upon itself in minority]
  c) Love of beauty
       +
The "Advent" – Confucian Jen, Buddhist compassion, Taoist
mercy – prepare for Gospel
  "L'effacement Taoiste est en quelque sorte une
  anticipation de l'humilité Chrétienne" . . . 47[35]
 "Si la Chine a été si difficile à convertir c'est parce que le
 christianisme n'a pas été présenté dans sa pureté." 48.[36] vg

---

against exterior practices."
  33. Sixth Ch'an (Zen) patriarch: see Thomas Merton, *Mystics and Zen Masters* (New York: Farrar, Straus and Giroux, 1967) 18-44 (subsequent references will be cited as "*MZM*").
  34. I.e., Chu Hsi.
  35. "Taoist effacement is in some sense an anticipation of Christian humility."
  36. "If China has been so difficult to convert, it is because Christianity has

opium war.

Hopes for future of China after present crisis – Calvary of Church preparing better times p. 50.

6

Confucius   H. Wilhelm – in Encyclopedia of World Art. Vol. 7[37]

The time – after centuries of anarchy under the Chou (11th to 3rd Cent. BC.)

Faith in the ancient traditions of archaic world dissolving.

C. "an attempt to reinforce tradition + to establish a comprehensive + integrated position within it for the human personality aware of its newly imposed responsibilities toward the civilization.

775 Education + cultivation of the personality were thus the cornerstones of his system. [38]

The exigencies of a constantly changing tradition could only be met by a comprehensively cultivated personality . . . who could assume leadership with regard to every aspect of this tradition at every level.[39]

The unity of ethics + aesthetics is a basic tenet of Confucianism.[40]

Wen = culture in tradition, mores, esthetic expression.

Culture creates an atmosphere of solidarity between cultivated persons promoting the aims of humanity.[41]

In Conf. tradition – Education of Gent. = 6 arts.[42]

Li – ritual + observances

Yueh – music

Shih – poetry

Shu – writing

charioteering

archery

When Confucians get power under Han (1st C. BC.)

Politics become all important, + culture, ethics etc subordinated to it.

---

not been presented in its purity."

37.   Helmut Wilhelm, "Confucianism," *Encyclopedia of World Art*, ed. Bernard Myers, 17 vols. (New York: McGraw-Hill, 1959-83) vol. 3, cols. 775-782.

38.   Text reads: ". . . reinforce the tradition and to . . . and integrated . . . ."

39.   Col. 775, which reads: "the exigencies . . . met only by . . . at any level."

40.   Col. 776, which reads: ". . . esthetics being a basic . . . ."

41.   See col. 776: "Only in this way can an atmosphere be created which favors the solidarity of cultivated persons endeavoring to promote the aims of humanity" (referencing *Analects* XII.xxiv).

42.   See col. 776.

The preservation of the esthetic side of Confucianism
guarantees its wholeness + humanism
Classics. Ching[43]
    Bk of Documents
    Bk of Songs (Odes)
    Bk of Changes "As divination was supposed to make man
       master of his fate this has always been the favorite
       Classic for the one who strove for the autonomy +
       universality of the human personality."[44]
    Bk of Rites
    Spring + Autumn Annals
       Analects. (Lun Yü)
       Mencius.

7

THE FOUR BOOKS

Analects.
Mencius
Great Learning
The Mean (Chung Yung)
These 4 books – primer of C. education – memorized by students,
– basis for civil service exams from 1313 to 1905
The Great Learning + Chung Yung are excerpts from the
Confucian Book of Rites.

            +

Confucius Kung Tzu = 孔子 – d. 479 B.C.
    Philos of Kung = meekness + ritual = Ju 儒
Importance 1) stressed benevolence in govt. – relationship of
           mutual trust between ruler + people
       2) Transformed ancient ritualism into a
          universal code of ethics
       3) Stresses basic virtues. 忠 = chung = fidelity.
          恕 = shu = altruism.
          仁 = jen = human heartedness. Pursuit of Tao
          義 = yi = righteousness.   道
          禮 = Li = rites – propriety
          知 = chih = wisdom[45]

---

    43. See cols. 776-77.
    44. Col. 776, which reads: ". . . fate, this . . . Classic of those . . . autonomy
and . . . ."
    45. This is actually the character for the verb "chih": "to know" – it is missing
the lower section that is part of the character for the noun "chih": "wisdom" – both

信 hsin – sincerity realness.

Followers of Kung.

Tsung Ts'an 曾參 – strong on filial piety ("source of
all virtue.")

Examined self daily on 3 things.

1) Had he been self-interested in working for others
2) Had he been unfaithful in intercourse with friends
3) Had he embodied in life teachings of Master.

7A

Confucius + Previous Tradition

It is by the odes that the mind is roused
It is by the Rules of Propriety that the character is established
It is from music that the finish is received
An. VIII.8.[46]

8

THE ANALECTS – Testament of Kung school – compiled by
disciples of K. + their students –
I. *Going to the Root* – The Superior Man.

Goes to the root – i.e. to that from which all good (benevolent)[47]
action follows

Legge. p. 13.[48]   root = filial piety (obedience. Leg. 17.[49])
fraternal submission.

Always acts acc. to virtue. Leg. 24.[50] C's own principles

---

are found correctly on page 106 below.

46. *The Chinese Classics*. A Translation by James Legge, D.D. Part I
Confucius (New York: John B. Alden, Publisher, 1891) 43-44, which reads: ". . .
Odes . . . is aroused . . . propriety . . . Music . . ." (subsequent references will be
cited as "Legge, *Classics* 1").

47. Interlined above "good action".

48. "Filial piety and fraternal submission! – are they not the root of all
benevolent actions?" (*Analects* I.ii.2).

49. "Mang E asked what filial piety was. The Master said, 'It is not being
disobedient'" (*Analects* II.v.1).

50. "The superior man does not, even for the space of a single meal, act
contrary to virtue" (*Analects* IV.v.3 [24-25]).

– (Leg. 31,[51] 37,[52] 39,[53] 46,[54]

II. *Sincerity, knowing the Heart*

The whole content of the Odes – summed up in 1 sentence –
"Have no depraved thoughts." (Leg. 16[55])

His reluctance to pronounce a man perfectly virtuous. "I don't
know."[56] [cf. Ta Hio – Pound pp. 39-43.[57]

III. *Action + Speech*

Action without impetuous passion. Leg. 38.[58]

Superior man acts before he speaks + speaks according to his
actions. Leg. 18[59]

Readiness of tongue no asset (Leg. 28[60]

---

51. "The Master said, 'Fine words, an insinuating appearance, and excessive respect; – Tso-k'ew Ming was ashamed of them. I also am ashamed of them. To conceal resentment against a person, and appear friendly with him; – Tso-k'ew Ming was ashamed of such conduct. I also am ashamed of it'" (*Analects* V.xxiv).

52. "The Master said, 'The leaving virtue without proper cultivation; the not thoroughly discussing what is learned; not being able to move towards righteousness of which a knowledge is gained; and not being able to change what is not good: – these are the things which occasion me solicitude'" (*Analects* VII.iii).

53. "The Master said, 'With coarse rice to eat, with water to drink, and my bended arm for a pillow; – I have still joy in the midst of these things. Riches and honours acquired by unrighteousness are to me as a floating cloud'" (*Analects* VII.xv).

54. "There were four things from which the Master was entirely free He had no foregone conclusions, no arbitrary predeterminations, no obstinacy, and no egoism" (*Analects* IX.iv).

55. *Analects* II.ii.

56. Legge, *Classics* 1.28, which reads: "I do not know" (*Analects* V.vii).

57. *The Great Digest* (or *Great Learning*) is *Ta Hsio* in Chinese (*Ta Hio* in an earlier version of Ezra Pound's translation: *Ta Hio: The Great Learning* [1928; New York: New Directions, 1939]); these pages refer to the third chapter of the commentary of Tseng Tsze as found in *Confucius: The Great Digest & Unwobbling Pivot*, translation and commentary by Ezra Pound (New York: New Directions, 1951) 35-89 (subsequent references will be cited as "Pound"), presumably referenced here because it consists of quotations from the *Odes*, followed by comments.

58. "The Master said, 'I would not have him to act with me, who will unarmed attack a tiger, or cross a river without a boat, dying without any regret. My associate must be the man who proceeds to action full of solicitude, who is fond of adjusting his plans, and then carries them into execution'" (*Analects* VII.x.3).

59. "Tsze-kung asked what constituted the superior man. The Master said, 'He acts before he speaks, and afterwards speaks according to his actions'" (*Analects* II.xiii).

60. "1. Some one said, 'Yung is truly virtuous, but he is not ready with his tongue.' 2. The Master said, 'What is the good of being ready with the tongue? They who meet men with smartnesses of speech, for the most part procure themselves hatred. I know not whether he be truly virtuous, but why should he show readiness

Hearing + practicing one thing at a time. (Leg. 29[61]
Does heaven say anything. (Leg. 98[62]
All according to propriety. Leg 62[63]
Virtue – Leg. 67.[64]

IV *Jen* – Basis of propriety + music (Leg 20[65])
Depends on true virtuousness – True to principles of nature. (Leg. 26[66])
To love all men – Leg 67.[67]

V *Li* – The mystery of the great sacrifice + its relation to govt. (Leg 21[68])
"He who offends agst Heaven has none to whom he can pray." (Leg. 22[69]

VI Relation to good + bad situations around one.
Sage praised for acting stupid during disorder (Leg. 31.[70]

---

of the tongue?'" (*Analects* V.ɪᴠ).

61. "When Tsze-loo heard anything, if he had not yet carried it into practice, he was only afraid lest he should hear *something else*" (*Analects* V.xɪɪɪ).

62. "The Master said, 'Does Heaven speak? The four seasons pursue their courses, and all things are *continually* being produced, *but* does Heaven say anything?'" (*Analects* XVII.xɪx).

63. "The Master said, 'To subdue one's-self and return to propriety, is perfect virtue. If a man can for one day subdue himself and return to propriety, all under heaven will ascribe perfect virtue to him" (*Analects* XII.ɪ).

64. "1. Fan-ch'e rambling with the Master under *the trees* about the rain-altars, said, 'I venture to ask how to exalt virtue, to correct cherished evil, and to discover delusions.' 2. The Master said, 'Truly a good question! 3. 'If doing what is to be done be made the first business, and success a secondary consideration; – is not this the way to exalt virtue? To assail one's own wickedness and not assail that of others; – is not this the way to correct cherished evil? For a morning's anger, to disregard one's own life, and involve that of his parents; – is not this a case of delusion?'" (*Analects* XII.xxɪ).

65. "The Master said, 'If a man be without the virtues proper to humanity, what has he to do with the rites of propriety? If a man be without the virtues proper to humanity, what has he to do with music?'" (*Analects* III.ɪɪɪ).

66. "Tsang said, 'The doctrine of our master is to be true to the principles of our nature and the benevolent exercise of them to others, – this and nothing more'" (*Analects* IV.xv.2).

67. "Fan ch'e asked about benevolence. The Master said, 'It is to love *all* men'" (*Analects* XII.xxɪɪ.1).

68. "Some one asked the meaning of the great sacrifice. The Master said, 'I do not know. He who knew its meaning would find it as easy to govern the empire as to look on this;' – pointing to his palm." (*Analects* III.xɪ).

69. *Analects* III.xɪɪɪ.2.

70. "The Master said, 'When good order prevailed in his country, Ning Woo acted the part of a wise man. When his country was in disorder, he acted the part of a stupid man. Others may equal his wisdom, but they cannot equal his stupidity'" (*Analects* V.xx).

Hiding when govt is bad. (Leg.44[71]
VII Government. agst cap. Punishment. Leg 66[72]
   As ruler, so people. Leg 66.[73]
   Employ the upright. Leg 67[74]
9

THE GREAT LEARNING (TA HSÜEH) 大學

A chapter from the Book of Rites.
   Title means "Adult Education" – is in fact addressed to Ruler
or Potential Ruler.
? Written by Tzu Ssu. (483-402 BC.)[75] or II Cent??
Theme – self-cultivation, in relation to problem of good government (oversimplified – led to impractical idealism.)[76]
inadequate confusing[77]
8 points.   Illustrious virtue
           Loving the People
           Resting in the Highest Good.
           Fixed purpose (due to rest)
           Calmness of mind (due to f p.)
           Serene repose
           Careful deliberation (for which S. R. is necessary)
           Achievement (follows from careful deliberation).[78]

---

71. "When right principles of government prevail in the empire, he will show himself; when they are prostrated, he will keep concealed" (*Analects* VIII.XIII.2).

72. "Ke K'ang asked Confucius about government, saying, 'What do you say to killing the unprincipled for the good of the principled?' Confucius replied, 'Sir, in carrying on your government, why should you use killing at all? Let your *evinced* desires be for what is good, and the people will be good. The relations between superiors and inferiors, is like that between the wind and the grass. The grass must bend, when the wind blows across it'" (*Analects* XII.XIX).

73. "Ke K'ang asked Confucius about government. Confucius replied, 'To govern means to rectify. If you lead on *the people* with correctness, who will dare not to be correct?'" (*Analects* XII.XVII).

74. "The Master said, 'Employ the upright and put aside all the crooked; – in this way, the crooked can be made to be upright'" (*Analects* XII.XXII.3).

75. Grandson of Confucius.

76. Information drawn from the introduction to "THE GREAT LEARNING (TA HSÜEH)" in *Sources of Chinese Tradition*, compiled by Wm. Theodore de Bary, Wing-tsit Chan and Burton Watson (New York: Columbia University Press, 1960) 127-28 (subsequent references will be cited as "*Sources*").

77. *Added in left margin.*

78. See "*Selections from the Great Learning*" (*Sources* 129).

Cultivation of virtue + peace in person affects family + govt.
Cultivation of person it involves = *rectification of mind* – see p.
   129-30.[79] freedom from Passion.[80]

          which requires
             sincerity of thought
             extension of knowledge   cultivation of individual
             investigation of things   character is the root.[81]

Read STC. p 129[82]   (right action)
Jen in the Great Learning. p 131[83]
Pound. points (Pounds #'s + pages)

---

79. "What is meant by saying that 'the cultivation of the person depends on the rectification of the mind' is this: When one is under the influence of anger, one's mind will not be correct; when one is under the influence of fear, it will not be correct; when one is under the influence of fond regard, it will not be correct; when one is under the influence of anxiety, it will not be correct. When the mind is not there, we gaze at things but do not see; we listen but do not hear; we eat but do not know the flavors. This is what is meant by saying that the cultivation of the person depends on the rectification of the mind."

80. "see . . . Passion." *added in right margin and marked for insertion.*

81. See Merton's discussion of *The Great Learning* in his essay "Classic Chinese Thought" (*MZM* 45-68), in which he writes: "The whole meaning of the *Great Learning* is that right action depends on the awareness of the person acting. . . . It means awareness of the personal root and the inner truth which is the center and source of all well-ordered action" (60-61); it is this "sacred awareness at the heart of Kung's doctrine" which Merton finds in this work that leads to his conclusion that "The *Great Learning* remains the key to classic Chinese thought" (62).

82. "The ancients who wished clearly to exemplify illustrious virtue throughout the world would first set up good government in their states. Wishing to govern well their states, they would first regulate their families. Wishing to regulate their families, they would first cultivate their persons. Wishing to cultivate their persons, they would first rectify their minds. Wishing to rectify their minds, they would first seek sincerity in their thoughts. Wishing for sincerity in their thoughts, they would first extend their knowledge. The extension of knowledge lay in the investigation of things. For only when things are investigated is knowledge extended; only when knowledge is extended are thoughts sincere; only when thoughts are sincere are minds rectified; only when minds are rectified are our persons cultivated; only when our persons are cultivated are our families regulated; only when families are regulated are states well governed; and only when states are well governed is there peace in the world."

83. On p. 131, in the Introduction to "THE MEAN (CHUNG YUNG)," *jên* is defined as "Confucius' concept of humanity," but it is on the previous page that the concept is found in *The Great Learning*: "If one family exemplifies humanity, humanity will abound in the whole country. . . . Yao and Shun ruled the empire with humanity, and the people followed them." See *MZM* 52: "The Confucians believed that a society governed by a just and 'human-hearted' prince would once again bring out the concealed goodness in the subjects." On the previous page Merton had defined *jên* as "humanity" or "human-heartedness."

#1 (p.27 – Clarifying the way *intelligence increases*[84] by look-
ing into heart + acting on results.

	Tseng's comment. p. 35-36.		
Renewing the people	"	"	p 36-39.
(29) coming to rest in equity	"	"	39-45*[85]
Sincerity ("precise verbal			
expression for inarticulate			
thoughts."[86])	"	"	47-51

(Pound – gets "heart giving off tones[87] from 意)

    self-discipline rooted in rectifying heart (passions blind it).

                                          Tseng. 51-53

    order in home depends on self discipline.   " 54-57.

    order in state dep. on humanity in families.   "   58-65

                                     (esp 63-65 odes)

              people follow the prince

      Prince + people.   Tseng 65 to end. (89)

10[88]

性 Hsing – nature   心 Hsin – mind (heart)

---

84. the way . . . *increases interlined above cancelled* intelligence

85. The asterisk here presumably indicates Merton's sense of the significance of this third chapter of commentary, which, as noted above (see n. 57), consists of quotations from the *Book of Odes* (relevant to the idea of resting in equity) with Tseng's brief explanations.

86. Pound 33.

87. Pound 31, which reads: "the tones given off by the heart" as a gloss on "inarticulate thoughts"; in his note on Tseng's commentary Pound writes: *"This is the sixth chapter of the comment, sorting out the grist of the sentence about finding precise verbal expression for the heart's tone, for the inarticulate thoughts. The dominant ideograms in the chapter are the sun's lance falling true on the word, and the heart giving off tone"* (51). After mentioning the first of these interpretations in his discussion of the text in "Classic Chinese Thought," Merton goes on to say: "It is a matter of semantic focus, as well as a sapiential clarification of what was hitherto unknown and inarticulate, the bringing forth of the unconscious and the obscure into the focus of clarity by meaningful action at the right moment, with the right purpose, in the right manner, with the proper splendor of rite, that is to say, with sacred and aesthetic awareness and with the correct definition of what was to be done" (*MZM* 61-62), suggesting that he understood "the heart's tone" to be both an interior harmony and one expressed in Confucian ritual as well as in appropriate action.

88. The characters on notebook pages 10-11 are drawn mainly from the Appendix (paginated separately 1-44) to I. A. Richards, *Mencius on the Mind: Experiments in Multiple Definition* (New York: Harcourt, Brace, 1932), which includes passages from Mencius in Chinese characters, with transliterations and literal interlinear translations (subsequent references will be cited as "Richards").

智 Chih – wisdom, wise
天 Tien – Heaven　　天 下 = heaven below = earth.
仁 Jên – Love　　人 Jen = men
固 Ku – inborn
禮 Li – rites, good form　　理 Li = Truth.
知 Chih – know　　智 Chih = wisdom.
道 Tao.
日 Ji – day　夜 yeh – night　旦 Tan – morning[89]　　母 mu = eye
　夜 気 Yeh-chih "night spirit." – (cf ox mountain parable of Mencius)
水 shui = water
言 yen = words
[　][90] p'ing = peace
無事 = Wu Shih. without laboring
善 Shan – good
爲 Wei – action　　[　]? coming to rest?[91]
情 Ching[92]
有 Yu – have
聖人 Sheng Jen = sage
山 Shan – mountain
雨 Yü – rain
11
之 chih – (possessive particle. etc) (is[93])
足 Tsu = sufficient.
見 chien = see.
而 erh = and
亡 wang = vanish　　王 wang = king
交 chiao = friendship

---

89. This is, more precisely, "dawn".

90. This character as drawn by Merton, found repeatedly in Richards, is not the standard character for p'ing (平); the triangular shape at the top points upward rather than downward, evidently a more archaic form of the word; it is not available for reproduction.

91. This is apparently one of a pair of mistaken identifications made by Merton: in the version of the *Great Learning* found in Pound, rubbings made from early stone tablets, the character "hou" (后), generally meaning "after" and the like, takes on a more rounded shape, copied by Merton, but not recognized as the same as the standard character, which he includes below, and evidently considered here to have the meaning "coming to rest" from its positioning in the *Great Learning* text, though the question mark indicates Merton's uncertainty about the identification.

92. Properly "ch'ing"; translated as "propensity" in Richards, Appendix 3, 13.

93. Merton presumably means "'s" here.

父母 = fu mu = parents
德 = "virtue" etc. quality
誠 – "precise verbal definition" = sincerity
吾 wu = I.
聞 wen = hear.
強 chiang = strong
否 fou = no   不 pu = not 不 可 知 – cannot be known
                              pu ko chih
高 hsi = glad
太 tu = great
信 hsin = true
美 mei – beautiful
光 Kuang = light.
聖 sheng = holy
[ ] shun ? = Hand which grasps cover uniting extremes = discipline.[94]
近 chin = near

12

Great Learning –
任 jen   (better[95] 任) = office, responsibility.
明 bright
德 Te   virtue
親 Chin   love[96]
民 Min (Matthews 4508[97]) – People, Mankind
止 Chih   halt, cease, rest.
於 Yü – with
至 ?[98]

---

94. This is the other apparent mistake; it is evidently the character "erh" (而), meaning "and," but in the stone rubbing, as copied by Merton here, the four "legs" are shorter and more rounded, apparently giving Merton the impression that it was an altogether different character; used together, as they are repeatedly in the *Great Learning*, 而 后 mean "and then" or "after that"; it is unclear where he came up with his definition and Chinese term here.

95. Merton evidently considers his second attempt to copy this character preferable to the first, though there is little difference between them.

96. i.e. "cherish"; *Sources* 129 interprets as "love" ; Legge, *Classics* 1.112 translates as "renovate".

97. *A Chinese–English Dictionary: Compiled for the China Inland Mission by R. H. Mathews* (Shanghai: China Inland Mission Press, 1931); revised edition: *Mathews' Chinese–English Dictionary* (Cambridge, MA: Harvard University Press, 1943).

98. "Chih" – which has a variety of meanings, including "arrive," "to," "until" which explains Merton's uncertainty, but which apparently means "most"

(土 Earth T'u)　　　士shih – scholar – gentleman

善 Shan – good, benevolent.

知[99]

F.158[100] 后 Hou. (Empress?[101]

F638　有 Yu have = br.

定 Ting – fix – stop – determine[102] – tranquil.

君 chün　superior man.

子 tzu.

13

　　　止[103]

Great learning cont[d]

能[104]　　　　　　　　　月 F. 654

　　　　　　　　　Yueh – moon.

靜[105]

14

THE MEAN

　Chung Yung.

Eur. Trans. *Doctrine of* the Mean (word Doctrine inserted by ua.)

Chinese words.　　中庸 chung yung

　　　　　　　　chung = center, mean,

　　　　　　　　yung = workman, work

　　　trans.　　functioning mean? 'The Mean in action.'[106]

---

or "highest" in the context of the *Great Learning*.

　99. "Chih" – "know": see above.

　100. The references here and twice more subsequently are to an unidentified source; it may be to a book referred to in an August 1960 letter to Merton from his friend the artist and printer Victor Hammer, who writes, "I am sorry I cannot re-dedicate the book on Chinese characters to you, it has already been dedicated to me by the printer. But you can keep it as long as you want, and I hope it will be of some use to you." In his response of August 17, 1960, Merton writes, "I am enjoying the Chinese ideograms" (Thomas Merton and Victor and Carolyn Hammer, *The Letters of Thomas Merton and Victor and Carolyn Hammer: Ad Majorem Dei Gloriam*, ed. F. Douglas Scutchfield and Paul Evans Holbrook Jr. [Lexington: University Press of Kentucky, 2014] 112, 113).

　101. This is the same Chinese character "hou" referred to above, which can mean "Empress" as well as "after" etc. Merton's question mark indicates that he is evidently puzzled by this definition as it has no relevance to the *Great Learning*.

　102. *Interlined with a caret.*

　103. It is not clear why Merton repeats this character for "rest" here.

　104. "neng": "can, be able".

　105. "ching": "quiet, calm".

　106. See *MZM* 59: "Other suggestions by various translators include the 'Working Center' and the 'Functioning Mean' or the 'Mean in Action.'"

Pound's "unwobbling" – for yung – seems gratuitous[107]
Central idea – 眞 – cheng.

　　　　　　　'Reality in heaven + realness in man.'

15

THE MEAN (Chung Yung.) by Tzu Ssu – 子 思[108]
Trad. ascribed to Tzu Ssu. – But a medley of texts.

Central conc　1) chung. "centrality" yung "normality."

　　　　　　　2) cheng – sincerity, truth. Moral integrity that
　　　　　　　makes a man real.
　　　　　　　is genuine with all + united to underlying
　　　　　　　reality of universe
　　　　　　　"self-realization in mystic unity between
　　　　　　　self – heaven – earth."[109]

A confucian response to Taoism:[110] *– quest for harmony in action.*
　　　　　　　Emphasis on cheng 眞 reality –

　　　　　　　　　　　　　in heaven
　　　　　　　　　　　　　in man

The Way STC. p. 132, 135[111]　The Mean – 133.
　　　Distinguish metaphysical *Tao* – the way of heaven
　　　　　　　　　　　ethical *Tao* – the way of man[112]
　　centrality + harmony. 133
　　Sincerity is the Way of Heaven. 134, 135 – leads to Jên 135.

　　　　　　　　　+

---

107. But see *MZM* 58-59: "Actually, to call the *Chung Yung* the *Doctrine of the Mean* is very inadequate. Ezra Pound's rendering, the 'Unwobbling Pivot,' is perhaps closer to the author's intention."

108. Information drawn from the introduction to "THE MEAN (CHUNG YUNG)" (*Sources* 131-32).

109. *Sources* 132, which reads: "through ethical cultivation the individual not only achieves human perfection but also 'realizes' himself in a mystic unity with Heaven and earth."

110. See *MZM* 58: "The main difference between the *Ju* school and the Taoists is that the latter are concerned with the metaphysical, the former with the ethical *Tao*. Needless to say, this comparison itself is not always clear, except in the *Doctrine of the Mean*, or *Chung Yung*, which is one of the four Confucian classics, and which was a kind of Confucian reply to Taoism."

111. "*Selections from The Mean*" (chs. I-III, XIV, XX, XXI-XXII, XXV-XXVI).

112. "Distinguish . . . man" *added on opposite page and marked for insertion.* See *MZM* 58: "The basis of Kung's philosophy . . . is the *Tao* itself, but the ethical *Tao*, the way of man, rather than the metaphysical *Tao* or the inscrutable way of God."

Pound.

I. Heaven "disposes + seals" inborn nature[113] –
    Realization of nature = Tao
    Clarification of this = education.
    The Tao[114] is always there – we do not depart from it but we
        seem to – we become estranged by passion –
        + no longer live "in the center"[115] – the axis – in harmony
    – unmoved by passion – in *axis*
    – moved properly by passion – in *harmony*.

II. Sup. man[116] finds center
    mean man goes in circles
    sup. man finds center *in season* (can vary, adapt.)
    small man is rigid – pays no att^n to times + seasons – because
    he *lacks reverence.* 103, 105.

III-IX. Sup. man – having found center, *stays there –*
        moving with the Tao (not exceeding or falling short).

X. Harmonizing southern + northern energy. (nb. Taoists – from
    South, Kung from North.)

XII – Highest ethic also simplest + most universal

XIII. Tao inborn in man "not far"[117] – Jen
                    – fidelity to word.

XIV. The man of quality[118] + the archer – when they miss they
    seek the cause in themselves

XV. Love begins with those nearest to us.

XVI. – Inborn principles of virtue.

XVII-XIX. Examples of piety + rites. Conclusion: *He who*
    understands the meaning + the justice of the rites to Earth
    + Heaven will govern a kingdom as if he held it lit up in the
    palm of his hand. (p. 147)

XX. JEN – the 'pure contents of man'[119]

---

113. See Pound 99: "What heaven has disposed and sealed is called the inborn nature."

114. Pound translates Tao as "process" throughout, but Merton in these notes retains the Chinese term.

115. Pound 103.

116. Pound uses the term "master man" while Merton keeps the term "superior man" used by Legge and others.

117. Pound 119.

118. Pound uses the term "man of breed" – another way of describing the "*chun tzu*" or superior man.

119. See Pound 149: "this *humanitas* [i.e. *jen*, human-heartedness] is the full contents of man, it is the contents of the full man."

based on affection – love for growth (linked with agriculture
says P. p. 149[120])
rites = based on affection, on degrees of affection.
Relationships – Knowledge. (p 151ff)
*Duke Ngai's question[121]
XX (cont'd).[122] Knowledge, humanity + energy.
Nine rules – (p 157) + application –
Calm preparation for important affairs. p 165.
Sincerity Sincerity – precision of terms – important development.
Sincerity = Ch'eng
= reality in heaven + in man[123]
169. "Sincere man finds the axis without forcing himself to do so."[124]
He arrives at it without thinking" (close to Taoism)
171. He does not leave loose ends.
XXI ff. *Sincerity* – Statement of thesis – developed in later
– natural
– acquired
XXII. – sincerity + emptiness? Note Nominalism of Pound – cf
other translations.[125]
XXIV. sage can read signs of future good + evil.
XXV. – *Reality* ("sincerity") the goal.
XXVI. – Tao. – end – Sapiential Hymn. cf Job etc.[126]

---

120. *"The ideogram represents the sacrificial vase. Ethics are born from agriculture; the nomad gets no further than the concept of my sheep and thy sheep."*

121. Duke Ngai's question, simply "about government" (147), is raised at the beginning of chapter XX and occupies the rest of this lengthy chapter of 21 sections (147-71).

122. The remainder of this summary of the treatise is found on the opposite page.

123. "Sincerity . . . man." *added above and marked for insertion.*

124. Text reads: "The sincere . . ." (167, 169).

125. Pound's translation reads: "Only the most absolute sincerity under heaven can bring the inborn talent to the full and empty the chalice of the nature" (173). Legge translates: "It is only he who is possessed of the most complete sincerity that can exist under heaven, who can give its full development to his nature" (*Classics* 1.138). *Sources* translation reads: "Only he who possesses absolute sincerity can give full development to his nature" (134).

126. The final chapter is a hymn celebrating cosmic harmony and integration encompassing sun, moon and stars, mountains, rivers and oceans, "wild fowl and the partridge, the four-footed beasts and stags," "terrapin and great turtles, monsters, crocodiles, dragons, fish and crustaceans" (183, 185, 187), recalling the Lord's speech from the whirlwind on creation in Job 38-41 and other passages on the dynamic, creative action of divine wisdom in the Old Testament.

No duality bet heaven + earth p 183.

16

孟子

MENCIUS. (Meng-Tzu). 372-289 bc.[127]

Native of Chi – studied under Confucius' grandson Tzu Ssu.
Time of war + chaos. M. argues against Moists.
Principles – *jen* (humanity)   AW. 84.[128]
(for true ruler)
"To Mencius, goodness meant compassion, it meant not being
able to bear that others should suffer. It meant a feeling of
responsibility for the sufferings of others." 83.[129]

   i – righteousness – propriety – duty. *Not* equal love to all
      men (Mo Tzu) but according to degrees, relationships
      etc (filial piety) STC 112[130]

   Innate goodness of man – "his child-like heart"[131]
      perverted by downward trends due to neglect
      man should strive to recover his innate goodness.
      see quotes STC. – 104, 105,[132]   AW. 83, (Bull Mt.) 84*.

---

127. Merton relies for his introductory material here on *Sources* 100-102,
which however says that Mencius studied under a disciple of Tzu Ssu rather than
Tzu Ssu himself.

128. Arthur Waley, *Three Ways of Thought in Ancient China* ([1939] Garden
City, NY: Doubleday Anchor, 1956) (subsequent references will be cited as
"Waley"). It is on the previous page, the beginning of his discussion of Mencius,
that Waley states that *jên*, which he translates as goodness or compassion, is the
basis for the teaching of Mencius; his version of the "allegory of the Bull Mountain"
that explains the process of the loss of innate good feelings is found on 84-85.
These references to Waley on Mencius seem to have been added subsequently to
Merton's initial summary of material from *Sources*.

129. "To Mencius . . . others." *added on opposite page and marked for
insertion*; text reads: "But to . . . Goodness . . . compassion; . . ."

130. "Mencius is known in later tradition for his defense of Confucian filial
piety against Yang Chu, the individualist, and Mo Tzu, the exponent of universal
love. By thus making a special point of it, he gave added importance to filial
piety among the Confucian virtues" (111) (see *Mencius* III B:9; IV A:19, 26, 27).

131. *Sources* 102.

132. The reference to quotes on these pages evidently refers to the passage
from the *Book of Odes* and the comment of Confucius on this passage: "Heaven so
produced the teeming multitudes that / For everything there is its principle. / The
people will keep to the constant principles, / And all will love a beautiful character.
Confucius said, regarding this poem, 'The writer of this poem understands indeed
the nature of the Way! For wherever there are things and affairs there must be
their principles. As the people keep to the constant principles, they will come to
love a beautiful character'" (Mencius VI A:6).

Not utilitarian – as agst Mo Tsu.

"Why must you speak of profit?" STC. 106.[133]

The 4 beginnings – cf child in the well parable.[134]

1) Pity – sympathy (Tse-yin) of mind is love's (jen) beginning

2) Shame – dislike of mind (hsiu-wu) – is righteousness's (yi's) beginning

3) Declining yielding of mind (tsu-jang) is propriety's (Li's) beginning

4) Right-wrong of mind (shih-fei) – wisdom's beginning (chih). (approving – disapproving)[135]

'A great man is not bent on having his words believed nor on making his actions effective.

He takes his stand on righteousness + nothing else'
    Mencius IV B.

Yet acting for good of people – for good of all – be comes an unconditional obligation for all.[136]

Violence does not bring good fruits – STC. 107-108. AW. 91;[137] 109ˣ[138]

"States have been won by men without humanity, but the world, never."[139]

---

133. This is the reply of Mencius to King Hui of Liang, who remarks that having come so far, Mencius must have "something of profit to offer." Mencius replies, "Why must you speak of profit? What I have to offer is humanity and righteousness, nothing more" (*Mencius* I A:1).

134. This parable (*Mencius* II A:6) says that anyone who becomes aware of a child about to fall into a well will feel "a sense of alarm and compassion" not motivated by desire to gain the approval of the child's parents or of friends and neighbors, nor by a fear of blame should he fail to rescue the child, but moved by an innate sense of commiseration (*Sources* 105).

135. "The 4 . . . disapproving) *added on opposite page.* See *Sources* 105, which does not however include the Chinese terms and uses different English terms as well ("approving – disapproving" is apparently taken from Legge's translation: *The Chinese Classics. A Translation by James Legge, D.D. Part II Mencius* [New York: John B. Alden, Publisher, 1891] 54).

136. 'A great . . . for all. *added on opposite page and marked for insertion*; quotation from Fung Yu-lan, *The Spirit of Chinese Philosophy*, trans. E. R. Hughes (Boston: Beacon Press, 1962) 14 (subsequent references will be cited as "Fung").

137. Mencius tells the newly enthroned King Hsiang of Wei that a ruler who did not delight in slaughter could unite the entire world.

138. Mencius tells King Hsüan of Ch'i, who asks how to become a true king, that his preparations for war are fundamentally about the desire to expand territory, which he compares to trying to get fish from a tree, except that while the latter is futile, it has no evil consequences, whereas the former will lead to calamity.

139. *Sources* 107 (*Mencius* VII B:13).

vg. Punishment for crime. – STC p. 107[140]

Providing for all. 108.[141] – division of land. 108[142] "well-field system." STC 109[143] AW. 88.[144]

"Heaven sees as my people see . . ." 110.[145]

Individual – foundation of all. 110[146] The "great man." AW. 119.[147]

Relation of Ruler + ministers – 110[148]

Breathing techniques – as aid to jên. AW. 85.[149]

Economic basis of goodness. – AW. 86,[150] Socialism (?) AW

---

140. Mencius points out to King Hsüan of Ch'i that the multitude will not have a steadfast heart without having a means of attaining a decent standard of living, and therefore may well turn to depraved behavior, so that "If you wait till they have lapsed into crime and then mete out punishment, it is like placing traps for the people" (*Mencius* I A:7).

141. Mencius maintains that when everyone has a sufficiency of land for raising food and material (silk) for clothing, the ruler becomes a true king (*Mencius* I A:7, found also in I A:3 and VIII A:22).

142. According to Mencius, "At the bottom of all humane government, we might say, lies the system of land division and demarcation" (*Mencius* III A:3).

143. The "well-field system" is the supposed ancient "system of equal landholding which [Mencius] believed had been maintained by the Chou dynasty" (108) and which he advocated reviving in his own time; it consisted of nine lots of equal size, eight of them owned by individual households and the ninth held and cultivated in common (*Mencius* III A:3, 13-20).

144. This section not only summarizes Mencius' approbation of the well-field system but his condemnation of the current oppressive tribute system of sharecropping.

145. The "Great Declaration" found in the *Book of History* states: "Heaven sees as my people see, Heaven hears as my people hear," meaning that popular acceptance of a just ruler indicates acceptance by Heaven (Mencius V A:5).

146. According to Mencius, "the foundation of the world lies in the state, the foundation of the state lies in the family, and the foundation of the family lies in the individual" (*Mencius* IV A:5).

147. Mencius contrasts the conventional understanding of the "great man" as someone who is powerful and to be feared with a true definition of such a person who when successful lets the people receive the benefits of his success but remains faithful to his values whether successful or unsuccessful.

148. According to Mencius, "When the ruler regards his ministers as his hands and feet, the ministers regard their ruler as their heart and bowels. When the ruler regards his ministers as his dogs and horses, the ministers regard their ruler as a stranger. When the ruler regards his ministers as dust and grass, the ministers regard their ruler as a brigand or foe" (*Mencius* IV B:3).

149. Mencius recommends breathing techniques similar to yoga in a passage that is textually corrupt, but indicates his endorsement of such practices as a way to remain calm and focused.

150. The advice of Mencius to various rulers on good government focuses principally on "land tenure, taxation and what we should call Old Age Pensions."

87.[151] – AW. 110 (importance of econ. conditions)[152]
["The 3 years' mourning. AW. 96-97[153]]
"Leave a loose thread hanging." 99.[154]
Government by goodness. AW. 104[155] (practical? 105[156]), 108,[157]
   110,[158] 112,[159] (sharing music. AW. 128[160])
17
I. A. Richards. Mencius on the Mind. London 1932.
   Unless the thinking which has been fundamental to historic

---

151. According to Waley, the conclusion of an unidentified "recent writer" that the economic theory of Mencius has "socialistic implications" has "not a single passage . . . which supports such an interpretation."

152. Here Waley summarizes the passage from *Mencius* I A:7 about oppressive policies toward the common people being equivalent to setting traps for them (see n. 140 above).

153. This Confucian recommendation for withdrawal from public life for an extended period, supposedly based on ancient practice, is impractical in its specifics but could serve as a kind of "sabbatical" allowing for a mid-career time of reflection for public officials, if not for lower-class laborers.

154. The "gentleman" (*chun tzu* or superior person) "leaves a loose thread hanging" in the sense that he realizes that he cannot complete all his plans himself but must depend upon his successors continuing his work.

155. A disciple of Mencius laments the fate of the principality of Sung which attempted to implement the vision of Mencius for good government and was attacked and overrun by more powerful neighboring states, a result that contradicted his master's conclusion that such a state would attract the respect and imitation of other states.

156. The response of Mencius that Sung must therefore not have been such a state is judged by Waley as representing an "ostrich-like attitude" about the actual political situation "that brought Confucianism into discredit as a practical morality and paved the way for the Realists."

157. Mencius distinguishes between saying that someone cannot do something that is indeed impossible and saying that someone cannot do something because he chooses not to, and that a failure to implement good government is a case of mistaking the second for the first.

158. As part of his conversation on good kingship with King Hsüan of Ch'i Mencius asserts his belief that government according to goodness would attract people of all classes to his land.

159. Mencius tells the governor of P'ing-lu that his strictness toward dereliction of duty on the part of a bodyguard is not matched by a comparable strictness toward his own failures to care for his people in time of famine, and the governor acknowledges his fault.

160. Mencius uses the Confucian emphasis on the importance of music to illustrate the contrasting attitudes of a ruler's people: if they perceive that he is taking private pleasure in entertainment while neglecting his duties toward his people, resentment arises, while if he shares his enjoyment with his people, a sense of loyalty and solidarity develops.

China can somehow be explained in Western terms it seems inevitably doomed to oblivion. p 9.

We have to suspend some of our most valued distinctions if we are to read Mencius with any hope of success. p. 11.[161]

We have to submit our minds to him in a fashion very difficult to reconcile with a clear understanding of what we are doing. id.

+

Hsing 性.[162] Mencius does not consider nature from a metaphysical viewpoint.

(Sung commentators of 13th cent gave it a metaphysical slant[163]). Hsing = that in man which makes him different from animals. Common humanity of all men. (illustrated by common tastes – inclination to sympathy etc)[164]

A complex of impulsions – which can be *interfered with by bad conditions*

vg. famine, tyranny[165]

*Rest + especially the breath of dawn + the night breath restore them. (cf Ox mountain parable[166])

[ ][167] 旦 之 気 夜 気
Ping Tan Chih Ch'i yeh chih[168]

----

161. Text reads: "We have therefore to suspend . . ."

162. Richards defines *Hsing* as "stand[ing] both for Human Nature – the subject inquired about in most of these passages from Mencius – and for Nature in general" (5).

163. See Richards 66: "Mencius – it is part of his eschewal of problems of knowledge – entirely avoids metaphysics. It is true that since A.D. 1200, when Chu Hsi, the great Sung philosopher, reinterpreted Mencius, *hsing* has had deep metaphysical significances attached to it, but our business is with Mencius."

164. See Richards 66, which reads: "*Hsing* is that in man which, though slight, makes him different from the animals . . . ; it is common to all men, and indeed is that which, as regards the mind, men have in common . . . – their common humanity in things of the mind . . . parallel to their common size, roughly, in feet . . . and their common tastes in meats, music, and beauty."

165. See Richards 66: "These impulsions can be interfered with by bad conditions. Famine, for example . . . , can entrap and drown the mind and thus distort them. So can bad government. The impulsions tend to be frustrated and curtailed by daily affairs . . . . Rest and especially the breath of dawn and the night-breath restore them."

166. Richards Appendix 9-12 (*Mencius* VI-I-8).

167. Here again Merton has the variant form of "ping": see n. 90 above.

168. Richards Appendix 10, 11, which should read: "*p'ing tan chih ch'i*"

['night spirit not sufficient to sustain (mind – like shoots of trees
cut on the mtn – then he differs from birds beasts not far.'[169]]
    These impulsions show themselves in the '4 beginnings'
        which are native to man.
    He seems much more at home with pity + shame than with
        the other two.[170]
'Those who make the most of their capacities who 'seek then
get it, do not 'give up so lose it'
become virtuous + in the highest examples become sages.'[171]
'As Yi Ya the Epicure was the first to grasp what all mouths
agree in liking, so the sage is the first to grasp what all *human*
minds agree in. *He is the sage because he is the most human
of men.*[172]

18

The Ox Mountain Parable of [173]*Meng-Tzu.*[174]

I.

Master Meng said
"There was once a fine forest on the Ox Mountain,

(dawn-spirit) and "*yeh ch'i*" (night-spirit); the Chinese character for the last word
is correct.

169. Richards Appendix 11, the interlinear literal translation which reads:
"night-spirit not sufficient to sustain/preserve (itself); night-spirit not sufficient
to sustain, then he differs from birds-beasts not far."

170. See Richards 67: "These impulsions show themselves in a minimal
degree in such universal promptings as pity, shame, reverence, and sense of right
and wrong, which are not due to inculcation or example or social pressure in the
first place, but are native to man. Mencius, however, seems much more at home
with pity and shame than with the other two."

171. See Richards 68, which reads: "Those who make the most of their
capacities (common to all men), 'who seek then get it' and do not 'give up so lose
it' . . . become virtuous and in the highest examples, become sages."

172. See Richards 15: "As the epicure Yi Ya surpassed and led others in
recognizing (grasping consciously) what all mouths like, so the sage leads in
recognizing (and 'making the most of', p. 4) the common human endowment
of propensities"; and Appendix 7-9 (interlinear literal translation of *Mencius*
VI-I-7[5-8]).

173. *Followed by cancelled Mencius.*

174. Draft of Merton's version of *Mencius* VI-I-7(5-8) first published with
a brief introduction in a limited edition by his friend Victor Hammer on his hand
press: *The Ox Mountain Parable of Meng Tzu*, translated with an introduction by
Thomas Merton (Lexington, KY: Stamperia del Santuccio, 1960); subsequently
included as an appendix to Merton's essay "Classic Chinese Thought" (*MZM*
65-68).

Near[175] a great capital.
They came out with axes and cut down the trees.
Was[176] it still a fine forest?
Yet rested in the alternation of day + night
Freshened by dew, the stumps sprouted + the trees[177]
Began to grow again.
Then came goats + cattle
To browse on the young shoots.
The Ox[178] Mountain was[179] stripped utterly bare.

And the people, seeing it stripped[180] utterly bare,
Think[181] the Ox Mountain never had any[182] woods on it at all![183]
II.
What is left to us of our humanity
Cannot be without some love[184] for our right mind
But just as men with axes, cutting down trees every morning
Destroy the beauty of the forest
So we, (by our daily actions,)
Lose our right mind.

The alternation of day + night, (resting the murdered forest)
And[185] The moisture of the dawn spirit,

---

175. *Preceded by cancelled* Over
176. *Preceded by cancelled* Could they
177. *Followed by cancelled* grew began to gr
178. *Interlined.*
179. *Interlined above cancelled* is
180. *Followed by cancelled* bare
181. *Added in left margin before cancelled* Thought
182. *Interlined with a caret.*
183. The published version of this section reads:
    Master Meng said: There was once a fine forest on the Ox Mountain,
    Near the capital of a populous country.
    The men came out with axes and cut down the trees. Was it still a fine forest?
    Yet, resting in the alternation of days and nights, moistened by dew,
    The stumps sprouted, the trees began to grow again.
    Then out came goats and cattle to browse on the young shoots.
    The Ox Mountain was stripped utterly bare.
    And the people, seeing it stripped utterly bare,
    Think the Ox Mountain never had any woods on it at all.
184. *Preceded by cancelled* vestige of conscience
185. *Added in left margin.*

Are like our natural[186] inclination to love others.

With the acts of one morning
We stifle[187] that love, stifle it again + again[188]

Our night spirit is no longer able
To bring[189] love back to life

Then are we[190] different from birds + animals?
Not much!

Men see us + say we never had any capacity for love.
Is this man's nature?[191]

III

Whatever[192] is cultivated[193] it must grow
Whatever is not cultivated must perish.

IV

K said "grasp it + keep it!
Let go + it will disappear[194]

---

186. *Preceded by cancelled* love
187. *Followed by cancelled* + kill
188. *Followed by mark in left margin indicating line space.*
189. *Followed by cancelled* back our
190. *Interlined above cancelled* we are not much different
191. The published version of this section reads:
    Our mind too, stripped bare, like the mountain,
    Still cannot be without some basic tendency to love.
    But just as men with axes, cutting down the trees every morning,
    Destroy the beauty of the forest,
    So we, by our daily actions, destroy our right mind.

    Day follows night, giving rest to the murdered forest,
    The moisture of the dawn spirit
    Awakens in us the right loves, the right aversions.

    With the actions of one morning we cut down this love,
    And destroy it again. At last the night spirit
    Is no longer able to revive our right mind.

    Where, then, do our likes and dislikes differ from those of animals?
    In nothing much.
    Men see us, and say we never had in us anything but evil.
    Is this man's nature?
192. *Interlined above cancelled* Nothing If our nature
193. *Interlined above cancelled* nourished
194. *Preceded by cancelled* vanish

No time[195] for it to come in or go out –
No one knows its country!"
Of the mind, the mind only, does he speak.[196]

19

Mo Tzu (Mo Ti) 470-391 BC.[197]
born in Sung or Lu.

> Opposition to Confucius – opp. to skepticism + fatalism +
> > ritualism of C's followers.
> > – goes back beyond Chou to *Hsia*
> > dynasty.[198]

> Characteristic Doctrines – Heaven – *active power* manifesting
> love for all men.

> Therefore Men should follow heaven by *universal love +
> identification with Superior*

> Therefore condemns exterior ritualism – (AW. 123[199]
> > war – (exc. punitive expeditions). (AW. 130[200]

---

195. *Preceded by cancelled* As our know

196. The published version of these sections (combined into a single section) reads:

> Whatever is cultivated rightly, will surely grow.
> Whatever is not cultivated rightly must surely perish.
> Master Kung (Confucius) said:
> > Grasp it firmly and you will keep it.
> > Grasp it loosely, and it will vanish out of your hand.
> > Its comings and goings have no fixed times:
> > No one knows its country!
>
> Of man's right mind, of this only does he speak!

197. The background material here is drawn principally from the introduction to Chapter III, "Mo Tzu: Universal Love, Utilitarianism, and Uniformity" (*Sources* 36-37).

198. This information is found in the last chapter of the Han-era work *Hainan Tzu*, on "The Historical Mission of Mo Tzu" (*Sources* 203), which states that Mo Tzu eventually rejected Confucianism and "turned his back upon the ways of Chou and used the practices of Hsia," the legendary or mythic earliest Chinese dynasty, preceding the Shang and Chou, holding up Yü, its founder, as a model, who devoted himself personally to repairing the land and guiding the people during the time of a great flood.

199. "Under the heading harmful he included all lavish ritual expenditure, in particular the wholesale waste of property that accompanied an orthodox Chinese burial" (as with the Mencius notes, these references to Waley were added subsequently to Merton's initial summary of material from *Sources*).

200. "But, like the Confucians, Mo Tzu believed in the Righteous War, in which a good king, at the command of Heaven, punishes a bad one" (Waley 130-31).

nb. on not letting war criminals escape. AW. 131.[201]

"diversion" (music) AW 125, 126.[202]

is a rigorist – a missionary for ideals of peace + brotherhood.
anti-emotional.

His "love" is mental + utilitarian – it pays.

Identification with Superior[203]

Interpolations in the Mo Tzu – ch. 1-7 by later disciples They
were debaters + prosyletizers.[204]

29 – later addition (unhistorical)

40-45 by disciples after MT.

His social philos. – 1 primitive times every man for himself
(cf Hobbes[205]) *hence need of Ruler* (Son of Heaven)

SCT. 38.

2 All evil to be reported to superiors – identification with
Superior + not with subordinates[206]

3 Exaltation of the worthy[207] (without personal favoritism)
– zeal of the "worthy" for the state

They must be rewarded, their authority confirmed.

4 *universal* love[208] (not favoritism) – bec. hatred + selfishness dismember society "U. love is the cause of the major

---

201. Mo Tzu criticizes the Confucian precept allowing a defeated enemy to withdraw unmolested: "if this is done, the violent and disorderly will escape with their lives and the world will not be rid of its pest. . . . There could be no greater injustice than that they should be allowed to escape."

202. "Mo Tzu condemned 'music.' But the Chinese word in question had a much wider sense than our term 'music.' What Mo Tzu had in mind were elaborate and costly dance rituals, demanding expensive costumes, the maintenance of large companies of dancers and musicians, all of which were paid out of the public funds. . . . '. . . It is clear then that if rulers and their ministers encourage musical performances, the common people will go short of food and clothing, so great is the drain of such performances upon their resources. That is why Mo Tzu said that it is wrong to go in for music.'"

203. "Identification with the Superior" is the title of chapter 2, the first selected excerpt (*Sources* 38-39).

204. Added in right margin; see *Sources* 37: "their evangelistic approach and readiness to discuss or debate with anyone may explain why the later Mo-ist canon is so much concerned with logic and dialectics."

205. In his treatise *Leviathan*, English philosopher Thomas Hobbes (1588-1679) discusses the state of nature as a "war of each against all" in which life was "poor, nasty, brutish and short," leading people to surrender their freedom to an authoritarian ruler for the sake of stability and security.

206. See *Mo Tzu* c. 2 (*Sources* 38-39).

207. Title of chapter 9, the second selected excerpt (*Sources* 39-41).

208. Title of chapter 16, the third selected excerpt (*Sources* 42-46).

benefits of the world . . ." SCT. 43.[209]

partial love – relies on *force*[210]

    5 The will of Heaven[211] – righteousness. SCT. 47
      (universal love)
      Heaven sends calamities for the murder of the innocent[212]
          (evil kings condemned by posterity[213])
     "   rewards good actions of the worthy.[214]
    Rule of force for selfish ends violates will of heaven.[215]

20

MO TZU. 5th Cent BC.[216]

Of lower class origin (unlike Kung)

Went back to legendary sages like KT, but to Yü the self-sacrificing king who combated floods

Ascetic discipline + hard work.

Attacked lavish burials of nobles as exhausting treasury + bleeding the people.

Emphasis on Providence – a revival of ancient faith agst skepticism of Kung + Lao

---

209. Text reads: "Now, since universal love is the cause of the major benefits in the world, therefore Mo Tzu proclaims that universal love is right."

210. See *Sources* 49: "According to the doctrine of universality the standard of conduct is righteousness; according to the doctrine of partiality the standard is force."

211. Title of chapter 28, the fourth selected excerpt (*Sources* 46-49).

212. See *Sources* 48: "In all the countries in the world and among all the peoples who live on grain, the murder of one innocent individual is invariably followed by a calamity. Now, who is it that murders the innocent individual? It is man. Who is it that sends forth the calamity? It is Heaven."

213. See *Sources* 49: "the multitude condemned them, the condemnation lasting through countless generations and the people calling them the lost kings. Here we have the proof of Heaven's punishment of the evil."

214. See *Sources* 48: "[Heaven] invariably rewards the good and punishes the evil. We know this from the record of the sage kings of the Three Dynasties . . . Yao, Shun, Yü, T'ang, Wen, and Wu" (legendary kings of the Hsia, Shang and Chou eras).

215. See *Sources* 49: "what is it like when force becomes the standard of conduct? The great will attack the small, the strong will plunder the weak, the many will oppress the few, the cunning will deceive the simple, the noble will disdain the humble, the rich will mock the poor, and the young will encroach upon the old. And the states in the empire will ruin each other with water, fire, poison, and weapons. . . . This is called the violation of Heaven. . . . Why? Because such conduct is in opposition to the will of Heaven."

216. This material is drawn from Liu Wu-Chi, *A Short History of Confucian Philosophy* (Baltimore: Penguin, 1955) 43-46 (subsequent references will be cited parenthetically as "Liu").

Founded a popular military anti-war organization
Mencius said
    "If the doctrines of Yang + Mo are not checked + the
doctrine of Master K'ung is not promoted, perverse teachings
will delude the people + block the road to human-heartedness
+ righteousness. And when that way is blocked beasts will
devour men + men will devour one another"[217]
    "Anyone who lifts his voice against Yang + Mo is worthy to
be a disciple of the sages"[218]
    "To acknowledge neither king nor father is to be a brute."[219]

20A

    "Those who know the way will untiringly instruct others." MT[220]
Critique of Mo Tzu by Chuang Tzu.[221] SCT. p. 81.[222]
Praises his austerity for himself, but condemns it in rel. to
others as inhuman. 82*[223]
    "Their way is too harsh. It makes of life a sad + dreary
business. Their standard of conduct is impossible to live up to
. . . *It is contrary to the heart of the world* + the world at large
could never endure it." Chuang Tzu in AW. p 134[224]
The self-sacrifice of the Mo-ists of China today 82, 83.[225]
    "Mo Tzu produced something better than disorder but still far

---

217. Quoted in Liu 69.
218. Quoted in Liu 69.
219. Quoted in Liu 69.
220. Quoted in H. G. Creel, *Chinese Thought from Confucius to Mao Tse-tung* (London: Eyer & Spottiswoode, 1954) 62; subsequent references will be cited as "Creel" parenthetically in the text.
221. This critique is found in chapter 33 of the *Chuang Tzu*, but is generally considered by scholars to come from "a later hand" (*Sources* 80).
222. "To leave no examples of extravagance to future generations, to show no wastefulness in the use of things, to indulge in no excess of measures and institutions, but to keep themselves under the restraint of strict rules so as to be prepared for relieving others in emergencies – these were some of the aspects of the system of the Tao among the ancients. Mo Ti (Mo Tzu) and Ch'in Ku-li heard of them and cherished them. But in practicing them themselves they went to extremes and in restricting other people they were too arbitrary."
223. "I fear it cannot be regarded as the Tao of the sages. It is contrary to human nature and few people can stand it. Though Mo Tzu himself was able to carry it out, how about the rest of mankind? Being alien to mankind, his teaching is far removed from the way of the kings."
224. Text reads: "Way"; emphasis added.
225. "The intentions of Mo Tzu and Ch'in Ku-li were right; their practice was wrong. They would make the Mo-ists of later ages feel it necessary to encourage each other in self-sacrifice until their legs were worn thin and their shins hairless."

from perfect order."[226]
Style of Mo Tzu critique by Arthur Waley. p. 121.
"Feeble, repetitive, heavy, unimaginative, unentertaining,
devoid of a single passage that could possibly be said to have
wit, beauty or force." 121[227]
[contrast SCT 44.[228]

21

+

HSÜN TZU

22

+

HSÜN TZU – 298-238[229]
Leads to Legalism
Lives in period when Ch'in is taking over all the other states.
More of a *writer* than his predecessors.
Attacks magic + superstition – is skeptical of Heaven as personal
Providence.
Rationalistic view of rites, of the past (he does not idealize).
Emphasis on *present* – solving problems *now*.
Discrimination bet. wisdom + folly.
Suspicious of human nature as evil. (agst Mencius)
Hence emphasizes *training* in good – optimistic for future.
Hsün Tzu – finally divorced religion from philosophy (3rd Cent BC)[230]
"The Chinese people lost their faith in Hsün Tzu's time +
have not yet found it."[231]

---

226. Text reads: "The effect of such teachings would be to produce something better than disorder but still far from perfect order. Nevertheless, Mo Tzu was truly a fine man, of whom there are only too few to be found. Despite all personal hardships, he held fast to his ideal – a man of excellence indeed!" (*Sources* 83).

227. Text reads: "feeble, repetitive (and I am not referring to the fact that many of the chapters occur in alternative forms), unimaginative and unentertaining, . . ."

228. Presumably the reference here is to a striking image that does not correspond to this negative stylistic critique: "A man's life on earth is of short duration; it is like a galloping horse rushing past a crack in the wall." The general evaluation of Mo Tzu as writer and thinker is less vehement but not incompatible with that of Waley: "Mo Tzu has been much less admired for his literary style, or even for his ideas, that for the nobility of soul which he revealed in his life of service to others" (*Sources* 37).

229. The background material here is drawn from the introduction to "Rationalism and Realism in Hsün Tzu" (*Sources* 112-14).

230. This material, from Liu, is added subsequent to Merton's original notes from *Sources* on the lower half of the page and marked for insertion.

231. Liu 96, which reads: ". . . their spiritual faith in Hsu'n Ch'ing's time,

(ie. intellectuals – have been agnostics.

Buddhism – did not go deep enough

Taoism – degenerated into superstition + magic.

Man's relation to Heaven.[232] – cf Wu Wei. STC. 114-115[233]

(Hsün Tzu was a *complete agnostic*)[234]

The Superior man develops himself + does not depend on or fight against Heaven. 116[235] – but "controls" it. 117. (sayings)[236]

"Human Portents." 117.[237]

"The Nature of man is evil: his goodness is acquired."[238] 118, 120, (gt. controversy with Mencius on this)[239]

"man *wishes to be good* because his nature is evil."[240]

followers of Mencius defeated him + he fell into disrepute[241]

Li. 122 + 123,[242] objectivity, "centrality" of rites 124.[243]

Sacrifice. 124. (only understood by Sage.)[244]

---

and they have . . ."; Merton quotes this passage, as found here, in "Classic Chinese Thought" (*MZM* 55).

232. Chapter 17, "Concerning Heaven," is the first selected excerpt from the *Hsün Tzu* (*Sources* 114-18).

233. On *Wu Wei*, or non-action, see *MZM* 75-76; the relevant statement here is: "To accomplish without exertion and to obtain without effort, this is what is meant by the office of Heaven" (*Sources* 115).

234. (Hsün . . . *agnostic*) *added on line*.

235. Text reads: "Because the gentleman carefully develops what is within his power, and does not desire what comes from Heaven, he progresses every day."

236. The set of couplets that concludes this chapter includes the following: "You obey Heaven and sing praises to it: / Why not control its course and employ it?"

237. Hsün Tzu is contrasting what he considers the superstitious search for supernatural omens and signs, which are beyond human control in any case, with what he calls "human portents," behavior that affects the quality of life and can be altered by human insight and effort, including poor agricultural practices, reckless or unjust governing policies, neglect of basic tasks, flouting of the rules of decorum and righteousness, leading to invasion and disaster. "Of all occurrences and phenomena, human portents are the most to be feared."

238. In chapter 23, "Human Nature Is Evil," the second selected excerpt (*Sources* 118-22), this assertion is repeated several times.

239. (gt. . . . this) *added on line*; Hsün Tzu refers to and argues against the claim of Mencius that human nature is originally good in this chapter (*Sources* 119; see also Waley 155, 204-205).

240. *Sources* 120 (emphasis added).

241. *Added on line*; see *Sources* 114.

242. See chapter 19, "On the Rules of Decorum (or Rites, Li)," the third selected excerpt (*Sources* 122-24).

243. Hsün Tzu praises "the middle path of rites" that achieves balance and moderation, avoiding the extremes of behavior in mourning and rejoicing.

244. "Sacrifice is something that the sage clearly understands, the scholar-

Hsün Tzu on Li.[245]

"Li arises from the necessity of regulating human desires."[246]
"Perfect indeed is Li (as a sacramental act symbolizing) the
heavens + earth in their harmony, the sun + moon in their
splendour, the four seasons in their succession, the stars in
their movements, the rivers + streams in their flow, the myriad
creatures in their abundance, liking + disliking in due (expression), delight + vexation with fitting (force), in the lower orders
of society (the expression of) obedience, in the higher orders
(the expression of) shining intelligence, with all creations
unceasingly changing, yet without confusion, for if the unity of
creation were lost the loss would be irredeemable"
Hsün Tzu quoted in Liu Wu Chi Hist. Conf. Philos. p. 99.[247]
The Reason for Having Names: 125.[248] (Nominalism?)
Names – conventional[249] (as opp. to Hebrews etc[250]) 126.
Music – "The ancient kings invented musical notes so that the
sounds might express happiness but excite no riot . . . + that

---

gentlemen contentedly perform, the officials consider as a duty, and the common
people regard as established custom. Among gentlemen it is considered the way of
man; among the common people it is considered as having to do with the spirits."

245. *Added on opposite page and marked for insertion.*

246. Liu 99.

247. Liu 99-100; the same passage is found, in a different translation, in
Sources 123.

248. See chapter 22, "On the Correct Use of Terminology," the fourth
selected excerpt (*Sources* 125-27).

249. "There are no names necessarily appropriate of themselves. Upon
agreement things were named. . . . Names have no actualities necessarily
corresponding to them" (126).

250. The biblical sense is that the name, above all the Name of the Lord,
is a revelation of true identity; see "The Name of the Lord" in Thomas Merton,
Seasons of Celebration (New York: Farrar, Straus & Giroux, 1965) 183-203.
See also Thomas Merton, *The New Man* (New York: Farrar, Straus and Cudahy,
1961) 83-84: "Adam's function is to *look* at creation, see it, recognize it, and thus
give it a new and spiritual existence within himself. He imitates and reproduces
the creative action of God first of all by repeating, within the silence of his own
intelligence, the creative word by which God made each living thing. The most
interesting point in the story is the freedom left to Adam in this work of 'creation.'
The name is decided, chosen, not by God but by Adam. 'For that which the man
called each of them, *would be its name.*' . . . It was for Adam to draw each being
notionally out of the silence and hold it up to the light of his own intelligence,
coining the brand new word that would signify the correspondence between the
thought in the mind of Adam and the *reality* in the mind of God. Thus Adam's
science was a discovery not only of names but of *essences.*"

composition + orchestration might inspire good thoughts +
suppress evil notions." In Liu Wu Chi. p 101.
Dancing – important (objectivity. "The Dancers eyes do not
look at himself + his ears do not listen to himself" in Liu Wu
Chi p 102.)

23

THE LEGALISTS.

Prin of Legalist school was *political*. Triumph of this pragmatic
doctrine due to alliance with government party. Ch'in.
– In beginning – nobles governed by rites
                                peasants by reward + punishment
Legalism – leveling – equal punishments for all (bec. ancients
had failed in their responsibility)
        – legalists – against the "well field" system.
        – Two great exponents of legalism – Han Fei
                                                Li Szu
                                        both students of Hsün Tzu.

24

THE LEGALISTS

Most influential of Classical Schools in *practical* politics
Helped organize Ch'in Empire
Anti-intellectual, anti-philosophical.[251]

Han Fei Tzu (d. 233 BC)
Student of Hsün Tzu.
Theories – emphasis on increasing the power of the Ruler. –
centralization.
        – emphasis on good of the state first, + on power.
        – rejecting Jên as impractical.[252] – *Antithesis of
            Confucianism* – cf. SCT. 142.[253]
        (reasons – 146[254])
        – *Law* important thing – sanctioned by *punishment*

---

251. The background material here is drawn from the introduction to chapter
VII: "The Legalists" (*Sources* 136-38).

252. See Waley 155.

253. Han Fei Tzu compares Confucians to priests and witches as equally
unrealistic, promising order not on the basis of current realities but by exalting "the
reputed glories of remote antiquity and the achievements of the ancient kings."

254. Han Fei Tzu maintains that even in the days of the early kings so
lauded by Confucians, human nature was such that rulers' good example and
paternal feelings were not enough; "humanity could not be depended upon for
good government" and the penalties of law had to be imposed.

+ *reward* –
– Agriculture – frugality – obedience encouraged.
Intellectual life + commerce discouraged

Texts.[255] *The stupidity of traditionalism which cannot rest on evidence* – SCT. 139.[256] (stump + hare. 144[257])

Stupidity of a Ruler patronizing opposing schools of philos. – encourages confusion. 140.[258]

Stupidity of giving land to poor, who deserve poverty because lazy 140[259]

To tax farmers + reward intellectuals is to discourage hard work + encourage idleness – 141.[260]

Stupid to expect people to do good by themselves. 141[261]

Hence – "straightening + bending" – rewards + punishments 142.[262]

---

255. *"Selections from the Han Fei Tzu"* (*Sources* 138-50: c. 50: "On the Dominant Systems of Learning" [138-43]; c. 49: "The Five Vermin of the State" [143-50]).

256. "To claim certainty without corroborating evidence is stupid; to refer to anything that one cannot be certain of is self-deceptive. Therefore those who explicitly refer to the ancient kings and dogmatically claim the authority of Yao and Shun [i.e. the Confucians and Mo-ists] must be either stupid or deceitful."

257. This anecdote of a hare who ran into a stump in a field and broke its neck, and the farmer who stopped his plowing and waited for the incident to recur and provide him with another hare, is a satiric commentary on traditionalists who expect the policies of the legendary early kings to be repeated in the present age.

258. "[H]eretical and contradictory teachings cannot be expected to prevail simultaneously and result in orderly government. Now that heretical teachings are equally listened to and contradictory talk is absurdly acted upon, how can there be anything else but chaos? Since such is the way the ruler listens to advice, it will also, of course, be the way he will govern the people."

259. "It is the extravagant and lazy people who have become poor; it is the diligent and frugal people who have become rich. Now the sovereign would tax the rich to give to the poor. This amounts to robbing the diligent and frugal and rewarding the extravagant and lazy" (another translation of the same passage is found in Waley 173).

260. "As long as heavy taxes are collected from the farmers while rich rewards are given to the learned gentlemen, it will be impossible to expect the people to work hard and talk little."

261. "When the sage rules the state, he does not count on people doing good of themselves, but employs such measures as will keep them from doing any evil. If he counts on people doing good of themselves, there will not be enough such people to be numbered by the tens in the whole country."

262. Just as it is impractical to rely for arrows on pieces of wood that are already straight or for wheels on pieces of wood that are already round, so people must be straightened and bent through a system of rewards and punishments for their behavior to be properly shaped.

. People – to be treated as babies who don't know their own good. 143.[263]
To consult the people is to invite chaos. 143.[264]
Government by fear of punishment. 146.[265]
A *Waley*.[266] Legalists (*Realists*) = Fa Chia (School of Law)
  "Held that law should replace morality" 151
  "They rejected all appeals to tradition, all reliance on supernatural sanctions + trust in supernatural guidance" 151
    Rejection of private standards of right + wrong. Authoritarianism
* *Mutual espionage* – groups "mutually responsible for each other – obliged to denounce each other's crimes" AW. 152[267]
157 Language – Terms (esp. in edicts) have meanings defined by the Leader.[268]
    Laws to be very clear + detailed + known to all.
    Punishments very strict – so that no one will transgress the Law. People[269]
160 "The ultimate goal of penalties is that there should be no

263. As a baby cries when its head is shaved to keep sores from recurring, or its boil is lanced to prevent further infection, because it "does not understand that suffering a small pain is the way to obtain a great benefit," so the ruler must do what is best for the people despite their objections, for "the intelligence of the people is not to be relied upon any more than the mind of a baby" (another translation of the same passage is found in Waley 162).

264. Because of their ignorance, the people misinterpret the ruler as being cruel when he regulates agricultural practices, or severe when he increases penalties for wicked behavior, or greedy when he imposes taxes or collects grain to deal with famine or feed the army, or violent when he imposes military service and urges his army to fight hard, so trying to please the people in establishing policies is "the cause of chaos and not the means for attaining order."

265. Han Fei Tzu uses as an example a bad young man who is unresponsive to the love of his parents, the reproof of his fellow villagers and the admonishments of teachers and elders, but becomes fearful and changes his ways when the authorities send out soldiers to search out and apprehend wicked individuals.

266. Waley, "The Realists" (149-88). In his discussion of legalism in "Classic Chinese Thought" (*MZM* 54-57), Merton relies principally on Waley, including most of the points outlined below, and concluding with a lengthy quotation from Waley 161-62, 167-68 focusing on the shortsightedness of subjects, the benefits of severe laws and the misfortune of not being at war, since peacetime promotes the cultivation of the "maggots" of music and ritual, filial piety and the like.

267. Quoted from *The Book of the Lord Shang*, the other main text of legalism along with the *Han Fei Tzu*.

268. "The ruler must define by statute the sense in which he wishes them to be understood, and in course of time these meanings will be popularly accepted as 'right' and 'true.'"

269. Evidently Merton intended to include a further comment here but left it unfinished.

penalties"[270]

161– Make the state so powerful that all enemies are wiped out –
then there will be peace.

Every sacrifice[271] must then be made for this end: esp. by
the people.

25

SUNG PHILOSOPHERS

"Just as the Chinese intellect burst forth (in the Chou) with its colorful 'hundred schools' so it now ripened through the cultivation
of the Sung scholars into a more mature, complete + well-rounded
system of philosophy that was to reign supreme in Chinese intellectual circles for more than 700 years."[272]

Liu Wu Chi p 151

Kung thinkers of Sung dyn. – using Taoism + Buddhism – include
cosmology + metaphysics in their doctrines.[273]

25A

Shao Yung 邵 雍 (1011-1077)[274]
"Master of Tranquil Delight"[275] Hermit outside Lao Yang
Primeval diagram – circle of 64 hexagrams[276]
in refuge – visited by friends out of favor with Wang An Shih
– radical reformer in capital with his friends Ch'eng Hao +
Ch'eng I etc. initiated neo-Ju movement

    Ch'eng Hao – active – monistic (mind – Hsin –) school
    Ch'eng I – retired – dualistic (Li – law) school.
    Distin of Li – immaterial cosmic principle from Ch'i – ether[277]
    Esp Chou Tun I (1017-1075) – forerunner of Chou Hsi[278]

---

270. Quoted from *The Book of the Lord Shang.*

271. The sacrifices referred to here include food production as well as
preparation for war.

272. Text reads: "Just as the Chinese intellect suddenly burst forth into bloom
in the earlier period with its colourful 'hundred schools', . . . complete, and . . ."

273. Text reads: "This fruition of thought was brought about by the K'ung
followers who were versed in the Buddhist and Taoist ideologies, and who
therefore were able to extend the horizon of the orthodox doctrine of ethics and
politics to include cosmology and metaphysics" (Liu 151).

274. This material is drawn from Liu 151-53, 155-56, 159-60.

275. Liu 152.

276. "Primeval . . . hexagrams" *added in upper right margin and marked
for insertion.*

277. "Ch'eng Hao . . . ether" *added below* "Works . . . *Ching*" and *marked
for transposition.*

278. i.e Chu Hsi.

Works out metaphysic + ethic based on *I Ching*

26

SUNG Neo-Confucians.[279]

The 4 books. (Analects – Mencius – Great Learning – Chung-Yung (D of Mean.)).[280]

2 schools (debated at Goose Lake monastery[281]

1 CHU HSI. 1130-1200.[282]

Had been Buddhist monk??

Extensive commentaries on Classics – approved as "correct" in govt exams down to 1905.

idea of *Li chi* – "form" + matter. Li – (form without form – empty.)

In man – all have same Li – but Chi may be pure or impure – return to original nature – benevolence – righteousness – li = courtesy – wisdom.

Desire obscures true nature.

Knowledge as root of understanding.

Ruler should be a sage, understand Li (Tao) of events. This not happened for 1500 yrs (since Conf)

"Chu Hsi fashioned a superb product by combining with the early Ju doctrine the cosmological discoveries of Chou Tun I, the numerical wonders of Shao Yung, the theory of matter (ch'i) of Chang Tsai, and the concept of Law (Li) of the Ch'eng brothers – (in him) the Neo-Ju philosophy reached its highest development." Liu Wu Chi p. 161[283]

CHU HSI[284]

Became the orthodox norm of Confucianism – greatest single influence on Chinese thought

Instituted universal study of 4 classics

Put Meng Tzu in the hierarchy, excluding Hsün – Put end to tendency to deify Kung

Formulated complete system of thought.

Ethic: desire obscures man's true nature.

---

279. This material is based principally on Creel, with additional notations from Liu.

280. See Creel 216.

281. "(debated at Goose Lake monastery" from Liu 165.

282. This material is drawn from Creel 217-20.

283. Text reads: ". . . fashioned a supreme product . . . law (*li*) . . ."

284. *"CHU HSI . . .* Hsiang Chan" based on Liu 161-64, *added on opposite page and marked for insertion.*

To restore nature – a) exercise of attentiveness (to luminous
          princ in oneself)
          b) extension of knowledge (of celestial Li –
          through li of individual objects) leading to
          sudden enlightenment criticized by
          Lu Hsiang Chan

2. *Lu Hsiang Shan* (1139-1193)[285] – heavy Buddhist leanings[286]
Emphasis on meditation + intuition.
Monism – all consists of Li. (not ch'i) "The universe is my
mind + my mind is the universe."[287]
Morality = rediscovery of one's lost nature, which is good.
(cf Mencius) – *Enlightenment.*

MING. *Wang-Yang-Ming*. (1472-1529)[288] (man of action)[289]
– follows Lu Hsiang Shan – rejects search for principles
through things – only in one's own nature. "The streets are
full of sages"[290]
close to Zen. "apart from the mind there is neither law nor
object."[291]

Huang Tsung Hsi – (1610-1695)[292]
Enemy of imperial Eunuchs who killed his father.
Critic of degenerate monarchy.

Yen Yüan (1635-1704)[293] Criticizes Chu Hsi (official philos –
see above) – *Historical criticism.*[294]
Necessity of action, not mere speculation.
Wanted partition of land to all.

(CH'ING.) *Tai chen* (1724-1777)[295] Mathematician. Critic of Chu Hsi.
Materialist? (all is ch'i – substance. No li) Empiricism.
comments on Mencius – with modern psych insight.

School of Han Learning[296] – Mod. Textual criticism of Han

---

285. This material is drawn from Creel 220-24.

286. "heavy Buddhist leanings" from Liu 167.

287. *Hsiang-shan chuan-chi* 36.56 (Creel 222).

288. This material is drawn from Creel 224-27.

289. "(1472-1529) (man of action)" from Liu 167, 172 (*added on line*).

290. "The streets . . . sages" from Liu 170 (*interlined and marked with an arrow for insertion*).

291. "apart . . . object." from Liu 169 (*added on line*).

292. This material is drawn from Creel 233-35.

293. This material is drawn from Creel 235-37.

294. *"Historical criticism."* from Liu 175.

295. This material is drawn from Creel 237-43.

296. See Creel 244-45.

commentators.

Led by Tai Chen.

Modern[297] Kang Yu Wei – 1858-1927. irresponsible – see his
Utopia – LWC p. 181.[298] Cf. Mao Tse Tung
tries to make Ju a national religion
Ch'en Tu hsiu – "throw out Kung"[299] – incompatible with
modern life"[300] feudalist – retrogressive
Li = "Cannibalism."[301]
Kuomintang – encouraged study of Kung[302]

27

Influence of West. – after 1905[303]
Note – inefficiency of Old China. Despotism but lack of
obedience. Graft etc. compromise.
Final reaction agst Confucianism as "feudal" + reactionary force
[Confucianism used by unscrupulous warlords + by
Japanese]
The Classical lit. Chinese language has become incompre-
hensible
However Sun Yat Sen said "What we need to learn from
Europe is science, not political philosophy. As for the true
principles of political philosophy the Europeans need to learn

---

297. This material is drawn from Liu 179-90.

298. Liu provides a list of twelve points summarizing K'ang's plans for a
global utopia drawn from his book *Ta Tung* or *The Great Commonwealth*, ranging
from abolishing all states and forming a world government, to reducing marriage
to a series of one-year contracts, to requiring cremation of the dead and locating
cremation grounds in the vicinity of fertilizer factories, a gathering of what Liu
calls "a hodgepodge of indigested and incongruous ideas introduced from the West
at the end of the nineteenth century" (182) but put forth as a Confucian program.

299. Text reads: "Down with K'ung and sons" (185, 187).

300. Text reads: "Furthermore, as a system of ethical teaching, which is in
fact all that it amounts to, its ideals are incompatible with modern life, science,
and the republican form of government" (186).

301. See Liu 187: "They likewise made capital of the traditional subjection
of Chinese women, blaming it all on Master K'ung and his 'cannibalistic doctrine
of *li*,' and declared that the emancipation of women . . . demanded a prior
emancipation from the K'ung orthodoxy."

302. See Liu 190: "the Kuomintang government began to encourage the
study of the K'ung classics"; the Kuomintang was the political party formed by
Sun Yat-sen at the time of the establishment of the Chinese Republic in 1911 and
later led by Chiang Kai-shek; its defeat by the Communists in 1949 led to exile
in Taiwan, where it was the dominant party for decades.

303. This material is drawn from Creel 252-54.

them from China."[304]
Chinese Communism [305]– *Peasant* supported – with *intellectuals*.
  – West had made capitalism odious in China (+ ancient
    tradition was already against this)
  – West itself became odious – esp. in its patronage.
  – Russia joined China as an *equal*.

28

TAOISM

Lin Yutang. on Tao te Ching[306]
Most translated of Chinese Texts – 12 trans. In English + 9 in
German. Probably more.[307]
Taoism – admired openly or secretly by the poets.[308]
  Influence of Taoism on the T'ang poets + painters
+

Basic teaching of Lao Tzu not paralleled in Chuang Tzu:[309] his
emphasis on humanity, on non resistance.
  the strength of weakness.
  Chuang Tzu – more a matter of tranquillity.
  "Laotse praised the humble, Chuangtse lambasted the great"[310]
+

Laotse – self realization by self forgetfulness. "He who loses his
life shall find it"[311] but – for *my sake*.
+

Lin Yutang – finds Taoism in Eddington's statement about elec-
tion. "Something unknown is doing we know not what."[312]
Also – comparisons with Edison.[313]
+

"The chaos of the modern world I believe is due to the total lack
of a philosophy of the rhythm of life such as we find in Lao Tze or

---

304. Sun Yat-sen, *San Min Chu I, The Three Principles of the People* (Creel
254).

305. This material is drawn from Creel 255-59.

306. *The Wisdom of Laotse*, translated and edited by Lin Yutang (New York:
Modern Library, 1948) (subsequent references will be cited as "Yutang, *Laotse*")

307. See Yutang, *Laotse* 3.

308. See Yutang, *Laotse* 4.

309. See Yutang, *Laotse* 10.

310. Yutang, *Laotse* 11.

311. Mt. 10:39, 16:25, quoted in Yutang, *Laotse* 12.

312. Quoted in Yutang, *Laotse* 16.

313. Merton evidently meant to write "Eddington": see Yutang, *Laotse*
13-14, 20.

his brilliant disciple Chuang tse."[314]

29

TAOISM.   1 TAO-TE-CHING.[315]

Strong contrast to Confucianism: – anti-conventional – derides
  respectability

> unworldly –
> paradoxical – + poetic.
> mystical.
> > [but degenerated into
> > superstition, magic etc.

Lao Tse. – who?

  The Tao Te Ching. primarily a treatise for *Rulers* (as usual).
    but the Ruler must be in harmony with the Tao, + lead
      people back to innocence + emptiness.
    Retirement from public life is encouraged!! Chuang Tzu
      developed this emphasis.
  Implications of *Tao* in govt: 16[316] 17[317] 19[318] 65[319] – 3[320]

The Tao (Tao Te Ching).

  1[321] Nameless + Namable – two aspects *Namable – it is*

---

314. *The Wisdom of India and China*, edited by Lin Yutang (New York:
Random House, 1942) 579, which reads: ". . . world, I believe, is . . . Laotse and
. . . Chuangtse."

315. Background material here is drawn from the introduction to chapter
IV: "Taoism" (*Sources* 50-53).

316. To attain emptiness in quietude is to know the eternal and so to become
impartial, therefore kingly, at one with the Tao (see *Sources* 56-57).

317. The best government is one of which the people are aware only of
its existence, the next best that which is loved and praised, then that which is
despised (see *Sources* 57).

318. To live without (self-conscious) wisdom, righteousness and skill will
bring about spontaneous harmony and order (see *Sources* 57).

319. Ancient masters of the *Tao* left the people in the simplicity of ignorance;
too much knowledge breeds dissatisfaction and disorder (see *Sources* 62).

320. The sage ruler strives to keep the people unaware of knowledge and
desires and governs by *wu-wei*, whereby (paradoxically) nothing is unregulated
(see *Sources* 54).

321. See *Sources* 53.

mother of all things cf. 21^{322} 40^{323} 25^{324} 32^{325}

    Non-Existent + existent

        cf 4^{326} – a phenomenon "that apparently preceded the Lord."[327]

        *14^{328} 34^{329} 40^{330} 42^{331} – spirit of the valley. 6^{332}

Wu Wei – 3 "By doing nothing that interferes, nothing is left unregulated."[333] 37^{334} 43^{335} 48^{336}

    8 Since it (Tao) is without strife it is without reproach.[337] 78^{338} 67^{339}

    10^{340} – principles – wu wei + passivity, unknowing

---

322. The *Tao*, from which Vast Virtue (*te*) comes, is elusive and evasive (see *Sources* 57-58).

323. Everything in the world comes into being from being, while being comes into being from non-being (see *Sources* 61).

324. Born before heaven and earth, the mother of the world, was the *Tao*, self-sufficient and unchanging (see *Sources* 58).

325. The *Tao* is compared to the uncarved block, figure of the original state of complete simplicity, and its working to the flow of streams into river or sea (see *Sources* 59-60).

326. The *Tao* is empty and mysterious, its origin unknown (see *Sources* 54).

327. *Sources* 54.

328. The *Tao* is formless, soundless, bodiless unity (see *Sources* 55-56).

329. The *Tao* is the source of all, but is not possessive; its greatness is manifested in its refusal to claim greatness (see *Sources* 60).

330. See note 323 above.

331. The *Tao* gave birth to One, which in turn gave birth to Two, which gave birth to Three, which gave birth to all beings, marked by the interaction of *yin* and *yang* (see *Sources* 61).

332. The spirit of the valley is associated with the mysterious feminine, apparently insubstantial yet inexhaustible (see Yutang, *Laotse* 99; not in *Sources*).

333. *Sources* 54, which reads: ". . . interferes with anything (*wu-wei*), nothing . . ."

334. "Tao invariably does nothing (*wu-wei*), / And yet there is nothing that is not done" (see *Sources* 60).

335. Few in the world realize the instructiveness of silence, the value of non-action (see *Sources* 61).

336. The process of seeking the *Tao* involves letting go and leaving behind, until one reaches the complete (receptive) passivity of doing nothing (see *Sources* 61).

337. *Sources* 55.

338. Nothing is superior to water, weak and yielding, in overcoming that which is strong and unyielding (see *Sources* 63).

339. The greatness of Tao is in its apparent impertinence, for its mercy, frugality and refusal to put itself forward bring courage, abundance and distinguished service, but to choose these latter qualities for themselves is disastrous (see *Sources* 62-63).

340. *Sources* 55.

especially the final 4 lines. ("To beget but not to claim" etc[341]) give real meaning of non-action. It is not mere negation. It is highly positive + productive but it achieves "in emptiness." cf. 14 end.[342] 28[343] *34[344] 37[345] 43[346] 67[347] 78[348]

Returning to the root – 16[349] 25[350] 28[351] 34[352]

The "uncarved block." 28[353] 32[354]

Praise of Lao T. by Chuang Tzu. SCT 85*[355]

The Sage – accomplishes without acting 2[356] 10[357] 34[358]

---

341. "To beget but not to claim, / To achieve but not to cherish, / To be leader but not master – / This is called the Mystic Virtue (*te*)."

342. The Tao is the formless form whose face cannot be seen in confronting it nor its back in following it, but by holding fast to it one can grasp the events of the present and know the beginnings of the past (see *Sources* 56).

343. To know the masculine but keep to the feminine is to dwell in constant virtue and innocence; to know the white but keep to the black is to rest in constant virtue and return to the infinite; to know glory but keep to disgrace is to be content with constant virtue and return to the uncarved block (see *Sources* 59); Merton quotes and comments on part of this section (along with section 18) in "Classic Chinese Thought" (*MZM* 49-50).

344. See note 329 above.

345. See note 334 above.

346. See note 335 above.

347. See note 339 above.

348. See note 338 above.

349. "To return to the root is called quietude, / Which is also said to be reversion to one's destiny" (*Sources* 56).

350. See note 324 above.

351. See note 343 above.

352. See note 329 above.

353. See note 343 above.

354. See note 325 above.

355. "Silent and formless, changing and impermanent! Are life and death one? Do I coexist with heaven and earth? Where do the spirits move? Disappearing whither, going whence, so mysteriously and suddenly? All things lie spread before me, but in none of them can be found my destiny – these were some aspects of the system of the Tao among the ancients. Chuang Chou [Chuang Tzu] heard of them and cherished them." This passage it part of the survey of ancient Chinese thought in chapter 33 of the *Chuang Tzu*, generally not considered to be written by himself. It should be noted that this passage does not refer explicitly to Lao Tzu, whose ideas are summarized in the preceding paragraph; the same formula (referring to different "aspects") was actually used to describe Lao Tzu's own response to the Tao in introducing him.

356. The true sage accomplishes his work without effort and without drawing attention to himself (see Yutang, *Laotse* 95-96; not in *Sources*).

357. See note 340 above.

358. See note 329 above.

puts himself last. 8[359] 7[360]

disappears when his work is done. 9[361]   hidden, looks like nothing. 15[362] 20[363]

by his humility – overcomes all. 22[364] 23[365]

30

comparisons – Tao Te King + Ta Hsüeh[366]

> cf Legge p 107.[367] "reporting they have fulfilled their end"?[368]

Tao – #16. returning to root.[369]

> cf Great Learning – "resting" in action achieved.
>> Chung Yung. –
> but cf 19.[370] rel. to simplicity of Tao.

Tao #17.[371] in highest antiquity ruler ruled without ruling – people *did not know they had rulers.*

> later – as rulers lose faith in Tao people lose faith in rulers.
>> cf. Bks of Kings. I K. 3:1?[372]

* 18[373] crucial difference. Benevolence + righteousness *came*

---

359. Like water, the highest good seeks out the lowly places that most people disregard (see *Sources* 55).

360. Because he puts himself last the sage is a leader; because of his selflessness his self is realized (see Yutang, *Laotse* 100; not in *Sources*).

361. The Way of Heaven is to retire when one's work is done (see Yutang, *Laotse* 101; not in *Sources*).

362. One who remains with the Tao does not seek fullness, and so is like a hidden sprout, not rushing to ripen (see Yutang, *Laotse* 106-107; not in *Sources*).

363. Dim and quiet like a child, the sage differs from others in knowing how to receive nourishment from the Mother (see Yutang, *Laotse* 110-11; not in *Sources*).

364. Refusing all self-display, the sage shines; to the one who has attained wholeness, all things will be attracted (see Yutang, *Laotse* 113; not in *Sources*).

365. As violent weather does not last, neither do rash human efforts; only simple, quiet words ripen gradually (see Yutang, *Laotse* 113-14; not in *Sources*).

366. I.e., The *Great Learning*.

367. *The Texts of Taoism: The Tao Te Ching and the Writings of Chuang-Tzu*, trans. James Legge, Introduction by D. T. Suzuki (New York: Julian Press, 1959) (subsequent references will be cited as "Legge, *Taoism*").

368. Text reads: "reporting that they have fulfilled their appointed end" (16.1).

369. Legge, *Taoism* 107-108.

370. Legge, *Taoism* 110.

371. Legge, *Taoism* 108-109.

372. The reference here is unclear: it may in fact refer to 1 Kings (i.e. 1 Samuel) 4:1ff., in which the continued wickedness of the sons of Eli leads to the defeat of Israel at the hands of the Philistines and the capture of the ark of the covenant.

373. Legge, *Taoism* 109.

into vogue when Tao is abandoned.

Then appeared wisdom etc. Then hypocrisy.

Hence need of filial sons + loyal ministers.

Leg.109.[374] *Decay of innocence affords opportunity for di play of virtue*[375]

19[376] – return to simplicity of Tao.

cf. 28.[377] "uncarved block."

31

The Tao

無源 = without fountain (no source) [378]

用 = emptiness.[379]

歸 根 returning to the root.[380]

無為而無不為無為 Doing nothing yet doing all things.[381]

益謙 – The increase granted to humility. #22.[382]

虛無 "emptiness + nothingness" 23[383]

反樸 returning to simplicity[384]

眞 人 – The true man.[385]

仙 人 – The mountain man.[386]

---

374. Added in left margin.

375. Text reads: "the general decay of manners afforded opportunity for the display of certain virtues by individuals" (Legge's note on c. 18).

376. Legge, *Taoism* 110.

377. Legge, *Taoism* 119, where the phrase "unwrought material" is used rather than "uncarved block."

378. Title of *Tao Te Ching*, c. 4 (see Legge, *Taoism* 98, which reads: "The Fountainless").

379. Part of title of c. 5: "The Use of Emptiness" (see Legge, *Taoism* 98).

380. Title of c. 16 (see Legge, *Taoism* 108).

381. See Legge, *Taoism* 108, which reads: '. . . nothing and yet . . ." [Legge's note on c. 16]).

382. Title of c. 22 (see Legge, *Taoism* 113).

383. Title of c. 23 (see Legge, *Taoism* 114, where Legge interprets this title as "Absolute Vacancy").

384. Title of c. 28 (see Legge, *Taoism* 119).

385. Title used extensively by Chuang Tzu to describe the "Master of the Tao," particularly in Book 6: see Legge, *Taoism* 284-306.

386. Title associated with the Taoist hermit.

32

(MW = Waley 3 Ways of Thought)[387]

Chuang Tzu.[388] 莊 周

? 369-286 bc. (contemporary of Mencius).

Warning to those who do not understand. The Han-Tan Walk
AW. 36.[389]

Explanation of CT's approach – see SCT. 85.*[390]

stories + examples, not abstract doctrine

Tao less as guide than for its own sake. More
indifferent to human society + its affairs. "Essentially a
plea for the freedom of the individual. But it is a kind of
spiritual freedom liberating the individual more from the
confines of his own mind than from external restraints."[391]

Princ.

What is of man is artificial + unnatural

What of nature or Tao alone is "enduringly true."[392]

Is his vision of life selfish? SEE *first of all the Tortoise of King
of Ch'u – 79*;*[393] + also 83.[394]

---

387. Added in upper left margin; as in previous sections, references to
Waley were added later.

388. Background material here is drawn from introduction to second part of
chapter IV: "Skepticism and Mysticism in Chuang Tzu" (*Sources* 64-65).

389. A child is sent to Han-Tan to learn its particular way of walking, which
not only does he fail to do, but forgets how to walk normally and is reduced to
crawling back home.

390. This summary from chapter 33 of the *Chuang Tzu* emphasizes the
profound yet playful nature of Chuang Tzu's approach to the paradoxical nature of
the Tao, beyond the grasp of the intellect, employing different methods to convey
different aspects of the mystery of the *Tao*, "effervescent words" for wide-ranging
discussions to "weighty words" for conveying truths to illustrative allegories; it
notes his unwillingness to engage in polemics about morality or philosophical
positions, yet the rootedness of his principles in the *Tao*. "He is mysterious,
obscure and boundless" (85-86).

391. *Sources* 64-65, which reads: ". . . freedom, liberating . . ."

392. *Sources* 65, which reads: "what is of nature or the Tao alone is
enduringly and universally true."

393. When the King of Ch'u sends messengers to Chuang Tzu to invite
him to become his chief minister, Chuang Tzu refers to the remains of a sacred
tortoise kept in the king's temple, and asks whether the tortoise is better off dead
and venerated or alive and dragging his tail in the mud; when the messengers
favor the latter, Chuang Tzu sends them away, saying he will continue to drag his
own tail in the mud (c. 17). This story is included as "The Turtle" in *WCT* 93-94.

394. Taking things as they come and being without worry or care, rather
than relying on one's own cleverness, are considered as key aspects of the Tao as

+
Tao – no beginning or end. 78,[395] 84,[396] AW. 52[397] fragmented
  by philosophers. 81.[398]
Wu Wei – Plant your tree in Nothingness. p. 70.[399] cf cook of
  Wen Hui. 76,[400] cf 79*,[401] Shen Tao etc. 83-84.[402]
  cf AW. 39,[403] 44,[404] 46,[405] 47,[406] (machines) 70,[407]

---

recognized by the ancients (c. 33).

395. "The Tao is without beginning and without end," whereas all discrete things are impermanent, every end giving rise to a new beginning (c. 17).

396. The Tao is identified by Lao Tzu with eternal non-being and recognized as supreme unity (c. 33).

397. According to the *Tao Te Ching*, the Tao existed from the beginning, before heaven and earth, to which it gave life, yet it has no duration, never aging.

398. After the era of the early sages and worthies, the world fell into chaos and recognition of the unity of the Tao was lost; various schools of thought focused on a limited dimension of this unity and mistook it for the whole. "The system of the Tao has been scattered in fragments throughout the world!" (c. 33).

399. Chuang Tzu responds to the complaint of Hui Tzu that his tree is so twisted that it is useless by counseling him to plant it "in the realm of Nothingness, in the expanse of Infinitude" (c. 1). This passage, entitled "The Useless Tree," is the opening selection in *WCT* (35-36).

400. For this story of the cook who is able to carve an ox with such precision that his blade is never dulled (c. 3), see "Cutting Up an Ox" (*WCT* 45-47).

401. To recognize the contrast between the natural and the artificial and to be in harmony with the former is to act with genuine virtue (*te*) and recover original innocence (c. 17).

402. The approach to the *Tao* of Shen Tao is one of pure passivity, a renunciation of all striving, even for knowledge – judged by the commentator as "often contrary to human nature" and not fully in touch with the authentic *Tao* (c. 33).

403. The Lord of Lu is desolate because despite his best efforts his land is full of troubles; the sage Shih-nan I-liau advises him to journey to the Land where Tê Rules, where the people live unselfconsciously and in apparent ignorance, but are in perfect accord with the "Great Plan."

404. Unlike those who seek after superiority, or idleness, or physical perfection, the wise live in "Quietness, stillness, emptiness, not-having, inactivity . . . the very substance of the Way and its Power."

405. The way of wholeness or integrity is for the soul to be in accord with the movements of Heaven.

406. Here is the story of the King of Wei's cook and his marvelous skill in carving; see note 400 above.

407. The Taoist rejection of machinery as having a deleterious effect on those who make use of it is illustrated by the story of the peasant gardener who rejects the advice of Tzu-kung, a disciple of Confucius, to employ a well-sweep in irrigating his land, having been taught that using a cunning contrivance would lead to having a cunning heart in which the Tao would not dwell.

Unity

"The other arises out of the self." etc. p. 70 (SCT)[408] – 73,[409] 77,[410] *78,[411]

"When the self + the other lose their contrariety, there we have the very essence of the Tao." SCT. 71.[412]

Three in the Morning – SCT. 72.,[413] cf. 73.[414]

"Confucius + you are both in a dream." 74[415]

Being + non-being – + anterior to both "no-non-being" 72,[416] 84.[417]

Beyond "right + wrong" 74-75,[418] 79,*[419] 83[420] (cf 81[421])

---

408. Reflecting the awareness of relativity and complementarity in all limited things, "it is said, the other arises out of the self, just as the self arises out of the other. This is the theory that self and other give rise to each other" (c. 2) (70-71).

409. Being and non-being appear simultaneously, but how to discern which is which is difficult to know (c. 2).

410. Given the relativity of all finite things, calling one thing great and another small, or one thing noble and another mean, is to fail to recognize that such terms describe not essential qualities but are meaningful only in relation to other things (c. 17).

411. According to the Spirit of the Ocean, what is noble and what is mean are "but phrases in a process of alternation" (c. 17).

412. C. 2.

413. For this story of the zookeeper who willingly changes the monkeys' rations from three measures in the morning and four in the afternoon to four in the morning and three in the afternoon (c. 2), see "Three in the Morning" (*WCT* 44) and Merton's comments at the conclusion of his introduction to the volume (*WCT* 32).

414. The sage is one who is able to blend everything into a harmonious whole, transcending confusion and gloom, beyond strife and toil, equalizing the humble and the honorable (c. 2).

415. Fools think they are awake and able to distinguish the great and the lowly, whereas Confucius, who rejects the Taoist understanding of the sage, and Ch'ü-ch'iao Tzu, who accepts it, are seen by Ch'ang-wu Tzu as both still awaiting the "great awakening" of full awareness (c. 2).

416. The text goes on to say that before "no-nonbeing" there was "no-no-nonbeing"! (c. 2).

417. See note 396 above.

418. Ch'ang-wu Tzu points out that arguing about right and wrong may produce a winner and a loser but to win an argument is not to assure the truth of one's position, and choosing a third party to decide who is correct is an exercise in futility, so he counsels that the claims of right and wrong should be put aside and one should abide in the realm of the infinite, transcending partial views (c. 2).

419. See note 401 above.

420. "Realizing that all things have their capacities and limitations, they said: 'Selection cannot embrace the whole; instruction cannot exhaust the ultimate; only the Tao is all-inclusive'" (c. 33).

421. Mo Tzu and his disciple Ch'in Ku-li recognized aspects of the true Tao but "in practicing them themselves they went to extremes and in restricting other

– esp. 85*[422] AW 45,[423] 54,[424] 76*[425]
The cook of Prince Wen Hui. 36.[426] cf. 77.[427] AW 47[428]
Impartiality – cf. "be ye perfect."[429] 78*,[430] 79,[431] 83.[432] AW 45,[433] 76.[434]
Agst. Confucius – re mourning. 77,[435] also 74-75.,[436]   Yü
(interior journey.) see AW 37ff.[437] 42[438] – discipline insuffi-
cient. AW 38-39,[439] 43 f.[440]   controversies AW 73.[441]

---

people they were too arbitrary" (c. 33).

422. Chuang Tzu "did not quarrel with what others regard as right and wrong, and so he was able to mingle with conventional society" (c. 33).

423. Sadness and joy, delight and anger, love and hate, are alike in undermining authentic Power – "to have in oneself no contraries, is the climax of purity."

424. To be known is to be lost; to be known for being unknown is a double curse.

425. The wise man in the court of an evil king must try to improve himself rather than to improve the king, to be outwardly accommodating without undermining his inward integrity.

426. See note 400 above.

427. Those who abide by the principle of nature in their coming into and leaving this life are beyond sorrow and joy (c. 3).

428. See notes 400, 406 above.

429. Matthew 5:48.

430. To be impartial is to embrace all creation, without favoring one part or another (c. 17).

431. If one is aware of the course of nature as fundamental, one may advance or retreat, contract or expand, always returning to the essential (c. 17).

432. To be impartial and without prejudice, taking things as they happen, has been recognized since ancient times as corresponding to the Tao (c. 33).

433. See note 423 above.

434. See note 425 above.

435. For this story of Lao Tzu's funeral rites and the excessive behavior of mourning that took place (c. 3), see "Lao Tzu's Wake" (*WCT* 56-57).

436. The question is raised whether love of life may be a delusion, and whether the dead might repent their former craving for life; one should submit to the process of change in order to complete one's life span, forgetting the passage of time and experiencing the infinite (c. 2).

437. The common term *yü*, understood by Confucians to refer to moving from court to court to propagate the Master's teachings, takes on a very different meaning for Taoism: Lieh Tzu, a great traveler before his acceptance of Taoism, learns that the true journey is interior, the discovery of the highest reality within himself.

438. King Mu is taken by a wizard on a magical journey into otherworldly realms, only to discover that in fact he has not left his own palace, that his actual journey was interior, after which he devoted himself to journeys of the soul.

439. See note 403 above.

440. Early Taoists distinguished between various physiological practices and exercises, said to conserve vital powers, and genuine inner transformation, between *yang-hsing* – "nurturing the bodily frame" – and *yang-shêng* – "nurturing life."

441. While the oppressed and maimed lie prostrate, Confucians and Mo-ists

The Natural + *the artificial* – Taoism non antinomian, but agst
   artificial norms – for Tao "do not let the artificial obliterate
   the natural" 79.[442] Nb. on Mo Tzu pro + con 81*,[443] ethic of
   Tao 83.[444]
but cf critique of Shen Tao's quietism. 84*[445] – cf. AW. 45,[446]
   46,[447] 70[448] (Heart of man) 71,[449] 72,[450]
Political + social implications – *not* anarchy. Sage + king both
   come from Tao. SCT. 80,[451] 81[452]
   – importance of *love* + *peace* – 83,[453] AW 76[454] AW 66,[455]

---

dispute with one another, as it were, straddling the bodies of those stretched out on the ground.

442. C. 17.

443. Mo Tzu's rigidity is criticized as being alien to human nature, his intentions are praised but his practice is rejected as better than disorder but far from perfect order, but he is held up as "truly a fine man, of whom there are only too few to be found," who "held fast to his ideal – a man of excellence indeed" (c. 33) (83).

444. Indifference to popular fashions and external display, care for others and devotion to peace, commitment to moderation, devotion to the harmony of joy through warmth of affection toward all, were the principles of Sung Hsing and Yin Wen, which they preached incessantly to little effect on the multitude.

445. See note 402 above.

446. See note 423 above.

447. See note 405 above.

448. See note 407 above.

449. When asked how men's hearts are to be improved if there is no government, Lao Tzu replies that the last thing one should do is to tamper with men's hearts, which are by nature as quiet in repose as a pool and as mysterious in action as Heaven itself.

450. From the earliest days of organized society down to the age of Confucius and Mo Tzu controversies and disagreements were rampant, conflicts erupted, all because of tampering with the heart of man.

451. "There is that which brings forth sages; there is that which produces kings. The all originate in the One" (c. 33).

452. When the unified vision of Tao fragmented, "the Tao of 'sageliness within and kingliness without' became obscure and unclear, repressed and suspended," and everyone became a law unto himself (c. 33).

453. Devotion to peace in the world so as to preserve life for all, to setting one's own heart at peace, to showing that reacting to an insult with violence was unnecessary, to condemning aggression and fostering disarmament were central to the message of Sung Hsing and Yin Wen, though "the people would have none of it" (c. 33).

454. See note 425 above.

455. According to Hua Tzu, both those who counsel the King of Wei to attack Ch'u and those who plead for peace with Ch'u are scoundrels, as are those who fail to identify both parties as such; in such situations, the king must see the *Tao* rather than the advice of men.

70,[456] 71,[457]

"Pure Man."

The way of wholeness, purity etc. AW 46,[458] 49[459] (not packing for the brigands AW 75[460]) Man of Tê AW 78*[461]
Hiddenness. AW 55,[462] 56,[463] 76[464] – to follow others without losing yourself AW 75-76.[465] 78*[466]
P'u (uncarved wood) AW 66.[467]

   (cf. the Dismembered Criminal – AW 73[468])

---

456. Both the sages who invent artificial rules of duty and goodness and the tyrants who torture are violators of the integrity of the heart.

457. See note 449 above.

458. "A purity unspoiled by any contamination, a peace and unity not disturbed by any variation, detachment and inactivity broken only by such movement as in accord with the motions of Heaven – such are the secrets that conserve the soul."

459. The true or pure man is preserved from catastrophe not by knowledge or skill, nor by determination or courage, but "by the purity of his breath."

460. Accumulating and carefully preserving material property can be regarded as simply saving thieves the labor of doing their own packing when stealing; such is the case with what is commonly regarded as wisdom and holiness, which simply organize society in such a way as to make it easy for tyrants to seize power (74-75).

461. The Man of *Tê* (power or virtue), indifferent to the future or to human opinion, seems as bewildered as a motherless child or a lost traveler, but has all he needs despite not knowing whence or how it comes to him.

462. Lieh Tzu's effort to avoid all notoriety became itself a trait that attracted disciples.

463. On his journey to Ch'u, Confucius recognizes the person in a neighboring house as a sage who has hidden himself away from the world; when Confucius' companion volunteers to invite the sage to meet them Confucius forbids it, realizing that the sage knows he has been recognized and fears his retreat will be disturbed when his whereabouts are revealed to the king of Ch'u; in fact they soon notice that the house has already been evacuated.

464. See note 425 above.

465. "The Taoist does not 'hide himself away in the woods and hills.' What he hides is not his body, but his *tê*, his inborn powers. He knows how to 'follow others without losing his Self.'"

466. See note 461 above.

467. "*P'u* means wood in its natural condition, uncarved and unpainted. It is the Taoist symbol of man's natural state, when his inborn powers (*tê*) have not been tampered with by knowledge or circumscribed by morality."

468. Po Chü finds the drawn and quartered corpse of a criminal, binds up its limbs and clothes it in his own court dress, and addresses it, saying that its fate is actually universal, and that those who forbid murder and theft are the same ones whose accumulation of power and possessions drives others to commit those very crimes.

34[469]

Chuang Tzu. Legge trans.[470]

Bk IV[471] 1+ 2 252-253 Kung speaking as Taoist – important
#1.[472] Telling Hui not to go to a state where disorder prevails.
fine psych. analysis of the professional "sage" striving to
improve a king.

1) Virtue is dissipated in pursuit of the name (for it).

2) Even if virtue is firm, if not understanding the other's mind
we try to force righteousness on him, we pervert our own
virtue + endanger our life

3) 254. how the king justifies himself in opposition to 'ordinary men.' cf Chung Yung.[473]

4) 255 – Hui's false application of the *Chung* – his pretense to
be a co-worker with heaven, with other men + with antiquity.

Answer. Right procedure. *Fasting of the Mind.* See 257
  + *Hearing of the spirit.* –

[The "useless tree etc."[474] 6-9. especially 9.[475] The madman of
Khu + the advantage of being useless 269

Bk V[476] §1 – Wang Tai, the sage with no feet. Said nothing but
taught many. Why?

"Men do not look into running water as a mirror but into still
water." 273.

2-3. other sages without feet etc.

*5 281-282. "The sage has that in which his mind finds its enjoy-
ment + looks on wisdom as but the shoots from an old stump;
agreement with others are to him but as so much glue etc.[477]

see all[478]

---

469. The preceding page, headed "Dharma" and summarizing an article on
this topic by A. K. Coomaraswamy, is not included in this transcription since it
is not on East Asian material.

470. This heading, written at the top of the page, is followed by almost a
half page of blank space, evidently left for notes on the first three books of the
Chuang Tzu, but never filled in.

471. Legge, *Taoism* 251-70.

472. See "The Fasting of the Heart" (*WCT* 50-53).

473. *Added in left margin.*

474. See "The Useless Tree" (*WCT* 35-36).

475. See "Confucius and the Madman" (*WCT* 58-59).

476. Legge, *Taoism* 271-83.

477. Text reads: ". . . sagely man . . . and (looks on) . . . as (but) . . ."

478. This includes no plans, no goals, without passions and desires,
indifferent to public opinion.

35

Chuang Tzu

Bk. VIII[479] "webbed toes"[480]

"When I pronounce men to be good I am not speaking of their benevolence and righteousness but simply of their allowing the nature with which they are endowed to have its free course."[481]

VIII. 5 p. 322.

Bk. IX[482] Horses hooves. (cf. image. nature of horse ruined by training)

#2 "In the age of perfect virtue men lived in common with birds + beasts + were on terms of equality with all creatures as forming one family – how could they know among themselves the distinctions of Superior men + small men. Equally without knowledge they did not leave the path of their natural virtue. Equally free of desires they were in the state of pure simplicity . . ."[483] p. 326[484]

But when the sagely men appeared, limping and wheeling about in benevolence, pressing along and standing on tiptoe in the doing of righteousness, then men universally began to be perplexed.[485]

Bk. XI.[486] "Letting be"[487]

#1 "always occupied with rewards + punishments what leisure have men to rest in the instincts of the nature with which they are endowed."[488]

"Delight in the power of vision leads to excess in the pursuit of colors . . . etc. 8 delights which lead to excess. Incl. delight in benevolence, righteousness, wisdom + knowledge also in

---

479. Legge, *Taoism* 316-23.

480. The introductory note to this book (Legge, *Taoism* 186-87) points out that from its perspective what are called benevolence and righteousness are not natural to the person but excrescences, like an extra finger or webs between the toes.

481. Text reads: ". . . righteousness; – . . ."

482. Legge, *Taoism* 324-28.

483. Text reads: ". . . virtue, . . . beasts, were . . . creatures, as . . . family; – . . . men? . . . knowledge, they . . . (the path of) . . . virtue; – equally . . . free from desires, they . . ."

484. "p. 326." added in left margin.

485. Text reads: ". . . in (the exercise of) benevolence, . . ."

486. Legge, *Taoism* 339-54.

487. See "Leaving Things Alone" (*WCT* 70-71).

488. Text reads: "Always . . . punishments, what . . . men had to . . . endowed?" (340).

ceremonies.[489]

#5. Teaching of chaos.

"Do nothing + things of themselves will be transformed . . . unloose your mind; set your spirit free, be still as if you had no soul of all the multitude of things every one returns to its root . . . They are all in the state of chaos + during their existence they do not leave it.[490] 350-51[491]

If they knew (they were returning to their root) they would be leaving it.

They do not ask its name; they do not seek to spy out their nature, + thus it is that things come to life of themselves.[492] right attitude toward action, benevolence etc. detached work.

#6-7

2 Taos – way of heaven, way of man –

Doing nothing yet attracting all honor = way of heaven

Doing + being embarrassed thereby = way of man

36

Chuang Tzu

Bk. XIV.[493] (largely spurious – Legge[494])

#5. "The perfect men of old trod the path of benevolence on a path which they borrowed for the occasion, + dwelt in righteousness as in a lodging which they used for a night. Then they rambled in the vacancy of untroubled ease + found their food in the fields of indifference + stood in the gardens which they had not borrowed.

untroubled ease requires the doing of nothing; indifference is easily supplied with nourishment; not borrowing needs no outlay. The ancients called this the enjoyment that collects the true.[495]

#6. The snow-goose does not bathe every day to make itself white nor the crow blacken itself every day to make itself

---

489. Text reads: ". . . of (ornamental) colours . . ." (340-41).

490. Text reads: "take the position of doing nothing and things of themselves become transformed . . . all as in . . . chaos, and during all their . . ."

491. "350-351" *added in left margin.*

492. Text reads: ". . . (that they . . . be (consciously) leaving it. . . . nature; and thus . . ."

493. Legge, *Taoism* 393-410.

494. See 193-94.

495. Text reads: ". . . Righteousness . . . Untroubled Ease, found . . . Untroubled Ease requires . . . Indifference, and . . . . Untroubled Ease . . . Indifference . . . Enjoyment . . . Collects . . ." (404).

black. The natural simplicity of their black + white does not
afford any ground for controversy; + the fame + praise which
men like to contemplate do not make them any greater than
they naturally are."[496]

#7.   The wisdom of the three kings was opposed to the bright-
ness of the sun and moon above, contrary to the exquisite
purity of the hills + streams below, + subversive of the benefi-
cence of the four seasons between. Their wisdom has been
more fatal than the sting of a scorpion or the bite of a dangerous beast. Unable to rest in the true attributes of their nature
+ constitution they still regarded themselves as sages – was it
not a thing to be ashamed of? But they were shameless"[497]

#8.   If you get the Tao there is no effect that cannot be pro-
duced; if you miss it there is no effect that can.[498]

Bk. XV[499]

#1.   Placidity, indifference, silence, quietude, absolute vacancy
+ non-action – these are the qualities which maintain the level
of heaven + earth + are the substance of the Tao.[500]

#2.   (The Sage) does not take the initiative in producing either
happiness or calamity. He responds to the influence acting
on him + moves as he feels the pressure. He rises to act only
when he is obliged to do so He discards wisdom + the memo-
ries of the past, He follows the lines of his Heaven + therefore
suffers no calamity from heaven, no involvement from things,
no blame from men + no reproof from the spirits of the
dead. . . . He does not indulge any anxious doubts, he does not
lay plans beforehand. His light is without display, his good
faith is without previous arrangement. His sleep is untroubled
by dreams; his waking is followed by no sorrows. His spirit is
guileless and pure; his soul is not subject to weariness. Vacant
+ without self-assertion, placid + indifferent, he agrees with
the virtue of heaven.[501]

---

496. Text reads: ". . . white, nor . . . them greater . . ." (405).

497. Text reads: ". . . of the beneficent gifts of . . . sages; – was . . ." (408).

498. Text reads: ". . . Tao, there . . . it, there . . ." (409).

499. Legge, *Taoism* 411-15.

500. Text reads: ". . . vacancy, – and nonaction: – . . ." (413).

501. Text reads ". . . him, and . . . so. He . . . past; He . . . Heaven (-given
nature); and therefore he suffers . . . Heaven, no . . . men, and no . . . doubts; he
. . . display; his . . . Heaven" (413-14).

37

Bk. XVI[502] Correcting the nature
on returning to the paradisiacal state.

#2. a The men of old, while the chaotic condition was yet unde-
veloped, shared the placid tranquility which belonged to the
whole world . . . Men might be possessed of the faculty of
knowledge but they had no occasion for its use. That is what
is called the state of Perfect unity. *At this time there was no
action on the part of anyone but a constant manifestation of
spontaneity.*[503]

b This condition deteriorated + decayed till Sui-Jan (cf. Prometheus) + Fu-hsi arose + commenced their administration of
the world, on which the people rested, but did not themselves
comply with them.[504]

c The deterioration + decay continued until the Lords of
Thang + Yü began to administer the world . . .

They left the Tao + substituted the good for it + pursued
the course of haphazard virtue. After this they forsook their
nature + followed the promptings of their minds One mind +
another associated their knowledge but were unable to give
rest to the world.

Then they added to this knowledge elegant forms . . .

The forms extinguished the primal simplicity till the mind
was drowned by their multiplicity.

After this the people began to be perplexed + disordered
+ had no way by which to return to their true nature + bring
back their original condition.[505]

Bk XVII[506] "Autumn Floods"[507]

---

502. Legge, *Taoism* 416-21.

503. Text reads: ". . . of (the faculty of) knowledge, but . . . That was what
. . . Unity. . . . any one . . ." (417-18; emphasis added).

504. Text reads: "This condition (of excellence) . . . decayed, till . . . world;
on which came a compliance (with their methods), but the state of unity was
lost. The condition going on to deteriorate and decay. Shan Nang and Hwang-Ti
arose, and took the administration of the world, on which (the people) rested (in
their methods), but did not themselves comply with them" (418; apparently an
instance of eye-skip).

505. Text reads: ". . . Tao, and . . . Good for it, and . . . Haphazard Virtue. . .
. (promptings of) . . . knowledge, but . . . this knowledge (external and) elegant
. . . (primal) simplicity, . . . disordered, and . . . nature, and . . ." (418-19).

506. Legge, *Taoism* 422-40.

507. See "Autumn Floods" (*WCT* 84-86).

#4[508]   "The Man of Tao does not become distinguished, the
greatest virtue is unsuccessful."[509]
Bk XIX[510]
(like drunk who is not hurt falling from carriage)
"The sagely man is kept hid in his Heavenly constitution +
therefore nothing can injure him."[511]
#4   All who attach importance to what is external show stupidity
in themselves.[512]
      (vg archer thinking of prize rather than the shot[513]
*(carving the bell-stand – see #10.[514] cf. #12[515] #13[516]
Also the fighting cock #8.[517]

38

Chuang Tzu (cont^d)
Bk XIX
#14 p. 465   The perfect man seems lost and aimless beyond the
dust and dirt of the world + enjoys himself at ease in occupations
untroubled by the affairs of business. He may be described as
acting + yet not relying on what he does, as being superior + yet
not using his superiority to exercise any control. But *you* would
make a display of your wisdom to astonish the ignorant . . . etc.[518]
Bk XX[519]   Who can rid himself of the ideas of merit + fame +
return + put himself on the level of the masses of men[520]
The straight tree is the first to be cut down, the well of sweet
water is the first to be exhausted.[521]

---

508.   Actually #3; text reads: ". . . distinguished; the . . ."
509.   See "The Man of Tao" (*WCT* 91-92 [referenced as xvii.3]).
510.   Legge, *Taoism* 451-66.
511.   Text reads: ". . . constitution, and . . ." (454); see "Wholeness" (*WCT* 105-106).
512.   Legge, *Taoism* 456.
513.   See "The Need to Win" (*WCT* 107).
514.   Legge, *Taoism* 462; see "The Woodcarver" (*WCT* 110-11).
515.   The artisan is more exact creating free-hand than using artificial aids (463-64); see "When the Shoe Fits" (*WCT* 112-13).
516.   The properly made object attracts no attention or thought (456).
517.   The properly trained cock is not changed by external conditions (460); see "The Fighting Cock" (*WCT* 109).
518.   Text reads "Have you not heard how the perfect man deals with himself? . . . He seems . . . world, and . . . But now you . . ."
519.   Legge, *Taoism* 467-81.
520.   Text reads: "of (the ideas of) merit and fame, and . . ." (473).
521.   Text reads: ". . . down; the well . . ."; see "The Empty Boat" (*WCT* 115).

Bk XXII.[522]   When we walk we should not know where we are going, when we stop + rest we should not know what to occupy ourselves with; when we eat we should not know the taste of our food . . . How then can you get the Tao + hold it as your own?[523]

505   Man's life between heaven and earth is like a white colt's passing a crevice + suddenly disappearing.[524]

506   The Tao cannot be heard with the ears it is better to shut the ears than to try and hear it.[525]

513   Perfect speech is to put speech away; perfect action is to put action away; to digest all knowledge this is known is a thing to be despised.

Bk XXI[526] p. 516 Men who wish to preserve their bodies + lives keep their persons concealed + they do so in the deepest retirement possible.[527]

*523   The Tower of intelligence has its guardian (the Tao) who acts unconsciously + whose care will not be effective if there be any conscious purpose in it. If one who has not this entire sincerity in himself make any outward demonstration, any such demonstration will be incorrect. The thing will enter into him + not let go its hold. Then with every fresh demonstration there will be still greater failure. If he do what is not good in the light of day men will have the opportunity of punishing him; if he do it in darkness + secrecy, spirits will inflict the punishment. Let a man understand this – his relation both to men + spirits + then he will do what is good in the solitude of himself.[528]

---

522. Legge, *Taoism* 497-513.

523. Text reads: ". . . walk, we . . . going; when . . . rest, we . . . eat, we . . . get (the Tao) . . ." (502-503).

524. Text reads: "Men's life . . . crevice, and . . ."

525. Text reads: ". . . ears; – . . ."

526. Should read: "XXIII".

527. Text reads: ". . . concealed, and . . ."

528. Text reads: ". . . guardian who acts . . . effective, if . . . demonstration, every such . . . into him, and . . . of open day, men . . . spirits, and then . . ."; see "The Tower of the Spirit" (*WCT* 134-35).

39

Two Chinese Classic[529]

1 Intro.[530] Personalism in the ancient world.
   Need for study –
   Asian instincts.
2 The concept of *Ching* – a "classic" or authoritative book[531]
   The concept of Tzu – at once child + Master.[532]
3 Taoism + Confucianism – as reflected in these two books
   Tao Te Ching – Classic of Tao + of its mysterious action.
   Hsiao Ching – classic of Filial piety, or better filial love and
   its *mysterious* action as related to ethical Tao.
      Not superficial contrast bet. Confucianism + Taoism.[533]
      But ethical rather than mystical
      conceives Love as a basic force which acts everywhere + man
      is to make himself a conscious instrument of this love-force
      by entering into his right relationships with Father – brothers etc.
   Common – our being is received – is for another – HC.
   Stresses cultivation of personality + talents because received as gift[534]
       Return to root
       In order to advance
   Difference. – Taoism more passive + contemplative
       Its influence in poetry + art – its combining with
       Buddhism to produce Zen.
4 Tao Te Ching – its popularity.
   Tao. Chuang Tzu said "Even the one who asks about Tao has
   not heard Tao. Tao cannot be asked about + to the question

---

529. The essay outlined here was published as Thomas Merton, "Two Chinese Classics," *Chinese Culture Quarterly* 4 (June 1962) 34-41, and reprinted in *Mystics and Zen Masters* as "Love and Tao" (69-80); a somewhat different version was published as Thomas Merton, "Christian Culture Needs Oriental Wisdom," *Catholic World* 195 (May 1962) 72-79, reprinted in *A Thomas Merton Reader*, ed. Thomas P. McDonnell (New York: Harcourt, Brace, 1962) 319-26; rev. ed. (Garden City, NY: Doubleday Image, 1974) 295-303; a version of the essay incorporating all the material from both versions, retaining the more evocative title from the *Catholic World* article, is included in Thomas Merton, *Selected Essays*, ed. Patrick F. O'Connell (Maryknoll, NY: Orbis, 2013) 102-12; see the headnote to this last version and the correspondence with Paul Sih above (8-10, 22, 24-26, 29-30, 55) for the details of the different versions and their publication.
530. The essay as written has a different introduction.
531. See *MZM* 71-72.
532. See *MZM* 72.
533. See *MZM* 71.
534. See *MZM* 78.

there is no answer."[535]
outline of main features[536]
* The 3 Treasures 67. Love (Ts'e) – mercy.[537]
    End: "Blessed are the merciful . . ."[538]
    Lin Yutang. "Heaven arms with love those it would not see destroyed"[539]
        (resonance – the classic Greek saying. Those whom the gods would destroy they first make proud[540]).
5 Hsiao Ching – Not known – very good for beginners in language studies.
    Love of parents – basic + central
        5 basic relationships[541]
        3 powers. #7 – comment – princ. of heaven + earth
            Kings as standard + example[542]
            Music + rites teach love[543]
6 But – Chuang Tzu with his dishpan[544] – always going beyond formalities

40

Hsiao Ching. After Mencius – unknown author – circa 350-200 BC.[545]
    Filial love – basic to whole moral life.
        all other relationships based on this.[546] – NOT exterior
        formalism but interior love which rejoins Tao. it springs spontaneously from the heart of a child.[547]

---

535. Yutang, *Laotze* 43 (XXII.7: see Legge, *Taoism* 509-10).

536. *Added in left margin and marked for insertion.*

537. See Yutang, *Laotze* 291-92: the three treasures are love, not doing too much, and never being first.

538. See *MZM* 77.

539. Yutang, *Laotze* 292; see *MZM* 77, which quotes this verse and those immediately preceding it.

540. The traditional saying is actually: "Those whom the gods would destroy they first make mad."

541. See *MZM* 78-79.

542. See *MZM* 79.

543. See *MZM* 79.

544. This story of Chuang Tzu drumming on a pan after his wife's death (XVIII.2: Legge, *Taoism* 444-45; also Waley 6-7) is not used in the final version of the essay.

545. See *The Hsiao Ching*, translated by Mary Lelia Makra, edited by Paul K. T. Sih, Asian Institute Translations 2 (New York: St. John's University Press, 1961) x (subsequent references will be cited as "*Hsiao Ching*").

546. See *Hsiao Ching* ix.

547. See *Hsiao Ching* vii.

This is what communism wants to destroy
> p vii. story of Duke who praises son that witnesses against theft of Father[548]

Serving parents when they are old – meaning of old age – relationship reversed.

> LOVE acts in all situations we are instruments

> How this leads to Xtian notion of love – *disinterestedness*.

"No greater sorrow than to be unable to render such service." p vii.

Comparison of East + West p viii –

> West – centers on husband wife relationship
> East   "   "   father–son   "   [549]

Paul Sih – says it is "one of the deepest revelations ever made to us of the soul of Chinese culture."[550]

> Best text for beginner in Chinese language studies[551] –
> Notes valuable for this.

Sr Mary Lelia Makra. "Some measure of proof that the conclusions reached by Chinese Classical philosophers, aided by only natural reason, are in reality a segment of the whole Truth."[552]

Doctrine.

> Our being is *received* – + is *for* Another. Cultivating one's personality + character – because received as gift (Parable of Talents[553])

> Gratitude
> Return to root
> In order to advance

41

Hsiao Ching. 孝

Classic of Filial Piety.

I.[554] Ancient Kings following the Yao Tao[555] (way of life)

---

548. See *Hsiao Ching* vii (from *Tzu Lu* [*Analects*]).

549. See *Hsiao Ching* viii.

550. *Hsiao Ching* xi.

551. See *Hsiao Ching* xi.

552. *Hsiao Ching* xiv, which reads: "It has long been my secret desire that this translation of the *Hsiao Ching* might bring about not only a dissemination of the noble ideas it contains but also that it might serve as some measure of proof that the conclusions reached by classical Chinese philosophers, aided only by natural reason, are in reality a segment of the whole Truth."

553. Mt. 25:14-30; Lk. 19:12-27.

554. *Hsiao Ching* 3.

555. See *Hsiao Ching* 45 (n. 4), where *yao tao* is translated "the vital way" or "the right way."

They knew filiality was the foundation of virtue +
civilization.
a What is filiality?
    a) beginning *Respect for one's own person + body as a gift
    which has been received.*
    b) end. Cultivation of one's own person to hand on the gift.
b another view – Service of parents   fruit is building
      up of own character.
              Service of prince (society)
[Hence fact that character Tzu 子 means at once child + master.[556]]
Filiality is the proof that a man is human.
Expression of inmost nature, very liable to be hidden. (cf Ox
Mountain parable.)
5 basic relationships[557] – Father Son – justice
                     Mother son – compassion
                     Son parents – filiality
                     Elder bro – younger bro. – friendship
                     Younger bro elder bro. – respect.
II.[558] Love of parents – leads to love of all.
    (conversely – if you hate others, lack of love for parents.)
Reverence for parents – leads to reverence for all.
By these two one becomes a pattern + an influence for good.
III.[559] The Prince – Filiality of a Prince – to preserve his
inheritance rightly.
To be worthy of this he must be humble + kind, prudent,
moderate, not wasteful
Thus he protects the altars to the gods of grain in his fields.
IV.[560] The High Officers – must also preserve their ancestral altars.
They do not make rash innovations
Their words are well chosen, acc. to tradition, so as not to
offend anyone.
Their actions are well-considered. + no one complains of them.

---

556. See *Hsiao Ching* 44 (n. 2); see *MZM* 72, where this is noted in reference
to Lao Tzu.

557. See *Hsiao Ching* 45-46 (n. 10), where the virtues are listed as
"righteous," "compassionate," " friendly," "reverent" and "filial."

558. *Hsiao Ching* 5 (this chapter is entitled "The Son of Heaven" and is
applied specifically to the emperor: see 47, n. 13).

559. *Hsiao Ching* 7.

560. *Hsiao Ching* 9.

comment. a Senator Joe McCarthy[561] – *least* fit to preserve
traditions of society + freedom]

42

V.[562] *The Scholars.*[563] Filiality of scholars – to be worthy of their
rank + to carry on their sacrifices.

owe love   owe reverence
↙ ↘ ↙ ↘

Mother   Father   prince.

Filiality is expressed in loyalty to prince (learned by loyalty to
    Father)

Civic obedience – based on reverent service to parents.

VI.[564] *The Common People* – Filiality for them – based on living
contact with nature

observation of + conformity to its cycles + conditions.

Fitting their lives + needs in to this

Resumé: Peace + safety[565] of society depends on filiality in
every hierarchy from Emperor on down.

Otherwise a disaster will follow.

VII[566] *The 3 Powers* – Heaven 人行 Jen Hsing[567] – normal
conduct for man making heaven + earth his pattern

cf XVI[568]   Earth

                  Man

Filiality = 1ˢᵗ principle of heaven

    ultimate standard (rectitude – I[569]) of Earth

    men – imitating kings who imitate heaven by universal love

    Kings – helped in teaching univ. love by ritual + music.

VIII.[570] *Government by Filiality* –

---

561. Joseph McCarthy (1908-1957), Republican Senator from Wisconsin
from 1947 until his death, became famous for his allegations of widespread
Communist infiltration of the American government and military; the term
"McCarthyism" became synonymous with unsubstantiated charges of subversion
and treason.

562. *Hsiao Ching* 11.

563. "Scholars" in this era referred to a group of retired warriors who became
advisors of the prince (see 52 [n. 24]).

564. *Hsiao Ching* 13.

565. + safety *interlined with a caret.*

566. *Hsiao Ching* 15.

567. See *Hsiao Ching* 53-54 (n. 29).

568. *Added in left margin* (the reference is to how the emperor serves heaven
and earth and rules over men [*Hsiao Ching* 35]).

569. See *Hsiao Ching* 54 (n. 30).

570. *Hsiao Ching* 17.

Ancient kings governed by filiality.

The powerful respected those beneath them.

Those beneath them were grateful + acted accordingly.

IX.[571] *Government of the Sage*.* Sheng[572] 聖 whose conduct corresponds to that of heaven.

why filiality is the most important virtue

1 Rule of sage is based on love, is not severe, but efficacious.

2 Because of the foundation laid in love – the relation of father + son is rooted in nature

rel. of prince + ministers follows from it.

3 *Ordo caritatis*[573] – if one loves parents then love of other men has meaning.

otherwise – it is false.

X.[574] *Five duties of filiality* – reverence

support

care in sickness

grief at death

sacrifice.

* He who loves parents – not proud in high position, nor insubordinate as inferior, nor contentious with his equals.

43

XI.[575] Five punishments for worst offences.[576]

No worse than unfiliality – this is the road to chaos.

+ irreverence to king + sage.

XII.[577] *The Right Way* – mutual love among men –

aided by music which transforms + harmonizes manners

propriety + reverence – to the right ones.

all are happy when the proper ones are reverenced.

---

571. *Hsiao Ching* 19, 21.

572. See *Hsiao Ching* 55-56 (n. 36).

573. "The order of charity," a phrase based on Song of Songs 2:4 ("*Ordinavit in me caritatem*") and used extensively by the early Cistercians, notably St. Bernard in *Sermons on the Canticle* 49-50 (see Thomas Merton, *The Cistercian Fathers and Their Monastic Theology: Initiation into the Monastic Tradition* 8, ed. Patrick F. O'Connell [Collegeville, MN: Cistercian Publications, 2016] xcvi-xcvii, 338-55).

574. *Hsiao Ching* 23 (the title of this chapter is actually "The Practice of Filiality").

575. *Hsiao Ching* 25 (the title of this chapter is "The Five Punishments").

576. The traditional five punishments were branding, cutting off the nose, cutting off the feet, castration and execution (*Hsiao Ching* 58 [n. 47]).

577. *Hsiao Ching* 27 (the full title of this chapter is "The 'Right Way' Further Explained").

XIII.[578] *Highest Virtue further Explained*
How the Superior man radiates kindness, teaches all, is a center from whom filialilty + respect radiate outward practiced by all.
His ability to educate effectively is the sign he possesses virtue + hence assiduous + evident works in practice of virtue (visiting families) not so necessary.

XIV.[579] Perpetuating the Name
important notes on *chung hsin* (fidelity)[580] 忠 (middle – heart)
Fidelity to parents ⟶ fidelity to prince ⟶ perpetuation of name.

XV.[581] *Duty of correction*
cf XVII[582]
* *Important* – Not simply blind obedience to father – in good + evil – unquestioning
Kung indignant. "What kind of talk is this?"
    Duty to father to warn him if he is on an evil course.
    This is filiality (also to prince)
    It leads to preservation of *good name*[583] (note concrete moral realism)

XVI[584] (cf VII) Filiality to Father ⟶ intelligent service of heaven
Filiality to Mother ⟶ intelligent service of earth
"Because heaven was well served + earth honored the spirits manifested themselves brilliantly"
* The "contemplation" of the Son of Heaven – due to order of his life by filiality.
And because of this, all obey

XVII.[585] "Serving the Ruler"
Action + contemplation – Fidelity in service
                        Duty to guide Superior with real love.
                        Self- examination in Solitude

XVIII.[586] Mourning for Parents –

---

578. *Hsiao Ching* 29.
579. *Hsiao Ching* 31(the full title of this chapter is "'Perpetuating the Name' Further Explained").
580. See *Hsiao Ching* 61 (n. 53).
581. *Hsiao Ching* 33.
582. *Added in left margin.*
583. See *Hsiao Ching* 61 (n. 54).
584. *Hsiao Ching* 33 (the title of this chapter is "Evocation and Response").
585. *Hsiao Ching* 37.
586. *Hsiao Ching* 39.

Filial completion of service to parents –
   laid in ground chose by divination.
   real grief.
   with a term – to show dead do not hurt the living –
   mourning ends "to show that all things come to an end"[587]
"fulfillment of mutual relations bet. living + dead."[588]

44

+

Influence + perversions of Taoism.
Yang Chu[589] – from Taoist simplicity – deriding virtue + effort
– comes to pure sensualism, emphasis on sensual pleasure as
only object of life.

---

587. Text reads: "The period of mourning is not allowed to exceed three years, thus showing the people that all things come to an end" (see *Hsiao Ching* 64 [n. 58]).

588. The full text of this final sentence reads: "When parents are alive, to serve them with love and reverence; when deceased, to cherish their memory with deep grief – this is the sum total of man's fundamental duty, the fulfillment of the mutual relations between the living and the dead, the accomplishment of the filial son's service of his parents."

589. The Taoist philosopher Yang Chu (c. 440-360 B.C.) was a contemporary of Mencius, who mentions him in his writings; in a chapter from the later Taoist treatise *Lieh Tzu* (*Sources* 290-91), he is said to have recommended living for pleasure in the face of human mortality that destroys all indiscriminately, though according to the headnote in *Sources* this passage was attributed to him erroneously. In his introduction to *The Way of Chuang Tzu* Merton writes that there may be some "difficulty in distinguishing [Chuang Tzu] at first sight from the sophists and hedonists of his own time. For example, Yang Chu resembles Chuang Tzu in his praise of reclusion and his contempt for politics." But his "philosophy of evasion . . . is frankly egotistical," so that the "avoidance of political responsibility was, therefore, essential to Yang's idea of personal happiness, and he carried this to such an extent that Mencius said of him, 'Though he might have benefited the whole world by plucking out a single hair, he would not have done it.' However, even in Yang Chu's hedonism we can find elements which remind us of our own modern concern with the person: for instance the idea that the life and integrity of the person remain of greater value than any object or any function to which the person may be called to devote himself, at the risk of alienation. But a personalism that has nothing to offer but evasion will not be a genuine personalism at all, since it destroys the relationships without which the person cannot truly develop" (*WCT* 17; the quotation from Mencius is taken from Fung 30).

CONFUCIANISM IN MERTON'S NOVITIATE CONFERENCES

THE CONFUCIAN *ANALECTS*
IN CONFERENCES ON THE VOWS

Natural law[1] is a promulgation of that part of the eternal Law which concerns our nature. It is impressed on our very soul itself; *it is promulgated in our very nature*, in our intelligence, where it reflects the light of God, the wisdom of God. It is known intuitively by every reasonable man – it is the "light which illumines every man coming into the world" (John 1). If we follow the light of the natural law imprinted in us, *we will certainly receive the higher illumination of grace and faith in order to arrive at our end, God*. This is true of everyone – pagan, Jew, Moslem, Red. Ignoring the natural law, man is held guilty for his ignorance of God (Romans 1). It is of no avail to be baptized and to have the faith if we refuse to keep the natural law. *We have to follow the law of our nature in order to be children of God*. He is our Father in the natural order first of all – our Father supernaturally after this. Since, in the actual order established by God, nature is fulfilled and perfected by grace, it is in fact sin that is *against nature* and *virtue that fulfills and elevates nature*, with grace, to the charity for which in fact we were created and without which we cannot be what we are intended to be by God.

The natural law tells us that we must do good and avoid evil. It tells us that children must love and honor their parents, that parents must care for their children, that husbands and wives must love one another and assist one another and particularly work together for the procreation and education of their children. It tells us that we must not hurt others without reason, that we must not do to others what we would not have them do to us, that we must give every man his due.

For instance {see} the great principle of "human-heartedness"

---

1. See *Prima Secundae*, q. 94 (*Sancti Thomae Aquinatis Doctoris Angelici Ordinis Praedicatorum Opera Omnia, secundum Impressionem Petri Fiaccadori Parmae 1852-1873 Photolithographice Reimpressa*, 25 vols. [New York: Misurgia, 1948] 2.342-47).

which is one of the foundation stones of the ethic of Confucius. It is the ability to understand others by realizing that they suffer what we suffer and desire what we desire – to reach out by empathy and put ourselves in their place and act accordingly. This is one of the very great principles of the natural law, and it also finds its place in St. Bernard[2] – a very central place too. Confucius says: "If a man be really bent on human-heartedness, there is no wickedness in him[3] . . . . A human-hearted ruler wants security for himself, and so he makes others secure. He wishes to get a wider sphere of influence, and so he extends other people's spheres of influence. The ability to draw parallels from matters very near to oneself may be called the art of human-heartedness.[4] . . . The man bent on public service, if he be human-hearted, will under no circumstances seek to live at the expense of his human-heartedness. There are occasions when he will lay down his life to preserve his human-heartedness."[5] {This is} a magnificent statement, comparable to Our Lord's own words, "Greater love than this hath no man, than that he lay down his life for his friend."[6] For Confucius, the "man of honor" is the human-hearted man – and the man of principle who realizes that if wealth and high station cannot be obtained without disobeying the law (*Tao*), then they must be relinquished, and that if poverty and low station cannot be avoided without contravention of principle, then they must be accepted.[7] The first thing for the "man of honor" is loyalty and keeping his word. "If he does wrong he will not shirk

---

2. In *De Diligendo Deo*, VIII.23 (J. P. Migne, ed., *Patrologiae Cursus Completus, Series Latina,* 221 vols. [Paris: Garnier, 1844-1865] vol. 182, cols. 987D-988A), on the first degree of love, Bernard points out that carnal love for self becomes social love when it is extended to others: "It is just indeed that he who shares the same nature should not be deprived of the same benefits, especially that benefit which is grafted in that nature. . . . I think you will not find it a burden to share with those of your nature that which you have withheld from the enemy of your soul. Then your love will be sober and just if you do not refuse your brother that which he needs of what you have denied yourself in pleasure" (*On Loving God*, trans. Robert Walton, OSB, *The Works of Bernard of Clairvaux*, vol. 5: *Treatises II*, Cistercian Fathers 13 [Washington, DC: Cistercian Publications, 1973] 115-16).

3. Confucius, *Analects*, 4.4, in *Chinese Philosophy in Classical Times*, ed. and trans. E. R. Hughes (London: J. M. Dent, 1942) 19, which reads: ". . . human-heartedenss, then there is . . .".

4. Confucius, *Analects*, 6.28 (Hughes 19).

5. Confucius, *Analects*, 15.8 (Hughes 20, which reads: ". . . be the human-hearted kind of man, under no circumstances will he seek . . .").

6. Jn. 15:13.

7. See Confucius, *Analects*, 4.5 (Hughes 20).

mending his ways."[8] "Amongst men of honor there is nothing to cause selfish rivalry.[9] {. . .} The man of honor in relation to the Great Society has no private preferences . . . . He sees matters in relation to the right."[10] "The man of true breeding sets his heart on spiritual power in himself: the man of no breeding sets his heart on land."[11] Four characteristics of the man of honor {are} modesty in private, respectfulness in relations with superiors, benevolence in providing for inferiors, justice in the organization of labor.[12] Finally, "Be trustworthy in every respect, devoted to the acquisition of learning, steadfast unto death for the good."[13] These maxims should be to us a revelation of the depth and wonder of the natural law. How sad that by ignoring these depths, imagining ourselves more "supernatural," we are in fact very poor Christians at times. So much for the great importance of the natural law. No one can hope to ignore it and yet become a saint!

---

8. Confucius, *Analects*, 1.8 (Hughes 21).

9. Confucius, *Analects*, 3.7 (Hughes 21).

10. Confucius, *Analects*, 4.10 (Hughes 21, which reads: "The true man . . . He sees these matters . . .").

11. Confucius, *Analects*, 4.11 (Hughes 21, which reads: "A man . . .").

12. See Confucius, *Analects*, 4.15 (Hughes 21).

13. Confucius, *Analects*, 8.13 (Hughes 21, which reads: ". . . respect, be devoted . . . the Good.").

CONFUCIANISM IN MERTON'S NOVITIATE CONFERENCES

NOVITIATE CONFERENCES ON CONFUCIANISM
AND CHINESE CULTURE

CONFERENCE 1: JUNE 3, 1965[1]

I finally want to get around to my favorite subject, of Greek tragedy, which we've been trying to get to for months and months
and months![2] This is a very important subject, and you'll see how
important it is, because actually this whole business, when you
start talking about Greek tragedy, you get yourself back in the
sixth and fifth centuries B.C., which are absolutely the most important period in the history of civilization. This is the time when
everything begins to pop.[3] What's happening in the fifth and sixth
century B.C.? Where are we at? What's going on? Who's around?
(Of course I'm not too absolutely convinced of all these dates myself. This is pretty rough – this is *around* the fifth and sixth century
B.C. and thereabouts.[4]) Who's around? Greek philosophy is starting up – Plato and so forth? These fellows are before the Greek
philosophers; Socrates comes a little after them,[5] so this is actually
preparing the way for the Greek philosophers. What else is going

---

1. The recording of this conference (Gethsemani #148.2), is commercially
available as "*The Search for Wholeness*: 1. Greek Tragedy and Chinese Thought,
Part 1" (Rockville, MD: Now You Know Media, 2012). It had previously been
issued by Credence Cassettes both as "The Search for Wholeness" (2370:1) and
"The Fully Human Being" (2906:1).

2. Merton's series of novitiate conferences on literature began on October
31, 1964.

3. Merton is probably drawing here on the ideas of German philosopher
Karl Jaspers (1883-1969) first articulated in his 1949 book *The Origin and Goal
of History*, which posited that this period was the "axial age" in which a sense
of human individuality and dignity began to emerge in various civilizations
throughout Eurasia.

4. The generally accepted dates for the great Greek tragedians are: Aeschylus,
c. 525-456 B.C.; Sophocles, c. 496-406 B.C.; Euripides, c. 485-c. 406 B.C.

5. B. 469 B.C.; d. 399 B.C.

on elsewhere? Babylonian captivity[6] – and then who's around in the Babylonian Captivity? Who's writing around that time in that area? The Hebrew prophets![7] You've got the Greek tragedy and the Hebrew prophets are doing very much the same kind of thing.[8] You find the same sort of development in Greek tragedy and the Hebrew prophets – same kind of thought. In certain ways, of course, there's definitely a difference. Push the thing a little farther out in the East and what have you got – what's going on, say, like India? You've got Buddha floating around in India;[9] and then you push the thing further into China, and you get Confucius[10] and those people, and there's a great deal in common with all this.[11]

They're all thinking pretty much the same kind of thing, and what is happening – and this is the thing that comes up in Greek tragedy – the thing that is happening is one of the most important things that's happened in the history of man: man acquiring the sense of identity and destiny. People are asking the question: what is man and what is he all about? People are beginning to see that man can stand on his own feet and can make decisions, and

---

6. The exile of the Jews in Babylon after the fall of Jerusalem (586-539 B.C.).

7. The prophets Jeremiah, Ezekiel and Deutero-Isaiah were active in the years leading up to and during the Babylonian exile.

8. See Merton's journal entry for January 17, 1960 on reading the *Prometheus Bound* of Aeschylus: "Shattered by it. I do not know when I have read anything so stupendous and so completely contemporary. . . . A great religious experience. Prometheus, archetypal representation of the suffering Christ. . . . Prometheus startles us by being more fully Christ than the Lord of our own cliches" (Thomas Merton, *A Search for Solitude: Pursuing the Monk's True Life. Journals, vol. 3: 1952-1960*, ed. Lawrence S. Cunningham [San Francisco: HarperCollins, 1996] 370); also the journal entry for July 18, 1961: "Looked over notes on Sophocles' *Antigone*. Must read it again and again. How great are the Greeks, how much we owe them, how foolish to set them aside in silly contrasts with the Bible. Sophocles throws light on his contemporaries Isaiah and Jeremiah" (Thomas Merton, *Turning Toward the World: The Pivotal Years. Journals, vol. 4: 1960-1963*, ed. Victor A. Kramer [San Francisco: HarperCollins, 1996] 146; subsequent references will be cited as "*TTW*").

9. The traditional dates for the Buddha are 563-483 B.C.

10. The traditional dates for Confucius are 551-479 B.C.

11. Merton makes the same point in his essay "Classic Chinese Thought" in Thomas Merton, *Mystics and Zen Masters* (New York: Farrar, Straus and Giroux, 1967) 47-48 (subsequent references will be cited as "*MZM*"). See also Thomas Merton, *The Way of Chuang Tzu* (New York: New Directions, 1965) 22: "Chuang Tzu's concern with the problem that the very goodness of the good and the nobility of the great may contain the hidden seed of ruin is analogous to the concern that Sophocles or Aeschylus felt a little earlier, in the west" (subsequent references will be cited as "*WCT*").

he's got freedom and he's responsible for his life. All this stuff is coming up now. It hadn't come up before. Before this, man wasn't thinking in these terms.

For thousands and thousands of years, man simply lived with a bunch of other men – don't get the impression that these people were all a bunch of fools. They were very deep, and they had all kinds of gifts and so forth that we don't have. They can throw boomerangs and things like that; they can do all kinds of things that we can't do. They had all kinds of physical and spiritual and mental gifts that we lack; but they sort of lived without any profound self-consciousness. They lived in this simplicity that Philoxenos was talking about,[12] which was natural to them. They just simply lived. They didn't reflect on themselves much. If they had any get up and go, they got up and went! They just did what they did: there came a time the sun rose and you were hungry, so you went out and bam – let's stop and think – nowadays we think that an antelope is pretty fast. These characters could catch an antelope! This is true! These men could run after an antelope and catch it – like to have a few of those around in the Olympic games! There were things that they could do like that; they didn't even need to boffle. They just caught them and run them back and ate them. They had all sorts of things they did. They didn't just catch them and eat them whole! They had a very elaborate kind of society. They caught him in a certain way, and then having caught him, there were certain things that they did – certain religious ways of dealing with this thing. They had a totally different view of life than we have, a great respect. They didn't just go around catching antelopes when they thought of catching antelopes. They caught one if they needed one. They

---

12. Between March 31 and August 15, 1965, Merton was giving conferences on the Eastern Christian ascetic, spiritual writer and bishop Philoxenos of Mabbug, with particular emphasis on his teaching of simplicity in homilies 4 and 5 (conferences of May 16 and 27 and June 4, 1965); see Thomas Merton, *Pre-Benedictine Monasticism: Initiation into the Monastic Tradition* 2, ed. Patrick F. O'Connell (Kalamazoo, MI: Cistercian Publications, 2006) xliii-li, 279-325; after quoting a passage from the fourth homily, Merton writes: "compare here the idea of man's natural simplicity in Chinese thought (Mencius)" (292). See also his essay "Rain and the Rhinoceros" in Thomas Merton, *Raids on the Unspeakable* (New York: New Directions, 1966) 9-23, and his letter of May 3, 1965 to D. T. Suzuki, in which he highlights this doctrine of primordial simplicity, quoting from the fourth homily (Thomas Merton, *The Hidden Ground of Love: Letters on Religious Experience and Social Concerns*, ed. William H. Shannon [New York: Farrar, Straus, Giroux, 1985] 570-71; subsequent references will be cited as "*HGL*").

didn't kill animals just for the sake of killing animals the way we do: go out hunting and blast a lot of rabbits on a Sunday afternoon because they couldn't think of anything else to do.

Quite on the contrary, they lived with the same respect for life and nature that animals themselves have.[13] You seldom find an animal that just goes and kills another animal just for the heck of it. Supposing you go to Africa and you get into one of these big areas where they still have a lot of game around. Well they're all around – the antelopes and the zebras and the lions and so forth, all in the same place, and the zebras don't decide, let's get the heck out of here, where there aren't any lions or anything. They just live there together and a certain time of the day, the lions are hungry and at a certain time of the day the lions spread out and they pick this one zebra or antelope or something, and kill it, and then all the other zebras scatter while this is going on, and after the lions aren't hungry anymore, so they're just sitting around eating peacefully; then the next day they get another one. But they don't just go killing zebras for the sake of killing zebras. They kill one when they're hungry.

So in these early days, you've got men embedded, so to speak, in nature – but somewhat above the rest of nature. He's man, and he definitely has a spiritual life. He lives like the way the Indians used to live. He's in the Stone Age still, or in the Bronze Age – he's getting into metals – but he's been living for thousands of years with stone implements and a very developed religion, although quite a simple religion perhaps; and of course in this early period you get the rise of literature. Literature appears: you get poetry; you get religious hymns and things like that. Some of the earliest literature is religious literature: it's oral. They don't sit down and write. They didn't whip out a typewriter and bat out a poem and then send it to the magazine or something like that! It's the oral tradition literature – very little written literature. The first use of writing is more for records than literary. The normal way of transmission is oral. Writing is for things you're liable to forget. Writing gets to be important when you have cities. Writing comes with business, with city civilization. City civilization is late. When you get cities and

13. See Merton's reflections on Paleolithic cave painting and his speculation that "one of the peculiar sources of power and life in Asian art and philosophy is in its greater fidelity to immemorial modes of vision going back into the prehistoric past," with particular mention of Lao Tzu and Chuang Tzu, in Thomas Merton, *Conjectures of a Guilty Bystander* (Garden City, NY: Doubleday, 1966) 280-81.

when you get history, this is the last age of man. For thousands and thousands of years, man lived very well without cities and without history, but when you get cities and history then you get the present age that we're in, and we are now at the tail end of the age of cities and history. We're going into a new one – the age of computers and post-history or something like that – I don't know what you want to call it. We're going through a new revolution now, a whole new development. We're going through the kind of development that man went through thousands and thousands of years back, when he discovered fire. That was a revolution, and now that we've got into mechanization, that's an even bigger revolution, and we haven't the faintest idea what's going to come out of it! Anything can come out of it. You don't know where we're going to go.

But anyway, in Greek tragedy and in Oriental philosophy, like Confucianism and so forth, you come up against the idea of man, and before you can start discussing Greek tragedy or anything like that, you have to realize what this emergence of man meant, this sense of the individual person, and the sense of the fact of the individual person, with an individual destiny. This is one of the big things that comes up in Greek tragedy – the problem of the person whose destiny is different from that of the group. Before, this doesn't arise too much. The hero of early literature – what is he? He is not a person necessarily; he is a type, a mythical figure who just embodies in himself the destiny of the group. What would be one of the earliest ones? Gilgamesh would probably be one of the first ones – Babylonian Gilgamesh.[14] He's moving along. The Homeric heroes tend to be types, but as they get into tragedy they become personalized. Achilles gets into tragedy as a person.[15] Divinity – that's what goes with being a type of the people, because the people is also partly divine – the people itself is related to gods. They always try to give the king a divine background and all that. But the further up you come, especially in Israel, the king is in a

---

14. Among the most celebrated contemporary versions of this ancient poem is *Gilgamesh: A Verse Narrative* (Boston: Houghton Mifflin, 1971), by Merton's friend and correspondent Herbert Mason; Merton refers to *Gilgamesh* in his August 24 and September 3, 1959 letters to Mason: see Thomas Merton, *Witness to Freedom: Letters in Times of Crisis*, ed. William H. Shannon (New York: Farrar, Straus, Giroux, 1994) 263, 264.

15. The reference here is vague: Achilles, the central figure of Homer's *Iliad*, is not a major character in any of the surviving Greek tragedies, though he could certainly be regarded as a tragic figure in the *Iliad* itself.

different position than he is in Egypt, because you've got Yahweh to contend with, which was the real boss. These early figures are mythical figures; they're not persons, they're types. They exemplify in themselves all the strivings of the people and the desires of the people and that sort of thing, and they just embody certain myths about the people.

But now you start to get persons who stand out as different, and their life develops in a different way, and their decision helps the development. This is a total new thing in literature, and this is what you get in Greek tragedy. You get people faced with decisions that have to be made, and they have to make decisions – not just, shall I buy a house, or shall I buy a car or something like that, but decisions on which everything depends, and the thing that you run into is the person making a decision when he knows that it's going to mean his ruin, but he makes it anyway, because he believes that it's the right decision. This is the standard situation you get in Sophocles.[16] So therefore you can see how terribly important this is. You get the presentation of really important human problems, deep human problems. So deep are these human problems that nowadays our old friend Siggi Freud comes along and takes these as the type of the deepest possible psychological problem. The whole business of the tragedy of Oedipus – the Oedipus trilogy[17] – comes from the decisions that he had to make, after a whole lot of other decisions, extremely unpleasant, that were made for him without his knowing, and this is the situation that you usually get into in tragedy. The person standing face to face with a situation which he hasn't chosen and which has been sort of made for him by the gods or something, and then he is put on the spot and he makes a decision which elevates him above his fate, and he is a

---

16. See Merton's July 14, 1962 letter to Etta Gullick: "I find that the *Antigone* or *Oedipus at Colonus* is most helpful in a shattering sort of way. We simply have to get away from this business of weighing spiritual values in the balance against one another especially in the night when in any case it is almost impossible anyway. In the night it is intolerable to raise the question of right and wrong because we are in a sense simply wrong and in another sense out of the whole area of argument altogether. That is precisely the atmosphere of Greek religious tragedy. . . . In the night optimism and pessimism are both meaningless" (*HGL* 354).

17. The so-called Theban trilogy – *Oedipus the King* (c. 430 B.C.), *Oedipus at Colonus* (401 B.C.) and *Antigone* (441 B.C.) – three plays about the royal family of Thebes, though not written and performed at the same time as were, for example, Aeschylus' *Oresteia* trilogy (*Agamemnon*, *The Libation Bearers* and *The Eumenides*), presented in 458 B.C.

great and noble person insofar as he is capable of rising above what has been thrust on him. What Greek tragedy usually does, then, it makes this person stand out as superior to his destiny and even in a certain sense superior to the gods who determine the destiny for him, because he is on top of it; he is capable of choice; he is capable of choosing. His choice may be limited. He doesn't have an ultimate choice, but he chooses. Between one or two things, he chooses the one that he thinks is the best.

Now let's switch a little bit to China, and to get the picture in China, you don't have tragedy because to have tragedy you've got to have this sense of conflict, and in China they didn't have this sense of conflict. But in China you do get preoccupation with the question of what is the superior man. This is the idea that Confucius comes along with. The philosophy of Confucius aims at developing the person in such a way that he is a superior person.[18] But what do you mean, superior? It's not that he is a superman or any of this kind of nonsense; and it is not at all that he stands out over other people by kind of winning. The superior person: don't read by that, the winner. Confucius does not have a philosophy of how to be a winner. It's not that. On the contrary, the superior man in Confucius is the self-sacrificing man, the man who is formed in such a way that he knows how to give himself for others, in such a way that in giving himself, he realizes himself. This is what Confucius discovered, and this is a great discovery – that in giving oneself, one realizes oneself.

This is just as fundamental as anything can be, so if you want to understand how Confucius arrives at this, and how men are supposed to develop according to his mind, you have to see some of the four-fold setup that he's got; and these are what you may call not just cardinal virtues. They're something deeper than that. They are the four things that make life fully and completely human.[19] These

18. The *Chun Tzu*, sometimes translated "gentleman," reinterpreted by Confucius to refer to the person whose authentic humanity (*jên*) is most fully developed.

19. Merton probably first encountered this grouping by Mencius of "the four great virtues" in the Confucian system, "*Jên* (Love or Benevolence), *Yi* (Righteousness, the Right), *Li* (Good Form or Propriety), and *Chih* (Wisdom)" in I. A. Richards, *Mencius on the Mind: Experiments in Multiple Definition* (New York: Harcourt, Brace, 1932) 14. See his comments in his July 10, 1960 journal entry, at the time he was reading Richards: "Is this discipline that leads a man to love 仁 and righteousness 義 injurious to his nature? From the way many people talk, one would think [it] is. Not Mencius – and not St. Bernard. An interesting comparison

are the four qualities of a completely full and human life. These four qualities – we'll make a kind of little pattern out of it. (We haven't forgotten these ideas of symbols and symbolic patterns – the way things build up and so forth.) We'll put the Chinese names first: *jên*, *yi*, *li* and *chih*.[20] These are four qualities and four conditions of a fully human life. This first one means – let's translate it as love. Each one of these is very deep. This is not just something that you can rattle off. You have to understand these things in depth and see their relationship to one another to get the picture of the wholeness of man, as these people saw it. This first one, this love here, is not just well-wishing. It is a profoundly compassionate love, by which a person is able to identify himself completely with somebody else and to empathize with another person and to understand the other person in depth and to really go out to him with a charity which appreciates him as a person. It's a full notion of love. It isn't just, you feel well-disposed and you see a man in the street. The poor fellow, he hasn't got any shoes, and you give him a nickel. It's much deeper than this.

This next one is a very important one – and of course you read these things in translations and you don't get the full – I'm not saying I know it in Chinese! – even the translations don't give you any kind of a notion what it's all about. They translate this one as righteousness or justice or something like that, but what it really means is it involves a distinction between doing things for profit and doing things because they're right.[21] Now one of the big things that Confucius insists on[22] is that a man who acts purely for the sake

---

could be made between them especially as regards the 'four beginnings' – the four roots in nature from which love, righteousness, Li, 禮 – and wisdom can always spring provided they are not completely killed" (*TTW* 19).

20. In this conference he is following Fung Yu-lan, *The Spirit of Chinese Philosophy*, trans. E. R. Hughes (Boston: Beacon Press, 1962) 11-19 (subsequent references will be cited as "Fung"). Merton provides an extended discussion, also based on Fung, of this "four-sided mandala of basic virtues" that characterizes "the 'Superior Man' or 'Noble Minded Man'" in his introduction to *The Way of Chuang Tzu* (*WCT* 18-19); Merton completed writing this introduction on June 3, 1965, the same day he presented this conference (see Thomas Merton, *Dancing in the Water of Life: Seeking Peace in the Hermitage. Journals, vol. 5: 1963-1965*, ed. Robert E. Daggy [San Francisco: HarperCollins, 1997] 253; subsequent references will be cited as "*DWL*").

21. See Fung 13-16.

22. Fung quotes Book IV of the *Lun Yu* (*Analects*): "The noble-minded man comprehends righteousness, the low-minded man comprehends profit" (13).

of profit, a man who acts to be a winner or to get something out of it, or to get a reward out of it, or because it's profitable to him, or because it's pleasurable to him, is not capable of moral action. He is not a fully developed human being. He hasn't made it yet; he's not grown up yet. He only acts for profit. His action may or may not be in accordance with moral standards. It may be according to the law and so forth, but if he's acting only for profit, he's not acting as a man, because he doesn't act according to righteousness. That is to say, he doesn't do the thing because it's right. The right way to act is to do the thing because you know it is the right thing, irrespective of whether you're going to get anything out of it or not. Have we made a great deal of progress beyond this point? It would be kind of nice if we could make a little progress back to this point, because this is a very deep concept – the idea of doing things not for profit but because they're right.

You've got this developing in Israel at the same time, and the prophets bring this out and the psalms bring it out. This is one of the big problems that comes up in the psalms – the problem of the guy who acts for profit and in acting for profit doesn't care whether it's right or not, and he makes it, and you get a lot of this. In several of the psalms you get this problem.[23] The psalmist is complaining to God: here are these fellows just out for themselves and they go ahead and do what they want to do and they're rewarded! Where do we get off? What's the use of being just men? And then you sort of reflect, well, it comes to the kind of answer that the psalmist comes to, which usually isn't terribly deep actually: well, they get it in the end. Sooner or later they'll fail, or something like that.

Now this *li* here is liturgy or rites, and this again is something very, very deep. It is not just a question. Of course if you start reading Confucius you find all sorts of strange things that they do in the name of liturgy and rituals. They had an extremely elaborate liturgy. But what this is, is an expression, an acting out in liturgy, in ritual expression, of one's real sense of the relationship that he's in with other people, and his relationship with heaven. In Confucianism you don't get a great deal of talk about God; you've got a great deal of talk about heaven, and what liturgy is, is something that grows out of a profound consideration of the relations of man to man, especially relations to your ancestors, because Confucian liturgy is all centered around ancestors. And liturgy is an expression of

---

23. See for example Psalms 72[73], 93[94].

man's relationship to the universe. It's not just simply an arbitrary thing, where you come out with a censer and swing it around and that sort of thing, and go back. It is an expression of the way the universe is constructed: this is the way things are built, and this is acted out in liturgy.

Finally this last thing is a kind of an all-embracing wisdom, which does all this with a complete understanding of what it's all about.

If you put those four things together, you find you've really got something, and if you put these four things together, incidentally, it's a very Benedictine setup.[24] If you transfer this into our life, you have got a very monastic viewpoint – especially the kind of monastic viewpoint that's in the black Benedictine tradition, where you've got a lot of liturgy and a lot of ceremony and a lot of rather formal relationship and so forth, because this is all based on a lot of rather formal relationships. This is the sort of thing that most monks haven't yet got, so I think it is worth thinking about. It doesn't hurt us a bit to give a little thought to this pattern that Confucius is setting up for the fully developed human being. You start thinking in terms of monastic formation – monastic formation could very well, could easily put in about three years on Confucius, exclusively! I suppose it would be nice to get a little bit of the Bible in, just so that you don't forget that you're Christians and so forth, but a few years of Confucius wouldn't hurt! Confucius is difficult to read, although he's relatively simple compared to some of the other Chinese philosophers, but if a monk really lived the monastic life in such a way that he absorbed all this and molded it all together in a unity, and topped it all off with this wisdom, which understands the whole thing, he would really be ready to become a real monk.

Whereas Confucius' view of the man who is not living according to this and who is therefore an inferior man – I suppose you could put it, he's just simply a rube or something like that – this is really an ideal of civilization. This isn't an ideal of being a saint or anything. This is just how to be civilized, or how to grow up, or something like that. The inferior man does not act out of love and righteousness. He acts because it's profitable, or because he gets

---

24. Merton makes the same point at the conclusion of "Classic Chinese Thought": "Benedictines can hardly find it difficult to understand and to admire the tradition of Kung Tzu, which has in it so many elements in common with the tradition and spirit of St. Benedict" (*MZM* 65).

pleasure out of it. All right, this isn't wrong, but it's not enough. He doesn't act according to the *li* of ritual, which understands ritual. He acts purely because the rites are there, and he goes through them mechanically. Let us examine our conscience, brethren, and see how we stack up on this particular point! The inferior man is one who goes through rites without understanding them – aren't we in a nice box! But if you stop and think, this is no way to be! We're dealing with it: this is why they're going to bring in English. This is why they're going to do different things to make the thing more comprehensible. The Church is working on this, but it's not a tolerable situation to be going through movements and gestures that you don't understand. This isn't human. It's not right. A person shouldn't accept that kind of thing – although you have to, to some extent.

Then there is finally this business of wisdom, which makes the whole thing completely interior, which means that the person understands why he's doing it, does it because he really wants to do it, because it really comes from inside himself, because he himself has become the principle of this. In other words he wants to love other people not because it's nice – it says so in a book someplace it's nice to love other people; if you love other people you'll be popular, you'll win friends and influence everybody. He wants to love other people because that is the way to be – that is the way a man should be, and he does things because they're right, because that's the way it should be, that's the way it is. If you push the thing right down to the root, you get the idea that this is based on a vision of reality, on a sense of the way things are, an awareness of the way things are, and this means really a kind of a contemplation of reality, a contemplative awareness of the way things are; and then finally that this manifests itself in liturgy, because a person knows how to express this in liturgy. His liturgy is an expression, first of all, of love. When is our liturgy an expression of love? Well, we're trying; we're working at it. I think that's the real attraction of the concelebration.[25] I think that that's the point of it. It does bring out more. You can see that it's supposed to bring out more that

---

25. For Merton's initially somewhat ambivalent attitude toward liturgical concelebration see the journal entries for January 27, July 5, July 12 and July 19, 1965 (*DWL* 196, 264, 268, 273) and the March 28, 1965 letter to Dame Marcella Van Bruyn, OSB (Thomas Merton, *The School of Charity: Letters on Religious Renewal and Spiritual Direction*, ed. Patrick Hart [New York: Farrar, Straus, Giroux, 1990] 270-71).

we love one another, or maybe it does. God knows! I think they should sing with a little more enthusiasm and perhaps put a little life into it. It should be less of a com*miseration* and a little more of a con*celebration*. This would all be helpful. This would all lift up the heart a little more. Wait till Pentecost, where the old gang is going to be in there, at Pentecost! It'll liven things up, if only by forgetting all the rubrics and falling all over each other, fighting for the chalice – see you Sunday![26]

CONFERENCE 2: JUNE 10, 1965[27]

This is going to be a wild conference this morning. Remember what we were talking about last time. We were in China. We're still in China. We're working on the wholeness of the development of man. Behind this whole idea of Greek tragedy is the question of the wholeness of man. What is man? What is a whole man, and how does man live in such a way that he is not necessarily whole by himself. This is one of the things that Greek tragedy understands: that his destiny is given to him in which a man can make something out of it or not.[28] As I was saying before, everyone is getting conscious of this around the sixth century B.C. They're all suddenly realizing that life isn't just something that happens. You're in it. You come into it, and you go out of it, and you just follow it along with all the other living beings, and sometimes you have a toothache or something like that, but on the whole you just live. But now comes the idea that you have to make something out of your life. You can make a wholeness out of your life – or not. Then if this is true, you have to understand the principle of life. There is something to

---

26. Pentecost in 1965 was celebrated on June 6.

27. The recording of this conference (Gethsemani #148.4), is commercially available as "*The Search for Wholeness*: 2. Greek Tragedy and Chinese Thought, Part 2" (Rockville, MD: Now You Know Media, 2012). It had previously been issued by Credence Cassettes both as "The Search for Wholeness" (2370:2) and "The Fully Human Being" (2906:2).

28. See Merton's comments in his essay "'Baptism in the Forest': Wisdom and Initiation in William Faulkner" about "the facts that Greek tragedy deals religiously with the great basic problems of human destiny and that one can accept this without committing oneself to a particular dogmatic faith. The 'religious' elements in Greek tragedy . . . . are embedded in human nature itself, or, if that expression is no longer acceptable to some readers, then in the very constitution of man's psyche, whether his collective unconscious or his individual character structure" (Thomas Merton, *The Literary Essays of Thomas Merton*, ed. Patrick Hart, OCSO [New York: New Directions, 1981] 95).

discover about life that one needs to know, some central principle which is not evident to everybody, and if you find it and put it into practice, then you become a whole person, and if you don't, if you miss the boat, there is this idea coming up everywhere that you can lose your way, you can get lost and not find the answer, not find the central thing. Now Confucius, who was not an original philosopher by any means, was just simply resuming the old Chinese tradition going back thousands of years, probably. He had this sort of a four-fold setup: we're going to be talking in sort of screwball symbols today anyway – so you've got a symbolic wholeness there. What I'm going to be dealing with today are expressions of this spiritual wholeness in various symbolic forms, and this underlying symbolic structure of wholeness that you find in philosophy and in poetry and in liturgy and in religion and so forth. It crops up everywhere, and of course one of the standards is, this is already a picture of a kind of wholeness. You get four things like this, you've got a whole; and underlying this idea of a four-fold structure, you've got a deep symbolic treatment of this takes place in Central Asia and places like that, where Tibetan Buddhist contemplation is centered on achieving a kind of spiritual wholeness by a contemplation of a kind of four-fold psychological structure within yourself, which is called a mandala,[29] and if you get to be a real big shot in Tibetan Buddhism you can come up and construct a mandala of what's going on inside. It's kind of a very complex four-fold design. Don't do this – it's not what you're supposed to be doing here.

Now these four elements here are, in case you've forgotten, are *jên*, *yi*, *li* and *chih* – and this is love; this is righteousness, justice and so forth; this is worship, liturgy, fittingness – all these things mean much more than just the words – and this *chih* is wisdom. So now you've got this four-fold structure. Now the basic thesis that I'm working on to make this useful for us is that in all these pagan philosophies and Chinese philosophies and these structures – what you have there is not simply a new answer. These are natural adumbrations or sort of patterns calling for a fulfillment, so that when the Chinese are talking in terms of this, we as Christians

29. Merton has extensive discussion of the mandala, based largely on Giuseppe Tucci, *The Theory and Practice of the Mandala*, trans. A. H. Broderick (London: Rider, 1961), in his journal during his trip to Asia (see Thomas Merton, *The Asian Journal*, ed. Naomi Burton Stone, Brother Patrick Hart and James Laughlin [New York: New Directions, 1973] 56-57, 59, 67-68, 80-81, 82, 84, 85-86, 87-88, 90, 105-107, 270-71).

should see not only the fact that this is very interesting and very wise and that there is this human-heartedness and all this sort of thing, and perhaps tie it in with a Christian morality and say, oh yes, you can find a very close link between Chinese morality and Christian morality and the link is in the natural law, if you want to put it that way, and the golden rule: treating others as you would be treated yourself. But there's a deeper link, and this deeper link is that not only do mad people who think along these lines see types in the Old Testament which are fulfilled in the New,[30] but we also see types in pagan philosophy calling for fulfillment in the New, and this four-fold structure, for example, has a fulfillment very obvious, very simple, in First Corinthians, where you read the following – we were talking about this just the other day so let's just get the picture.

Of course for us, where is the wholeness that the Christian seeks? Where does a Christian find wholeness? In Christ, obviously. So consequently this Confucian wholeness for us is going to have meaning in so far as this is something that is going to be fulfilled perfectly in Christ. So Confucius has got a setup which takes you so far but it doesn't take you all the way, because it calls for something that Confucius can't provide, and that nobody in China can provide, Buddha can't provide and so forth – nobody can provide. Christ has to provide it; the Holy Spirit has to provide it. This lifts the whole thing to a higher plane, and it's really quite an extraordinary correspondence here! This is the passage we were reading the other day. The context of this passage is that in the wisdom of the cross, the Jewish hope is fulfilled, and the philosophers', the gentiles' hope is fulfilled – which backs up the statement I made a minute ago that Christ is the fulfillment of the aspirations of Jew and gentile. When God showed us His wisdom, the world in all its wisdom could not find its way to God and now God would use a foolish thing, our preaching, to save those who believe it. "Here are the Jews asking for signs and wonders; here are the Greeks" – or the Chinese – "intent on their philosophy, but what we preach is Christ crucified, to the Jews a discouragement, to the gentiles mere folly, but to us who have been called, Jew and gentile alike,

---

30. For extensive discussion of this traditional typological reading of scripture, see Thomas Merton, *A Monastic Introduction to Sacred Scripture*, ed. Patrick F. O'Connell (Eugene, OR: Cascade, 2020) xxxiv-xxxvi, xlii-xliii, xlv-xlvi, 129-37.

Christ the power of God, Christ the wisdom of God"[31] – and then he goes on and talks about this, and then what do you get all of a sudden? No human creature is to have any ground of boasting in the presence of God; and then what? "It is from him that you take your origin, from Christ Jesus, whom God gave us to be all our wisdom, our justification, our sanctification and our atonement, so that the scripture might be fulfilled. If anyone boasts, let him make his boast in the Lord."[32] So now what you've got here is this elevated to a higher plane. You've got the same four – here now is redemption, justification, sanctification, wisdom. It's exactly the same four-fold structure! It's the same thing. Here, instead of just a human love, human-heartedness, you have love lifted to the level of a redemptive love, a divine human-heartedness, and this is something you find developed in Orthodox theology. They go into this – this idea of the human love of God for man, a human redemptive love, which is the supernatural perfection of this Confucian *jên*. Justice is perfected by a supernatural justification, which is something more than just simply my just acts. It's the justice of God communicated to me in the passion of Christ, and this is terribly important, to see the relation, because this is the Christian dimension of these wisdoms – of these non-Christian wisdoms which can't fulfill things by themselves; all they can do is place an aspiration which needs to be fulfilled from somewhere else. It's fulfilled from a totally unexpected quarter, not through our efforts but through the grace of God. And then sanctification ties in beautifully with this idea of the Chinese notion of liturgy and Christ the sanctifier – you find him written about in the epistle to the Hebrews – this whole idea of the sanctifying power of the sacrifice of Christ.[33] And then wisdom of course comes up with the same thing. Now that's the first complicated step in this long thing.

Now this gets you, I'm sorry to say, this gets you into numbers. Now I'm not going to get too excited about numbers at this particular point, but nevertheless there is something involved here with this question of numbers. Here you've got four things in the unit, which makes five. Now don't get mad! I don't know anything about science, but I'm told on good authority that in point of fact we're getting

31. 1 Corinthians 1:22-24 (*The New Testament of Our Lord and Saviour Jesus Christ*, trans. Ronald A. Knox [New York: Sheed & Ward, 1944] 342; subsequent references will be cited as "Knox").

32. 1 Corinthians 1:30-31 (Knox 343).

33. See especially Hebrews 9:11-10:18.

back to this sort of thing in science. The most way-out people are looking for simple symbolic numeric statements of the basic structure of something or other. They are looking for ways in which you can reduce everything to a few simple numbers that you can play with. This isn't as far out as it seems. So you've got four, and you've got one, so you've got five. Now five is an important number. The ancient Chinese symbol for five is this: [五]. It's a cross; and then twice five is ten, which is the perfect number, so the Chinese symbol for ten is this: [十]. It's another cross. So whatever way you look at it, whatever you want to do with it, there is a connection between these numbers and this visual representation, because you can get a five out of these lines and so forth. There is a connection between this numerical statement and the visual statement, and it ends up with something like a cross, so that at the center of this pattern of wholeness and so forth is the idea of a cross, and here you've got a cross. You can run it any way you like, you've got a cross in there. So it turns out that all these basic patterns of wholeness land you sooner or later in a cruciform pattern. This is one of the fundamental patterns, one of the fundamental symbolic patterns.

Now hold on to that; and now we start moving into something else. This is a Chinese ideogram [中] and that ideogram is *chung*; and one of the big Confucian classics is a book called the *Chung Yung*, the Doctrine of the Mean.[34] But it means much more than the doctrine of the mean. The word *chung* – this is really a picture of an arrow going through a target, or an arrow in the center of a target. It's reduced to two dimensions. The real meaning of *chung* is a pivot around which everything centers.[35] Now if you look behind this particular ideogram, which is a very important ideogram, you find that this is giving you a development of this picture of wholeness. The whole idea of this *Chung Yung* is developing the idea of wholeness. It isn't just wholeness by practicing the virtue of the mean which is in between extremes, which is the Greek approach.[36] It is achieving wholeness by attaining to the central pivot around

---

34. See Merton's discussion in "Classic Chinese Thought" (*MZM* 58-59) and his reading notes on the *Chung Yung* above (108-12).

35. This is the interpretation of Ezra Pound in *Confucius: The Great Digest & Unwobbling Pivot*, translation and commentary by Ezra Pound (New York: New Directions, 1951) 95.

36. I.e. in Aristotle's *Nicomachean Ethics* (see Frederic Copleston, SJ, *A History of Philosophy, Vol. I: Greece and Rome*, Part II [1946; Garden City, NY: Doubleday Image, 1962] 78-80).

which everything moves, and if you're in the center, then you are with everything, and this is wholeness.

Now let's see how this develops. This is two-dimensional, but what it really is, you have to see it with more dimensions. So this now is supposed to be perspective. Here's this part of the thing as a plane surface going back there and this instead of just running through the middle of the thing is actually coming down and hitting the center of this, coming out the other side, so now you've got this thing spread out in space. This is a better picture of *chung*. First of all, this is a figure that they use for almost anything that they want to talk about that's fundamental. In cosmology, for example, *chung* signifies the world, with its cardinal points and the center, so north, south, east and west, and the middle: five. This is everything. Everything is reducible to this, these directions. In Chinese thought, Chinese cosmology, Chinese cosmology is always reduced to two basic realities, earth and heaven, and this dimension is earth [土], and this dimension is heaven [天], and in point of fact what you've actually got is heaven as a kind of a dome over this plane of earth. So now you're getting a picture of what this completeness is. True completeness is heaven and earth in diverse relations to each other and the thing to do is to get into the center of the pivot around which everything turns and then you are a whole person, because you are united with the whole, and wherever you are in the whole, you can do this, and you get united with it. So what happens then is that in the center of all this you not only see this in perspective but see it moving around. You should have a mobile or something and get the thing moving. Now while it's moving, there is one point that is still, and that is the point right at the center, so there once again, the sage who is seeking for wholeness is not going to seek to be out here or up here or down here or out there or somewhere. He's going to seek to be here, at the one still point around which everything is moving.

Now if you remember back a little bit to T. S. Eliot,[37] we get this out of one of T. S. Eliot's *Four Quartets*. This is from "Burnt Norton": "At the still point of the turning world. Neither flesh nor fleshless; / Neither from nor towards; at the still point, there the dance is, / But neither arrest nor movement. And do not call it fixity, / Where past and future are gathered. Neither movement from

37. Merton had given conferences on Eliot as part of his series on literature on April 22, May 6 and May 13, 1965.

nor towards, / Neither ascent nor decline. Except for the point, the still point, / There would be no dance, and there is only the dance. . . . not in movement / But abstention from movement; while the world moves / In appetency, on its metalled ways / Of time past and time future."[38] So now what he is saying here – this is tied up in the ascetic approach of *Four Quartets* – he is saying: how do you reach this still point? What's the statement he's making about reaching the still point here? This is in familiar ascetic terms: how do you reach the still point according to Eliot in this particular passage? He's thinking of the Carthusian symbol of the globe, a cross on top and the globe turning and the cross standing still, with the motto "the world turns and the cross stands still."[39] This is the same idea, except that here, metaphysically this still point is that on which the dance depends. Now this is obvious to anybody who has ever danced. If there's not a place from which you start and to which you return, there's no dance. It may be a cross-country race or something like that – a cross-country race, you end up right back where you started most of the time. With any form of dance, you have to have a beginning and an end. There's a place where the step starts and then you go away from there, and then you come back to it, and no matter how elaborate your dance gets – you can be here and your partner can be the other end of the room and there can be fifty million people in between – but there is still something that you are doing that has reference to a place where you started and where you're coming back to. So the dance therefore depends on this still point to which you return, and the movement has meaning in so far as it always refers to this still point. Now this has great implications for contemplation for example, because contemplation, in this sense, is not simply getting in the middle, the still point in the middle, and then hanging on there for dear life, and not getting into any kind of movement – on the contrary, it is a question of moving and acting and being involved in activity with reference to the still point which is at the center. This is all therefore tied up with this Chinese idea. The Chinese are definitely looking at it this way. This is a Chinese idea that Eliot's got here.

This is their view of wholeness, and if you push the thing a

---

38. T. S. Eliot, "Burnt Norton" II.16-21, III.34-37, in T. S. Eliot, *The Complete Poems and Plays: 1909-1950* (New York: Harcourt, Brace & World, 1962) 119.

39. "*Stat Crux dum volvitur orbis*" (the motto of the Carthusian Order).

little further – we've just got enough time to this last most elaborate diagram, which is really going to be the diagram to end all diagrams – turning this now to the realm of wholeness in thought and in a certain kind of logic, this gives you an indication of how Asian people think. This is *the* expression of Asian thought, which I have copyrighted, which I now give you absolutely free, and it goes like this – and I think it's correct. Two dimensions will be enough this time. Let's just have a square . . . at the center. Let's take these as an opposite. If you affirm this, you negate this. This isn't arbitrary; this is the way people think. You think in terms of affirmations and negations, obviously. Everything that you ordinarily think is in these terms. If you affirm, this you negate this; if you say this one, you exclude this. But the point is, you don't have to think that way. There are other ways of thinking. This is the ordinary way – if I think of me, it's not you. You're not him. You can reduce all thought to that kind of a structure. Now one way you can think is this: you can say, all right, I affirm this, so this is my position, and anybody wants to fight about it, we will fight. I'm going to affirm this against all comers. That's nice. That's true, you can affirm this and you can get out here on this corner of the square and stay there if you want to, but the trouble is that if you affirm this and don't remember that your affirmation implies this denial, you are already in trouble; you're already out of touch with the center. As long as you affirm this realizing that this is there as the basis for your affirmation, then you are in implicit touch with the center; or you can get down here and cling to this. So you've got several positions you can take. You can take the position: I just affirm this; you can take the position I just deny this; or you can take the position – now this is the way the Asians develop the thing – you can say, okay, I accept both this and this.[40] I accept this as affirmative and since these are correlatives then I accept this as denying this. They go together; and this is a better position, right

---

40. While Merton's examples are his own, he is drawing on the ideas of the Chinese dialecticians and logicians that in the empirical realm of "shapes and features," contrary elements, "the big and the small, the square and the round, the long and the short, the black and the white" (Fung 45) are all relative: an object that is large in relation to some objects is small in relation to others; only by an intuitive awareness of an absolute that transcends the experiential does one come to awareness of that which is beyond such relativity (see Fung 45-51). This points toward the Taoist position of transcending relative distinctions by living at "the axis of the Tao" (Fung 72) in order to experience "the Great Whole" (Fung 74).

at the middle, and I've got both, and that is already a much better position. This is already a more mature and broadminded position, because you see these as they really are. This is a true position. Why is this position more true than this one? It sees that these two are correlatives, so this is a very important thing. It is very important to see that not only is it important to affirm this or to deny it but to see that once I have one I've got the other, and the two go together all the time, so that they're always there. Now you can apply that to any important information, statement, that you want. Supposing I say I am a good religious; then I say, okay, I'm going to defend this against all comers and this is my position: I am a good religious. This is very impractical position to take, because from the moment I affirm I am a good religious, I also immediately affirm I am a bad religious, and both are equally in some way or other true, and somebody can immediately say, you say you're a good religious; I say you're a bad religious, and if I don't admit that he's got something, right away we're in trouble, so it's much more important for us to realize that from the moment I say I'm a good religious, I'm a good religious in so far as I'm bad, and I'm bad in so far as I'm good. After all, was I immaculately conceived? The only way to be a good religious is to be a bad religious who's trying to be good, and of course the success doesn't consist in having no mixture between good and bad, it just consists in how well you mix them, and no matter how bad a religious I am, I'm still a good religious to some extent.

Now with this kind of thinking you're going to get all kind of interesting stuff in China, where the Chinese logicians come up with the idea that a white horse is not a horse![41] I won't argue that one out, but that has to be understood in the light of this sort of thing, and now there's another position you can have, which is *neither* this *nor* this, and that is a highly mystical position. For a person to take the neither position, as long as he is there, he's wrong, because this position of neither this nor this is not feasible as long as you have a square and a plane and so forth. It only becomes possible when the whole thing has been reduced to a complete sphere, in which there are no corners and in which therefore you can't have this opposition, because the opposition has totally vanished, and

41. A paradox of the logician Kung-sun Lung: that is, a particular concrete horse is not "horse" in the universal sense (further developed to claim that a white horse is not even white) (see Fung 53-55).

there is nothing but the sphere, which is the perfect figure, which is *the* wholeness, and of course in this the individual himself disappears. Again, this is not something practical for you to strive after, because if you do – good, I'll bank on this position – I will adopt the perfect position of such and such, and then you start all over again. Now this, I think, if you ever read anything about Asian philosophy or Asian spirituality or anything like that you've got to keep this kind of thing in mind.

CONFERENCE 3: JULY 1, 1965[42]

Last time we had one of these talks on art, literature and allied subjects, we got into all kinds of obscure diagrams, and what is the big idea? What are we trying to get at? I suppose what I am trying to get out at this particular point is: what is the religious sense, and how does this religious sense operate? And in the case we're going to talk about, Greek tragedy, how does this happen to be religious? How does the religious sense operate in literature, and particularly in Greek tragedy? Now instead of talking about Greek tragedy, what we've been talking about is Chinese philosophy! Well that's just typical; it's par for the course around here. We do it that way, and the last thing I remember before I lost consciousness last time was that we were talking about a Chinese ideogram called *chung*, and what this really is all about. I was saying this is what we want to get back to, is this idea of ideograms and symbols and symbolic expressions that kind of sum up everything. Now the one that we have, the Christian symbol that we have that sums up everything, is the cross, and it is a good thing to stop and think and pay a little attention and meditate a bit to see in what way the cross symbolizes everything, how everything gets centered on the cross; and this ideogram *chung* is rather like a cross and it has very much the same kind of configuration as a cross, but it also has another dimension. Remember how we did it – this is supposed to be in perspective, and this thing going through the middle here, this is really a picture of this. Now what I want to get at – remember last time we were talking about this and talking about contrary ideas meeting in this center, and what I'm trying to work back to now – this gets us situated – what we're trying to hit, what we're trying

42. The recording of this conference (Gethsemani #150.1) was previously issued by Credence Cassettes both as "Chinese Thought/Symbol of Chung" (3284.2) and "The Religious Intuition" (2374.1).

to talk about – the religious sense is in this center, and the deeply philosophical sense is in this center, and the contemplative sense is in this center.[43]

Now the only way I can illustrate that is to give you concrete examples. Suppose now we are talking about God. There are all kinds of statements can be made about God. Now remember what I was saying last time: that you can take contraries and put them in opposite corners of this square here. Let's take two statements about God: one, the statement God exists. All right, well what's the contrary to that: God non-exists. He exists but He non-exists. Now what we were saying before was that once you make one of these two contrary statements, you immediately start implying the other one. Supposing I stand up in a hall full of freemasons, or reds, or something like this, and I stand up and say: "God exists." Well the immediate reaction of all the people who don't think that God exists, or would like Him not to exist, will be: "Okay, prove it – I say He doesn't." This shows that in a certain sphere of thought, as soon as you raise one of these things, the other comes up with it, so from a certain point of view, as soon as you say God exists, you are raising the possibility that He might not exist, and as soon as you say that, what's your comment on that statement? As soon as I say God exists I raise the possibility that He might not exist! Well that statement is not a religious statement. If I state that God exists in such a way that it's immediately implied that He might not exist, my statement lacks religious values. From the very moment – it can be a philosophical statement, it can be a scientific statement or something like that, but if you look at God from a religious point of view, you cannot consider His existence in such a way that it implies His non-existence. Now this is another personal discovery which I pass on to you absolutely free of charge at this particular moment. This is the religious way of looking at God and the religious way therefore is not saying God exists in such a way that He doesn't exist or saying He doesn't exist in such a way that it implies that He does exist, which is what the atheist does, and

---

43. See "Classic Chinese Thought": "*Reality* is the goal, and reality in act is the 'axis' or 'pivot' of man's being. The 'superior man' is one who finds this axis in himself and lives always centered upon it. Other men do not find the center, the axis, and spend their lives aimlessly carried this way and that by winds of fortune and of passion. Their center is not in themselves but somewhere outside them, and their lives are consequently a turmoil of frustration, self-seeking, and confusion" (*MZM* 59).

the atheist is running around with a chip on his shoulder trying to prove to everybody that God exists is actually the one man in the world today who is making the most fuss about the existence of God, but he's not usually doing it in a religious way. It's not a religious statement.

So now here in the middle, you have another way of looking at the thing, which is neither a statement that God exists or that He doesn't exist. What is this middle position? It's the existential fact of God. What's the biblical statement of this middle position: I am who am.[44] When Moses comes along and says, what is your name, God doesn't come up and say, well now, sit down and I'll prove that I exist. Just be patient and listen for a while, and I'll give you all the steps, and then when you get down to Egypt, when these wise guys start arguing with you I don't exist, you tell them this; tell them that all these things are created, aren't they? There's a watch, isn't there? Can't have a watch without a watchmaker. You tell them that. This is fine. The watch and the watchmaker is all very nice, but it's not a religious statement. It lacks religious value; it lacks religious force. It's not enough. This middle one is actually the position of Saint Anselm in his argument: that from the moment that I am aware that existence exists, or that is is, in that very fact I am aware that He who is cannot not be, and it's not a proof that He exists, it's not a proof that He doesn't exist, it's a direct grasp of what is implied in the fact of existence, in the fact of being. It's a direct grasp of being or is-ness, and that is your middle position.[45] It isn't at all a question of just latching on to one of these things and then trying to fight the other one off. Supposing that I do try to get on the outside and then try to hold on to this one position, what I am trying to do is in fact to move the center all the way over to

44. Exodus 3:14.
45. See Merton's essay "St. Anselm and His Argument" in Thomas Merton, *Cistercian Fathers and Forefathers: Essays and Conferences*, ed. Patrick F. O'Connell (Hyde Park, NY: New City Press, 2018) 102-33. In this essay Merton also relates Anselm's satisfaction theory of redemption to Confucian thought: "We must not think of feudal honor merely in terms of self-esteem and wounded feelings, offended dignity, injured reputation, loss of face and so on. In the eleventh century, the honor of a feudal Lord was quite concrete and objective. It concerned his estate and the network of relationships and loyalties in which he functioned. The concept is much more in the spirit of those Classical Chinese social relationships expounded in the Confucian *Analects* or the *Hsiao Ching*. For St. Anselm, also, the loyalties of man to man in the social hierarchy tend to reflect something of the order built into the universe by its Creator" (126).

the end, where I am out here. It can't be done.

If you get somebody like St. Thomas giving it out, somebody like St. Bonaventure giving it out, if it implies a basically religious position, then it has religious undertones or overtones; you have to have scientific theology and you have to be able to get out there and make statements on this other level, but when St. Thomas got through writing the *Summa*, what did he say? That the whole thing was all straw. Let's burn it, because without this religious center the whole thing *is* all straw, but with this center, it has worth. Where you get into trouble with this kind of thing is when you get into the Cartesian position, where Descartes gets himself way out here somewhere, on one of the ends of the stick, and then tries to operate from there. It's no place to operate. You've got to get in the middle. What St. Augustine starts with is faith, and then the intuition of God, and the intuition of God as his end, to whom he has to go to rest in Him and so forth. He heads right for the center, and having his sights set on the center of the target, then he also thinks in terms of things that might be on the periphery and sort of relates them to where he is in the center.

Now take another two opposites about God. What are some other favorite opposites about God? What's one of the big apparent contradictions: mercy and justice. Okay, you can whirl around those two for the rest of your life if you want to – make a real technical argument about it: this business of predestination, grace and free will. How do I know I'm free? If I have the grace to do it, can I resist? If I resist, whose fault is it – my fault or God's fault? and so forth. Go round and round and round the mulberry bush and never get anywhere! So once again, it isn't a question of getting out here and trying to reconcile these two things from way out at the extremes. But you get in the middle, and the middle position is the position that is taken. Where? How? Why? Give me an example of the middle position in this – an existential position. There is a perfectly normal way in which we do this all the time; we're all the time doing it. We all did this today. We all sat right down in the middle of this thing, at one time today at least. What I'm trying to do is not get you to think of this in terms of mental acts. It isn't a question of mental acts. It's a question of a living act of the whole being, in which God's justice and mercy come to me reconciled, without my thinking about it at all. When you go to communion for example – this puts the thing in a different dimension. You go to communion – you're not thinking, now let me see: this half of the host is justice, this half of the host is mercy. This would be ridiculous! You wouldn't think that way. You receive communion, and here's a totally different dimension. Here's an existential act. He gives Himself to me, and once He gives Himself totally to me, what am I going to fool around worrying about justice and mercy for – two abstractions – because in point of fact, God *is* His justice, and God *is* His mercy, and they're not divided in Him. They're divided in my own head. Now if after I have received Him in His totality, as He is in Himself – which I'm not capable of understanding – I'm still batting around these two abstractions, I am in fact dealing with something that has nothing to do with Him anymore. These abstractions have a certain point. They help a little bit to understand, to approach certain things, but when I come directly in contact with Him, then the whole thing is forgotten – the abstractions. Here we are celebrating the Feast of the Precious Blood[46] – the meaning of something like the Feast of the Precious Blood, or the mystery of the Precious Blood – it means forget this business of justice and mercy and plunge into the precious blood, or whatever corny metaphor you want to use (because some of these metaphors are pretty naïve), but you use these things because they indicate something that can't be indicated otherwise, and so constantly in religious statements about God, the thing to do is to get away from these extremes and to get into this central position, and the central position is the position whereby an act of love or an act of surrender or something like that – or receiving a sacrament – you just go direct to Him, and it's you and Him and you're there.

There's a very good little passage in Jeremiah, for example. What we're doing here, we're not doing it with the head, we're doing it with the heart, and the heart not just meaning sentimentality, or feeling or something, but the heart as a center of a divine instinct of love which draws us to direct contact with God. Let's for example take this one little passage from Jeremias: "Why then is this people in Jerusalem turned away with a stubborn revolting? they have laid hold on lying, and have refused to return. I attended, and hearkened; no man speaketh what is good, there is none that

---

46. Feast instituted by Pope Pius IX in 1849, originally celebrated on the first Sunday of July, transferred to July 1 by Pope Pius X and removed from the liturgical calendar in 1969.

doth penance for his sin, saying: What have I done? They are all turned to their own course, as a horse rushing to the battle. The kite in the air [now the kite is not a paper kite; it's a hawk] hath known her time: the turtle, and the swallow, and the stork [now the turtle is not a turtle – you all know what the turtle is] have observed the time of their coming: but my people have not known the judgment of the Lord."[47] Now here is a very good example of this business of being in the center. The hawk knows the time – well for example, the hawk knows where there's something going on. You observe the hawks around here, some of which are not dead I understand. (I don't know what got into the red-shouldered hawks – they're no longer around.) But anyway, you see a cooper's hawk go over here every once in a while; he knows where he's going, and he usually goes over about the same time, and he usually has the same end in view, somewhere. In other words, birds have their way of knowing when to migrate, when to do this and so forth.

We have something like that, which has been put in our hearts by God, first of all a natural basis, and then God's grace on top of it, and if we follow this, we follow the voice of God in our heart; and of course, being human beings, we just can't do this on our own. You have to have the Church to help you do this, so God has given us the Church, given the Holy Spirit to the Church, guides us and so forth. If we follow these things then we know the judgment of the Lord, and this is this central position: to know the judgment, the concrete judgment of the Lord – not some abstract statement about His goodness or His greatness or something like that, but his concrete judgment; and where we go off on this question of the judgment of the Lord is that we actually project into God's mind judgments of our own. The judgments of the Lord are unknown to us until they happen, and when they happen they are still unknown to us; we still don't quite know what's cooking. We just know that it happened, and this is the way in which we function in a religious context.

Now in Second Corinthians we've got another one, a very good one, using more of the supernatural view with this. (Now this Bible's great – you can never find the Epistles of St. Paul in it!) Second Corinthians 4: "Our gospel is a mystery, yes, but it is only a mystery to those who are on the road to perdition; those whose unbelieving minds have been blinded by the god this world

---

47. Jeremiah 8:5-7 (Douay-Rheims translation).

worships, so that the glorious gospel of Christ, God's matchless image, cannot reach them with the rays of its illumination [the rays of the illumination of Christ strike in this center]. After all, it is not ourselves we proclaim; we proclaim Christ Jesus as Lord, and ourselves as your servants for Jesus' sake. The same God who bade light shine out of darkness has kindled a light in our hearts, whose shining is to make known his glory as he has revealed it in the features of Jesus Christ"[48] and so forth. So therefore, again, this central position here is the light of the heart, the light of faith, the light of grace in the heart, which God kindles there, and therefore there's a corollary to that. If we're too anxious to be all the time out at one of the ends of these things, and all the time thinking in terms of these oppositions and trying to reconcile them and so forth, we get out of contact with this invisible center where faith operates.

Well what's the answer? How are you going to apply this in practice? Well there are all sorts of ordinary answers that you have. First of all it's a question of being silent; being able to listen; being able to be attentive to the meaning of life as time goes on, and so forth, and not trying to push everything ourselves, and not trying to answer all the questions before they answer themselves and so forth. All these things are kind of traditional answers in the monastic life, but very important for us. Where would you say that monastic tradition came in here for us, or any other tradition when it comes to that – theological tradition, patristic tradition? There is a bit of a problem about finding this central spot – to begin with it's different every day. What you get in monastic tradition and in ecclesiastical tradition and in liturgical tradition, you have a means by which something that is known only by experience can be passed on in such a way that it's experienced by other people. This is why tradition is necessary. If it were not so difficult to pass on an experience, there wouldn't be any need for this. There's no need for a tradition for example in mathematics. All you need is to know how it's done and then do it. You know what you're supposed to do, so you pass it on, but whatever Euclid experienced when he was working out these theorems of his, that's his affair; that's his business. I don't care how he felt. But in the things of religion, the religious experience, it's very important to be able to relive in our hearts the things that the fathers of monasticism lived, because that's the only way in which we can know what they were doing, and so

---

48. 2 Corinthians 4:3-6 (Knox 380).

what we have to do is, in our lives, approximate to the experience of God which our fathers arrived at in their life of prayer and in their life of renunciation and so forth; and how do we do that? Well we just have to do what they did. We have to do it in the same way that they did, and with the same dispositions as they did, as far as we know; and of course it's most important that this tradition should be a living tradition, because if it becomes a book tradition, right away the thing is already very risky. For example just take the way you learn how to do anything that is completely practical and that can't be transmitted by words. What would be an example of that? Well, in sports, for example, or play the piano: if you want to learn one of these things you have to be shown by somebody who knows how to do it. You can learn it from a book, but much less well, and most of us not at all. You just get a book on how to play the harp in three easy lessons. You can do it – there are diagrams and you can sort of sit and look – but it's much easier if you just get somebody who really knows how to play the harp, because if this person sits down and starts playing it, you get a whole lot of stuff that can't be put in a book. For example what do you get? You can tell the particular way in which he is enjoying this. The book will tell you people who play the harp have a tremendous amount of fun which other people never have because it's a unique experience. Try it! But it's a very different thing with a fellow playing this thing, and it obviously means a great deal to him and he's having a wonderful time, and you see it, because there's something in us that latches on to that, and we can to some extent imitate it, and we can begin to reproduce this in our own life.

So it is with monasticism. There has to be a living tradition, and above all a tradition of people who get something out of monasticism. That's why the most important thing about monastic formation is to have a lot of people around who are getting something out of it. It's no use to have an ideal system and then beat a lot of people over the head to make them do it! But from the moment when you've got a monastery in which you've got people really getting something out of monastic life, 95 per cent of it is done. If you have a monastery in which people are just running around like mad trying to get a lot of stuff finished or trying to get something done or something like that, it's not the same, because there you have a monastery in which a lot of people are wishing they did live the monastic life, or not realizing that they could be living it, even though they're rushed off their feet and so forth. All this creates is a tradition of people who wished that they were living the monastic life! That not a good enough tradition. We've got a fine tradition here of people who wish they had a better monastic life, but I think it's up to us to realize that really what we've got isn't so bad! There are possibilities. The fact that we've got feast days and things like that, and people obviously are getting something, things out of them, and things are going well in that respect, that's 95 per cent of it! That is the way these things are passed on, and that's why it's so important to make good use out of what you have got, and to really get something out of it, and really find God and really be at peace and so forth, because that's the way you get into this central thing and you're not just whirling around on the outside thinking about we could do this or we could do that or we might do this or we might do that, but here and now, this is what we've got. So the most important thing is, as far as possible, to be right where you are, to be present where you are, and to be in it and to live it and to share it with other people in a simple way, whatever simple way you can, and the man who lives life that way and shares it to some extent with other people is doing good. He's doing something for the monastery, whereas if you're living a miserable life, and you don't know where it's all going, and you're griping about it and so forth, and you're getting everybody else to gripe about it, you're getting everybody blinded to the possibilities of what's there, so I think we really ought to take care of that.

What I was really going to get around to was Chinese art, but we'll try that next time.

CONFERENCE 4: JULY 8, 1965.[49]

Now we're going back again to these primitive ideas, trying to get the background of the way people thought – about the fifth century B.C. – which is very important. It's good to know this. It has a great deal of importance for our life, and for our understanding, for example, of the liturgy. Now remember, I've been putting these crazy diagrams on the board. What have you been getting out of this? Has any light of any kind whatever percolated through from all this? What on earth is this all about, or is it just funny to see me standing up here and running back and forth to the blackboard,

---

49. Gethsemani #153 (never made available commercially).

yelling my head off? Is anything coming through at all? What has this got to do with us though? This contemplative center – what do you suppose I mean? What does it mean in our everyday experience, this contemplative center that I'm talking about? How is reality experienced? It's not experienced in terms of: this equals that, or this is that, or this is not that. It's neither one nor the other. It just *is* – the experience of is-ness, which is central our life. This isn't anything mystical, or anything strange. It's the ordinary experience if is-ness in life, the direct experience of being, which however is very important for the contemplative approach, because if you don't have any capacity for this basic intuition, if everything that you do is always in the form of a dialectical judgment or something like that – this equals this, and this equals this, therefore this equals this – you're always working the thing out, you're always out on the end of the thing and trying to get things related to each other.

This is no process. You just simply go straight to it, and it is experienced; for example one of the ways in which this clicks is in the form of a kind of silence that sums everything up. Sometimes you just see something, and then bing! Everything is silent and that's it. Well now that is this *chung*, this pivot. What you experience when you see that you're not seeing something in your head. You're not reaching out for something here and reaching out for something there and putting them together. You're just simply aware of being in yourself, and in this awareness of being comes the contact with Being with a great big B. So you experience being with a little b, and in this you experience Being with a big B, and then what else is there? Anything you add to it is embroidery. But of course you have to get down again to the ordinary level of human behavior, in which you do have to say this equals this, and this goes together with that, and this belongs here and so forth. The whole purpose of the contemplative life is to live in a dimension where you see that the embroidery is nothing but embroidery, and you can sure get along without it, and the more you get along without it the better off you are.

But this is the sort of basic outlook that you get in Oriental thought, in Chinese thought, in Japanese thought, and Indian thought, to some extent, and you get it in Western medieval thought. You get it in the Fathers of the Church and so forth; and where you don't get it is in modern thought, because in modern thought

you start out with the Cartesian split,[50] in which you as subject are
split off from everything else and then you run around looking
for objects, and you've just got division. So therefore one of the
ancient Chinese books on liturgies says, "Acts of the greatest reverence admit of no ornament,"[51] so this points to this idea of liturgy
is supposed to bring us into contact with this center of silence and
being and fullness. This is obvious. If liturgy is perfect – bing! – the
whole thing is fixed. Everything falls into place. Where liturgy is
not perfect, then there's a lot of mickey mouse and flimflam, useless gestures, useless this and that, even though we're trying real
hard. The more nonsense you can get into it, the better it seems:
multiply all kinds of other activities. So that's why we're trying
now to get the liturgy simple. In liturgical action, for example, you
are supposed to have this kind of a result: that liturgy makes you
aware of the presence of the invisible in the midst of the visible.
If our liturgy is going properly, it should be such that we become
aware of the truth that's expressed by Our Lord in the Gospel, that
"Where two or three are gathered together in My name there am
I in the midst of you."[52] The whole function of liturgy is basically
to keep us aware of this presence. If it's not getting us aware of
this presence, then there's something the matter with it, or with us
– either with the liturgy or with us – it's hard to say which sometimes. Sometimes it's the matter with both! But this is the whole
purpose of liturgy. Liturgy should be such that when we are doing
the thing right, then it becomes obvious to everybody who's there
that Christ is present in the midst, and it becomes easy to see this;
and if it's not easy to see this, well there's something the matter.

Now let me read you a quote from a Chinese sage. You're prepared for this now. You've had your background and now this sort
of stuff just comes right in – no obstacle! "If there is desistence from
movement, this is quiescence, but quiescence is not the opposite to
movement. To desist from speaking is silence, but silence is not the
opposite to speaking. That being so, although Heaven-and-Earth is

50. For Merton's rejection of the position of Descartes separating the interior
world of the mind from the exterior world of objects (extension), see Thomas
Merton, *New Seeds of Contemplation* (New York: New Directions, 1961) 8;
Thomas Merton, *Zen and the Birds of Appetite* (New York: New Directions,
1968) 22-23.

51. *The Book of Rites* (*Li Ki*) 8.14, trans. James Legge, *Sacred Books of the
East*, ed. Max Muller, 50 vols. (Oxford: Clarendon Press, 1879-1910) 27.400.

52. Matthew 18:20.

so vast and is filled with myriads of things, with such transforma-
tions as thunder moving and the wind traveling, yet the silence of
non-being is the original root of it all."[53] Now this is just a very
simple statement of the kind of thing that we've been talking about.
First of all, what does he do? This is very important for the contemplative life. He breaks down this artificial division: movement/
not movement; talking/silence. As long as we think that silence is
the opposite to talking, we never have any silence – impossible.
It's got nothing to do with it. Silence is something else. It's a different dimension. It's the thing in the center. It's the pivot. Action
and non-action, or action and contemplation: the whole house is
full of people running around – not you necessarily – but the place
is full of people who are worried about this action/contemplation
thing – one or the other. Which is it going to be? And then you've
got people running around saying, "Action is it. Everybody gotta
act. Get in there and fight"; and then you've got other people saying, "Too much action; slow down; be quiet. You're never going
to make it that way." The thing is, quiescence is not the opposite
of movement. Quiescence has got nothing to do with movement,
because it's in the center. It's not on which end of the thing, and
if you want to be a contemplative, you have to learn how to be
quiescent even though you're going ninety miles an hour, and to
see that it makes no difference whether you're going ninety miles
an hour or two miles an hour. You get up in space – what are they
doing? He's doing 20,000 miles an hour, and he's motionless!
He's just out there floating around, but he's doing 20,000 miles
an hour, and he's not excited, he's not sweating or anything! So
this is the kind of dimension that you want to get into. And then he
says, what you should do is, you should "be aware of the hidden
spring or pivot of what is likely to happen."[54] Well of course this
is a different dimension.

Now this brings us to the question of Chinese landscape painting. Have you ever seen any Chinese painting? There's good and
there's bad – there's some awful stuff. The house must be full
of books on Chinese painting and Japanese painting – one of the
most terrific paintings in the world! I forget the name of the Japanese artist who did it, but it's a famous one – you see it all over

---

53. Wang Pi (third century A.D.), quoted in Fung 99, which reads: ". . .
quiescence. Quiescence . . . is to be silent . . . ."
54. Fung 100.

the place. It's just a big blank space – it's supposed to be the sea, and with mist, and in the middle of it is just a little fishing boat, kind of towed up, and there's a little fellow sitting on the end of the fishing boat and he's fishing, and he's just hanging in space, but you know it's on water and so forth.[55] This doesn't look like anything; it's a nice picture, nicely drawn and so forth, but if you know what these people are trying to say with these pictures, you see what this says. It says this is the quintessence of everything! What he is saying is, what an artist does in a Japanese or Chinese painting is, he gives you just enough visible indication to point to the invisible, and what you see in any Japanese or Chinese painting is always invisible. The visible elements are only valuable insofar as they point to something invisible in the painting. For example, they have a whole technique of painting bamboo in such a way that you see the wind; but it isn't just a question of seeing the wind – it isn't just a trick of painting bamboo so that you can see the wind, but in seeing bamboo in the wind, the way it's painted, you also see this central silence and quiescence and so forth, and that's the purpose. Chinese painting is profoundly contemplative. Now first of all, this means to say that you can't just do this by a trick. You have to learn this, and obviously this comes from inside the painter. It isn't a trick you learn by a coupon you clip out of a magazine and send it in, you get ten lessons free and then you pay for the rest and then after you're through, wham! – you do a painting and you can see the invisible! It comes obviously from a contemplative disposition in the painting. So here you get one of the painters, one of these Chinese painters – and there are a lot of nice quotes from Chinese painters here – he says, "He who is learning to paint must first learn to still his heart, and thus to clarify his understanding and increase his wisdom."[56] This is before you do anything, before

---

55. The reference seems to be to an anonymous vintage Japanese woodblock given the title "Lonely Fisherman," which closely matches the description provided by Merton, but does not seem to be nearly as well known as he indicates; see the illustration at www.worthpoint.com/worthopedia/vintage-japanese-woodblock-print-1904067062.

56. Mai-Mai Sze, *The Tao of Painting: A Study of the Ritual Disposition of Chinese Painting*, 2nd ed., 2 vols. in 1 (New York: Pantheon, 1963) 2.26; subsequent references will be cited as "Sze." Merton borrowed this book from his friends Victor and Carolyn Hammer when he was in Lexington for a medical check-up: see his journal entry for June 6, 1965 (*DWL* 253); five days later he writes: "I take delight in Mai Mai Sze's *Tao of Painting*, a deep and contemplative book. I am reading it slowly with great profit. She is becoming . . . one of my secret

you even take the first lesson or draw a line or anything. Before you start anything, you have to learn how to still your heart, to be quiet inside and so forth, because where the painting is going to come from is from the silence inside, and if a person doesn't have that silence, it doesn't matter how well he paints, it isn't going to be any good, because it's got to be a picture of this silence. It's got to communicate this central pivot of silence. "Then he should begin to study the basic brushstroke technique of one school and he should be sure that he is learning what he set out to learn, and that his heart and hand are in accord."[57] When he starts he gets everything silent inside, and then he learns the technique and learns to paint it in such a way that the silence is supposed to come down his arm, out his hand and through the brush and wham! It's on the paper; and if it isn't inside him it never gets on the paper, and the need to learn the brushstrokes – he has to learn the discipline that will get the silence from here down his arm onto the paper, and that is what he is trying to do; and of course what this silence is – another word is that it is spirit. He has to paint spirit, so that what he's got on the paper, what you see when you look at the paper when he's through, is spirit. Of course they don't paint on paper; they paint on silk. Well, they paint on a lot of things; they paint on paper too, but they paint on silk; and the chief concern is this spirit, which is a kind of integration. In terms of the picture, it's a kind of integration of visible and invisible elements, white spaces and black lines – that's what a picture is. A picture is not made up just of lines and colors; it's made up of lines and colors and blank spaces. This is true of all good art.

But sometimes you get European art, or the Renaissance – the chief idea was to fill in all the spaces. Well all right, if you fill in all the spaces you get a very elaborate painting, it takes longer, and there's a lot of things you can do, but the best art is that which speaks by means of blank spaces to a great extent, and the mere idea of just filling up everything for the sake of filling it up doesn't make sense, although that's the way kids paint. Kids draw pictures; when a kid draws a picture, you can't have him have too much sky left. You've got to have the whole blamed thing full of birds! It's easy to make birds because you just make a v, so a kid draws

---

loves" (*DWL* 255).

57. Sze 2.26-27, which reads: "He should then . . . School. He should be sure . . . that heart . . . ."

a house and having drawn the house he puts in every brick on the house and in every window there's somebody looking out, and then he puts every blade of grass on the lawn and then he puts a few animals on the lawn and then he fills the sky with v's for birds and where there's a little space further up where he hasn't got a bird, he puts a cloud.[58] Okay, this is fine; there's nothing wrong with it, but there are other ways of doing it.

You can express something by a blank space, but the blank space is meaningful insofar as the heart and the hand are attuned. Now there's an African proverb that says that if the heart of the dancer isn't right the rhythm of the drum is going to go wrong. This gets into the idea of communal participation in the thing. This is a very true thing, because here again you get a different dimension. You've got people participating together but where the heart is right then everything can get together and it can start moving and this is true. You think in terms of dancing or that sort of thing. Thus you have to think of it in terms of our choir too. We depend on our choir to make our heart right, whereas it's the other way around. If the heart's right, the choir is going to be great. If the heart isn't right, no matter what you're going to do with the choir, it's not going to mean anything. It starts inside and it's a communion of what's inside various different people.

Now let's get down to this idea of Chinese landscape. The Chinese landscape has got to show you the invisible. Chinese landscape – it's a picture of the Chinese idea of how things are constituted. The Chinese idea of how things are constituted is that you've got two principles working together, and that the combination of these two principles brings out the reality. The two principles are *yang* and *yin*. You've heard of this before: one is the masculine, the strong principle, and the other is the feminine and passive principle. Now that's not as simple as it looks, but nevertheless all through these landscape paintings, you get an expression of these two principles. So you have to have certain elements that are strong and rugged and black and dark and so forth, and then you have to have empty spaces. But now the funny thing is, it isn't the way you think it. You have, for example, the Chinese word for landscape painting

58. This description is reminiscent of Merton's well-known poem "Grace's House" (Thomas Merton, *Emblems of a Season of Fury* [New York: New Directions, 1963] 28-29; Thomas Merton, *The Collected Poems of Thomas Merton* [New York: New Directions, 1977] 330-31), though the perspective of the poem on the child's drawing is much more positive.

is mountain-water painting. It's painting in which you've got mountain and water and you've also got sky, and you've also got people, and you've got a path, usually, and you've got a house or something like that, with some trees and so forth. All these elements have to be in it in order to get the desired effect. Now you would say, okay, the strong, masculine element is the mountains, and then the passive feminine element is the water and the sky. Not necessarily so at all, because in Chinese thought the most masculine thing is heaven, or the sky. It is from heaven and the sky and the light and so forth that everything comes, so you're painting a landscape picture, you have to do it in such a way that the power comes from the sky and from the empty spaces, and whereas earth and so forth is feminine, your mountains have a tendency to have a feminine aspect – but on the other hand since they're big and rugged and rocky they're also masculine. Now what have you got to have in a landscape? The mountains have to be full of life, and so in a Chinese landscape, what doesn't it have to be? What's the obvious thing that it doesn't have to be? And if you've ever seen a Chinese landscape, you'll see it isn't. What are they not trying to be? It doesn't have to be at all an absolutely realistic representation. For example if the Chinese landscape painter wants to paint a landscape, the last thing he does is pick up his paper and pencil and run out to a landscape and look at it. That's just what he doesn't do. That's the last thing in the world that he does. It's the first thing that we would do. You tell somebody to paint a landscape, they're going to pick up their trappings and run out there and look at this landscape and copy it down on a piece of paper and come back with something that's like a photograph, only not quite so good.

No, what they do is, this landscape has to be the spirit of landscape, and so they have different ways of rendering cliffs and waterfalls and so forth. Now there's a rule for what you do with water in a Chinese landscape: what must water do? It must suggest the source from which it comes. Okay, so now you've got your sky, and you've got your mountains and you've got a waterfall; and what you get then is the idea of the water coming from someplace that you don't see. This is always very important. That's one very important element. Another thing that is necessary in this picture of mountains and so forth is, the mountains always have to have many inaccessible places where you obviously can't get. This isn't something that you think about, but it's just there. It has an effect.

That's one of the things about Chinese mountains, is that obviously you couldn't climb most of them. It would be utterly impossible to get to the top of most of these mountains. So you've got inaccessible tops of mountains; you've got water coming from an invisible source; then the thing that you have to have, is if you've got people in the picture – they're not always obviously going someplace, but they obviously have someplace to go to or to come from. Very often they're on a road that's leading off someplace up into the mountains, you don't know where. You can see now from the explanation I gave you about the silence business and this inaccessible stuff, you can see how this all suggests this journey to what you don't see, to what you can't touch, to what isn't evident to the senses and so forth, so there's always a road going back up into the mountains, into the woods and so forth, and usually there's a couple of people on the road, and they're sort of going along; they're not in a rush; they're obviously going quite slowly and quietly; maybe they've got an oxcart or something, they're just riding along in an oxcart, back into this place – you don't know where it is. This is very important too; or else they're just standing around, looking off somewhere. What do you suppose something like this does? Well it gives it as a kind of contemplative atmosphere, and usually the figures are sort of solitary figures. (In some Chinese paintings you get these armies going through – it's a different style.) They're just quiet and solitary and alone, and they're thinking. You can see that their mind is going off into this silent, distant place, and then finally you may have somebody just sitting there and thinking. Now the general effect of all this, you put all this together, and what happens? It's that if you have all this kind and background and you start looking at this kind of picture, you can see that what it does, it simply puts you in contact with something that is not visible and which is present in the mind of the artist, and which is present in you, although you didn't know it.

So the function of this kind of art, then, is to bring out in you something that you didn't know was there, an awareness that you didn't think you had. This is the purpose of this kind of art. It's the purpose of good poetry; it's the purpose of liturgy; it's the purpose of anything; and this is the purpose of the monastic life. We have to learn how to live in such a way that everything that we do and the way in which we do it and so forth brings us into contact with this invisible center that we just don't see and so forth. The essential thing in monastic formation is learning this. If you put this now in terms of virtues – because it can be reduced to something else; it can be reduced to terms of virtues – how would you tie this in with some of the familiar monastic virtues? Humility does in the moral and ascetic order what all these other things do in art and poetry and so forth. Why does humility do this? because humility brings us into contact with this center, with this pivot, because it is the law of being to humble that which is not humble. The word that I've been using has been pivot or center, but the Chinese word for this – you might as well know it now – is *tao*, and this is one of the great central ideas of Chinese thought, and that just means the idea of the pivot, the center and so forth. When John Wu was translating the Gospel of St. John into Chinese, he opened the translation with "In the beginning was the Tao"[59] – "In the beginning was the Word"[60] – the Logos and so forth. It can represent what we mean by the Word of God. In fact it can represent God, if you like. The highest concept of the *tao* is the ineffable, and then the next highest concept is the creative power that comes from this hidden ineffableness, and finally, on the lower level there is the *tao* of man, which is the level on which we in our conduct are in union with these hidden principles which come from God – union with the will of God. Now what *tao* does, it is itself the most humble of all beings. It is infinite littleness, and therefore infinite greatness – not the other way around. You could put it other way around if you want to – the reason why it's invisible is it's too little; it's not that it's too great, put it that way – and out of this littleness, which is so little it's nothing, comes everything. Now the force and power of this littleness is to diminish everything that's great and you'll find that this is the law of the New Testament, and this comes in the Magnificat of Our Blessed Mother: "He has put down . . ."[61] The law of *tao* is that all the mighty are going to be put down from their seats because the greatest power is little, and everything that is great is going to be put down and destroyed by this littleness. So now here you get this idea: "It is the tao of Heaven to diminish the puffed up and to augment the modest."[62] It goes two ways, because that which is little is in accord with the *tao* and therefore

---

59. See Merton, "Love and Tao" (*MZM* 72).

60. John 1:1.

61. Luke 1:52.

62. Commentary on the modesty hexagram of the *I Ching*, quoted in Fung 101.

it is full of power and presence and so forth. "It is the tao of Earth to subvert the puffed up and give free course to the modest and it is the tao of man to hate the puffed up and delight in the modest. Modesty in a high position sheds lustre on it; in a low position it cannot pass unobserved. This is the final goal of the man of moral intelligence."[63] So the whole center of the moral life, then, is just like your picture, in which the blank spaces and so forth lead the mind to that which is nothing and which is not visible.

The whole idea of the moral life and of the ascetic life is reducing our self-esteem and reducing our aggressiveness and reducing our desire to make an impression. Once we get rid of all that, we are in the center, but if we don't do this, if all we do all the time is aimed at affirming ourselves, then in the end we're building something that is going to have to be destroyed. I can see you're not clicking too well on this! Maybe you don't like this idea, but it's really very fundamental. It's most important. The silence that's in ourself, the silence that we find in our heart, is actually proportionate to humility. A person who is not humble is not silent – I don't mean in terms of making signs and so forth but in terms of interior silence.

CONFERENCE 5: JULY 15, 1965[64]

Let's get back into this mysterious Chinese business that we were talking about here. Now what we're talking about really – this is a very urgent kind of subject in a way, because what we're talking about is just life, and here you have the wisdom of hundreds of years ago when people had reached a very deep apprehension of what life was all about, and this stuff that we've been talking about, with these diagrams – it's all deceptively simple, although it perhaps isn't as simple as all that either. It looks as though I'm giving you something. I draw these things and then I put an "a" there and a "b" there, and then I put something in the center. It looks great. It looks as though there's an answer to something. But right away you have to understand that this isn't an answer to anything, because to begin with – what about finding this center? All this stuff is nice – to sit here and talk about this center, the spiritual center, but what's it

---

63. Quoted in Fung 101, which reads: ". . . and to give free . . . modest. It is . . . and to delight in . . . sheds a lustre . . . pass by unobserved. . . ."

64. The recording of this conference (Gethsemani #151.2) was previously issued by Credence Cassettes as "Community and Transformation" (2371.2).

all about? What is it? What are we really talking about here? To begin with, it's highly figurative language. It's purely myth, if you like. What actually is this whole thing? How can you find this particular kind of a center? Do you just sort of go to the library and look up a book: *How to Find the Center*? There are answers on how to find God, but on the other hand, when you talk in terms of this center thing, you're talking in terms of mysticism. The only way to really find this thing that we're talking about on the board, the only answer, is mystical. Now when you say mystical, that's no help to anybody! Why is that no help? I mean, supposing I tell you that something is mystical, what good does that do anybody? Why? What's the problem? What comes out of that if I say, it's mystical? What about it? Everybody has the capacity to reach this mystical center, but on the other hand it's not up to you – it is and it isn't. When I say, okay, this whole business about the center is mystical, it means to say that you can desire it if you want, but that doesn't guarantee that you're going to find it, because it isn't up to us in this realm.

Now okay, that having been said, that's as far as I'm going to go with that. I'm not going to give you any recipes or anything like that. All I'm going to say is that since this thing turns out to be mystical, and therefore not exactly up to us, human beings being what they are, and perfectly reasonable too, the idea is that you want to find some kind of a center that you *can* reach, which takes it off the mystical level and puts it on another level and on that level is what? If it's not on the mystical level, if it's on a level where our powers can attain to it, you call it what? On the level of metaphysical speculation – okay, that's a possibility. The more obvious one, because not everyone is a metaphysician? – faith? Alright, okay, if you put it on the level of faith you're getting once again back into the supernatural, but now we're talking about sixth-century B.C. China – they had faith, actually, but they didn't know it, perhaps. What I'm getting at mainly is the moral level. The moral level, you can find certain practical central positions that do sort of keep you in the middle where you're supposed to go.

The reason I bring this in is this brings us to the idea that's behind Greek tragedy. Greek tragedy is actually built around this whole concept of a center that's very hard to find, and of course how this comes into Greek tragedy, when we get to it, is in Greek tragedy what you always have is a character who is in some way extraordinary. He is, to begin with, an extraordinary person – it may be a woman:[65] she is an extraordinary person, and in an extraordinary situation, with an extraordinary kind of a problem, which they may not completely understand. They are put in a position where usually they are caught between two conflicting choices, and the whole idea of the tragedy is: what are they going to choose? Now of course this depends. This isn't so clear in the earliest tragedies, of Aeschylus and so forth, because Aeschylus hasn't quite developed this idea of choice so much. But in Sophocles this is the central thing. Sophocles always puts his people more or less in a position where they have to choose, make a difficult kind of choice, and what happens then is, in point of fact, as a result of their choice, they are destroyed, and the whole interest of the tragedy consists in seeing the relationship between the choosing and the destruction, and how does it happen that this person, having made this choice, is destroyed on account of it. Was he wrong or was he right? And the greatest of the tragedies are the ones where the person knows that he's going to be destroyed, and yet makes a choice, which is a heroic and right one, and yet is destroyed anyway; or you get other tragedies where he is sort of led into a choice that looks good, seems like the only obvious choice to make, and he makes it and it turns out to be extremely wrong, but for some reason that he didn't know; there's something involved in it that he didn't see; and so in Greek tragedy you've got people who, so to speak look for this center, and instead of finding it, they get destroyed.

So now this is where this begins to get interesting, because when you are talking about the center of everything in life, it's awful nice for us to sit back here and say, oh there is this beautiful center that we're going to head for and so forth. You've got to realize that one of things you're facing – you're facing not only fulfillment, but in the same breath, destruction; and if you want to talk seriously about the spiritual life or the mystical life, you have to take this into account. You don't play with this business, and that is why this life, with all its security and everything nice about it, it's a dangerous life. All life is dangerous, but especially the kind of life where you have done what you have done, where we're doing what we're doing: we're looking for the answer to everything. Because the thing is, as soon as you locate this center in some definite spot, you change the whole situation, because it isn't in any definite spot,

---

65. Merton is probably thinking particularly of Antigone here.

and if you say, on Tuesday the center was here, and that's where it's going to be all the time, and from then on out, everything else is in reference to this and Tuesday the center was to the right of this post in the conference room, and so therefore that's where it's going to be Wednesday, Thursday, Friday, Saturday and Sunday – you may come here Sunday and find God knows what – death sitting there or something like that – because the center is very closely related to death, and this business of finding the center is also the business of facing death, and that's where this power of Greek tragedy comes in, because Greek tragedy is very aware of this, and so Greek tragedy doesn't talk about the center in these Chinese terms, but it does talk about death.

Hence that puts it on a very existentialist kind of a plane; and then talking about death it also talks about humility, because after all what is more humiliating than to die? Humiliation takes you down, reduces you to about as low as you can get. Well, death does that. After you're dead, there's nothing left. There's a body, but your soul is gone and so forth, but I mean, to die, you're just about as reduced as you can get. If you can think of any more effective way of getting reduced to nothing than die, well let me know! But you are diminished, shall we say, by death, and in Greek tragedy the conflict comes always between death and the gods and fate and all that sort of thing, and somebody whose life force is very well developed, and is so well developed that it's too well developed, and it develops into a form of pride; and so you have therefore in Greek tragedy this question of the person who seeks the center, so to speak, with pride, which means it's impossible to find it. It can't be done, and so therefore this shows you that life is full of these very curious and mysterious problems.

From the moment you say you're going to be a mystic, this is a very dangerous proposition, because it depends how you say it, and it depends what you mean by it, and if a person suddenly says, "Okay, here we go, let's jump on the bus marked mysticism and move," what he may mean by that could be something completely the opposite to what he thinks he means. What would be the wrong thing to mean by that – which everybody inevitably means, and which means he has to get it in the neck sooner or later? "I'm going to be bigger than I am now when this is over!" If this is the attitude that we have – and who hasn't – this is the attitude that means trouble. "I have tried this, and I have tried baseball, and that didn't go; then I've tried the bottle, and that was all right but it was too expensive and I ran out of money, so I entered the monastery [now this may be closer to autobiography than you realize!] but then I heard that there was this other trick kind of fulfillment and so that is what I'm going to shoot for. There's a lot of people outside that don't know about this, and I'm ahead of them, I'm smarter than these people, and I found my way into a Trappist monastery and I'm going to go for this, and then it's going to make me much more real than I am now."

Now if I have that idea in view, most of the time what this means is that what is most unreal about me is going to be stabilized for keeps, and I've won – and this isn't what you want. This isn't it, and so therefore, once again this gets you back to this kind of situation that we're looking for. It is not an affirmation of self, and to find this center is not to be fully affirmed, and what we are looking for is not a way of fully affirming ourselves, and we have to be quite careful about this in our life, because as distinct from the Asian traditions, in the Christian tradition, we don't have enough safeguards on this. The true safeguards – they're real obvious ones and so forth – but we don't pay too much attention to them. What are the safeguards? In Buddhism you've got all kinds of built-in safeguards telling you that you aren't there in the first place. Anything that you build up, you're building up nothing, so don't waste your time. Stop doing it, that kind of thing. We don't have that. On the contrary, with our emphasis on personalism and so forth, we're quite likely to mistake the whole thing, and think of this question of building up – a personal affirmation – and at the end of the road too there is sanctity: there I am, on a pedestal, with a halo and vigil lights all around me – not a very good likeness, but there it is.

But of course, what is the guarantee against that in Christianity? How do we get around that? What is the big safeguard – it isn't that somebody is always humiliating you – the Christian common life. In Christianity, if we realize what Christianity is all about, we realize that our perfection is Christ, in Christ, and that our perfection consists in being found fully in Christ, which is in the Mystical Body of Christ, which is in the Church, which means to say, losing ourselves, in a superficial sense, by giving ourselves in charity for the other, so that by charity, by constant renunciation of our own interests and our own projects and so forth, we disappear, so to speak. This is the way that one really does become

Christ – by constant surrender of his own preferences and so forth for somebody else. This is the Christian view of it. If you push the thing back far enough, you find that this is universal. This isn't just Christian. This is a universal solution.

So one last fling, then, on this Chinese philosophy thing and then I guess we will get back to the Greeks. Back in this period of Confucianism, around the time of Christ, you have this picture of man in the universe and what the answer's going to be now here. Confucianism is not mystical. The mind of Confucius is the mind of China. Chinese people aren't that mystical. They're moral, they're practical, and there's a lot of common sense involved in it, and there's a lot of humor involved in it, and it's right down to earth and your feet are on the ground and so forth. But this is a sort of a moral center that you can attain, so the practical answer to this is that if you aim at something that you really can attain, and what the center is going to be for each one is his place. This is the way this thing stacks up. If you find your place, if it's your place, for you you're in the center. If you're trying to get into somebody else's place, then you're no longer in the center, because what's the center for you isn't the center for him. The Confucian idea here is this *tao*, this moral *tao*, is your own place. This ties in with the Christian view because it's your place in relation to the other guy and his place. So now let me just give you the rundown on this. First of all, you've got the idea of a kind of a trinity, a trinity of heaven, earth and man.[66] Now this is a trinity that's sort of centered around the idea of life and growth and development and so forth, a trinity of creation. Now it's all symbolic, except that this business about man is to a great extent literally true. In this work of creation you've got three forces. (It's very interesting to think of this in terms of the theological trinity.) You've got three forces at work: you've got heaven, which produces all creatures – all creatures are

66. See *Chung Yung* (*Doctrine of the Mean*), quoted in Fung 109-10: "It is only the man who is entirely real in this world who has the capacity to give full development to his human nature. If he has that capacity, it follows that he has the capacity to give full development to other men's human nature. If he has that capacity, it follows that he has the capacity to give full development to the natures of all species of things. Thus it is possible for him to be assisting the transforming and nourishing work of Heaven-and-Earth. That being so, it is possible for him to be part of a trinity of Heaven, Earth and himself. . . . It is only the man who is completely real in the world, who can weave the fabric of the great basic strands in human society, who can establish the great foundations of this world, and who can understand the transforming and nourishing work of Heaven-and-Earth."

produced and brought into being by heaven; and you've got earth, which nourishes all creatures and this is all very nice. This is sort of a standard Chinese cosmology and everything's great so far. But now you've got one other element that comes in, and what is this other element going to be? water? fire? uranium? You've got heaven which produces all creatures, and you've got earth, which nourishes all creatures. What does the world need? We've got our picture of the world. It needs one more thing to be the world: man – and this is a very beautiful idea, actually. Man is necessary to complete all creatures. I think this is a terrific philosophical idea. This is one of the best things that came out of Confucianism. It's a beautiful idea of heaven producing all things, earth nourishing all things, and man completing all things. We're going to see how this works, because this isn't just man completing all things just by being around, just by walking upright and looking them over and so forth. He appreciates all these things, but there is also a real active contribution that he brings into this.

To see this active contribution we've got to see the two things that man has to do. (We've got a lot to say in ten minutes – I'll have to say as much as I can and try and get it as clear as possible.) This gets to be very like St. Bernard. This is very Cistercian, what he's going to say now, because the power that gives man this ability to complete the whole creation is the power to appreciate and, push it one further, what's the highest power that man has – to love. Man has this capacity to love and it's by his capacity to love right away you can see it's going to be creative. It's going to be free. By this capacity to love, he completes all creation, and this capacity to love is not automatic. This capacity to love involves, right away, in itself, in man's actual existential condition, it involves a problem. Why does it involve a problem? This is old stuff. You've had all this many times. What is the big problem? If man has a faculty to love, why doesn't he just love and complete the universe? He can either love in a greedy way or in an unselfish way. His love can be greed or his love can be, in the Chinese term, what they call human-heartedness,[67] which is to say charity, which is to say, that he can love disinterestedly; he can love other people, he can love his brother as himself, and so this is not automatic. It depends what he chooses. This is as close to Christianity as anything I can see, except it hasn't got Our Lord in it, but this is a basically Christian

67. I.e. *jên*.

philosophy. It's a Christian view of life. So here you have the earth and all this productive force and life and so forth, and then of course suffering comes in, as a result of the wrong choice. If man chooses to love selfishly, then automatically suffering follows, because selfish love means suffering – although it seems to mean pleasure. That of course is one of the big ambiguities of life: as soon as I choose a pleasure for myself, I am automatically by that same act choosing suffering for myself and suffering for somebody else, and this follows – this never fails. You may not see it right away. It may not be immediately evident. But it never fails. This is one of the laws, and Greek tragedy again is full of this, and Asian mysticism is full of this too. It's this idea that certain choices having been made, suffering has to inevitably follow, because the choice was a bad one, even though it looked like a good one – and again you find this in Greek tragedy: something happens to somebody of the third generation as a result of a choice that was made way back by somebody else, a selfish choice made by a father. It results in suffering for the daughter, and that becomes the tragedy, which is worked out, and the thing that they're always very clear about is the effect of these choices.

So now what's a man going to do with this love? He's got this power to love and he can love badly or he can love well; what's he going to do about it? How does he know? Well first of all, in life itself there is a law which says, this is still the right way to love. It's built into nature; it's built into man; it's built into the way things are constructed. What is this law? Formulate the law. This is the basic law of nature, the basic moral law. What is this basic moral law, the law by which our love is regulated: do to the other what you want him to do to you.[68] It has to be awful simple and it has to be obvious. It has to be right in us, and not just way down in the depths – on the surface. This is something that is hard to hide. No matter how selfish a person is, this remains obvious to him, although he may not pay any attention to it any more. It's quite obvious that when you're dealing with other people, this is always there to some extent, the idea that if I do this to him, would I like him to do that to me? We may not think about it, but it's implicit in our actions.

68. This is the phrasing of the so-called "Golden Rule" of Matthew 7:12; the Confucian equivalent, sometimes referred to as the "Silver Rule," is expressed negatively, as found in *Analects* 15.23: "What you do not want done to yourself, do not do to others" (*The Chinese Classics*. A Translation by James Legge, D.D. Part I Confucius [New York: John B. Alden, Publisher, 1891] 86); see also 12.2 (63).

So okay, a man lives according to this. He conforms to this, and by conforming to this law, which he has to do – if he doesn't do this he's punished – then he is already completing heaven and earth. That being the case, that's one part of it. That is the level of nature, but on top of this is another level. Now this is very important, and also it's very good. There is an area of freedom where he no longer is bound not to do this because it's bad, or to do this because it's good. There is the area where he can choose, and what area is this now, and what has this got to do with anything and why should we bother about and so forth? This is a very important area. What are some of the things that we can choose to do – not in a monastery necessarily; there are a lot of things that we can't choose in the monastery but you are normally free to choose. These are important things and they've got a very important place in this. What is something that you have chosen recently that you were allowed to choose? The way you wear your hair; the kind of clothes you wear; what you eat; the kind of music you listen to; the kind of pictures you like; the kind of books you read – you can choose all these things. This is very important. This is where you live. This is life. This is the area of culture. The way you wear your hair is a matter of culture. (We're more cultured now than when we had those nasty old crowns – horrible thing full of fleas all the time – it was most unsanitary, those things. It's a very good thing we finally got rid of them after the hundreds of years of medieval superstition!) Here's the thing where I think that this is extremely important. It's important because we neglect it. It took about a half-hour of fishing to get around to the fact that we admit that things like this even exist at all, but they're actually very important from the point of view of man completing in the world what has been left undone by heaven and earth. Therefore, heaven produces all creatures; earth nourishes all creatures; and man completes all creatures, first of all by loving in conformity with the laws of nature, and then by finishing the work. There's part of the job which is left for him to do, and that is the job of culture or civilization, and in this he's got an absolutely free choice – except of course when it runs into the question of the moral law: if I build myself a pagoda so high that it blocks off all the light for my neighbor's garden and he can't grow any more chop suey or something like that, this gets to be bad. I'm not doing right. My culture is interfering with his agriculture! The training of a man is a training of his freedom and his understanding and his intelligence and his tastes and so forth, so that he can, by his work and by his daily life and the things that he does, complete the work of heaven and earth.

Now actually, not every man gets into this as deeply as he should, and what is necessary is that certain men who are the ones that Confucius is most interested in training, the ones he calls the superior man or the noble man – these are the people. You're going to get a few rare people who fully develop in themselves this freedom and this capacity to complete the work of creation, and in doing this they bring out the same capacity in everybody else and so the real function of Confucian education – and you can put this right away on the basis of monastic formation too – the whole idea of monastic formation is to form people, some people anyway, who have a complete sense of what the monastic life is about, and who can develop the capacity of the monastic life and build up the monastic life so that it's worth living, and bring out these capacities in everybody else, so that you've got a society in which everybody is really living the life and really understanding what it's about and really doing something creative about it. The presence of us living here should add immensely to the value of just the woods and the trees and so forth that we've got around.

PART II
STUDIES

THOMAS MERTON
AND CONFUCIAN RITES:
"THE FIG LEAF FOR
THE PARADISE CONDITION"

John Wu, Jr.

INTRODUCTION: SEEKING PERSONAL INTEGRITY

As it has been well-documented, in the last decade of his life Thomas Merton tirelessly pointed directly to the hidden potential of ancient Asian traditions. The Christian monk had an abiding love affair with Asia and saw in the Asian a repository of an older wisdom that he felt the West lacked. Yet, however optimistically he may have felt about Asia and her hallowed past, Merton was never blind to her contemporary problems. Although he was never a Christian of the triumphalist persuasion, Merton nonetheless saw clearly the role that a revitalized Christianity might play in future cultural and spiritual revivals in the East. His concerns are clearly indicated in the following excerpt from a letter to a Chinese priest in California:

> I fully realize the complexity of the problem today. The Asians have renounced Asia. They want to be western, sometimes they are frantic about being western. . . . They feel that there have been centuries of inertia and stagnation, and there is a reaction against the humiliations and misunderstandings of colonialism, calling for a defeat of the west at its own technological game. All this is dangerous but inevitable. Christianity of course has a crucial part to play in saving all that is valuable in the east as well as in the west.[1]

Elsewhere, Merton appears to be echoing Mahatma Gandhi when

---

1. Thomas Merton, *The Road to Joy: Letters to New and Old Friends,* ed. Robert E. Daggy (New York: Farrar, Straus, Giroux, 1989) 322 (March 1962 letter to Rev. Thomas J. Liang).

he writes that Western man "is communicating his spiritual and mental sickness to men of the East. Asia is gravely tempted by the violence and activism of the West and is gradually losing hold of its traditional respect for silent wisdom."[2]

Merton's writings on the East show a boundless concern for nearly anything Asian. Many of his later writings and talks to his novices centered around Zen Buddhism, philosophical Taoism, and Sufism. I will examine an interest of Merton's which up to now few Mertonian scholars have dealt with, notably, *Ju Chia*, or Confucianism. I will show that Merton was able to see in Confucianism a dimension much overlooked until very recent decades. His essay "Classic Chinese Thought," in *Mystics and Zen Masters*,[3] along with my father's work on Confucius and Mencius, initially opened my eyes to Confucianism as an exceptional philosophy of the person aimed at social and political harmony and anchored solidly on an idea of ritual whose function is to disclose the dimension of the sacred in human society. To Merton, the main thrust of the thought of Confucius and Mencius (the latter, the greatest Confucian after the Master himself) lay in recovering one's humanity and in restoring the order of things as they are; this, in fact, meant the recovery of what he called the "paradise condition," which I shall also examine.

In an enlightening tape appropriately entitled "The Search for Wholeness," Merton the novice master connects scriptural writings with the basic concerns of Confucius. The American monk

---

2. "Honorable Reader," preface to the Japanese edition of *Thoughts in Solitude* in Thomas Merton, *"Honorable Reader": Reflections on My Work*, ed. Robert E. Daggy (New York: Crossroad, 1989) 115. See also *Beyond East and West* (New York: Sheed and Ward, 1951) in which my father, John C. H. Wu, writing of his beloved country two years after the Communist takeover, sings nostalgically of the old China and laments the new: "Now China has changed. She has been dragged into the swirl and whirl of the world. Like a leaf in the west wind, like a flower fallen upon the ever-flowing Yangtsze, she is no longer herself, but is being swept along against her will to an unknown destiny. I know she will survive all the storms and currents, and emerge victorious over all her trials and tribulations, but she will not recover the original tranquillity of her soul and sweetness of her temper. Her music will no longer be flute-like, reverberating with clear wind and running water: it will be turned into something metallic and coarse, like the Wagnerian masterpieces. To her son, she will no longer be the tender Mother that she was, but will be transformed into a stern Father, a Father who will be as severe as the summer sun. China my Motherland is dead, long live my Fatherland!" (16).

3. Thomas Merton, *Mystics and Zen Masters* (New York: Farrar, Straus and Giroux, 1967) 45-68.

enlists his unique perspective by cutting through the hard-crusted, centuries-old paraphernalia surrounding the much-maligned old sage of China. He says:

> The philosophy of Confucius aims at developing the person in such a way that he is a superior person. But what do you mean "superior"? It's not that he is a superman or any of this kind of nonsense, and it is not at all that he stands out over other people by winning. . . . Confucius doesn't have a philosophy on how to be a winner. . . . In contrast, the superior man in Confucius is the self-sacrificing man, the man who is formed in such a way that he knows how to give himself . . . that in giving himself, he realizes himself. This is what Confucius discovered, and this is a great discovery. . . . This is just as fundamental as anything can be.[4]

He goes on to say that Confucian love (*jen*), which we may also call humanheartedness or benevolence, implies full identification with and empathy for others. The proper carrying out of Confucian ritual or *li* (Merton, given his own experience as a monastic, understandably prefers the word liturgy) would in fact express the reality of humankind's relationship to the universe, in which we are given the insight into the way the universe is constructed; this is acted out in liturgy in both the sacred and secular realms, whose demarcation is, in fact, inseparable. Elsewhere in this same suggestive talk, Merton compares (if not actually raises) Confucian *li* to Christian notions of sanctification and sacramentality.

Merton then suggests that the basic Confucian virtues (which include righteousness and wisdom) resemble what he colloquially calls the "Benedictine setup" traditionally based on an elaborate structure of formal relationships whose ultimate goal is the "fully-developed personality." In fact, he hints that if monks live according to these basic principles, they will become complete persons. He does not elaborate as to whether he means "complete person" in the Confucian or Christian sense, or even if such a distinction ought to be entertained. Merton says the importance of Confucian wisdom is that it makes everything interior so that when one loves it is because:

---

4. Thomas Merton, "The Search for Wholeness," Credence Cassette, Merton AA2370, Side 2.

that is the way to be. . . . This is based on a vision of reality
. . . and this means really a kind of contemplation of reality,
a *contemplative* awareness of the way things are. And this
manifests itself in liturgy because a person knows how to
express himself in liturgy (since it is something learned
and/or handed down to him). *His liturgy is an expression
of . . . love.*[5]

To the monk of Gethsemani, the Confucian vision of reality is
"contemplative awareness" because he sees in it a preordained
wholeness imprinted indelibly in the heart of the person at birth.
Further, it is this deeply ingrained sense of wholeness, this sense
of oneness of life, that informs the Confucian person's relationships with others and with heaven. The true Confucian never goes
through ritualistic movements merely to fulfill personal and social
duties: rather, personal fulfillment is the perfect exchange of love
and compassion, of that deep commiserate feeling of identity with
the other, to wit, an exchange of human-heartedness (*jen*) and good
will at the sacred level of being.

Confucius shared with all dialogical thinkers the belief that
though the seeds of wholeness or the paradisaic condition may indeed be part and parcel of man, we nonetheless depend *existentially*
for our completion on others. There is, hence, the implicit belief in
the perfectibility of the person, that through proper study and the
learning and carrying out of rituals, the person may indeed come to
fulfill that original state of being for which he or she was destined
from the very beginning of his or her existence.[6]

To my mind, it is the spiritual and contemplative dimension and
not its rather prosaic ethical and social dimensions that gives Confucianism its true value and appeal. Without its *given* and encompassing wholeness, *Ju* could easily degenerate – and as Chinese history
so well attested to, has degenerated – into a rigid set of mechanized
social rituals whose sole aim would be to preserve a dead social
and political order or, at best, be a disconnected series of moral

---

5. Ibid. Emphasis added.

6. A thorough investigation into this question can be found in Donald J.
Munro, *The Concept of Man in Early China* (Stanford, CA: Stanford University
Press, 1969), in which the author's main thesis is that "men, lacking inner defects,
are perfectible through education." And adds, "The educational environment
determines whether or not men will be good or evil, and educational reform is
a key to the solution of urgent social and political problems" (preface, vii-viii).

aphorisms, both of which have been its fate since nearly its inception.

A close reading of *The Four Books* would convince us that these early Chinese classics were initially conceived as an organic way of life that long centuries of intensive systematization together with statecraft had emptied of their original energy and vision of wholeness. Merton's approach typifies his gifted ability to see through the deadly and choking provincialism of two millennia into what he felt was, at its core, perhaps, humanity's most universally-conceived *personalistic* philosophy.

When my wife, Terry, and I were at Merton's hermitage in June 1968, we noticed he had been reading Herbert Marcuse's *One-Dimensional Man*, which I too had just read for a college course. Nearly six months later, on the last day of his life on December 10, he was to make prominent mention of Marcuse in his last talk in Bangkok. At the time of our meeting, when I asked the monk why he was reading the neo-Marxist, instead of giving me the expected answer that Marcuse was "must reading" for his social and political thought – Marcuse then being the absolute darling on the more radical U.S. campuses – Merton confirmed for me what I, too, had hesitantly thought to be the real value of the book: Marcuse's fine critique regarding the utter usurpation and destruction of language by mass society, communistic *and* capitalistic. The socially prophetic Marcuse believed that society, with technology at its disposal, could order reality according to its own totalitarian or commercial ends, beginning with the control of the uses and abuses of language itself. The whole enterprise becomes ever more cynical when the services of psychology and other social sciences are enlisted to achieve their not-so-harmless aims. As the present world rides ever more enthusiastically on the shirttails of multinational enterprises that depend for their survival on the increasing utilization of language that is locked strictly into the language of the salesperson, we can see clearly the prophetic nature of Marcuse's warning of a coming world whose people have become immune to the inherent subtlety and beauty of words.

Beginning in the 1970s when I studied Confucianism in the Republic of China, I was reminded of Merton's interest in Marcuse and of his concern for the preservation of language, which, as I see it now, resembles the Confucian concern for *cheng ming* (正名) or what is conventionally accepted as *rectification of names*. This was the rather simple, common-sensical Confucian insight that the root of all social and political ills can largely be traced to the disharmony and personal and social alienation that ensue when we no longer give much thought to the importance of fitting names to realities. In a nutshell, we may say that disharmony and alienation occur when no one quite knows for certain who he or she is supposed to be; that is, when we have lost our identity or when, in the case of ideas, a concept such as love becomes for all practical purposes the dominant province of soap operas, ad agencies, and, most absurd and tragic of all, appropriated by totalitarian governments.

Both totalitarian regimes and capitalist societies (to which Merton fittingly gave the nicknames Gog and Magog, respectively[7]) abound with gross examples of such abuse. Societies as we know them could not flourish without conscious linguistic manipulations either by the state or Madison Avenue and Hollywood and, as I have suggested above, by worldwide multinationals in recent decades.

Confucius was able to see the root of both social and moral chaos in a person's inability to live according to who he or she is. The integral person – the famous Confucian gentleman, or what Merton calls the "superior man" – is the human being who has cultivated his or her ability to respond in a fully human way to each and every person and situation. This implies knowledge of one's identity and being free of all external coercion, political or commercial.

But cultivation also implies the understanding that there is in man and woman a constant growth in the realization of being, beginning with one's moral and aesthetic senses and finding its completion in spiritual fulfillment. The following well-known passage from *The Analects of Confucius* illustrates wonderfully the

---

7. See Thomas Merton, *The Courage for Truth: Letters to Writers*, ed. Christine M. Bochen (New York: Farrar, Straus & Giroux, 1993) 179. Bochen writes the following introduction to Thomas Merton's letters to the Nicaraguan poet Pablo Cuadra: "*In 1961, Merton wrote an article in the form of a letter to Cuadra. The well-known 'Letter to Pablo Antonio Cuadra Concerning Giants' was published in Nicaragua, Argentina, and El Salvador, as well as in Merton's* Emblems. *In it Merton denounced both the Soviet Union and the United States, whom he labeled Gog and Magog. 'Gog is a lover of power, Magog is absorbed in the cult of money: their idols differ and indeed their faces seem to be dead set against one another, but their madness is the same. . . . Be unlike the giants, Gog and Magog. Mark what they do, and act differently. . . . Their societies are becoming anthills, without purpose, without meaning, without spirit and joy.' The letter was 'a statement of where I stand morally, as a Christian writer,' Merton wrote to Cuadra on September 18, 1961.*"

Confucian sense of moral and spiritual progress, perhaps the only progress that really matters and is intrinsic to persons. It indicates quite clearly the unlimited spiritual potential suggested throughout early Confucianism and serves as a healthy counterbalance to notions of progress that govern our contemporary lives. To my mind, the progression the Chinese sage is pointing toward is a truer understanding of our being, for he is here resituating for us the entire notion of progress in the qualitative possibilities of life itself:

> The Master said, At fifteen I set my heart upon learning. At thirty, I had planted my feet firm upon the ground. At forty, I no longer suffered from perplexities. At fifty, I knew what were the biddings of Heaven. At sixty, I heard them with docile ear. At seventy, I could follow the dictates of my own heart, for what I desired no longer overstepped the boundaries of right.[8]

RITUALS AND THE WHOLENESS OF LIFE

Perhaps it is imprudent to lump together a monk/writer of the twentieth century with one of the paradigms of world history. Yet, one cannot help finding common ground in their thought. Like Confucius, Merton knew the importance of keeping the light of classical learning burning, which was, of course, an old monastic tradition. His talks and conferences to student novices and fellow monks are a testament of his respect for such studies. In fact, one of his main concerns with regard to his students was that, in entering monastic life, they had not sufficiently prepared themselves in either the basic classics or good literary works, past or present. To his credit, even though he was a religious, he did not find it necessary to make hard and fast distinctions between so-called sacred and secular literatures.

To Confucius, classical learning and all that it implies was the very lifeline of a race of people, the repository without which humans soon would degenerate into mere barbarians not only without social graces – which seems to have been the least of his concerns – but without any notion as to where he or she is rooted. In fact, one could conclude that his principal motivation was the very recovery of classical learning itself. For without classical learning – which

8. Arthur Waley, trans., *The Analects of Confucius* (New York: Vintage, 1938) 88.

Confucius considered the human person's essential didactic tool –
one becomes morally and spiritually directionless. To Merton, too,
an intimate knowledge and love of the classics was no less critical.
Here is what he had to say regarding the relationship among classical learning, Confucian humanism, and the human personality, on
the one hand, and his debunking of the shallow, modernist attempt
to come to terms with the person, on the other hand:

> The foundation of [the] Confucian system is first of all the
> *human person* and then his relations with other persons
> in society. This of course sounds quite modern – because
> one of our illusions about ourselves is that we have finally
> discovered "personality" and "personalism" in the twen-
> tieth century. Such are the advantages of not having had
> a classical education, which would do us the disservice
> of reminding us that personalism was very much alive in
> the sixth century B.C., and that, in fact, it existed then in a
> much more authentic form than it does among us with our
> "personality tests" and "personality problems" (the ultimate
> carving of the Taoist uncarved block!). *Ju* [Confucianism]
> is therefore a humanist and personalist doctrine, and this
> humanism is religious and sacred.[9]

Then Merton seems to draw directly from his own experience as a
member of a community of monks when he says:

> The society in which [men would once again be themselves,
> and would gradually recover the ability to act virtuously,
> kindly, and mercifully] must be very seriously and firmly
> held together by a social order that draws its strength not
> from the authority of law but from the deep and sacred
> significance of liturgical rites, *Li*.

And in the same vein, he adds almost rhapsodically: "These rites,
which bring earth into harmony with heaven, are not merely the cult
of heaven itself but also the expression of those affective relationships which, in their varying degrees, bind men to one another."[10]
Finally, he reveals what to me is the quintessential humanistic
Merton of the mid- and late-1960s, in which he speaks surely not
only for Confucianism but for himself as well: "The Confucian

9. *Mystics and Zen Masters* 51.
10. Ibid. 52.

system of rites was meant to give full expression to that natural and humane love which is the only genuine guarantee of peace and unity in society, and which produces that unity not by imposing it from without but by *bringing it out from within men themselves*."[11]

Confucianism in its purest form is a philosophy of the interior person and ought never to be associated with ideas that bespeak or are suggestive of determinism or social necessity. Merton's treatment of Confucian rituals may indeed be an idealization, but its great advantage is that it points out certain possibilities as to what rituals – particularly those that concern human relationships – may suggest when practiced to their fullest, that is, as vehicles revealing latent human tendencies that the Confucianists themselves may not have imagined existed. Merton points out the potentially rich *existential* content of what Confucius may have had only an inkling, but whose richly suggestive quality makes the idea worth exploring given the nature of its open-endedness.

Due to the sacredness with which Confucius regarded *any* ritual, religious or interpersonal, and the organic and holistic manner in which the early Confucianists naturally perceived the world – indeed, as *cosmos*, as had the Greeks – the potential for development of a truly flourishing and open-ended *personalist* philosophy of life would seem to be boundless. Merton helps us see the Chinese sage in an altogether new light.

The Confucian rectification of names and the notion of reciprocity[12] in human relations, rather than suggesting rigidification

---

11. Ibid.

12. As Confucius says in *The Analects*, trans. Arthur Waley (New York: Vintage, 1938): "The man of jen (仁) wishes to establish his own character, also helps others along the path" (VI, 28). For an explanation of the notion of reciprocity, see Y. F. Mei, "The Basis of Social, Ethical, and Spiritual Values in Chinese Philosophy," *The Chinese Mind*, ed. Charles A. Moore (Honolulu: University of Hawaii Press, 1967) 149-66, in which the author writes: "Confucius repeatedly spoke of his 'one unifying principle,' which is also rendered as 'an all-pervading unity.' This unifying principle is generally assumed to be shu (恕), reciprocity, which Confucius once said was the one word that might guide one's conduct throughout life, Reciprocity was stated to be 'what you would not have others do unto you, do not (do) unto others,' and this formula has usually been referred to as the Chinese Golden Rule. . . . *Jen* is . . . the cornerstone of Confucianism, and it may be assumed that reciprocity . . . is an expression of *jen*, and that it is just as proper to regard *jen* as the one unifying principle of all of Confucius' teachings. Historically, *jen* is a distinct Confucian concept, a concept little used before his time" (152). See also Wing-tsit Chan, "Chinese Theory and Practice," *The Chinese Mind*, trans. James Legge (Oxford: Oxford University Press, 1939) 11-30. Chan writes the following

of the family and social strata, can be regarded as ideas that, when carried out with deference, benevolence, and deep charity, lend themselves to the gradual actualization of those hidden qualities in all of us. How? Through an unmasking process brought about by commonplace, everyday ritual practices. It is essentially related to the understanding of human personality, not exclusively in a psychological sense within which we modernists tend to confine the whole of it, that is, as largely behaviorist phenomena, but in deeply existential, moral, and spiritual terms that emphasize the process of self-effacement and self-emptying, which are basic concerns of both the Taoist and the Zen Buddhist and of nearly all mystical traditions in the West. Further, it is related less to the absorption by the other – which is suggestive of a psychologically coercive relationship – than identification with the other at the level of being. When performed with the proper attitude, the action would naturally disclose what is deepest and, in the process, transform the participants.

Hence, the key to the progressive unfolding of the true self lies in reciprocity, which we may broadly define as the willingness of a person to allow the deepest yet most natural, expansive, and magnanimous impulses to come into play in his or her life. It says plainly to the other, I want to give to you because in the giving is revealed my true self. Further, it lies in never permitting this sacred exchange between persons – an exchange, as I have suggested above, at the level of *being* rather than *having* – to degenerate into the endless giving and returning of external favors, a social cult quite unrelated to genuine filial or fraternal feelings born fully of the spirit of benevolence and love. Surely it is not rooted in familial, social, or political pressure or coercion, that is, in the conventionally tiresome and perfunctorily carrying out of duty for the sole purpose of fulfilling an obligation, and, at its crudest form, mere face-saving.[13]

---

regarding the Golden Mean, or what he calls "central harmony": "Confucius said that 'there is one thread that runs through my doctrines.' . . . The thread is . . . generally to be identical with the Confucian doctrine of central harmony (*chung yung*, Golden Mean). Indeed, the doctrine is of supreme importance in Chinese philosophy; it is not only the backbone of Confucianism, both ancient and modern, but also of Chinese philosophy as a whole. Confucius said that 'to be central (*chung*) in our being and to be harmonious (*yung*) with all' is the supreme attainment in our moral life" (35).

13. For a rather extensive but wholly interesting elaboration and documentation on the ubiquitous issue of face in Chinese society, see "Face Saving

To Thomas Merton, the person or human personality is a manifestation of human nature transformed and divinized and made hallowed by the inherent sacredness of life. But the sacred, as he learned in his monastic experience, can only be experienced through the concrete ritual act which, if performed with a sincere and humble heart and directed wholly toward the other, goes a very long way in humanizing those involved. Yet, ironically, the real boon of any ritual act that is part and parcel of this humanizing process is the natural coming together of the sacred and the secular, the experience of the wholeness of being in which we, in finding identity in the other, become one with the universe as well. This, I think, is Confucianism at its most profound and the reason Merton felt he could speak so affirmatively of classical Confucianism as having understood the meaning of true personality and universal harmony that mirror one another. Confucianists have never made any Procrustean distinctions about harmony found in people, society, and the universe.

In Merton's delightful essay "A Study of Chuang Tzu," preceding his "imitations" of the great Chinese Taoist sage, he says, "To give priority to the person means respecting the unique and inalienable value of the *other* person, as well as one's own."[14] No doubt "inalienable value" refers to that sacred element in the person without which rituals would be wholly empty, a mere going through the motion. In fact, the end of ritual is partial fulfillment of one's personality through a mutual exchange on a very deep level of the mystery of being informed by the guiding light of *Tien* (天) or heaven. The ritual act, while taking the two persons to an altogether different depth, makes the participants aware of the ground of being upon which their lives are anchored. The sacred is never "out there" as much as it is in us as a guiding principle of life; in fact, it is irrevocably there for all eternity, and the deference we show toward others in relationship is to predispose the ever-present sacred to show its face whenever it sees fit to do so. And if we understand Confucius correctly, we may infer that *Tien* – the sacred – when listened to "with docile ear," indeed can inform the heart in such a way that all words will find their rightful resting place in actions

as a Way of Life" in Richard W. Hartzell's book *Harmony in Conflict* (Taipei, Taiwan, ROC: Caves Books Ltd., 1988) 305-76.

14. Thomas Merton, *The Way of Chuang Tzu* (New York: New Directions, 1965) 17.

that will keep within "the boundaries of right," that is, within the measure and pivot of central harmony (*chung yung*).

Perhaps for this reason the Sinologist Julia Ching has written so enthusiastically about the possible future revival of Confucianism, not as statecraft, but as perennial philosophy. As she puts it so aptly, "To survive and to be of use to modern man, Confucianism must become young again, as in the days of its first gestation."[15]

The material form of Confucian ritual may follow a certain well-defined pattern, but what is encountered in the ritual (for example, the lovely tea ceremony) is conditioned primarily by the right attitude of the heart the participants bring into the act. The spirit, in other words, is free and undetermined, and the degree to which this freedom roams depends very much on the freedom, maturity, and depth of the persons involved. And this is as it should be, for the ritual – seemingly stylized and rigid – is never mechanical and, if performed with correctness of attitude, is wholly personal. What is exchanged is *unspeakable* and beyond language; more significantly, it is never repeated. In fact, because in any true action language and the concrete act merge into one, the act is the language itself.[16]

Rituals, then, properly performed, can play the role of con-

---

15. Julia Ching, *Confucianism and Christianity: A Comparative Study* (Tokyo/New York/San Francisco: Kodansha International/USA, 1978) 63.

16. Merton himself illustrates this point of *act* as *language*. In responding to my father's gift of Chinese calligraphy and the poem Mei Teng ("Silent Lamp"), a Chinese sobriquet that the older man gave the younger monk, Merton in a typically playful Zen mood replies: "So it was moving to be 'baptized' in Chinese with a name I must live up to. After all, a name indicates a divine demand. Hence I must be Mei Teng, a silent lamp, not a sputtering one. . . . Your calligraphy fascinates me, and of course so does the poem . . . . I wish I could reply in kind, calligraphy and all. In desperation, or rather no, in considerable joy, I resort again to the green tea, and in fact the kettle is whistling by the fire right at my elbow, and the sun is rising over the completely silver landscape. Instead of putting all this into a poem, I will let it be its own poem. The silent steam will rise from the teacup and make an ideogram for you. Maybe sometime I will add a poem to it as an exclamation point of my own. But are such exclamation points needed?" (Thomas Merton, *The Hidden Ground of Love*, selected and ed. William H. Shannon [New York: Farrar, Straus & Giroux, 1985] 632; letter dated December 28, 1965.) The above seems to be an extraordinary spiritual insight. Words can only serve as footnotes to what is. The action/act is always primary as long as it expresses the fullness of being. Hence the tree trees, the steam steams, man mans, brother brothers, etc. Anything less than "steam steams" is an alienation of/from being. In "man mans," man is both the substantive and the predicate, and, in the end, there is, in fact, only "man," a merging of the doer and the doing. And if we really took all this very seriously, the rest would be silence.

tinuously helping to redefine the self in the most concrete and flesh-and-blood way, directing us to our proper place in the world and gradually disclosing the latent potential that lies dormant in us, in others, and, in the process, in what is hidden in life itself. With rituals, life can assume a grace, dignity, and depth hitherto lost, even disposing us to true contemplation. For the final aim of ritual is not so much aesthetic or even moral, but realization of the deep mystery of being that unaccountably shapes each relationship.

Rituals, beginning with forgetfulness of self and informed by charity and deference toward others, remind us not to press forward aggressively with our plans and schemes, an attitude and behavior that would unwittingly shrink the possibilities of what lies before us and in us. On the contrary, in being deferential toward others, in learning to step back and refusing to impose our will – which is what interpersonal rituals encourage – we are able to see uncovering before us the full measure of dignity in each person so that in the process of discovering that dignity, we recover our own dignity as well. In that discovery lie the seeds for our transformation into our true selves, or, as it were, the Confucian gentleman, the *chun tzu*.

CONFUCIANISM AND THE REVIVAL OF HUMANISM

Confucius, at least for the more progressive Chinese today, has not and perhaps never will fully recover from the onslaught of the May Fourth Movement,[17] whose reverberations continue unmitigated to this day. In this century, no sage has been discredited and cast aside more often and indiscriminately than Confucius, first by the proponents of the May Fourth Movement, then by the Communists' ongoing polemic. How ironic it is, then, that it has taken Western thinkers such as Karl Jaspers, Donald Munro, Herbert Fingarette, Benjamin I. Schwartz, Merton and others, or Asian thinkers trained in the West such as Wing-tsit Chan, my father, John C. H. Wu, Julia Ching, and Tu Wei-ming, to see in the Chinese sage the seeds of a future renaissance. Others, even scholars who perhaps should know better, seem to be caught in endless political squabbles over what

---

17. For a good historical discussion of this very important social and intellectual revolution in early twentieth-century Republican China, see Chow Tse-tsung, *The May Fourth Movement: Intellectual Revolution in Modern China* (Cambridge, MA: Harvard University Press, 1960) especially 300-13, on the controversies surrounding the anti-Confucian movement, which seemed to have set the intellectual, social, and moral tone for the rest of the century in China.

ought to be done with Confucius. What we do know is that the old fellow refuses to go away.[18]

Toward the end of *Mystics and Zen Masters*, in the essay "The Other Side of Despair," Merton writes of the horrors of faceless or "mass man," a perfect contrast to what he felt was the essence of Confucian humanism and personalism:

> Mass society . . . isolates each individual subject from his immediate neighbor, reducing him to a state of impersonal, purely formal, and abstract relationship with other objectified individuals. In dissolving the more intimate and personal bonds of life in the family and of the small sub-group (the farm, the shop of the artisan, the village, the town, the small business), mass society segregates the individual from the concrete and human "other" and leaves him alone and unaided in the presence of the Faceless, the collective void, the public. Thus . . . mass-man finds himself related not to flesh and blood human beings with the same freedom, responsibility, and conflicts as himself, but with the idealized typological images: the Führer, the

---

18. See Ching, "Confucianism: A Critical Reassessment of the Heritage" (*Confucianism and Christianity* 34-67). Some choice excerpts will suffice: "The critics today judge [Confucius] to have been 'irrelevant' to his own time, indeed, a reactionary and counter revolutionary who impeded the course of history. . . . His class-biased teachings can have no universal meaning, his thought was unoriginal, 'eclectic,' compromising, his scholarship was mediocre, and even his personal character is being assailed: he was no sage, but a hypocrite" (52). "The fall of Confucianism as an ethical system is bringing about a total spiritual vacuum. The alternative is to be the new, still evolving Maoist ethic, with its emphasis of serving the people. But the new ethic still lacks complete structuring and comes to the people, not from below, but from above. The message of Legalism is obvious. Faith in authority, that characteristic so much criticized in Confucianism, is not being assailed in itself. But the final arbiter of conscience has changed. It is now the state" (60). Ching asks the question, "Is Confucianism relevant?" to which she gives the following rather upbeat comments: "If we . . . mean by it a dynamic discovery of the worth of the human person, of his possibilities of moral greatness and even sagehood, of his fundamental relationship to others in a human society based on ethical values, of a metaphysics of the self open to the transcendent, then Confucianism is very relevant, and will always be relevant. And if, going further, we desire for Confucianism an openness to change and transformation, through confrontation with new values and ideas coming from other teachings – such as earlier from Buddhism – through a readiness to evaluate itself critically as well, then Confucianism is not only relevant but in possession of a future" (63-64).

president, the sports star, the teen singer, the space man.[19]

One of Merton's chief concerns – and here I believe he was prophetic as he was in so many other areas of concern – was his fear that the milieu, "a certain cultural and spiritual atmosphere" that "favors the secret and spontaneous development of the inner self," has disappeared. In contrast to ancient cultural traditions in both the East and the West, which "favored the interior life and indeed transmitted certain common materials in the form of archetypal symbols, liturgical rites, art, poetry, philosophy, and myth which nourished the inner self from childhood to maturity," Merton resigned himself into believing that "such a cultural setting no longer exists in the West, or is no longer common property."[20] And we might add with some trepidation that with the dawning of modernization such a setting no longer exists in the East either. In fact, what has happened in the East would have confirmed his worst suspicions as to the direction the East has been taking since his passing.

Merton, beginning with his own student novices, was very concerned with the rediscovery and the uncovering of common cultural materials conducive to the recovery of the true self. He did not hesitate to explore geographies of the mind and heart that appeared to be esoteric and obscure to his readers. The monk was disturbed by the obsessive emphasis on discursive thought that he felt had disproportionately contributed to the problems of the contemporary West. He actively sought after more affective ways of thinking and living that would help bring us directly back to both ourselves and God.

On the first leg of his journey to Asia, while speaking at the Center for the Study of Democratic Institutions, a think tank in Santa Barbara, California (October 3, 1968), Merton made his position rather clear with regard to a society fostering a constant reductionism of the human person. Remaining in character, he made no effort to water down what he had to say, even at the expense of touching a few raw nerves:

> After all, we are living in a society that is absolutely sick.
> And one of the reasons why it is sick is that it's completely
> from the top of the head. It's completely cerebral. It has

---

19. *Mystics and Zen Masters* 274.
20. William H. Shannon, *Thomas Merton's Dark Path* (New York: Farrar, Straus & Giroux, 1987) 117-18.

utterly neglected everything to do with the rest of the human being; *the whole person is reduced to a very small part of who and what the person is*. . . . And Christianity has connived with this, you see. The official Christianity has simply gone along with this, that is, with this kind of repressive, partial, and fragmented view of the human person.[21]

I might add that in the West there is almost always the tendency toward one extreme orientation or another. One is either wholly mystical or intellectual or moral or practical and, as is so often the case today, even strictly psychological. By insisting on one extreme, we facilely and conveniently explain all the others away, as if it were really possible to live out of the tunnel of one of these extremes. And the East, of course, goes along with this aberration and creates its own caricatures of the fragmented self. Under such circumstances, there is rarely a healthy coming together of all the diverse elements and dimensions that naturally go into the making of the whole man and woman.

One has to wonder if there are indeed some built-in elements in contemporary life's milieu that would make wholeness impossible and fragmentation of the self inevitable. To Merton, steeped in the existential literature of the nineteenth and twentieth centuries, experiences of alienation and angst were commonplace, a given of contemporary life. Despite the wholeness and optimism of his own thought, he was never optimistic enough to believe that in his own lifetime such problems had bottomed out, or had even come close to it.

In the same session at the Center for the Study of Democratic Institutions in which he spoke of monastic renewal, Merton made his ideas concerning the relationship between external restructuring of institutions and renewal of the inner self quite clear. He understood the shortcomings of trying to cure what is fundamentally interior by manipulating what is external:

You hear this talk everywhere, or you hear it in monasteries, about monastic renewal, and it is confusing because, too often, it is employed to talk about the renewal of an institution. But as soon as people start talking in these terms, you can see that they are enveloped in what Sartre

---

21. Thomas Merton, *Preview of the Asian Journey*, ed. Walter H. Capps (New York: Crossroad, 1989) 48. Emphasis added.

calls bad faith: If the life we are living is not meaningful in itself, how are we going to make an institution meaningful to other people?[22]

Rather than putting all its efforts into making its institutions meaningful and relevant to the world, true monasticism, for Merton, "is a question of *renewing an age-old experience*," for the "real essence of monasticism is the handing down from master to disciple of an *uncommunicable experience*."[23] True education or learning in the classical sense, East and West, is, indeed, this sacred handing down of a something that is uncommunicable. Though necessarily couched in words, true words are always transparent words that point to that uncommunicable something that always is. What is authentic and vital can never live fully in cold formulas alone.

Both Confucius and, later, Mencius regarded human relationships as the very cornerstone of society, the existential lifeline of an entire culture. In their writings, it astonishes readers that there are essentially no obvious traces of either legalism or Machiavellianism (which are both manipulative and concerned with control) in their almost naive and pristine social and political schemes; we can only attribute this to their remarkable faith not only in the human person, but in that in which both persons and nature are squarely rooted: upon *Tien* itself. Confucius and Mencius were wise enough to leave *Tien* undefined and to accept it as either a universal metaphysical principle or a personal or suprapersonal God, depending upon the context. More concretely, they relied on what in the West we may call natural law that emanated from an undefined and undifferentiated heaven.[24]

---

22. Ibid. 30-31.

23. Ibid. 34. Emphasis added.

24. The opening passage to The Golden Mean, or *Chung Yung*, one of *The Four Books*, reads: "What is ordained by Heaven is called 'Nature.' Following out this Nature is called the *Tao* (or the natural law). The refinement of the natural law is called 'culture.'" Mencius, as if giving a teleological form to this basic ontological insight, says: "He who has exhaustively studied all his mental constitution knows his nature. Knowing his nature, he knows Heaven. To preserve one's mental constitution and nourish one's nature is the way to serve Heaven" (*The Four Books*, trans. James Legge [Oxford: Oxford University Press, 1939] 448-49 [Book 7, Part 1, ch. 1, art. 1]). My father comments: "Thus, the mandate of Heaven, human nature and culture form a continuous series. The natural law is to be found by the mind in human nature itself, and to be further developed and applied by the mind to the ever-widening human relations under infinitely variable circumstances" (John C. H. Wu, "Mencius' Philosophy of Human Nature and Natural Law," *Chinese Humanism*

Merton, writing of an institution of which he was an integral part for over half his life, lamented that "in the end monasticism [in the late Middle Ages], by a curious reversal that is so usual in the evolution of societies, identified the fig leaf with the Paradise condition" so that freedom "consisted in renouncing nakedness in favor of elaborate and ritual vestments."[25] Here he could have very easily been speaking of Confucianism as well.

THE HEART AS THE BASIS FOR SOCIAL REFORM

By way of parallel, when Confucianism was rationalized into a convenient vehicle and basis of statecraft in the Han Dynasty (202 B.C.E.-220 C.E.), it too could be likened to identifying "the fig leaf with the Paradise condition." If we examine the spirit of the *Analects* and the *Book of Mencius* carefully, especially in the light of what rituals and rites might have meant to ancient peoples in general and to the Chinese in particular, we can come to a better appreciation of these ancient books and what their authors and compilers might have had in mind even without their having spelled out in detail and depth the meaning of personal and social rites. My own conclusion is that the Chinese sages, seeing the chaos of the times throw the entire social fabric out of joint and into general confusion, thereby looked *inward* in an effort to find a solution to what nearly everyone else seemed to have felt were basically external political and military problems. Their true wisdom lay in their ability to view social and political chaos as mere symptoms of a deeper illness residing in humankind itself. This is doubtlessly what Merton meant when he spoke of Confucius's achievement: "This is a great discovery. . . . This is just as fundamental as anything can be."[26]

and Christian Spirituality: Essays, Asian Philosophical Studies 2, ed. Paul K. T. Sih [Jamaica, NY: St. John's University Press, 1965] 17).

25. "Learning to Live," in Thomas Merton, *Love and Living*, ed. Naomi Burton Stone and Brother Patrick Hart (New York: Farrar, Straus, Giroux, 1979) 8-9.

26. Julia Ching capsulizes the early fate of Confucianism in her *Confucianism and Christianity*: "In 213 B.C. [the first emperor of the Ch'in dynasty, 221-206 B.C.] ordered the burning of all books except those which dealt with medicine, divination and agriculture. Allegedly, he also ordered the burying alive of 460 scholars, in order to put an end to criticisms of his rule. It is not known how many of these were Confucians. Confucianism remained underground, to be revived and dominant during the Han dynasty, where Emperor Wu (r. 140-87 B.C.) made it the state philosophy, supported by government patronage and an official educational system. But this could only happen at a certain cost to the teachings

The writings of the sages make plain the demands they imposed on all of society, beginning particularly with the ruler down to the most humble. They called for nothing short of a total internal reconstruction, which, to Confucius and Mencius, was the only healthy and possible road toward the recovery of the lost and fragmented moral sense in the human person and of the spiritual and cultural milieu. Their sole aim was to save a society that they loved for the reason that their whole beings – the traditions and history that made them what they were and their love for the ruler down to the common folk – were inextricably bound up with the way they thought, felt, and lived. One cannot imagine their loving their people less than the way Socrates loved and wholly identified with his beloved Athenians even unto death.

Thomas Merton falls very much into this sapiential dimension so evident in the ancient sages, a wisdom centered on life as unity and harmony. In "Cold War Letter 25" to James Forest (dated January 29, 1962), a pacifist who continues to be politically active today, he talks of the necessity of "the complete change of heart," of "inner change," of praying "for a total and profound change in the mentality of the whole world," of "application of spiritual force and not the use of merely political pressure," of "the deep need for purity of soul," finally concluding: "This [and all the above] takes precedence over everything else" when one is involved in a social

---

of Confucians themselves. The Confucianism that triumphed was no longer the philosophy of Confucius and Mencius. It had already absorbed many extraneous ideas . . . from Legalism and yin-yang cosmology and religious philosophy It would emphasize – far more than Confucius and Mencius did – the vertical and authoritarian dimensions of the five moral relationships. . . . It was a triumph which has been described as a 'Pyrrhic victory'" (40). Writing on the Legalists in his essay "The Individual in Political and Legal Traditions," in *The Chinese Mind*, my father says: "By isolating the Rule of Law from the fundamental humanity of men [and women], [the Legalists] foredoomed it to a catastrophic collapse. Instead of securing the rights and freedom of the individual, as it normally should, it became actually a ruthless instrument for dehumanizing the people. . . . So far as China was concerned, this unhappy wedding spoiled the chance of a genuine balanced Rule of Law for over two millenniums. Of all these lines of thinking, the way of Confucius would seem to be the most balanced. It excels Mohism by its catholicity, and excels Buddhism by its sense of reality. It steers between the anarchistic tendencies of Taoism and the totalitarianism of the Legalists. It recognizes the need of unity, but at the same time it sees the desirability of diversity. As Confucius himself puts it, 'Men of superior quality aim at harmony not uniformity; while the small-minded aim at uniformity, not harmony.' This is in the best tradition of political wisdom, and is still a living ideal" (342-43).

and political movement.[27]

In a later letter to Forest in the same year, Merton speaks in a way that Confucius himself might have spoken on politics were the ancient sage living today:

> [T]he basic problem is not political, it is apolitical and human. One of the most important things to do is to keep cutting deliberately through political lines and barriers and emphasizing the fact that these are largely fabrications and that *there is another dimension, a genuine reality, totally opposed to the fictions of politics*: the human dimension which politics pretend to arrogate entirely to themselves. This is the necessary first step along the long way toward the perhaps impossible task of purifying, humanizing and somehow illuminating politics themselves.[28]

The thought of the early Confucians reflects an abiding faith in the "interiority of man" that is based first on the more fundamental and implicit faith in the basic goodness of humans and, second, in the intimately personal relationship between human persons and heaven, which they regarded as a given, that is, as both preordained and inherent in the very structure of life itself.

The fact that such a vision never got off the ground and failed to materialize in Chinese society is surely less the fault of the sages than that of later Confucianists who shifted the emphasis from a remarkably balanced philosophy of life and society where rituals are constantly informed by the spirit of love and benevolence, to a one-sided emphasis upon the mere carrying out of rituals as a means of securing social and political order. Chinese humanism seemed to have quickly degenerated into a system and thought devoid of that all-important organic feel for the wholeness of life. It substituted for this original wholeness a rather lame notion of an impersonal cosmos without a warm, throbbing heart at the center of the universe. Moreover, it was marked principally by an overwrought and obsessive emphasis on filial piety and ancestor worship that favored looking backward rather than emphasizing a dynamic present and future.

This nearly deterministic opting for a narrower notion of social order over and against what initially held great promises of

---

27. *Hidden Ground of Love* 262.
28. Ibid. 272. Emphasis added.

developing into a potentially powerful personal, social, and even spiritual philosophy was indeed an identifying of "the fig leaf with the Paradise condition." The cult of the family, great and important as it has been in China, alas, never seemed to have overcome the blight of the tribal and the provincial; in the end, the cult sapped whatever natural energy and inclinations the Chinese might have had for true brotherhood, which, I am convinced, was the original vision of the early sages. The Chinese Communists have tried to bring about "universal brotherhood," but have, in its agonizing train, summarily torn the heart out of the human person. Indeed, one wonders exactly how long the new fatherland can last.

The quiet and subtle Confucian vision of true brotherhood based on a healthy sense of personalism draws each generation to reappraise Confucianism not as a system conceived for statecraft and its preservation, but as an indispensable way of life with sacred and universal principles at its very core. Without such abiding principles that these sages fathomed at the heart of nature and heaven, Confucianism would be no more than a quaint cultural remnant from the dead past; as, indeed, Christianity would be if we were to identify its merely external structures, hierarchy, Canon Law, or moral theology as the whole of it.

In this generation, the East owes a great debt to Thomas Merton for reminding Easterners of a priceless treasure that a good number of us, anxious not to be left off the irrepressible express freight of modernization, have already abandoned. He saw in classical Confucianism part and parcel a paradise condition, the very roots of which lie dormant, yet, in fact, are very much alive in every man and woman. It remains vigorous because Confucius hit upon a principle of love that is rooted not in society, but squarely in nature, by way of *Tien* itself. Therefore, it is not a positivistic principle whose reality and validity are strictly dependent on social environment and reforms.

Both Confucius and Mencius were able to speak very confidently of the basic goodness of humanity only because they saw the unmistakable signature of heaven in the center of humankind's being. Any fruitful exchanges between Confucianism and Christianity would center on an investigation between the Confucian *Tien* and the living God of Christianity.[29]

---

29. For an excellent discussion on the affinities and disparities in the Confucian and Christian notions of God, respectively, see chapter four, "The

In August 1967, Pope Paul VI requested that Merton write a "message of contemplatives to the world." What resulted was a wonderfully rich outpouring of humanistic sentiments supported by love and compassion. Like Confucius' faith in heaven, Merton's faith in the living God by the late sixties was so profound that he was able to see God's epiphany everywhere. The following may indeed be seen as a beautiful flowering of Confucian humanism couched in the language of a twentieth-century monk whose sentiments would have done even Confucius proud:

> [I]f we once began to recognize . . . the real value of our own self, we would see that this value was the sign of God in our being . . . . Fortunately, the love of our fellow man is given us as the way of realizing this. For the love of our brother, our sister, our beloved, our wife, our child, is there to see with the clarity of God Himself that we are good. It is the love of my lover, my brothers or my child that sees God in me, makes God credible to myself in me. And it is my love for my lover, my child, my brother, that enables me to show God to him or her in himself or herself. Love is the epiphany of God in our poverty.[30]

The basic message of Thomas Merton is that we are not alone and that both social and political harmony and moral and spiritual salvation demand the constant help of everyone we know.

Problem of God" (112-50) in Ching's *Confucianism and Christianity*. Ching notes, for example, "the Confucian Classics clearly enunciate a belief in God as the source and principle of all things, the giver of life and the protector of the human race" (118).

30. *Hidden Ground of Love* 157 (letter to Dom Francis Decroix).

"WISDOM CRIES THE DAWN DEACON": THOMAS MERTON AND "THE OX MOUNTAIN PARABLE"

Paul M. Pearson

For devoted readers of Thomas Merton, the sixties were a traumatic and challenging time. The quiet voice of monasticism had seemingly disappeared into the Gethsemani woods, and the new Merton was disturbing and could grate on his reader's sensibilities. The reaction of some readers was noted by Merton, when he wrote in a 1968 letter to Czeslaw Milosz that "Conservative Catholics in Louisville are burning my books because I am opposed to the Viet Nam war. The whole thing is ridiculous."[1] In December of 1964, while Thomas Merton sat in his hermitage at Gethsemani, the SAC planes – Strategic Air Command bombers – disturbed his silence as did the thudding and thumping of the guns at Fort Knox, that quintessential symbol of American military power and wealth, not quite thirty miles from the Abbey of Gethsemani, as the crow flies.

Thomas Merton sat in his hermitage listening to the sound of the rain, allowing oatmeal to boil over on his recently purchased Coleman stove whilst he toasted some bread at his log fire. In the isolation of his hermitage, an isolation deepened by the darkness of the night and the cold winter rain, he thought deeply about the modern world against the background of Philoxenus, a sixth-century Syrian hermit whom he was reading, of the theater of the absurd, in particular Eugene Ionesco and his play *Rhinoceros*, and of his own predicament – living the most solitary life anyone in his own Cistercian order had been permitted to live in centuries as he moved towards becoming a full-time hermit in the summer of 1965. Against this background, Merton drafted one of his finest

---

1. Thomas Merton and Czeslaw Milosz, *Striving towards Being: The Letters of Thomas Merton and Czeslaw Milosz*, ed. Robert Faggen (New York: Farrar, Straus & Giroux, 1997) 175; subsequent references will be cited as "*STB*" parenthetically in the text.

essays, "Rain and the Rhinoceros,"[2] he worked on the manuscript of *Conjectures of a Guilty Bystander*,[3] and he prepared novitiate conferences that he would begin delivering the following spring on Philoxenus, conferences he humorously titled "In Church with Louie: Monastic Life in the Raw."[4]

In this essay, before turning our attention to Merton's version of "The Ox Mountain Parable" of the Confucian sage Mencius (or Meng Tzu), written at the very beginning of this tumultuous decade, I want to look in more detail at *Conjectures of a Guilty Bystander* and Merton's essay "Rain and the Rhinoceros," as I think in them Merton sets out most clearly his understanding of the role of the monk, his own role as a guilty bystander in an age when such voices could easily be overlooked against the bellowing of herds of rhinoceroses. Almost fifty years have passed since he penned *Conjectures* and "Rain and the Rhinoceros," yet his reflections on the role of the guilty bystander are still as relevant as when he wrote them, if not more so, and such voices are still mostly going unheard, still being drowned out by the grunting and bellowing of the herd.

The very title of this book, *Conjectures of a Guilty Bystander*, points to some of the changes and developments that had taken place in Merton's life up to this point.[5] Let us just take a moment to see the origins of Merton's use of this term. In an essay he published in 1958 entitled "Letter to an Innocent Bystander,"[6] Merton suggests that, if he, or another person, were "bystanding" from a sense of inertia this could be a "source of our guilt" (*RU* 56). He questions

---

2. Thomas Merton, *Raids on the Unspeakable* (New York: New Directions, 1966) 9-23; subsequent references will be cited as "*RU*" parenthetically in the text.

3. Thomas Merton, *Conjectures of a Guilty Bystander* (Garden City, NY: Doubleday, 1966); subsequent references will be cited as "*CGB*" parenthetically in the text.

4. Gethsemani recording #144.2 (April 25, 1965), archives of the Thomas Merton Center (TMC), Bellarmine University, Louisville, KY.

5. Merton suggested a number of different titles for this book to his publisher including *A Temperature of My Own*, an interesting title reflecting the personal nature of his thought in it (see Thomas Merton, *Witness to Freedom: Letters in Times of Crisis*, ed. William H. Shannon [New York: Farrar, Straus, Giroux, 1994] 144 [August 9, 1965 letter to Naomi Burton Stone]).

6. Thomas Merton, *The Behavior of Titans* (New York: New Directions, 1961) 51-64 (subsequent references will be cited as "*BT*" parenthetically in the text); *RU* 53-62; first published in French in *Informations Catholiques Internationales* 77 (Aug. 1958) 29-31.

whether non-participation is possible and whether complicity can be avoided. Merton then looks at the role of intellectuals as by-standers, pondering how they could stand between those in power and authority and the majority who find themselves subject to such people. From this position, Merton suggests that the vocation of the innocent bystander is to speak the truth at all costs.

"Letter to an Innocent Bystander" was written in the year of Merton's Louisville epiphany (see *CGB* 140-42) and at a time when his correspondence was burgeoning, particularly with his contacts in Latin America. It was a year marking a distinctive change in Merton. By 1959, Merton was beginning to question his description of himself as an "innocent" bystander, moving towards the term "guilty" bystander instead.[7] This can be seen most clearly in letters Merton wrote to Czeslaw Milosz, where he questions his use of the term "innocent," suggesting that the only answer he knows is "to be responsible to everybody, to take upon oneself *all* the guilt" (*STB* 43, 55). So, by the time he was preparing *Conjectures* for publication, the enormous broadening of his horizons in the fifties and early sixties resulted in Merton's changing his view of himself from that of an "innocent bystander" to a "guilty bystander."

Conjectures, he writes, is "a confrontation of twentieth-century questions in the light of a monastic commitment, which" Merton says, "inevitably makes one something of a 'bystander'" (*CGB* vi). But during the challenging events of this period, innocent by-standing was no longer possible; just to by-stand made a person guilty because they were a part of the human race and therefore deeply implicated. In his introduction to a Japanese edition of *The Seven Storey Mountain*, written in 1963 at the time Merton was working on *Conjectures*, he expressed this succinctly:

> the monastery is not an "escape" from the world. On the contrary, by being in the monastery I take my true part in all the struggles and sufferings of the world. . . . By my monastic life and vows I am saying NO to all the concentration camps, the aerial bombardments, the staged political trials, the judicial murders, the racial injustices, the economic tyrannies, and the whole socio-economic apparatus which seems geared for nothing but global

---

7. In 1961, for example, Merton had entitled Part 2 of *The Behavior of Titans*, of which "Letter to an Innocent Bystander" was the first of two essays, "The Guilty Bystander" (*BT* 49).

destruction in spite of all its fair words in favor of peace.[8]

And again, three years later in 1966, in his essay "Is the World a Problem?"[9] Merton addressed his involvement with the world in more personal terms: "That I should have been born in 1915, that I should be the contemporary of Auschwitz, Hiroshima, Viet Nam and the Watts riots, are things about which I was not first consulted. Yet they are also events in which, whether I like it or not, I am deeply and personally involved" (*CWA* 145). Merton comes to the conclusion in *Conjectures* that instead of bystanding, "You must be willing, if necessary, to become a disturbing and therefore an undesired person, one who is not wanted because he upsets the general dream" (*CGB* 83). Merton's awareness of events in the world prompted him to become for some, including his own order,[10] a disturbing and undesired person as he felt "the time had come to move from the role of bystander (guilty by association and silence) to that of declared witness."[11] His prophetic stance is reflected in one of the epigraphs Merton used on the title page of *Conjectures*:

My life is like the crane who cries a few times
    under the pine tree
And like the silent light from the lamp
    in the bamboo grove. (*CGB* iii)[12]

The other epigraph, taken from Deuteronomy – "Remember that you were a slave in the land of Egypt, and the Lord your God brought you out of there" (*CGB* iii) – reflects Merton's own experience of God's mercy, an experience which consequently enabled him to reach out to others with compassion and mercy.

Before moving on to reflect on the Ox Mountain Parable and the theme of mercy, I think it is worth looking briefly at Merton's arrangement of *Conjectures* as, like all the journals Merton himself

8. Thomas Merton, *"Honorable Reader": Reflections on My Work*, ed. Robert E. Daggy (New York: Crossroad, 1989) 65-66.

9. Thomas Merton, *Contemplation in a World of Action* (Garden City, NY: Doubleday, 1971) 143-56; subsequent references will be cited as "*CWA*" parenthetically in the text.

10. For a period in the early sixties Merton was prevented by the Cistercian Order from publishing on issues of war and the arms race.

11. Michael Mott, *The Seven Mountains of Thomas Merton* (Boston: Houghton Mifflin, 1984) 368; subsequent references will be cited as "Mott" parenthetically in the text.

12. A passage from Chinese poet Po Chu-i.

prepared for publication, it is carefully structured.

Conjectures is divided into five parts, each of which has a sub-title and epigraphs indicative of the essence of that chapter. In the first part, entitled "Barth's Dream" (*CGB* 1-49), Merton begins by recounting a dream experienced by Karl Barth, the theologian. In the dream the composer Mozart implies Barth would "be saved more by the Mozart in himself than by his theology." Merton suggests that Barth's attraction to the music of Mozart was an attempt to awaken "the hidden sophianic Mozart in himself," to awaken the "'divine' child," and concludes his account by telling Barth: "Trust in the divine mercy" as "Christ remains a child in you" and "Your books (and mine) matter less than we might think! There is in us a Mozart who will be our salvation" (*CGB* 3-4). In this first part of *Conjectures* Merton presents a myriad of issues to his reader: questions about the monastery, the Church, his relationship to the world, peace, Gandhi and race issues. The title of this chapter, "Barth's Dream," serves to present a contrast between the issues and questions Merton raises, and the presence of a higher wisdom, the wisdom of the monk on the margins.[13]

In the second part of *Conjectures*, "Truth and Violence: An Interesting Era" (*CGB* 51-113), Merton paints a picture of the early part of the sixties as "an interesting era," a phrase taken from a story told by the novelist Albert Camus. In Camus's story a wise man prayed regularly to be spared "from living in an interesting era" and Camus suggests that since we are not wise "the Divinity has not spared us, and we are living in an interesting era" (*CGB* 51). In this chapter Merton discusses many issues relating to truth and violence, suggesting that humanity has perverted its understanding of truth, that everyone is convinced they "desire the truth above all" but "what we desire is not 'the truth' so much as 'to be in the right'" (*CGB* 65), and violence comes from this perversion of truth. Following the truth will then be a way of love, of mercy and of compassion. The period in which Merton was writing this was the

---

13. His epigraphs for this chapter reflect this contrast. The first, from Kabir, is a few lines from a song to Sadhu advising him to stop his "Buying and selling" and to "have done with your good and your bad" as "there are no markets and shops in the land to which you go." The other quotation, from Thomas Traherne, suggests that, though an infant does not often realize it, when compared to the world and all its treasures the child is "the cream and crown of all that round about did lie" (*CGB* 1), pointing the reader in the direction of the important themes in part one, the wisdom figure of the child and the Mozart figure.

height of the cold war when truth was being perverted in so many areas of life, leading Merton to conclude this chapter by suggesting that calling this era "interesting" could be to underestimate it (see *CGB* 113).

Part three, "The Night Spirit and the Dawn Air" (*CGB* 115-94), is the central, pivotal chapter of the book that draws on wisdom images Merton employed in Part One and that lays key foundations for the remainder of the book.[14] Merton took the title for this chapter from "The Ox Mountain Parable" by Meng Tzu. He may have discovered this parable as early as 1950 when he asked his publisher, James Laughlin, to send him "anything good from the Chinese – Mencius for instance."[15] Among other volumes on Eastern philosophy, Laughlin had promised to let Merton see Ezra Pound's work on Mencius.[16] Merton, however, makes no further references to "The Ox Mountain Parable" until 1960, when, in a journal entry for July 10, he writes, "Mencius – 'The Ox Mountain parable.' Importance of 'night-spirit' and 'dawn-breath' in the restoration of the trees to life. Men cut them down, beasts browse on the new shoots, no night spirit and no dawn breath – no rest; no renewal – and then one is convinced at last that the mountain *never had* any trees on it."[17] But, through rest and recuperation "in the night and the dawn," the trees will return. Similarly, "with human nature. Without the night spirit, the dawn breath, silence, passivity, rest, man's nature cannot be itself" (*CGB* 122-23). Meng Tzu's approach is one that would obviously appeal to Merton with his longing for solitude, and in this chapter he presents it as a solution both for himself and for the world.

In a brief entry in the fourth section of *Conjectures*, Merton points to Thoreau as someone who experienced the night spirit and the dawn air. Set against the industrial and affluent image of America, "Thoreau's idleness (as 'inspector of snowstorms') was

14. Images such as the divine child, the monk and the solitary on the margins.

15. Thomas Merton and James Laughlin, *Selected Letters*, ed. David D. Cooper (New York: W. W. Norton, 1997) 70 [June 1, 1950].

16. In an unpublished letter of May 7, 1950, Laughlin tells Merton that he has "the original typescript of his [Pound's] Mencius" and that he could "bring it down with me the next time I come," as he would not want to trust it to the mail (TMC archives); see also Mott 264.

17. Thomas Merton, *Turning Toward the World: The Pivotal Years. Journals, vol. 4: 1960-1963*, ed. Victor A. Kramer (San Francisco: HarperCollins, 1996) 19; subsequent references will be cited as "*TTW*" parenthetically in the text.

an incomparable gift and its fruits were blessings that America has never really learned to appreciate." After offering his gift to America, Thoreau, in Merton's words, "went his way, without following the advice of his neighbors. He took the fork in the road" (*CGB* 227). Merton takes that phrase, "The Fork in the Road," as his title for this chapter (*CGB* 195-249), reflecting a movement in his life. After Merton's awakening to the importance of the night spirit and the dawn air (a gradual discovery over many years but one which, in *Conjectures*, he actually names for the first time) he can approach the questions and problems he was facing earlier in the book with a sense of freedom and a lightness of touch. The effect upon him of the night spirit and the dawn air is summed up in one of his epigraphs for this chapter where he quotes Lieh Tzu as saying, "Life comes without warning" (*CGB* 195).

The final chapter of *Conjectures*, "The Madman Runs to the East" (*CGB* 251-320), takes its title from one of Merton's epigraphs for the chapter, a Zen Proverb:

The madman runs to the East
and his keeper runs to the East:
Both are running to the East,
Their purposes differ. (*CGB* 251)

In writing *Conjectures* Merton has been asking questions about the problems facing society. Having turned his back on the world when he entered the monastery, Merton is now returning to the world but from a different perspective, the difference between the madman and his keeper. Both are going in the same direction, but their reasons for doing so are vastly different. His final section of *Conjectures* focuses much more on the immediate, placing an emphasis on the beauty of life that is present at all times, the beauty he originally pointed to in Mozart at the beginning of the book. This beauty is continually renewed by the night spirit and the dawn air and signifies God's presence in the world.

I want to return now to part three of *Conjectures*, the section titled "The Night Spirit and the Dawn Air," and in particular to look at "The Ox Mountain Parable," Merton's source for this phrase. In 1960, Merton's arrangement of "The Ox Mountain Parable," based on the translation of I. A. Richards from his book *Mencius on the Mind*,[18] was printed by Victor Hammer as Broadside 2 on

---

18. I. A. Richards, *Mencius on the Mind: Experiments in Multiple Definition*

his Stamperia del Santuccio press in Lexington, Kentucky, in a limited edition of one hundred copies.[19] It is interesting to see how soon after Merton's first reference to this parable he is discussing the possibility with Victor and Carolyn Hammer of bringing "The Ox Mountain Parable" out as a broadside, literally within days, and how quickly after their discussions it is published.[20] Merton enjoyed seeing his work printed in high-quality editions by specialty presses and only did this with works which were of special importance to him (see *TMVCH* xiv). Merton's arrangement of "The Ox Mountain Parable," along with his introduction to it, was also subsequently published in a number of other places.[21] Besides Richards' arrangement of the parable, Merton was familiar both with Arthur Waley's rendition in his book *Three Ways of Thought in Ancient China*,[22] where he called it the "Bull Mountain" parable, and also with Albert Felix Verwilghen's book *Mencius: The Man and His Ideas*.[23]

"The Night Spirit and the Dawn Air" section of *Conjectures* begins, appositely, with a description of the valley awakening in the early morning. Having spent Part Two of *Conjectures* looking at the challenges and questions raised by the modern world Merton, in his description of dawn and the gradual awakening of nature,

---

(New York: Harcourt, Brace, 1932).

19. *The Ox Mountain Parable of Meng Tzu*, translated with an introduction by Thomas Merton (Lexington, KY: Stamperia del Santuccio, 1960); subsequent references will be cited as *"OMP"* parenthetically in the text.

20. It is only a month after Merton's July 10, 1960 journal reference to "The Ox Mountain Parable" that Victor Hammer acknowledges receipt of the text in a letter of August 9, and by December 1, Merton is acknowledging receipt of the published broadside. See Thomas Merton and Victor and Carolyn Hammer, *The Letters of Thomas Merton and Victor and Carolyn Hammer: Ad Majorem Dei Gloriam*, ed. F. Douglas Scutchfield and Paul Evans Holbrook Jr. (Lexington: University Press of Kentucky, 2014) 113, 119; subsequent references will be cited as *"TMVCH"* parenthetically in the text.

21. *Commonweal* 74 (12 May 1961) 174; Thomas Merton, *Mystics and Zen Masters* (New York: Farrar, Straus and Giroux, 1967) 65-68 (subsequent references will be cited as *"MZM"* parenthetically in the text); Thomas Merton, *The Collected Poems of Thomas Merton* (New York: New Directions, 1977) 970-71. Merton's introduction was not included in the versions found in *Commonweal* or *The Collected Poems*.

22. Arthur Waley, *Three Ways of Thought in Ancient China* (Garden City, NY: Doubleday, 1956) 84; subsequent references will be cited as "Waley" parenthetically in the text.

23. Albert Felix Verwilghen, *Mencius: The Man and His Ideas* (Jamaica, NY: St. John's University Press, 1967).

points to a different kind of wisdom than that of the human world, the wisdom he had earlier highlighted in his references to Mozart and the wisdom of the divine child in chapter 1. He describes the early morning as "the most wonderful moment of the day . . . when creation in its innocence asks permission to 'be' once again, as it did on the first morning that ever was" and at that moment of dawn "All wisdom seeks to collect and manifest itself at that blind sweet point" (*CGB* 117).

As Merton becomes more aware of the natural world surrounding him at Gethsemani, so his attitude to place changes markedly from section 3 of *Conjectures* onwards. In one entry contained in the section "The Night Spirit and the Dawn Air," probably dating from the early 1960s, Merton begins by describing "the 'way' up through the woods" and how he "appreciate[s] the beauty and the solemnity" of it, going on to describe the sunrise before stating: "It is essential to experience all the times and moods of one good place. No one will ever be able to say how essential, how truly part of a genuine life this is" (*CGB* 161). Merton's deepening sense of his vow of stability here reflects another effect of the night spirit and the dawn air upon him.

In "The Ox Mountain Parable," Merton found an expression of his experience of the effect nature had on him, especially the effect of the woods and of nature in the very early hours of the morning, a time when he, as a Cistercian monk, was awake as nature itself began to awaken. The understanding of nature that Merton found in Mencius's parable fits into his own expression of "paradise consciousness." So, in the early morning, Merton discovers "an unspeakable secret: paradise is all around us and we do not understand," the "dawn deacon" cries out "Wisdom" but "we do not attend" (*CGB* 117-18). Or again:

> The first chirps of the waking birds – "*le point vierge* [the virgin point]" of the dawn, a moment of awe and inexpressible innocence, when the Father in silence opens their eyes and they speak to Him, wondering if it is time to "be"? And he tells them "Yes" . . . With my hair almost on end and the eyes of the soul wide open I am present, without knowing it at all, in this unspeakable Paradise. (*TTW* 7)

In a letter to his Pakistani friend Abdul Aziz, Merton spoke of "the hour of dawn when the world is silent and the new light is most pure," as "symbolizing the dawning of divine light in the stillness of our hearts" – a rekindling of Meister Eckhart's spark of God in the soul.[24]

In his introduction to the parable, Merton draws a parallel between the violence, war and chaos of Meng Tzu's age and the sixties. He wrote:

> One of his [Meng Tzu's] central intuitions was that human nature was basically good, but that this basic goodness was destroyed by evil acts, and had tactfully to be brought out by right education, education in "humaneness." The great man, said Mencius, is the man who has not lost the heart of a child. This statement was not meant to be sentimental. It implied the serious duty to preserve the spontaneous and deep natural instinct to love, that instinct which is protected by the mysterious action of life itself and of providence, but which is destroyed by the wilfulness, the passionate arbitrariness of man's greed. . . . This is a parable of mercy. Note especially the emphasis of Meng Tzu on the "night wind" which is here rendered "night spirit," the merciful, pervasive and mysterious influence of unconscious nature which, according to him, as long as it is not tampered with, heals and revives man's good tendencies, his "right mind." (OMP)[25]

It is interesting to note here Merton's stress on both the need to keep "the heart of a child" (MZM 66) and his understanding of the parable as a "parable of mercy." In his introduction to this parable, Arthur Waley wrote that all of Meng Tzu's teaching centered on the word Goodness – jên. Waley clarifies that for different schools within Confucianism this term could mean different things. But, for Meng Tzu, in a paragraph underlined by Merton in his edition of Waley's book: "Goodness meant compassion; it meant not being able to bear that others should suffer. It meant a feeling of responsibility for the sufferings of others" (Waley 83). This is a pertinent description of Merton at this time in his life. During the period covered by Conjectures of a Guilty Bystander Merton's horizons had begun to broaden rapidly. The mercy he felt so strongly in

---

24. Thomas Merton, *The Hidden Ground of Love: Letters on Religious Experience and Social Concerns*, ed. William H. Shannon (New York: Farrar, Straus, Giroux, 1985) 46.

25. See also the revised version of this preface in *MZM* 65-66.

The Sign of Jonas[26] led gradually to an overflowing of mercy and compassion towards others: beginning with those with whom he was in contact in the monastery, the scholastics and then novices, through his expanding correspondence, the stream of visitors who came to Gethsemani to see him and through his writings, especially his writings on the social issues of his day.

In Merton's essay "The Climate of Mercy"[27] he speaks of the way the mercy of God changes the inmost reality of the sinner so that it is "no longer sinfulness but sonship." This was Merton's experience of God's mercy and compassion. Having discovered himself in God's mercy he is able to extend that mercy to others. The revelatory experience Merton had on a visit to Louisville in March 1958 is a clear expression of these changes. Although the account was elaborated by Merton in his preparation of this material for publication, the essence was there in his original text. On the corner of a busy street in Louisville, Merton was "overwhelmed with the realization that I love all these people" seeing the "secret beauty of their hearts" and knowing "we could not be alien to one another even though we were total strangers" (*CGB* 140). As the birds hear the call to awaken, so, too, Merton awakens at Fourth and Walnut. Significantly, this incident is placed by Merton in the pivotal third chapter of *Conjectures*, "The Night Spirit and the Dawn Air," and is another illustration from Merton's life of the power of that night spirit and dawn air to bring healing to the human condition.

For Merton, the wind and the rain and the darkness and the solitude of the night in his hermitage at Gethsemani had a restoring effect similar to the night spirit and the dawn air in "The Ox Mountain Parable." The rain helped to heal the damage done to the woods by men who had "stripped the hillside," and it also had a similar effect on Merton as he says in his essay "Rain and the Rhinoceros": "in this wilderness I have learned how to sleep again.

26. In the "Firewatch" epilogue to *The Sign of Jonas* (New York: Harcourt, Brace, 1953), Merton writes of himself as being "overshadowed" by God's mercy, a word reminiscent of Yahweh overshadowing the Ark of the Covenant in the Hebrew Scriptures, or of Mary being overshadowed by God at the time of the Annunciation. This passage was so key to Merton's experience that, after his death in 1968, his fellow monks at the Abbey of Gethsemani would use a passage from it on his memorial card: "I have always overshadowed Jonas with My mercy . . . . Have you had sight of Me, Jonas My child? Mercy within mercy within mercy" (362).

27. Thomas Merton, *Love and Living*, ed. Naomi Burton Stone and Brother Patrick Hart (New York: Farrar, Straus, Giroux, 1979) 203-19.

Here I am not alien. The trees I know, the night I know, the rain I know. I close my eyes and instantly sink into the whole rainy world of which I am a part, and the world goes on with me in it, for I am not alien to it" (*RU* 10). In contrast, rhinoceritis is the sickness that lies in wait "for those who *have lost the sense and the taste for solitude*" (*RU* 21) – or, we could say, for those who are no longer open to the experience of the night spirit and the dawn air.

In his essay, "Rain and the Rhinoceros," Merton paints a picture of his life as a life lived in protest of the herd mentality of his day – whether the monastic or ecclesial herd, the political herd, the commercial herd, or we could add today the technological herd. His solitude in the forest and the rain in this essay are contrasted with modern society, especially through the SAC plane flying overhead and through the guns of Fort Knox thumping in the distance. The rain, the noise of the guns, and the SAC plane[28] occur again and again in Merton's personal journal at this time: "A constant thumping and pummeling of guns at Fort Knox. It began last night when I was going to bed. Then there were big 'whumps,' unlike cannon, more like some kind of missile. Now, it sounds like a new kind of rapid-fire artillery." Later the same day he adds, "2:15. Bumps and punches at Fort Knox faster and faster" (*DWL* 177). Or again: "the guns were pounding at Fort Knox while I was making my afternoon meditation, and I thought that after all this is no mere 'distraction,' and that I am here because they are there so that, indeed, I am supposed to hear them. They form part of an ever renewed 'decision' and commitment for peace" (*DWL* 182).

Recall that this is December 1964. The early sixties saw Merton's most intense writings on war and the nuclear arms race, his Cold War letters, *Breakthrough to Peace*,[29] and then the ban on his

---

28. "[T]he huge SAC plane announced its coming and immediately swooped exactly overhead not more than two or three hundred feet above the hilltops. It was fantastic, and sure enough I could see the trap door of the bomb bays. . . . During the day, in fact, five SAC planes went over, not exactly over this particular hollow but all visible from it, i.e., very close, within a mile (otherwise one could not see them, flying so low, with so many hills around)" (Thomas Merton, *Dancing in the Water of Life: Seeking Peace in the Hermitage. Journals, vol. 5: 1963-1965*, ed. Robert E. Daggy [San Francisco: HarperCollins, 1997] 188) (subsequent references will be cited as "*DWL*" parenthetically in the text); and again: "Yesterday afternoon as I was saying office on the walk below the novitiate, before seeing Reverend Father, the SAC plane swooped by right over the hermitage. I would say it was hardly 150 feet above the tree tops" (*DWL* 190).

29. Thomas Merton, ed., *Breakthrough to Peace: Twelve Views on the Threat*

publishing *Peace in the Post-Christian Era*.[30] November 1964 saw Daniel Berrigan, Philip Berrigan, Jim Forest, John Howard Yoder, A. J. Muste and others at Gethsemani at Merton's invitation for a meeting on violence and non-violence.[31] Merton's writing, along with this gathering and Berrigan's frequent description of Merton as the conscience of the peace movement, clearly shows Merton's "decision and commitment for peace" – these are not hollow words. As Merton wrote in a November 1961 letter to Alceu Amoroso Lima, "when speech is in danger of perishing or being perverted in the amplified noises of beasts [rhinoceroses], perhaps it becomes obligatory for a monk to try to speak."[32]

The age in which Mencius lived, as Merton points out, was a time of violence, war and chaos that he parallels to the time in which he was writing at the beginning of the sixties, and the message of "The Ox Mountain Parable" is as relevant to our present age of violence, war and chaos, technological upheaval and ecological vulnerability as it was for the times in which Merton and Mencius lived. For Merton, we can avoid the symptoms of rhinoceritis – we can stop ourselves calcifying, putting on armor, growing a horn, and starting to grunt – by being open to the experience of the night spirit and the dawn air, by preserving some silence and solitude, by our willingness to dissent from the general myth dream, and by our compassion and responsibility for the suffering of others. Merton came to realize that the night spirit and the dawn air, discovered through some "stability in a peaceful place,"[33] gave him life and enhanced his prophetic and poetic voice so he could declare that life to others in his final lines of *Conjectures of a Guilty Bystander*: "There is the hope, there is the world that remakes itself at God's command without consulting us. So the poet . . . sees only the world remaking itself in the live seed" (*CGB* 319-20). Merton calls us to awaken: to awaken to the mysterious action of the night spirit and

of Thermonuclear Extermination (New York: New Directions, 1962).

30. Thomas Merton, *Peace in the Post-Christian Era*, ed. Patricia A. Burton (Maryknoll, NY: Orbis, 2004).

31. See Gordon Oyer, *Pursuing the Spiritual Roots of Protest: Merton, Berrigan, Yoder, and Muste at the Gethsemani Abbey Peacemakers Retreat* (Eugene, OR: Cascade, 2014).

32. Thomas Merton, *The Courage for Truth: Letters to Writers*, ed. Christine M. Bochen (New York: Farrar, Straus, Giroux, 1993) 165.

33. Charles Cummings, *Monastic Practices*, Cistercian Studies 75 (Kalamazoo, MI: Cistercian Publications, 1986) 177.

the dawn air in our lives and in our world today; to awaken to the mercy of God that continues to fall like rain in our lives; and then to share that mercy, our Christian hope, with a world so desperately in need of that message.

THOMAS MERTON, MATTEO RICCI, AND CONFUCIANISM

Wm. Theodore de Bary

I'm not sure when I first met Tom Merton. It was probably in the middle of my college years at Columbia. Merton had graduated a few years before (1938), but as a part-time English instructor and half-serious graduate student he continued to hang out with other former and current editors of *Jester*, the college's humor magazine, in their office on the fourth floor of John Jay Hall. The "*Jester* crowd" included the poet Robert Lax; Robert Gerdy, later an editor at the *New Yorker*; and Edward Rice, who created *Jubilee*. Robert Giroux, who went on to the publisher Farrar, Straus, later published Merton's *Seven Storey Mountain*. Together this lively, fun-loving crowd liked to clown around in John Jay and do "stunts" they could write about in *Jester*. We shared a strong enthusiasm for the jazz then thriving in nearby Harlem – at the Apollo Theater, the Savoy Ballroom, in midtown at the Roseland, and in the Village at Nick's. The college quad echoed to the jazz emanating from Rice's phonograph in the first floor of Livingston Hall.

I was of a somewhat different sort – active in the debate council and later one of its presidents and active also in student government. In that connection it was Bob Gerdy, as a leader of the Fusion Party and my political mentor, who listed me on the *Jester* masthead even though I did not actually write for it.

In this group, what probably recommended me as a freak along with the other *Jester* clowns was the fact that I had started learning Chinese, one of just two undergraduates in a Chinese language class that included two missionaries, the singer Paul Robeson, and a German spy who used her studies at Columbia as a cover for her espionage. This was in one of the few American colleges that offered Chinese in the 1930s. It was only much later that Merton got around to studying Chinese – and then mostly the mystics.

What Merton and I shared early on was an admiration for Dorothy Day, the editor of the *Catholic Worker*, a religious, communitarian, pacifist, and anti-industrialist supporter of the craft movement (à la Gandhi). In high school, I had already been active as a young Socialist, participating in antiwar demonstrations in New York's Union Square. Merton, as everyone knows, was a longtime pacifist. I might even say he was a diehard pacifist, but after he committed himself to the monastic life (and thus was not subject to the military draft), it became only a theoretical issue.

In 1939–1940, when the peace movement was disrupted by the deal Stalin made with Hitler, dividing Europe between them and leaving Hitler free to make an all-out attack on Britain, I was persuaded by the likes of Reinhard [sic] Niebuhr at Union Seminary, whom I had known in my Young Socialist days, and by Carlton J. H. Hayes, a leading Catholic historian at Columbia, who was active in the Committee to Defend America by Aiding the Allies, to abandon the "Neutrality" movement and support Britain in its resistance to Hitler. My sympathies for this cause led me in 1940 as chair of the Student Governing Board to respond to a request from Eleanor Roosevelt (long a friend of youth movements) to join in a meeting at the White House in support of the Lend-Lease program, by which FDR provided aid (short of war) to the defense of Britain (during the so-called Battle of Britain). Later, after the Pearl Harbor attack, I was recruited by Naval Intelligence for my Chinese and Japanese language skills (such as they were in those early days) and then was sent to the Pacific for three years. As you know from *The Seven Storey Mountain*, Merton followed a very different path – the mystical and eremitical – engaged only in nonviolent struggle.

Nevertheless, after having taken a vow of silence as a Trappist, Merton found a way to be highly articulate, and though not engaged directly in a political or social sense, he managed to express himself on many issues that touched upon his own religiosity, especially the forms of Asian mysticism identified with Hinduism, Daoism, and Zen.

Whether Merton's interest in other religions arose from an ecumenical impulse is a real question. He did not pay much attention to the distinctive characteristics of other religions in their ritual, doctrinal, ecclesiastical, or social forms, and he did not engage them too much on other levels than the contemplative. In the introduction to the Japanese edition of his *The New Man*, his first words bespeak his singular focus: "You must be born again."[1]

Merton goes on to explain this in terms that reflect his earlier starting point in the English version of the essay, titled "Rebirth and the New Man in Christianity."

> These mysterious and challenging words of Jesus Christ reveal the inner meaning of Christianity as life and dynamism. More than that, spiritual rebirth is the key to the aspirations of all the higher religions. By "higher religions" I mean those like Buddhism, Hinduism, Judaism, Islam and Christianity, that are not content with the ritual tribal cults rooted in the cycle of the seasons and harvests. These "higher religions" answer a deeper need in man: a need that cannot be satisfied merely by the ritual celebration of man's oneness with nature. . . . Man seeks to be liberated from mere natural necessity, from servitude to fertility and the seasons, from the round of birth, growth and death. Man is not content with being a slave to need; making a living, raising a family, and leaving a good name to his posterity. There is in the depths of man's heart a voice that says: "You must be born again."[2]

There can be little doubt that being reborn is central to the theme of crucifixion and resurrection in Christianity, and Merton goes on to explain how this theme can be understood in those religions he identifies among the 'higher religions." These "higher" religions are defined by their supernatural character, their capacity for spiritual freedom from the limits of natural life, in most cases through a meditative or contemplative praxis such as that to which Merton had very early committed himself.

The essence of this is conveyed in his comments when contemplating the monuments of archaic Buddhist civilization at Polonnaruwa, Sri Lanka. Merton said,

> I don't know when in my life I have ever had such a sense of beauty and spiritual validity running together. . . . I mean I know and have seen what I was obscurely looking for. I have now seen and have pierced through the surface and got beyond the shadow and the disguise. This is Asia in its

---

1. Thomas Merton, *Introductions East and West* (Greensboro, NC: Unicorn, 1981) 110.
2. Ibid.

purity, not covered over with garbage – Asian, European
or American – and it is clear, pure and complete.[3]

The question of which religions qualify among the "higher" ones is
already prefigured by the titles of the books in which he expresses these
views: *Seeds of Contemplation*, *The Ascent to Truth*, and *Introductions
East and West*, and by his frequent references to "Asian religions" as a
coherent class. To a degree, these are an understandable response
to the fact that his early bestselling works were quickly translated
into Asian languages, and he felt called upon in the *Introductions*
to explain how his ideas related to his Asian audiences.

Among the "higher" religions of Asia, however, and among the
major systems of Asian thought to be so classed there is one striking
omission: Confucianism. One could explain this as simply a matter of
definitions. Many people think of Confucianism as a worldly or secular
teaching, merely a social ethic. Indeed, there are some grounds for
this, insofar as Confucianism does not fit the conventional notion
of religion as a cult of devotional worship in the Indo-European or
Semitic mold. But that would not be enough to explain Merton's
failure at this point to discuss Confucianism as a prominent alternative to the systems he included approvingly among the "higher
religions" of Asia, and one that other Christian writers had felt a
need to reckon with.

Before proceeding with this other reckoning, however, I feel
that in Merton's case there is at least one particular circumstance
that leads him in this direction: his obsession with the evil of
"modernity." The world he sought to liberate himself from was a
world of modernization – thoroughly corrupted by industrialization, capitalism, and war, from which he sought to liberate himself. I believe this was a powerful element in his turning from his
revulsion over a thoroughly corrupt modern world toward a life of
contemplation, a turn that he saw as the common characteristic of
the "higher religions." This same characteristic he did not recognize
in Confucianism, however, which for him did not measure up to
this lofty liberating ideal.

Indeed, much of Confucianism he saw as devoted to satisfying
those "natural necessities" – "making a living, raising a family, leaving a good name" – from which Merton says we should be liberated.

---

3. Thomas Merton, *Thoughts on the East* (New York: New Directions,
1968) 84.

But there is more . . .

> For modern man the old is often paradoxically that which claims to be new. Man in modern, technological society has begun to be callous and disillusioned. . . . The specious glitter of newness, the pretended glitter of a society in which youthfulness is commercialized and the young are old before they are twenty, fill some hearts with utter despair.[4]

In this respect Merton anticipated the Beats, who followed him at Columbia, "beaten" by a corrupt world and driven by revulsion with it into revolt and escape.

In the midst of this Merton says:

> Yet in the deepest ground of our lives we still hear the insistent voice which tells us "You must be born again. . . . We seek to awaken in ourselves a force which really changes our lives from within. In modern secular life men resort to many expedients. If you can . . . find a good psychiatrist, it is possible that you may appreciate a psychological breakthrough and liberation. . . . But in reality psychoanalysis and psychiatry tend toward more workable compromises which enable us to function without having to undergo an impossible transformation. We are not born again. We simply learn to put up with ourselves. . . .
>
> More usually the desperation of modern man drives him to seek a kind of new life and rebirth in mass movements. In these he tries to forget himself; in dedication to a more or less idealistic cause. But he is not born again.[5]

It is directly against this predicament of modern man and modern society that Merton poses the need for a radical spiritual transformation, which finds a parallel in Asian religions that put spiritual liberation ahead of any reform of human society. One can understand, then, why for him Confucianism fails to qualify as a higher religion: it sees self-improvement as integrally bound up with this-worldly social obligation and social melioration. Whether this actually precludes spiritual or religious transformation is another matter, to be discussed in what follows.

In judging this question, it is significant for us that Merton

---

4. Merton, *Introductions* 111.
5. Ibid.

relies on scriptural evidence, directly interpreted in terms congenial to his own conception of modern man's spiritual dilemma. While denying Confucianism a place among the "higher religions," he cannot be unaware of the prominence of Confucianism among the major Chinese traditions. He knows that Confucianism is widely referred to both in China and abroad as among the "Three Teachings" (*san jiao*) of China, often referred to as the "Three Religions of China." Merton is quick to dispute this latter characterization because it does not sufficiently differentiate Confucianism from Daoism and Buddhism and tends to treat it on a par with the latter. On the other hand, he cannot deny that Confucian texts recognized as canonical do have definite religious aspects.

Although Merton's writings on the whole have almost nothing to say about Confucianism, he does attempt to deal with this seeming contradiction in a short section squeezed into a book otherwise broadly and loosely entitled *Mystics and Zen Masters*. Here, he refers to major Confucian texts under the headings of "The Great Traditions of China" and "The Sources of Classical Thought," which lead him into a consideration of texts generally considered "classic" that define that early classical tradition.[6]

These are recognized as "authoritative" but nonetheless competing alternatives in early Chinese thought. They include Daoist and Legalist writings, but the main focus is on what Merton calls the "Four Confucian classics," including the *Great Learning*, the *Mean*, and *Mencius*, along with the *Analects* of Confucius. Merton's section also includes the *Classic of Filial Piety* (*Xiao jing*), which he renders as "Filial Love" (not without some justification, since it combines both love and piety).

Taking these texts as representative of classical Confucianism, Merton has some extraordinarily positive things to say about the Confucian classics themselves, along with other things that would explain why Confucianism as an organized teaching succumbed ultimately to negative forces.

First, some of the strong positive evaluations: Speaking of "Confucian humanism" as found in the classics, he says: "The foundation of the Confucian system is first of all the human person and then his relations with other persons in the society. . . . Confucianism is therefore a humanist and personalist doctrine, and this humanism is religious

---

6. Thomas Merton, *Mystics and Zen Masters* (New York: Farrar, Straus and Giroux, 1961 [*sic*]).

and sacred." Moreover, "Confucianism is not just a set of formalistic devotions which have been loosely dismissed as 'ancestor worship.' The Confucian system of rites was meant to give full expression to that natural and humane love which is the only guarantee of peace and security in society. For Merton, the true and essential Confucianism was seen in the *Analects* and *Mencius*, which "continued to be the most vital and effective spiritual force in China."[7]

If this is so, however, one naturally asks: why did or does Confucianism not qualify as one of the "higher religions"? Why does it not stand on a par with the other two of the "Three Teachings"? Merton does not address this question in the essay under consideration here, but we get clues along the way as to how, despite this enduring, vital essence of Confucianism as seen in the classics, the teaching came to be vitiated by powerful decadent forces.

As I say, we get only clues, not a full explanation, but these clues fall into a pattern. Explaining a crucial historical development in the third century b.c.e., the unification of China by the totalitarian Legalist movement, Merton says of the latter "that they brought the most vital and productive age of Chinese thought to a close and perhaps did more than anything else to create a society that would guarantee the formalization and even the ossification of Chinese thought for centuries to come. At any rate by the third century the really great development of Chinese philosophy ceased."[8]

So stated, the increasing decadence of Confucianism is explained in terms of external forces and circumstances, but there are also hints that the teaching itself acquiesced in or succumbed to this "ossification" process in the longer run, when a Confucian ideal that had been basically personalistic yielded to "the rigid formalism of Confucian ethics and became, over two thousand years, a suffocating system." Against this, we have contrasting assertions in the same essay. "But in spite of this corruption, the iniquity, the pessimism of human nature that were able to flourish in this climate of official cynicism, [Confucian] scholars remained untouched by what was around them and the Confucian tradition remained pure."[9]

What are we to make of this juxtaposition of two thousand years of decadence and suffocation with Merton's affirmation of the surviving purity of Confucian tradition? I believe what he means

7. Ibid. 51, 52, 58.
8. Ibid. 48.
9. Ibid. 78, 63.

is that the institutionalized forms of Confucianism, especially as sponsored by the state, were corrupted by the systemic process, yet individual Confucians, drawing directly on the inspiration of surviving classics, remained true to the original teaching.

These relatively isolated and exceptional cases, however "spirited" they might be, still did not qualify as a "religion," much less as a "higher religion."

At this point, one begins to wonder if this contradictory representation of Confucianism reflects not just the "facts" but some common assumptions in modern Western thought. One of these sees religions in general as tending to fall away from their original inspiration and succumb to a process of inevitable corruption in the all-too-human hands of those who claim its sanction for their own self-interested uses. The other tendency draws from this the further conclusion that organized religion is inherently corrupt as compared to personal "spiritualities" that rely on direct intuitive experience through forms of contemplative praxis that transcend religious dogma and sectarianism. Fortunately, we have more than such suppositions to help us in arriving at a fair judgment, and these appear in the same collection of disparate thoughts collected under the upside-down umbrella of Merton's *Mystics and Zen Masters*.

Under that same heading, we find a section called "The Jesuits in China." Here, drawing mostly on the work of George H. Dunne,[10] Merton credits the early Jesuit missionaries to China in the late sixteenth and early seventeenth century with a remarkable accommodation to Chinese culture, including most notably the sympathetic efforts of Matteo Ricci to achieve a genuine understanding of Confucianism.

Merton's title, "The Jesuits in China," is right in drawing attention to the large contributions of the Jesuits as a group – including other Jesuits in China, such as Adam Schall von Bell (1592-1669), and also those who performed a similar mission, such as Roberto DiNobile (1577-1656) in India and Alexandro Valignano (1539-1606) in Japan – who led in a similar adaptation of Christianity to the native cultures, different as these were from each other, to Hinduism in India and to a Zen Buddhism already much adapted to Shinto and Japanese culture.

---

10. George H. Dunne, SJ, *A Generation of Giants* (South Bend, Ind.: University of Notre Dame Press, 1962).

Spectacular as each of these cases was in their own local setting, together they could also be seen as an outgrowth of a fundamental impulse in the founding of the Jesuit order in the wake of the European Renaissance, which from the start sought to harmonize Judeo-Christian piety with the classical culture then being revived from Greece and Rome. Jesuits in each of these different cultural settings produced distinctive results, yet this success was not just in adapting Christianity to native cultures but in creatively reviving some of the essential elements in native philosophy and religion itself.

Merton's high estimate of Ricci in these respects is confirmed by the eminent European sinologue Wolfgang Franke (unknown to Merton):

> Looking back with our present understanding of Chinese civilization of the late Ming period, we find it almost incredible that a foreigner – however well educated and intelligent he might be – without any previous knowledge of the Chinese language and civilization was able within less than twenty years to take up residence in the capital, become a prominent member of this society, make friends with a number of the most eminent scholar-officials of the time, and even convert some of them to his Christian faith. . . . This accommodation included a thorough Chinese literary education in order to carry on discussions with Chinese scholars and to talk to them on the achievements of European science and development of thought in their own terms. Ricci himself was particularly able to master a highly sophisticated form of accommodation, and was therefore accepted by the Chinese scholar-officials as one of their own.
>
> Ricci's ingenious, gentle and kindly nature conformed to the highest Chinese standards. . . . It inclined him to appreciate and value the essence of Chinese culture. All in all Ricci may be considered the most outstanding cultural mediator of all times.[11]

Ricci's achievement in this respect is typified by his extraordinary effort to learn and master classical Chinese (simply as a missionary he would have had plenty to do just by learning vernacular Chinese

---

11. L. C. Goodrich and C. Y. Fang, *Dictionary of Ming Biography* (New York: Columbia University Press, 1976) 2:1143-1144.

so as to communicate with and convert ordinary people). But Ricci recognized the importance of educated Chinese leadership, and he did not just dismiss or sidestep them in the way that Merton tends to do when he denigrates Confucian scholars as in the following: "All China, at least all the ruling class of China, was supposed in theory to be educated along Confucian lines, but many and not the least successful of Chinese statesmen were men who with the outward facade of Confucianism, were inwardly either pedants, rigid and heartless conformists, or unprincipled crooks."[12]

Ricci himself could easily have taken Confucianism at this low level and used it to his own advantage in converting people from a debased Confucianism to an unsullied Christianity. As a post-Renaissance man, however, and like Erasmus a Christian humanist, Ricci was disposed to take the classical Chinese tradition at its own best professions and attempt to reconcile Confucianism with Christianity at the highest level.

That Ricci was successful in this is attributable not only to his own openness of mind but to a similar openness of many Confucian scholars whom he sought to engage in active dialogue. Reciprocity was at work here, not just solitary genius being impressed on credulous others. And this openness of his Chinese partners (so much in contrast to Merton's characterization of the Confucians as rigid, heartless pedants) reflected something in the Confucians' own background that contrasts with Merton's routine characterization of them.

This new element is to be seen in a revival of Confucianism that had started in the eleventh century. It has been called Neo-Confucianism because it was not only a revival of the old but a reformulation of it to meet the new needs of Song-dynasty China. History was not just to be seen as a tired repetition of ancient platitudes by entrenched bureaucrats but a concerted response by thoughtful Neo-Confucians to the challenge of a new situation.

In the eleventh century, this new situation arose from the need of the new Song dynasty both to stabilize society, after years of civil war, and to address the economic and social problems of a society that had developed and expanded to a new level. Hu Yuan (993-1059) was one of a generation of Confucian scholars who responded to this new need by his formula of "substance, function, and literate discourse." By "substance" he meant enduring truths in the Confucian classics still

---

12. Merton, *Mystics* 53.

relevant to the solution of contemporary problems (their "function" or "application"), and by literate discourse he meant the need for open, public discourse by which people could arrive at common agreement or consensus on what to do about their shared problems. The test of timeless truths was their adaptability to the needs of human society. These could be based on shared natural feelings, but they had to be expressible, communicable, or they would be as unavailable for practical use as the wordlessness of Laozi or the *koans* of Zen Buddhism were in dealing with the rampant civil war and suffering that had prevailed in the ninth and tenth centuries, while Buddhism and Daoism were flourishing (except for a prohibition on Buddhism in 845 engineered at court by the rival Daoists).

Politically in the eleventh century, this new Confucian reform movement called for a "restoration of the ancient order" (here in an idealized form), and its political and economic program was called the New Laws or New System (*Xin fa*). (In the twentieth century, it is sometimes analogized to Franklin D. Roosevelt's New Deal.) Although the success of this movement waxed and waned in time, its institutional ideals continued to inspire successive generations of new reformers. But among these ideals the most enduring (yet also much conflicted) was a new ideal of "classical" education based on a new curriculum.

By the end of the twelfth century, this new curriculum had been shaped for the long term by the great Neo-Confucian philosopher Zhu Xi (1130-1200), who was no less an educator than a metaphysician and who provided Confucianism with a curricular core that far outlasted and outdistanced the reformers' limited success in achieving universal schooling. Despite the failure of at least nominal attempts to implement universal schooling in China, the new core curriculum made its way in different parts of East Asia and on different levels down into the twentieth century.

Zhu Xi's core curriculum was identified by what were called the Four Books and Five Classics, of which the key and crucial components were the *Great Learning*, the *Analects* of Confucius, the text of Mencius, and the *Mean* (*Zhong yong*). Since together with the Five Classics the Four Books came to be known as "the classics," it is important to recognize that actually they were a very select group of texts, singled out for special attention by Zhu Xi. The *Great Learning* and the *Mean* were separate chapters drawn from a traditional classic known as the *Record of Rites* (*Li ji*), a large collection of materials dealing with ritual under many diverse headings, both theoretical and practical. Zhu Xi, following up on an earlier trend among his Song predecessors, singled these out because they provided a brief compact formulation of the basics of all learning, here made to serve as a guide to one's reading of the other classics. Indeed, Zhu Xi's formulation was so succinct and focused that it readily became the heart of a new Confucian education. First adopted on the local level in Song private academies, next under the Mongol Yuan dynasty in the curriculum of the Imperial College, then in the civil-service examination system, ultimately it reached beyond the borders of China into the schools of Korea, Japan, and Vietnam. In fact, so succinct, manageable, and memorable was this core formulation that it persisted even in the household instruction of many families not able to afford formal instruction.

I have already spoken of the enormous outreach of Zhu Xi's "core" in chapter 9, but let me offer just one recent example of its perduring influence: In 1989, when the Chinese Communist regime reversed Mao's anti-Confucian campaign (the Cultural Revolution), I was invited to speak on Confucianism at a state-sponsored celebration of Confucius's birthday in Beijing. On that occasion, I had a conversation with the president of the People's Republic of China, Jiang Zemin, who fondly recalled his childhood education, before he became caught up in the Chinese Communist revolution, when his father instructed him at home in the Four Books. These homespun lessons stayed with him through the years and were no doubt part of the underlying sensibility that led Jiang, Deng Xiaoping, and other moderates to recoil from the excesses of Mao Zedong and the so-called Gang of Four.

The relevance of all this to Thomas Merton is that so widely had the Four Books become accepted as the essential Confucian classics, when Merton chose to talk about the Confucian classics in his *Mystics and Zen Masters*, he referred to these same core texts as representative of classic Chinese thought, calling them not the Four Books but "the Four Confucian Classics."[13] Classic texts they were indeed, but Merton reads them as speaking for the original pure Confucianism, not the later "corrupt" and "decadent" Confucianism he so readily dismisses (as compared to Daoism and Zen Buddhism). He can appreciate these particular "classics" without recognizing them as neoclassical, Neo-Confucian texts because they speak to

---

13. Ibid. 57.

him personally and directly and are amenable to his own form of higher spirituality.

Another new feature of "Neo"-Confucianism was its development of a method of contemplative praxis (unacknowledged by Merton) to match Daoist and Zen meditation. It was called "quiet-sitting" (*jing zuo*). Since no such explicit practice appears in classical Confucianism, there cannot be much doubt that quiet-sitting was adapted from something like Zhuangzi's "sitting in forgetfulness," in which one was supposed to "forget humaneness and rightness." Mencius's rejoinder to Zhuangzi was that one should "neither forget (natural moral impulses) nor try to abet (or force) them willfully." Neo-Confucians associated this new/old contemplative practice with a holistic experience of "the humaneness that forms one body (including the bodily feelings) with Heaven-and-Earth and all things."

Zhu Xi explained this further in his commentary on the *Great Learning*'s dictum of *ge-wu*, often translated as the "investigation of things," a rendering that appeals to the modern preference for objective investigation but that is better understood as "the recognition of things," which combines both the subjective and objective aspects of knowing or learning. Zhu Xu [*sic*] explains *ge-wu* as follows:

> The teaching of the Great Learning insists that the learner, as he comes upon the things of this world, must proceed from principles already known and further fathom them until he reaches the limit. After exerting himself for a long time, he will one day experience a breakthrough to integral comprehension. Then the qualities of all things, whether internal or external, refined or coarse, will all be apprehended and the mind in its whole substance and great functioning will all be clearly manifested.[14]

Quiet-sitting became a widespread practice in Neo-Confucianism and accompanied it to the rest of East Asia. Some schools in Korea and Japan even considered it orthodox praxis. Though obviously this could not be part of any official-examination "orthodoxy" that emphasized measurable objectivity, it satisfied the more personal and subjective side of Cheng–Zhu learning. Its place and status in the whole system is indicated by the fact that while some of Zhu

---

14. W. T. de Bary et al., eds., *Sources of Chinese Tradition* (New York: Columbia University Press, 1991) 1:729.

Xi's predecessors went so far as to speak of "spending half the day in reading (study) and half in quiet-sitting," Zhu himself wondered how one could do this and still meet his essential social obligations.

In his section on "The Jesuits in China" (part of what goes under the title of *Mystics and Zen Masters*), Merton dwells not on these developments in Song Confucianism but on the undoubted achievements of Jesuits like Matteo Ricci in coming to terms with the Confucians of that day.

> The legend of the subtle Jesuit diplomatist who always has an ace up his sleeve (otherwise known as "Jesuit casuistry") has obscured the true meaning and profound importance of Ricci's originality. He not only made an intelligent diagnosis of a totally unfamiliar condition, but also, by implication diagnosed his own condition and that of western Christian civilization as a whole. Like a true missionary, he divested himself of all that belonged to his own country and his own race and adopted all the good customs and attributes of the land to which he had been sent.[15]

(So much for the typical "colonialist" view of Christian missionaries.)

Merton has much more to say about the Jesuits that need not detain us here. Suffice it for me to quote these lines: "Here were men who three hundred years ahead of their time, were profoundly concerned with issues which are now seen to be so important that the whole history of the church and Western civilization seems to be implicated in their solution."[16] Merton is right, even though he does not himself go as far into the issues (especially the Neo-Confucian ones) as we might like. We can offer two more illustrations of Ricci's accomplishments that confirm what has just been quoted from Merton. The first is Ricci's phenomenal effort to learn classical Chinese and apply it to a pioneering translation into Latin of the Four Books. To this extent Ricci extended the process of spreading Zhu Xi's influence, already felt throughout East Asia, to the West and even to Merton himself.

The second example is Ricci's translation into Chinese of a version of Cicero's *De Amicitia* in response to the ready interest shown by his Confucian scholars in the fundamental and universal value of friendship. Not only did this satisfy a need

---

15. Merton, *Mystics* 83.
16. Ibid. 89.

of sixteenth- and seventeenth-century Neo-Confucian scholars for whom human association was the key to "self-cultivation and human governance" (as Zhu Xi had put it), but it at the same time expressed a strong impulse in the post-Renaissance religious humanism of Erasmus (1466?-1538), shared by Ricci's Jesuits.

From this we can see how these historical developments in both the West and China converged on an enduring universal value – friendship and the virtue of trust or trustworthiness it depended on. From the Renaissance interest in Roman civility to Erasmus's sixteenth-century religious humanism and on to the eighteenth-century Enlightenment, there was an unceasing focus on the key human elements in a civil society. This appealed to sixteenth-century Neo-Confucians who, instead of simply succumbing to the corrupt, despotic tendencies referred to by Merton, were eager to learn from Ricci whatever he could bring from the West that would help them remain true to their principles of civility.

In "The Jesuits in China," Merton is highly appreciative of what Ricci and the Jesuits did, but he has little to say about their Confucian counterparts. Because he does not pay that much attention to Chinese history (except as recurring decline) and does not recognize the much broader significance of Neo-Confucianism and Zhu Xi's core curriculum as it spread to the rest of East Asia, he is in no position to recognize the continuing vitality of Confucianism inside and outside of China. His own "Confucianism," the true kind, is one he can draw directly from a personal reading of "timeless" classics, like the *Analects* and *Mencius*, not from history.

Nevertheless, the original Confucian classics themselves included history, poetry, and much else, and it was only Merton's early initiation into the Four Books that allowed him to take a foreshortened "timeless" view of Confucianism. Another way to look at it, however, is to note that Merton was, from the start, more of a poet than a historian. As a poet, he could resonate with nature – earthly, human, and divine – but he would have had to be more of a historian and perhaps somewhat less of a pure contemplative in order to be brought truly "down to earth" in a Confucian sense. But then, few Confucians themselves were both good poets and historians. And I myself was no poet, despite my association with Lax and Merton (and even being listed on the masthead of *Jester*!)

At least this is my thought or, rather, the open question that I leave with you in conclusion. Perhaps it is more than I could reasonably expect of Merton, the poet, considering all that he did accomplish in his all-too-brief lifetime. Except for his premature death, he might well have caught up with the history – or better yet, since he was not out looking for it, history would probably have caught up with him.

As for myself, since those early days with Merton, I have spent my life rather differently. Instead of listening for the Zen sound of one hand clapping, I have looked for two hands clapping or clasping in support of humanistic learning, liberal education, and humane governance of the university, combining as best I could spiritual cultivation with public service – as a teacher in a collegial core curriculum, as a scholar in the Asian humanities, and as a university administrator, while at home cultivating my organic garden in a suburban cooperative community. Merton, I think, would not have objected to any of that.

Thank you.

"A WAY OF LIFE IMPREGNATED WITH TRUTH": DID THOMAS MERTON UNDERVALUE CONFUCIANISM?

Patrick F. O'Connell

On October 11, 2010, Professor Wm. Theodore de Bary, perhaps the most eminent contemporary American authority on Confucianism,[1] delivered the annual Thomas Merton lecture at Columbia University, entitled "Merton, Matteo Ricci, and Confucianism."[2] In his lecture, Professor de Bary (a somewhat younger acquaintance of Merton at Columbia) addresses what he sees as Merton's failure to include Confucianism among the "higher religions" and attributes this omission to Merton's characterization of Confucianism as primarily practical and social in orientation rather than contemplative and aimed at personal transformation. After some engaging reminiscences about his Columbia days and fleeting contacts with

---

1. For a detailed timeline of de Bary's distinguished career and a complete bibliography, see "Wm. Theodore de Bary: A Life in Consultation and Conversation," the Appendix to Wm. Theodore de Bary, *The Great Civilized Conversation: Education for a World Community* (New York: Columbia University Press, 2013) 367-72; subsequent references will be cited as "de Bary, *Conversation*" parenthetically in the text. See also the profile by Jamie Katz, "Loyal to His Core," *Columbia College Today* 41.1 (Fall 2013) 20-25, which includes information on de Bary's undergraduate (Class of 1941) and graduate studies (Ph.D. 1953) at Columbia, his service in naval intelligence during World War II, his teaching career at Columbia, including a period (1971-78) as Executive Vice President and Provost, his commitment to undergraduate teaching and to the college's core curriculum, his conversion to Catholicism in the late 1940s, his 67-year marriage to Fanny Brett (Barnard Class of 1943) and the fact that he was still teaching two courses a semester (*pro bono*) at the time of publication, at the age of 94.

2. Published in slightly revised form as "Thomas Merton, Matteo Ricci, and Confucianism" (de Bary, *Conversation* 351-66). An edited, somewhat abridged version appeared under the more pointed title "Thomas Merton and Confucianism: Why the Contemplative Never Got the Religion Quite Right" in *First Things* 211 (March 2011) 41-46.

Merton and the other members of the *Jester* gang of that era,[3] de Bary quotes a passage (*Conversation* 353) from Merton's 1967 introduction to the Japanese translation of *The New Man*, in which Merton declares that the "spiritual rebirth" that is the central focus of this volume "is the key to the aspirations of all the higher religions," which he identifies as "those like Buddhism, Hinduism, Judaism, Islam and Christianity, that are not content with the ritual tribal cults rooted in the cycle of the seasons and harvests" but respond to "a deeper need in man: a need that cannot be satisfied merely by the ritual celebration of man's oneness with nature."[4] De Bary spends the rest of his lecture considering the reasons for what he regards as the "striking omission" (*Conversation* 354) of Confucianism from this list, an indication of what he sees as a general failure on Merton's part to appreciate Confucianism. He acknowledges that it could be "simply a matter of definitions," as "Confucianism does not fit the conventional notion of religion as a cult of devotional worship in the Indo-European or Semitic mold," and he notes that "Many people think of Confucianism as a worldly

---

3. De Bary mentions his acquaintance with Merton, whom he calls a "half-serious graduate student" at the time, through the "*Jester* crowd," particularly Robert Gerdy, his "mentor" in campus politics, who included de Bary on the masthead of the Columbia humor magazine even though he never actually wrote for it; he notes their common love for jazz and shared admiration for Dorothy Day (*Conversation* 351-52). See also Thomas Vinciguerra, "The Teacher and the Trappist," *Columbia Magazine* (Winter 2010-2011) 6-7, an interview at the time of the lecture that concludes with comments on a visit Merton and friends made to the home of de Bary's future wife: "Indeed, de Bary told with some amusement an anecdote from long ago. On New Year's Day 1941, Merton and his old *Jester* and Philo comrades Robert Gerdy '39CC and Ed Rice '40CC visited Fanny and her sister on Long Island. As Merton recalled in *The Secular Journal of Thomas Merton*, he shared 'three eggnogs out at Northport among those giggling Jane Austen girls.' 'Merton was a storyteller,' said de Bary. 'My wife was not a giggly girl'" (see Thomas Merton, *The Secular Journal* [New York: Farrar, Straus & Cudahy, 1959] 146-48, and the original journal entry: Thomas Merton, *Run to the Mountain: The Story of a Vocation. Journals, vol. 1: 1939-1941*, ed. Patrick Hart [San Francisco: HarperCollins, 1995] 283-84).

4. Thomas Merton, *"Honorable Reader": Reflections on My Work*, ed. Robert E. Daggy (New York: Crossroad, 1989) 130; de Bary references the earlier edition of this material: Thomas Merton, *Introductions East & West: The Foreign Prefaces of Thomas Merton* (Greensboro, NC: Unicorn Press, 1981) 110; see also the revised and expanded version from spring 1968 entitled "Rebirth and the New Man in Christianity," in Thomas Merton, *Love and Living*, ed. Naomi Burton Stone and Brother Patrick Hart (New York: Farrar, Straus, Giroux, 1979) 192-203, in which the passage in question (194) remains virtually the same.

or secular teaching, merely a social ethic" (354). But he maintains that this factor "would not be enough to explain Merton's failure at this point to discuss Confucianism as a prominent alternative to the systems he included approvingly among the 'higher religions' of Asia, and one that other Christian writers had felt a need to reckon with" (354). Instead, he posits that Merton's contemplative rejection of "modernity," his "revulsion" toward a world "thoroughly corrupted by industrialization, capitalism, and war" (355), made him fundamentally unsympathetic to the approach of Confucianism, which "sees self-improvement as integrally bound up with this-worldly social obligation and social melioration" rather than "put[ting] spiritual liberation ahead of any reform of human society" like other Asian religions (356). He finds confirmation for this conclusion in the fact that in *Mystics and Zen Masters*[5] Merton rejects the common classification of Chinese religion in terms of the "Three Teachings," according to de Bary "because it does not sufficiently differentiate Confucianism from Daoism and Buddhism and tends to treat it on a par with the latter" (356).

At this point he declares that "Merton's writings on the whole have almost nothing to say about Confucianism," but then goes on to point out that "in a short section squeezed into" *Mystics and Zen Masters* Merton does refer "to major Confucian texts under the headings of 'The Great Traditions of China' and 'The Sources of Classical Thought'" (356) – the so-called "'Four Confucian classics,' including the *Great Learning*, the *Mean*, and *Mencius*, along with the *Analects* of Confucius" (357). He adds, "Merton's section also includes the *Classic of Filial Piety*" (357). De Bary does admit that despite his apparent exclusion of Confucianism from the ranks of the higher religions, "Merton has some extraordinarily positive things to say about the Confucian classics themselves" (357) and quotes comments on "Confucian humanism" that bear out this perception (357-58). He explains this apparent inconsistency on Merton's part by positing a distinction between "institutionalized forms of Confucianism, especially as sponsored by the state, [which] were corrupted by the systemic process" and "individual Confucians, drawing directly on the inspiration of surviving classics, [who] remained true to the original teaching" (358).

---

5. See Thomas Merton, *Mystics and Zen Masters* (New York: Farrar, Straus and Giroux, 1967) 46-47; subsequent references will be cited as "*MZM*" parenthetically in the text.

But these latter, according to de Bary's interpretation of Merton, were "isolated and exceptional cases" who were not sufficiently numerous to give Confucianism as a whole the status of a genuine "'religion,' much less . . . a 'higher religion'" (358). He suggests that this preference for the charismatic over the institutional "reflects . . . some common assumptions in modern Western thought" that tends to see religions as inevitably declining from their original purity and to conclude "that organized religion is inherently corrupt as compared to personal 'spiritualities' that rely on direct intuitive experience through forms of contemplative praxis that transcend religious dogma and sectarianism" (358). He suggests, in other words, that Merton is at least implicitly making a distinction with respect to model Confucians: they are spiritual but not religious.

At this point he finally turns to the aspect of the topic indicated in the title of his presentation, the missionary activities of Matteo Ricci (1552-1610) and other sixteenth- and seventeenth-century Jesuits in China, the subject of another "section called 'The Jesuits in China'" found "in the same collection of disparate thoughts" (358-59), *Mystics and Zen Masters*. Here, de Bary says, can be found "more than such suppositions to help us in arriving at a fair judgment" (358) (though it is not completely clear if he means a fair judgment of Confucianism or a fair judgment of Merton's response to Confucianism). He points out "Merton's high estimate of Ricci" not only "in adapting Christianity to native cultures but in creatively reviving some of the essential elements in native philosophy and religion itself" (359). But he contrasts Ricci's own openness to Confucian culture and to a genuine reciprocal relationship with the Confucian leaders of his time with what he sees as Merton's tendency to "denigrate Confucian scholars" and to "just dismiss or sidestep" the important role in Chinese society played by "educated Chinese . . . scholars," whom he tends to characterize as "rigid heartless pedants" (360).[6] While "Merton is highly appreciative of what Ricci and the Jesuits did" (365), of Ricci's willingness, in Merton's words, to divest himself "of all that belonged to his own country and his own race" and to adopt "all the good customs and

---

6. Here de Bary compresses a passage which he himself had just quoted: "All China, at least all the ruling class of China, was supposed in theory to be educated along Confucian lines, but many and not the least successful of Chinese statesmen were men who with the outward façade of Confucianism, were inwardly either pedants, rigid and heartless conformists, or unprincipled crooks" (*MZM* 53; *Conversation* 360).

attitudes of the land to which he had been sent" (*MZM* 83; *Conversation* 364[7]), he "has little to say" about the Jesuits' "Confucian counterparts" (365) who showed a real openness and receptivity to these European strangers that in its own way was almost as remarkable as the "inculturation" developed by Ricci and his companions.

Merton's basic limitation, de Bary concludes, is that he was, "from the start, more of a poet than a historian" (366). He gave no attention to the historical development of Confucianism, particularly the neo-Confucian reform movement[8] that began in the eleventh century and included the formation of the Confucian curriculum as shaped by "the great Neo-Confucian philosopher Zhu Xi" (361) (1130-1200) that was responsible for making the Confucian "Four Books"[9] the central texts for Chinese education, particularly for prospective civil servants, from that time until the early twentieth century – including the Confucian officials with whom Matteo Ricci would form a deep bond at the turn of the seventeenth century. "The relevance of all this to Thomas Merton," de Bary suggests, is that by neglecting the historical context in which the very texts he valued so highly had become "classics" during the very period of "the later 'corrupt' and 'decadent' Confucianism he so readily dismisses" (363), Merton has taken "a foreshortened 'timeless' view of Confucianism" in which Confucianism as an institution can be distinguished from "the true kind" of Confucianism, "one he can draw directly from a personal reading of 'timeless' classics, like the *Analects* and *Mencius*, not from history" (365-66). This is de Bary's solution to the conundrum of Merton's seemingly con-

---

7. De Bary's citation reads: ". . . customs and attributes . . ."

8. This is the particular focus of de Bary's own scholarly research and expertise: see in particular *The Unfolding of Neo-Confucianism* (New York: Columbia University Press, 1975); *Principle and Practicality: Neo-Confucianism and Practical Learning* (New York: Columbia University Press, 1981); *The Rise of Neo-Confucianism in Korea* (New York: Columbia University Press, 1985); *The Message of the Mind in Neo-Confucianism* (New York: Columbia University Press, 1988); *Neo-Confucian Education* (Berkeley: University of California Press, 1989); and the essays in Part 2 of *The Great Civilized Conversation*, "Liberal Learning in Confucianism" (97-325), including "Zhu Xi and Liberal Education" (109-31) and "Zhu Xi's Educational Program" (166-202).

9. De Bary notes in passing (*Conversation* 357) Merton's somewhat misleading application of the term "Confucian classics," usually used to refer to the five ancient texts Confucius supposedly edited (the *Book of Odes*, the *Book of Changes*, the *Book of History/Documents*, the *Book of Rites*, the *Spring and Autumn Annals*), to the "Four Books" associated with Confucianism proper (the *Analects*, the *Great Learning*, the *Mean* and the *Mencius*).

tradictory attitudes toward Confucianism, an appreciation of the essence coexisting with a largely misinformed depreciation of the actual development of Confucianism over the course of time. De Bary concludes by noting that while a few of the great Confucians were "both good poets and historians" (366) it is perhaps too much to expect such a holistic synthesis of Merton, especially as he died at such a young age (particularly compared with de Bary himself, who was over ninety as he sat in the Columbia chapel speaking of his contemporary whose death had come over four decades before); he graciously notes that if Merton was too much of a poet and not enough of a historian, he himself was no poet at all, and suggests that had Merton lived longer "he might well have caught up with the history – or better yet . . . history would probably have caught up with him" (366).

Thus the great scholar of Confucianism concludes his response to what he sees as the limitations of Merton's understanding of and response to Confucianism. The question naturally arises: how valid is this critique? Given the eminence of the speaker and the paucity of other writings on the topic,[10] de Bary's judgment certainly carries a great deal of weight. But the answer that I hope to demonstrate by a closer and broader investigation of Merton's writings on Confucianism is that de Bary has fundamentally misconstrued Merton's attitude toward Confucianism and largely missed the point of what Merton says regarding this great Asian tradition, which he may not consider a religion, but which he certainly regards as a source of profound wisdom and insight into the human condition, not merely in the abstract, but in its concrete unfolding over the course of history.

First of all, it is simply inaccurate to say that "Merton's writings on the whole have almost nothing to say about Confucianism." While it is true that Merton writes significantly less about Confucianism than on Buddhism and Taoism, there are five published sources with a substantial focus on the Confucian tradition. Merton's very first article on Asian spirituality, "Classic Chinese Thought," originally appearing in *Jubilee* in January 1961 and

---

10. See Patrick F. O'Connell, "Confucianism," in William H. Shannon, Christine M. Bochen and Patrick F. O'Connell, *The Thomas Merton Encyclopedia* (Maryknoll, NY: Orbis, 2002) 74-75; Paul M. Pearson, "Let Mercy Fall like Rain: Thomas Merton and the Ox Mountain Parable," *The Merton Journal* 18.1 (Eastertide 2011) 42-49; John Wu, Jr., "Thomas Merton and Confucian Rites: 'The Fig Leaf for the Paradise Condition,'" *The Merton Annual* 9 (1996) 118-41.

subsequently included in *Mystics and Zen Masters*,[11] is mainly concerned with Confucianism, contrasted with the alternative visions of Taoist anarchism and Legalist authoritarianism. It is this 24-page article, which Prof. de Bary inaccurately describes as "a short section squeezed into a book otherwise broadly and loosely entitled *Mystics and Zen Masters*" (*Conversation* 356) that provides the majority of references for de Bary's lecture, though he quotes it very selectively.

Appended to the version of this article in *Mystics and Zen Masters* (65-68) but originally published in a limited edition by Merton's friend Victor Hammer in 1960 on his hand press, *The Ox Mountain Parable of Meng Tzu*[12] is Merton's poetic rendition of a selection from the second great figure of Confucian tradition (372-289 BCE), preceded by a brief introduction in which Merton describes the brief tale as a "parable of mercy" (*MZM* 66) expressing Mencius' belief in the basic goodness of human nature, perverted by selfish acts but capable of being restored by a properly "humane" education, that proposed by Confucius (551-479 BCE); while Prof. de Bary mentions Mencius in passing he takes no notice of Merton's poetic reworking of this evocative text.

A second article with substantial Confucian material appeared in 1962 in two slightly different versions, one entitled "Christian Culture Needs Oriental Wisdom" in *The Catholic World* and the other "Two Chinese Classics" in *Chinese Culture Quarterly*, retitled "Love and Tao" when included in *Mystics and Zen Masters*;[13] this article was an appreciative commentary on recent translations of

---

11. Thomas Merton, "Classic Chinese Thought," *Jubilee* 8.9 (January 1961) 26-32; *MZM* 45-68.

12. *The Ox Mountain Parable of Meng Tzu*, translated with an introduction by Thomas Merton (Lexington, KY: Stamperia del Santuccio, 1960).

13. Thomas Merton, "Christian Culture Needs Oriental Wisdom," *Catholic World* 195 (May 1962) 72-79, reprinted in *A Thomas Merton Reader*, ed. Thomas P. McDonnell (New York: Harcourt, Brace, 1962) 319-26; rev. ed. (Garden City, NY: Doubleday Image, 1974) 295-303; Thomas Merton, "Two Chinese Classics," *Chinese Culture Quarterly* 4 (June 1962) 34-41, reprinted in *Mystics and Zen Masters* as "Love and Tao" (69-80); a version of the essay incorporating all the material from both versions, retaining the more evocative title from the *Catholic World* article, is included in Thomas Merton, *Selected Essays*, ed. Patrick F. O'Connell (Maryknoll, NY: Orbis, 2013) 102-12; subsequent references will be cited as "*SE*" parenthetically in the text.

the Taoist *Tao Te Ching*[14] and the Confucian *Hsiao Ching*,[15] or *Classic of Filial Piety*; aside from his erroneous comment that "Merton's section also includes" the latter text along with the four "Confucian classics," whereas it is part of a completely different article, along with the remark that "he renders" the title "as 'Filial Love' (not without some justification, since it combines both love and piety)" (*Conversation* 357), Prof. de Bary does not consider this material at all.

A third article is "The Jesuits in China," also originally appearing in 1962 and included in *Mystics and Zen Masters*,[16] focusing on the remarkable missionary work of Matteo Ricci in the late sixteenth and early seventeenth century,[17] the ostensible topic of Prof. de Bary's presentation, in which Merton gives little attention to the Confucian dialogue partners of Ricci and his companions, leading Prof. de Bary to suggest that Merton is failing to appreciate the powerful positive influence of Confucianism on the development of Chinese political, social and spiritual life.

The final major published source for Merton's treatment of Confucianism is found in his introduction to *The Way of Chuang Tzu*,[18] his collection of poetic reworkings of selections from the fourth-century BC Taoist master, in which Merton considers the "four-sided mandala of basic virtues," compassion, justice, ritual and wisdom (*WCT* 18), as the heart of the Confucian ethic and the key to the character of the superior or noble-minded person, and points out that in contrast to Taoism, the Confucian spirit is drawn to the ethical Tao, the way of human life and action, "the Tao 'that

---

14. *Tao Teh Ching*, trans. John C. H. Wu, Asian Institute Translations 1 (New York: St. John's University Press, 1961).

15. *The Hsiao Ching*, ed. Paul K. T. Sih, trans. Mary Lelia Makra, MM, Asian Institute Translations 2 (New York: St. John's University Press, 1961).

16. Thomas Merton, "The Jesuits in China," *Jubilee* 10.5 (September 1962) 35-38; *MZM* 81-90.

17. The article is based on Merton's reading of George H. Dunne, SJ, *Generation of Giants: The Story of the Jesuits in China in the Last Decades of the Ming Dynasty* (Notre Dame, IN: University of Notre Dame Press, 1962). He was finishing the book in mid-June 1962, as in preliminary comments on Fr. Adam Schall, one of Ricci's successors, from a novitiate conference of that time (n. 9.2 [archives of the Thomas Merton Center [TMC], Bellarmine University, Louisville, KY] – undated but preceded and followed by conferences of June 19 and June 24, respectively), he remarks that he needs to return the book on the following day.

18. Thomas Merton, *The Way of Chuang Tzu* (New York: New Directions, 1965) 15-32; subsequent references will be cited as "*WCT*" parenthetically in the text.

can be named,' which is the 'Mother of all things,'" rather than
to the mysterious "Eternal Tao 'that can not be named,' which is
the nameless and unknowable source of all being" (*WCT* 20-21),
the focus of the teaching of Lao Tzu and Chuang Tzu. There is no
indication in his lecture that Prof. de Bary is aware of this material.

In addition to these major sources there are various comments
and quotations related to Confucianism in Merton's letters,[19] journals[20] and novitiate conferences,[21] including four classes devoted
to Confucian thought from mid-1965,[22] shortly before the end of
his tenure as novice master; there are also extensive notes on Confucianism in Merton's reading notebooks for 1960-61, as he was

19. Frequent references to Confucianism are found in Merton's letters to
Paul K. T. Sih (Thomas Merton, *The Hidden Ground of Love: Letters on Religious
Experience and Social Concerns*, ed. William H. Shannon [New York: Farrar,
Straus, Giroux, 1985] 548-56 (subsequent references will be cited as "*HGL*"
parenthetically in the text); and to John C. H. Wu (*HGL* 611-35). Both sides of the
latter correspondence are now available in Cristóbal Serrán-Pagán, ed., *Merton &
the Tao: Dialogues with John Wu and the Ancient Sages* [Louisville, KY: Fons
Vitae, 2013] 171-346; subsequent references will be cited as "*Merton & the Tao*"
parenthetically in the text).

20. See for example the journal entry of September 5, 1961: "Confucius said:
'The higher type of man is not like a vessel which is designed for some special
use.' He was wiser than we monks are" (Thomas Merton, *Turning Toward the
World: The Pivotal Years. Journals, vol. 4: 1960-1963*, ed. Victor A. Kramer
[San Francisco: HarperCollins, 1996] 158; subsequent references will be cited
as "*TTW*" parenthetically in the text). In *Conjectures of a Guilty Bystander* this
is expanded to: "Confucius said: 'The higher type of man is not like a vessel
which is designed for special use.' He was wiser than we monks are: we are very
much concerned with our 'special function.' But that is precisely what the monk
does not have" (Thomas Merton, *Conjectures of a Guilty Bystander* [Garden
City, NY: Doubleday, 1966] 179; subsequent references will be cited as "*CGB*"
parenthetically in the text).

21. See Merton's appreciative comments on and quotations from the *Analects*
in the context of his discussion of natural law in Thomas Merton, *The Life of
the Vows: Initiation into the Monastic Tradition* 6, ed. Patrick F. O'Connell,
Monastic Wisdom vol. 30 (Collegeville, MN: Cistercian Publications, 2012)
46-47; subsequent references will be cited as "*LV*" parenthetically in the text.

22. Conferences of June 10, July 1, 8 and 15, 1965 (remastered recordings
of these conferences are in the TMC archives: nn. 148.4, 150.1, 150.3, 151.2;
the first two are available commercially in the CD set *The Search for Wholeness*
[Rockville, MD: Now You Know Media, 2012]; the first, second and fourth had
previously been issued by Credence Cassettes as *The Search for Wholeness*, side 2
[n. 2370.2], *Chinese Thought and the Symbol of Chung* [n. 3284.2] and *Community
and Transformation* [n. 2371.2]); these are part of a long series of presentations
on art and literature and a kind of excursus in the midst of discussions on Greek
tragedy, roughly contemporaneous with the Chinese material.

preparing his early articles.[23] De Bary of course would have no ready access to most of this ancillary material, though some of it is quite germane to his critique of Merton's approach to Confucianism.

Sometimes the simpler answer is the better one. De Bary raises and rejects the possibility that the omission of Confucianism as a higher religion may simply be a matter of definition, and it is true that Merton would not have accepted de Bary's proposed alternative description of Confucianism "as a worldly or secular teaching, merely a social ethic."[24] But Merton does describe Confucianism at the beginning of "Classic Chinese Thought" as "certainly not a religion in the same sense as Christianity. Confucianism is less a 'faith' than a sacred philosophy, a way of life based on archaic religious wisdom . . . nothing more or less than natural ethics in a very refined and traditional form: the natural law expressed in a sacred culture" (*MZM* 46-47).[25] In what are probably his earliest developed citation and commentary on the resources provided by Asian wisdom for moral and spiritual insight, he says much the same

---

23. Reading Notebook 58A [TMC archives], 44 pages of material on Chinese philosophy (plus numerous additional notes on verso pages), including material on Taoism and on Mo Tzu, but principally concerned with Confucianism. There are also four pages of quotations from the *Analects*, plus a few notes later on, in Reading Notebook 52 from the same period.

24. This is basically the position taken by Liu Wu-Chi in *A Short History of Confucian Philosophy* (Baltimore: Penguin, 1955) (subsequent references will be cited as "Liu" parenthetically in the text), one of the sources Merton cites for "Classic Chinese Thought" (see *MZM* 290), who asserts, approvingly, that Confucianism is purely philosophical and non-religious, a practical and practicable moral system with no trace of the metaphysical or the supernatural. See also the quotations from Liu that in the third century BC, at the time of the rise of Legalism, "the Chinese people lost their faith . . . and have not yet found it" and that "From now on religion had to go underground, so to speak, and never again would it become the chief concern of Chinese intellectuals except for a few erratic souls" (Liu 96), a position Merton characterizes as "perhaps . . . a really gross exaggeration" (*MZM* 55).

25. Merton's perspective here is in fact quite similar to de Bary's own: "We are already aware from other references to Heaven in the *Analects* that Confucius felt some personal relation to it – a kind of religious relationship between Heaven theistically conceived (a divine creator) and its creation. Heaven spoke directly and personally to him, and he had a filial obligation to listen. Confucianism may not be thought of as a 'religion' in the usual sense, but Confucius bespoke a reverential attitude toward Heaven, and the deep respect in which he held all life was a reflection of this. . . . Indeed, the attitude and virtue of reverence remained a key element in later Confucianism. It was not a purely secular ethic, as some have supposed it to be" (*Conversation* 73; see also 335).

thing: quoting maxims of Confucius on "'human-heartedness' . . . the ability to understand others by realizing that they suffer what we suffer and desire what we desire – to reach out by empathy and put ourselves in their place and act accordingly," he compares the *Analects* to the work of St. Bernard and even to Christ's command to lay down one's life for one's friends, and calls Confucian teaching "a revelation of the depth and wonder of the natural law." He concludes: "How sad that by ignoring these depths, imagining ourselves more 'supernatural,' we are in fact very poor Christians at times. So much for the great importance of the natural law. No one can hope to ignore it and yet become a saint!" (*LV* 46-47).

There is no need to posit as de Bary does a revulsion on Merton's part, particularly in April 1967 when he wrote the preface for *The New Man* translation, toward the evils of the modern social world that would carry over to a rejection of the Confucian project of gradual social melioration rather than a spiritual liberation through contemplative transformation that Merton finds not only in Christianity but in other "higher religions." If such an attitude of "world rejection" characterized Merton's spiritual stance in the years immediately leading up to and following his entrance into the Trappists in 1941, it certainly had been profoundly modified by his turning toward the world in the final decade of his life, when he became an advocate and practitioner of interreligious and intercultural dialogue. Far from rejecting the Confucian emphasis on social relations, Merton celebrates it as "a much more authentic form" of genuine personalism than the contemporary preoccupation with "personality tests" and "personality problems" (*MZM* 51).[26] He writes: "The foundation of Confucian system is first of all the *human person* and then his relations with other persons in society. . . . *Ju* is therefore a humanist and personalist doctrine, and this

---

26. Merton's characteristic distinction between the individual and the person (see for example Thomas Merton, *New Seeds of Contemplation* [New York: New Directions, 1961] 38; Thomas Merton, *Disputed Questions* [New York: Farrar, Straus and Cudahy, 1960] x-xi) is expressed in remarkably similar terms by de Bary himself in his essay "Confucian Individualism and Personhood" (*Conversation* 132-65), in which he writes of the Confucian emphasis on self-cultivation: "I prefer the term 'personalism' to 'individualism,' since it shares some common ground with forms of personalism in Western tradition as distinct from a modern liberationist 'individualism.' Here, 'personalism' expresses the worth and dignity of the person not as a raw, 'rugged' individual but as a self shaped and formed in the context of a given cultural tradition, its own social community, and its natural environment to reach full personhood" (119).

humanism is religious and sacred . . . . intellectual and ethical, objective, social, and one might even say democratic. The greatest thing about it is its universality" (*MZM* 51).[27]

Professor de Bary thinks that in the introduction to "Classic Chinese Thought" Merton rejects the notion of the three traditions because it "does not sufficiently differentiate Confucianism from Daoism and Buddhism, and tends to treat it on a par with the latter," but in fact Merton's point is quite different. He is pointing out the inadequacy of drawing a parallel between the religious situation in America, with its three distinct, mutually exclusive religious identities – Catholicism, Protestantism, Judaism – and the situation in Asia, where "Oriental religions, while they may differ in philosophy and belief, have a way of interpenetrating quite freely with one another" (*MZM* 46), as evidenced by the mutual influence of Taoism and Mahayana Buddhism that led to the development of Zen, and above all by the capacity of Confucianism to coexist in the same person "with some other faith in religious revelation" (*MZM* 47), not only with Taoism and Buddhism but potentially even with Christianity.[28] Far from denigrating Confucianism here, Merton is emphasizing its compatibility with other traditions not only of Asia but of the West. His very first mention of Confucianism in the article calls attention to the rare ability of "the first Jesuits in China . . . to evaluate correctly the profound Catholicity of Confu-

---

27. "*Ju*" is the usual Chinese expression for what is called Confucianism in the West, which Merton picks up particularly from Liu Wu-Chi; its origin is somewhat vague, but its basic meaning (which Merton never explains) apparently was originally a denigratory term applied to scholars, meaning "weakling," that eventually came to be a term of respect for intellectuals trained in traditional ceremonial rites and especially disciples of "Master K'ung."

28. In his notes from another source he consulted, the Chinese convert and Oratorian priest François Huang's *Ame Chinoise et Christianisme* (Paris: Casterman, 1957), Merton writes "Rather than speak of the religions of China, more accurate to deal with concrete religious spirit of the Chinese people" (Reading Notebook 58A: 4). See Huang 17: "J'ai bien dit 'la religion' et non 'les religions.' Car, c'est l'esprit religieux du people chinois plutôt que le détail de chaque religion qu'il importe de mettre en lumière, d'autant plus que l'âme chinoise, répugnant à la distinction cartésienne, noie souvent les diverses doctrines religieuses dans une unité plus organique qu'organisée, plus vécue que systématique" ("I have specifically said 'religion' and not 'religions,' for it is the religious spirit of the Chinese people rather than the detail of each religion that it is important to bring to light, since the Chinese soul, repudiating the Cartesian distinction, often links diverse religious doctrines in a unity more organic than organized, more lived out than systematic").

cian philosophy" (*MZM* 46), an evaluation that he clearly endorses and seeks to place in a contemporary context.

It is indeed true that in "The Jesuits in China" Merton does not give equal attention and credit to the Confucian colleagues of Ricci and his fellow Jesuits for their remarkable mutual engagement and dialogue that allowed Christianity to flourish for a brief period in early seventeenth-century China. But it is equally true that he in no way impugns or otherwise dismisses their contributions or motivations. In fact, in his one explicit reference to "Confucian scholars converted to the faith" he states that "the finest of the early Chinese converts belonged to this class" (*MZM* 87). Merton's principal interest in this article is simply elsewhere, focused as he is on the missionaries' willingness to transcend their own cultural limitations, to distinguish "what was essentially Christian and truly Catholic – that is, universal – from cultural and accidental accretions proper to a certain time and place" (*MZM* 83), to reject the assumption "that all non-Christian philosophies were 'pagan' and indeed somehow diabolical" (*MZM* 83), to identify, and identify with, what they perceived as the genuine, deeply human and humane values of Chinese Confucianism, to follow the guidance of the Holy Spirit who "asks the Christian apostle to respect and preserve all that is good in the culture and philosophy of newly converted peoples" (*MZM* 85) – phrasing that remarkably anticipates that found in *Nostra Aetate*, the Vatican Council document on non-Christian religions that would appear a few years later.[29] Prof. de Bary implies that Merton is contrasting Ricci and his Confucian counterparts when he claims (*Conversation* 360) that "Ricci recognized the importance of educated Chinese leadership, and he did not just dismiss or sidestep them in the way that Merton tends to do when he denigrates Confucian scholars as in the follow-

29. See "Declaration on the Relationship of the Church to Non-Christian Religions" ("*Nostra Aetate*"), promulgated October 28, 1965, n. 2: "The Catholic Church rejects nothing which is true and holy in these religions. She looks with sincere respect upon those ways of conduct and of life, those rules and teachings which, though differing in many particulars from what she holds and sets forth, nevertheless often reflect a ray of that Truth which enlightens all men. . . . The Church therefore has this exhortation for her sons: prudently and lovingly, through dialogue and collaboration with the followers of other religions, and in witness of Christian faith and life, acknowledge, preserve, and promote the spiritual and moral goods found among these men, as well as the values in their society and culture" (*The Documents of Vatican II*, ed. Walter Abbott, SJ [New York: America Press, 1966] 662-63).

ing: 'All China, at least all the ruling class of China, was supposed in theory to be educated along Confucian lines, but many and not the least successful of Chinese statesman were men who with the outward façade of Confucianism, were inwardly either pedants, rigid and heartless conformists, or unprincipled crooks'" (*MZM* 53). But in fact Merton is not referring here to Ricci's Confucian contemporaries, as one might assume from the context: this quotation is not found in "The Jesuits in China" at all, but comes from "Classic Chinese Thought," where it immediately follows Merton's highly laudatory description of Confucius' success "in founding a system of education which, for all its eventual limitations, was able to survive, and to form generations of scholars who were to be the glory of their nation and a singular credit to the human race" (*MZM* 53). In other words, the Confucian system at its best – not merely individual Confucians but the system and its products generally – was one of the most admirable achievements in human history. In its original context, the statement Prof. de Bary quotes is not presented as a description of the typical state of affairs but a concessive caveat, a realistic recognition that human beings often fail to live up to their ideals, and sometimes even profess ideals in order to conceal considerably less elevated motives and ambitions. Merton certainly would not claim that such behavior is in any way particularly or peculiarly Confucian, and his statement is certainly not to be taken, as de Bary tends to do, as a blanket condemnation of Confucianism as practiced through the centuries. Toward the conclusion of "Classic Chinese Thought," Merton approvingly quotes the historian Christopher Dawson, who wrote that due to Confucianism, "in China alone among the advanced civilizations of the world, the law of nature had not been a philosophical abstraction but a living force which has had a religious appeal to the heart and conscience of the people . . . In this way Chinese civilization seems to have solved certain fundamental problems of the social and moral order more successfully than any other known culture" (*MZM* 64).[30] Such a declaration is hardly compatible with de Bary's hypothesis that Merton acknowledges Confucian values and approves of individuals faithful to the teachings of the "Confucian classics," but rejects a Confucian institution that failed utterly to live up to its professed ideals.

---

30. Christopher Dawson, *Religion and Culture* (New York: Meridian Books, 1959) 171.

This citation from a celebrated historian prompts a consideration of the final issue raised by Prof. de Bary: is it accurate to say that Merton the poet neglects the historical record and so constructs a "timeless" Confucianism detached from its actual setting in time and space, a perspective that "does not recognize," in particular, "the much broader significance of Neo-Confucianism and Zhu Xi's core curriculum as it spread to the rest of East Asia," so that "he is in no position to recognize the continuing vitality of Confucianism inside and outside of China" (*Conversation* 365)? Here de Bary's critique initially seems to be most cogent, as he broadly but effectively highlights the reforms of the eleventh and twelfth centuries, unmentioned by Merton, that were in place at the time of Ricci's mission and would continue to guide China until the end of the Empire early in the twentieth century. But there is at least a hint in "Classic Chinese Thought" that even this deficiency he detects may not be as applicable to Merton as it seems. In his notes for this article Merton lists among his resources the volume *Sources of Chinese Tradition*, a massive anthology of primary sources presented chronologically, with ample commentary, from antiquity to the present, edited by none other than Wm. Theodore de Bary,[31] as well as Liu Wu-Chi's *A Short History of Confucian Philosophy* and other texts.[32] The more than forty pages of notes that Merton took in preparation for writing his early articles on the Chinese tradition include abundant citations from both these works, among others.

---

31. *Sources of Chinese Tradition*, compiled by Wm. Theodore de Bary, Wing-tsit Chan and Burton Watson (New York: Columbia University Press, 1960), one of the three initial volumes (along with sourcebooks on Indian and Japanese traditions) of "Introduction to Oriental Civilizations" under the general editorship of de Bary, volumes LIV-LVI of Columbia's massive *Records of Civilization: Sources and Studies* series. It is clear from Notebook 58A that Merton relied heavily on this volume for texts and background material on the classic period of Confucian as well as Taoist thought. (A two-volume revised edition of this work, still under the general editorship of de Bary, was published by Columbia University Press in 1999-2000).

32. Merton also mentions in his notes to "Classic Chinese Thought" Arthur Waley, *Three Ways of Thought in Ancient China* ([1939] Garden City, NY: Doubleday Anchor, 1956) and *Confucius: The Great Digest & Unwobbling Pivot*, translation and commentary by Ezra Pound (New York: New Directions, 1951), both of which are cited extensively in Notebook 58A, as are Huang, I. A. Richards' *Mencius on the Mind: Experiments in Multiple Definition* (New York: Harcourt, Brace, 1932) and Helmut Wilhelm's article on Confucianism in *Encyclopedia of World Art*, ed. Bernard Myers, 17 vols. (New York: McGraw-Hill, 1959-83) vol. 3, cols. 775-782.

Merton begins his compilation with a page on "Poetry & Wisdom of the Ancients" situating China in the context of other cultures, followed by a century-by-century chronology of key figures and events from the sixth century BC through the seventeenth century AD. In particular, there are detailed notes from the *Short History* on the Sung philosophers and the rise of Neo-Confucianism, with its own "title page" (23) featuring a quotation from Liu Wu-Chi.[33] Merton's notes include the following on Chu Hsi (i.e. Zhu Xi[34]): "Became the orthodox source of Confucianism – greatest single influence on Chinese thought / Instituted universal study of 4 classics / Put Meng Tzu in the hierarchy, excluding Hsün – Put end to tendency to deify Kung / Formulated complete system of thought / *Ethic* – desire obscures man's true nature. / To restore nature – a) exercise of attentiveness (to luminous spirit in oneself) / b) extension of knowledge (of celestial Li – through li of individual objects) leading to *sudden enlightenment* . . . . Extensive commentaries on Classics – approved as 'correct' in govt exams down to 1905" – and considerably more of a rather technical nature, concluding with a quotation from Liu Wu-Chi stating that "(in him) the Neo-Ju philosophy reached its highest development."[35] Far from being unaware of Chu Hsi's importance, then, Merton takes particular note of it,[36]

33. "Just as the Chinese intellect burst forth (in the Chou) with its colorful 'hundred schools' so it now ripened through the cultivation of the Sung scholars into a more mature, complete and well-rounded system of philosophy that was to reign supreme in Chinese intellectual circles for more than 700 years" (Liu 151, which reads: ". . . intellect suddenly burst forth into bloom with its . . .").

34. Merton uses the Wade-Giles system of orthography (as does de Bary in 1960) rather than the Pinyin system now standard – hence the divergent spellings of the same name.

35. Reading Notebook 58A: 25A, 26; quotation from Liu 161.

36. It should be noted in connection with this issue that according to Dunne, the Jesuits in general and Matteo Ricci in particular differentiated what they considered to be "original Confucianism . . . from the materialistic interpretations of the Sung School" of Chu Hsi (*Generation of Giants* 27). "It was through his studies during these years at Shaochow that Ricci came to distinguish between the original doctrine of the classics and the interpretations given to the text by commentators of the Chu Hsi school. These interpretations had determined the character of Sung neo-Confucianism, the accepted orthodoxy of the day. . . . If Christianity were to enter deeply into the life of China, it had to find points of contact with Confucianism. If it were to receive a sympathetic hearing Ricci would have to persuade the scholars that the metaphysics of Chu Hsi, thoroughly materialistic and utterly opposed to the Christian world view, were not an integral part of original Confucian doctrine. This he attempted to do by appealing to the original texts" (32). Ricci aligned himself with the progressive, reformist movement of the

and follows it with capsule summaries, drawn from Liu, of eight

Tung-lin group, who were opposed both to the powerful and corrupt eunuchs at court and to the neo-Confucian establishment, "the self-seeking and reactionary type of officials who were allied with them" (42). It was "from the Tung-lin milieu," Dunne writes, that "all of the eminent Christian converts of the scholar class and many non-Christian friends of Christianity emerged" (43). *Generation of Giants* was still unpublished when Merton was taking notes on *A Short History of Confucianism*, so he would not have known about Ricci's negative attitude toward Chu Hsi, but he would have read Liu Wu-chi's assertion that "this rationalization of the Ju philosophy disposed of the last few religious elements that had strayed into the K'ung system. Once for all, the Neo-Ju rationalists put an end to the tendency to deify Master K'ung and to make his teaching a religion – a tendency that had occasionally asserted itself . . . in the Han and T'ang ages. Lastly, this attempt to humanize the K'ung doctrine had also the indirect effect of ultimately doing away with the ancient Sinitic conception of Heaven as a personalized god. This was in line with the position Master K'ung took, who refused to discuss the question of religion one way or the other. And now, with the mysteries of the creation satisfactorily explained in terms of metaphysics, it is obvious that there would be no further use for an almighty god as the ruling deity of men. At least, this was the belief of the Chinese intellectuals, who, like Master K'ung, kept aloof from spiritual beings while at the same time showing a sovereign contempt for the superstitions of the common people. In fact, the mind of Chinese scholars has been so long divorced from all religious ideas and beliefs that to this day they remain confirmed atheists in the best tradition of the Neo-Ju school" (164) – a perspective that seems clearly shared by the author himself and one that would confirm the rationale for the opposition of Ricci and his fellow Jesuits, and that represents a very different understanding of Confucius from that taken by Ricci – and by Merton (and de Bary as well). See also John Wu's November 28, 1961 letter to Merton in which he compares Chu Hsi with the later neo-Confucian Wang Yang-ming (1474-1529), writing: "Chu Hsi is theoretically more transcendent. Wang Yang Ming, more immanentist. But I feel that Wang is more spiritual than Chu. My conclusion was that if one is thorough-goingly immanentist, one is bound to arrive at a transcendence more authentic than a rationalist could conceive of" (*Merton & the Tao* 217).While de Bary does not consider Ricci's attitude toward Chu Hsi in his lecture, in the headnote (presumably by de Bary) to Li Chi-tsao's preface to Ricci's *The True Meaning of God* (*Sources of Chinese Tradition* 626-27) there is a brief reference to the fact that Ricci (and his Chinese friend Li, who became a Christian some time after writing this preface to Ricci's fundamental work on Christian beliefs) found "the speculations of the Neo-Confucianists . . . less compatible" than "the Confucian moral ideal with the Christian doctrines of divine justice and self-perfection." In *The Great Civilized Conversation* de Bary notes "the essential ambivalence of Neo-Confucian teaching" with respect to the religious foundations of Confucianism, pointing out "the number of later Neo-Confucians for whom this religiosity has a strong appeal, as well as those others for whom it was to become an abomination" (114); he finds in Zhu Xi himself "a religious attitude of reverence toward all life," a recognition of "a religious dimension in the moral cultivation of the self, bridging the active and contemplative sides of human life" (120), and refers to his "actually experiencing in some vague

more significant figures in Confucian intellectual history from the twelfth through the twentieth centuries.[37]

Why then does this important aspect of Confucian historical development remain unmentioned in *Mystics and Zen Masters*? Not taking account of the original provenance and audience of Merton's articles, de Bary assumes it is due to his ignorance of and/or disinterest in the historical development of Confucianism, but these extensive notes and their evidence of wide reading in the historical background of Confucianism demonstrate conclusively that this is not at all the case. Rather, writing for popular religious publications like *Jubilee* and *Catholic World*, most of whose readers probably had little or no previous acquaintance with Asian religious and philosophical traditions, Merton focuses in his articles on what he sees to be the essentials of Confucianism, providing a broad-based overview that doesn't overwhelm his readers with a plethora of details but nevertheless situates the rise of Confucianism in its original historical context and provides brief but insightful summaries and commentary on key texts. To trace in more detail the various phases of historical development would be ineffective and inappropriate with regard to Merton's purpose in writing these articles – to make the wisdom of Asian traditions more accessible, better known and more appreciated by his largely American Catholic audience. But this does not mean, as Prof. de Bary assumes, that these articles represent the extent of Merton's own acquaintance with and recognition of the key moments and movements in the history of his subject. He certainly does not claim to be an original scholar of Confucianism, or any of the other traditions he writes about, but he clearly values the work of scholars – including Prof. de Bary himself – and draws on them to the extent he considers appropriate in his project to share his own enthusiasm for and insight into these traditions, while remaining faithful to his own role as a practitioner, one who responds to the presence of wisdom primarily on the spiritual rather than a purely objective, intellectual level, who believes that "The values hidden in Oriental thought actually reveal themselves only on the plane of spiritual experience, or perhaps, if

manner a mystical enlightenment" as a young man (170).

37. In his notes on Chu Hsi's rival Lu Hsiang-shan (1139-1193), an exponent of the "Mind" school, Merton highlights his "heavy Buddhist leanings / Emphasis on meditation + intuition" and his conception of morality as a "rediscovery of one's lost nature, which is good. (cf Mencius) – *Enlightenment*" (26) – thus an alternative to Chu Hsi's materialism.

you like, of aesthetic experience" (*SE* 112).

It is certainly true that Merton responded to Taoist (as well as Buddhist) thought with deeper sympathy and greater enthusiasm than to Confucianism. In his first detailed journal comments on Chinese thought,[38] after his early July 1960 time in the hospital in Louisville where he occupied himself "reading Chinese philosophy" (*TTW* 17 [6/30/1960])[39] he writes of his appreciation of Mencius' Ox Mountain parable, comparing the Chinese Confucian's positive view of human nature with that of St. Bernard and remarking that "An interesting comparison could be made between them, especially as regards the 'four beginnings' – the four roots in nature from which love, righteousness, Li, 禮 – and wisdom can always spring provided they are not completely killed," but then concludes with the simple statement: "But I like Chuang Tzu better" (*TTW* 19 [7/10/1960]).[40] He recognizes the validity of much of the Taoist critique of Confucianism, particularly as found in Chuang Tzu,[41] who uses humor and parody to expose the limitations of the Confucian ethos and its potential for declining into a kind of formalism based on external behavior that does not express interior attitudes. Merton sees the Taoist stress on inner spontaneity and creativity as

38. He had earlier mentioned some experiments he had made with the *I Ching*, or *Book of Changes*, one of the five "Confucian Classics," under the influence of C. G. Jung's Foreword to that work (*The I Ching or Book of Changes*, trans. Richard Wilhelm and Cary Baynes, 2 vols. [New York: Pantheon, 1950]), during a period of vocation crisis connected with the request for exclaustration and a relocation to the primitive Benedictine monastery of Cuernavaca in Mexico (see Thomas Merton, *A Search for Solitude: Pursuing the Monk's True Life. Journals, vol. 3: 1952-1960*, ed. Lawrence S. Cunningham [San Francisco: HarperCollins, 1996] 266-67 [3/3/1959]; 267 [3/10/1959]; 279-81 [5/12/1959]; subsequent references will be cited as "*SS*" parenthetically in the text).

39. Almost certainly he was reading Waley's *Three Ways of Thought in Ancient China*, which includes sections on Chuang Tzu and Mencius, as well as the Legalists (or Realists as Waley calls them), since he refers explicitly to the first two in the July 10 entry that follows (though he mentions only Richards' *Mencius on the Mind* there).

40. This entry was reworked for inclusion in *Conjectures of a Guilty Bystander* (122-23), part of the second section of the book, entitled "The Night Spirit and the Dawn Air," images taken from this parable.

41. See in particular Merton's version of Chuang Tzu's "Confucius and the Madman" (*WCT* 58-59), with its suggestion that Confucian virtue is effective when the world is in order but useless when the world is "askew," and that in such circumstances the madman, the "fool" who can speak unpalatable truths in seemingly nonsensical words, with a deeper meaning not immediately perceptible, may have deeper insight than the sage.

a challenge, but also a complement, to the clearly defined patterns of behavior spelled out by Confucianism with its "self-conscious virtuousness" (*WCT* 26). He notes Chuang Tzu's complaint about Confucianism that while it produced "well-behaved and virtuous officials . . . . it nevertheless limited and imprisoned them within fixed external norms and consequently made it impossible for them to act really freely and creatively in response to the ever new demands of unforeseen situations" (*WCT* 20). The Confucian reliance on the "ethical Tao," the "Tao 'that can be named,'" was critiqued by Lao Tzu and Chuang Tzu as neglecting the "Eternal Tao . . . the nameless and unknowable source of all being" (*WCT* 20-21).

But if it is true that Merton was sympathetic to the Taoists' criticisms of Confucianism and resonated more deeply with the contemplative perspective he found in the *Tao Te Ching* and in Chuang Tzu, it is also true that he saw Confucianism as a salutary corrective to Taoist tendencies toward what he called in "Classic Chinese Thought" "the practical anarchism which is implicit in Taoist doctrine" that made it largely irrelevant to those struggling "with the problems of life in society." While Taoist withdrawal could and did lead some to an "evasion *upward* into the transcendent," for many it resulted in "the evasion downward into the Freudian id, an all too obvious consummation" (*MZM* 50). Thus his critique is not all one-sided, and in this first article on Oriental wisdom Confucianism is mainly presented as a kind of mean between the poles of Taoist anarchism and Legalist totalitarianism. More generally, he recognizes that Confucianism and Taoism, the ethical Tao and the eternal Tao, are not mutually exclusive alternatives but complements, providing a creative and fruitful tension needed for growth toward a fully integrated human existence. In *The Way of Chuang Tzu* he notes the tendency in later Confucianism for the ethical Tao to be subdivided into numerous "ways" of behaving properly in various social roles, but goes on to point out that "these various human taos could and did become fingers pointing to the invisible and divine Tao" (*WCT* 21), thus allowing for a synthesis rather than an unbridgeable opposition between Confucianism and Taoism.

In "Christian Culture Needs Oriental Wisdom" he emphasizes the crucial importance for contemporary Christians of recognizing and responding to "a dimension of *wisdom* oriented to contemplation as well as to wise action" (*MZM* 80; *SE* 111) as represented by these two traditions, respectively, articulated in the texts of the *Tao*

Te Ching and the *Hsiao Ching*.[42] Of the latter he remarks:

> Here in this "Classic of Filial Love" we find not so much
> a Confucianism that is arbitrarily opposed to Taoism, as
> what I would venture to call a *Confucian kind of Taoism*.
> We must not imagine that the classic Confucianism of the
> third century B.C. was something purely formalistic and
> external, without respect for the interior, the hidden mystery
> in which all life has its invisible roots. On the contrary, . . .
> filial love was, for these Confucians, the taproot which
> was sunk most deeply in the mystery of the ethical *Tao*
> and which, unless it was cut by selfishness, kept both the
> individual and society in living contact with the mysterious
> will of heaven. (*MZM* 71; *SE* 104)

He likewise finds in the *Doctrine of the Mean*, which he calls "a
kind of Confucian reply to Taoism" (*MZM* 58), not merely a practical treatise on ethics that recommends moderation in all things,
as the somewhat misleading English translation of the title might
suggest,[43] but a recognition "that at the very center of man's being is
an intimate, dynamic principle of reality" that seeks to express itself
in "right action" and in so doing brings the person into harmony with
"the hidden reality of heaven" (*MZM* 59). The *Great Learning* is
also much more than simply a treatise on the proper ordering of society; it emphasizes, according to Merton, that such order is the fruit
of "a way of enlightenment, of clarification by *intelligent action*"
in harmony with the ethical Tao, "the *fruit of spiritual awareness*"
that is celebrated in the liturgical ritual that is the context of authentic Confucianism (*MZM* 61). In such a "magnificently human,
contemplative, noble, and productive" vision of human flourishing
Merton finds the "key to classic Chinese thought" (*MZM* 62) and
a salutary model for a nominally Christian culture that has largely

---

42. In his May 23, 1961 letter to Paul Sih, thanking him for sending the
Hsiao Ching, Merton writes: "I enjoy the *Hsiao Ching* very much indeed. In its
simplicity it has roots in the highest wisdom and one is surprised at the 'modern'
sound of some of its basic intuitions" (*HGL* 549). In Reading Notebook 58A
Merton recorded extensive notes on Sih's Preface to the work and on each of the
book's eighteen chapters (40-43).

43. In his notes on this work in Reading Notebook 58A he points out the
"Doctrine" is an addition to the Chinese title (14), and in "Classic Chinese Thought"
he suggests that the title "Unwobbling Pivot" given the work by Ezra Pound "is
perhaps closer to the author's intention" (*MZM* 59).

lost touch with its sacred and spiritual foundations.

At the conclusion of "Classic Chinese Thought" Merton notes that "Benedictines can hardly find it difficult to understand and to admire the tradition of Kung Tzu, which has in it so many elements in common with the tradition and spirit of St. Benedict" (*MZM* 65), and in his series of conferences on Confucianism with the novices in mid-1965, while associating the pattern of Confucian life more particularly with the "Black Benedictines" (i.e. the Order of St. Benedict as distinguished from the Cistercians) with their emphasis on liturgical life and a more active, outward-directed form of monasticism, he goes on to indicate its relevance to their own process of monastic formation, noting that one could easily spend three years simply absorbing and interiorizing the wisdom of Confucius.[44] He returns to this point repeatedly, emphasizing two classes later that the whole point of formation is to learn humility by contact with the "pivot" of the Tao, the balance of active *yang* and passive *yin* as expressed in Chinese landscape painting;[45] and at the conclusion of the last of these four conferences[46] he focuses on Confucius' instruction of his disciples in the area of culture, identified with true freedom, so that they could complete his work by bringing out this same capacity in others, in those whom they would touch in their work, as a parallel to the work of monastic formation, guiding people with the capacity to do this creative work and to help others to do so as well – an implicit reflection on his own decade as master of novices as he prepared to retire to the hermitage a little more than a month later.

But he goes even further in the second of these presentations,[47] focusing on the Confucian reinterpretation of the "superior man" not as a figure of high social status but as a fully developed, humane person characterized by the fourfold qualities of *jen* (empathic love), *yi* (justice or righteousness), *li* (a "liturgical" connection to the cosmos) and *chih* (wisdom that interiorizes these values)[48] and presents as his "basic thesis" the suggestion that this natural pattern is a kind of preparation for the gospel and is fulfilled in Christ, in whom the same fourfold structure can be discerned on a higher plane: as

44. N. 148.4 [6/10/1965].

45. N. 150.3 [7/8/1965].

46. N. 151.2 [7/15/1965].

47. N. 150.1 [7/1/1965].

48. This is the same fourfold "mandala" that he describes in his introduction to *The Way of Chuang Tzu* (18-19), written at around the same time.

wisdom, justification, atonement and sanctification, so identified by St. Paul in 1 Corinthians 1:30, Christ embodies *chih*, *yi*, *jen* and *li*, respectively. Likewise the symbol of *chung*, the ideogram that represents an arrow going to the center of a target, found in the title of the *Doctrine of the Mean* or *Unwobbling Pivot* (*Chung Yung*) can be analogized to the cross and seen as a reflection of the "still point of the turning world" described by T. S. Eliot,[49] a basically contemplative Chinese perception of wholeness.

Making a similar point at the conclusion of "The Jesuits in China," Merton speaks of the encounter between East and West in Confucian Peking as "a kind of brief epiphany of the Son of Man as a Chinese scholar" (*MZM* 90), which seems at first to refer only to Ricci and his companions, in their Confucian robes, as bringing the presence of Christ to the Orient, but the subsequent reference to "the old tradition of the wise men from the East"[50] that "has always obscurely called for this epiphany" (*MZM* 90) suggests that Merton is referring not only to Ricci being Christ for but discovering Christ in the scholars he encountered, that he was able, as Merton writes in his conclusion to his essay "From Pilgrimage to Crusade," to recognize "the stranger" he met at the end of his long journey as being "no other than ourselves – which is the same as saying that we find Christ in him . . . Christ our fellow-pilgrim and our brother" (*MZM* 112). It is the recognition of this epiphany of Christ in the other, the realization, as Merton says elsewhere, that "God speaks, and God is to be heard, not only on Sinai, not only in my own heart, but in the *voice of the stranger*" (*SE* 121) that Merton affirms as the ultimate goal for dialogue with Eastern wisdom generally, and, pace Prof. de Bary, with Confucianism in particular.

In *Conjectures of a Guilty Bystander*, when he reflects on the "angels" who have been in some way revelatory in a "quasi-sacramental way" in his own life, providing "the tone and value of

49. T. S. Eliot, "Burnt Norton" II.16, in T. S. Eliot, *The Complete Poems and Plays: 1909-1950* (New York: Harcourt, Brace & World, 1962) 119; Merton quotes this same line in relation to Eastern religious traditions in his essay "The New Consciousness" (Thomas Merton, *Zen and the Birds of Appetite* [New York: New Directions, 1968] 24).

50. The reference may consciously or subconsciously have been suggested to Merton by the title of Vincent Cronin's biography of Ricci, *The Wise Man from the West* (New York: E. P. Dutton, 1955); Merton's June 22, 1958 journal reference to "Very good book on Fr. Matthew Ricci in refectory" (*SS* 207), his first recorded mention of Ricci, is almost certainly to this work.

my own interior world," Merton notes that this tone is not limited to the Latin West but "it is open also to China, to Confucianism and to Zen, to the great Taoists" (*CGB* 167);[51] he goes on to say that "it is . . . by means of this cultural matter with a mysterious Christian form, that God works in our lives, since we are creatures of history, and tradition is vitally important to us" (*CGB* 167). In his May 1965 essay *Day of a Stranger* he notes "the reassuring companionship of many silent Tzu's and Fu's: Kung Tzu, Lao Tzu, Meng Tzu, Tu Fu" as an essential part of the "mental ecology" of his hermitage, "a living balance of spirits in this corner of the woods."[52] Thus it is not a timeless, placeless spirituality that Merton values, but one rooted in history and tradition, experienced in a particular corner of a particular wood. In this "living balance of spirits," among these reassuring companions, the great figures of the Confucian tradition are prominently included, presented by Merton as playing an essential part, as representatives, if not of a "higher religion," then certainly of a deep spiritual wisdom, of "a *way of life* impregnated with truth" (*MZM* 59).

---

51. In the original August 6, 1961 journal passage from which Merton develops this reflection, he writes simply: "Thought much today of the tone and value of my own interior world, which is after all important, at least relatively. And culture, of a sort, has given it much of its tone. Christian and European culture, Christian spirituality, monastic life, occidental mysticism, plus a certain openness to other cultures and spiritualities, especially I think the Chinese. All this is not only relevant to my life and salvation but has crucial significance in my whole vocation" (*TTW* 147-48).

52. Thomas Merton, *Day of a Stranger* (Salt Lake City: Gibbs M. Smith, 1981) 35.

MO TZU AND THOMAS MERTON

Robert E. Daggy

Mo Tzu and Thomas Merton. Strange bedfellows, as we say in the West. Mo Tzu lived in China in the fifth century before Christ. Thomas Merton, basically our contemporary, was very much a twentieth-century person who died only twenty-five years ago. At first glance, it would seem that these two figures, separated in time by nearly two and a half millennia, have only one thing in common. As noted scholar Arthur Waley pointed out fifty years ago (and it still holds true today): "A good many people outside China have heard of Confucianism and Taoism; very few know even the name of Mo Tzu."[1] It is undoubtedly true that very few people in China know the name Thomas Merton. So why is there a paper being delivered at this conference that deals in some way with these two diverse and disparate men? One good reason would seem to be that both came to the conclusion that universal love – a benign, benevolent, non-discriminating love – might be the governing principle, indeed the remedy, which would allow the world and all humans (not just an individual culture) to live in peace and harmony – and this love might be the world's salvation.

Thomas Merton was a signal and significant figure in helping to introduce Chinese thought and make it explicable to readers in the West, particularly and primarily in the United States. When he wrote in nearly mystical fashion that he had the "reassuring companionship of many silent Tzu's and Fu's" in his hermitage in the woods, one of those "silent" voices was certainly Mo Tzu, even if Merton, as we shall see, was not immediately as "reassured" by Mo Tzu as he was by some other Chinese thinkers.[2] But, beyond the fact that Merton was definitely familiar with Mo Tzu, there are interesting connections between the two, always remembering, of course, their very different times, geographies and mind sets. First, however, let me try to introduce Thomas Merton to you.

---

1. Arthur Waley, *Three Ways of Thought in Ancient China* (1939; Garden City, NY: Doubleday, n.d.) 121; subsequent references are cited as "Waley" parenthetically in the text.
    2. Thomas Merton, *Day of a Stranger*, edited with an introduction by Robert E. Daggy (Salt Lake City: Gibbs M. Smith, 1981) 35.

WHO IS THOMAS MERTON?

People are already calling Thomas Merton a symbol that will speak for our time in centuries to come. That may be true, but we're not in those centuries, though sometimes a period is symbolized by the most unlikely person. Merton was a monk of the Roman Catholic Order of Trappists, or Cistercians, decidedly an unlikely person given United States society in the so-called "post-Christian" world. Yet Merton enunciated a response to our world which seems to speak for our time.

He died in Bangkok, Thailand, on December 10, 1968, victim of accidental electrocution. His death ironically occurred twenty-seven years to the day after his entrance into the Abbey of Gethsemani near Bardstown, Kentucky, on December 10, 1941. The next day his obituary in *The New York Times* called him a person "who spoke from the world of silence to questing millions who sought God. . . . He was a writer of singular grace about the City of God and an essayist of penetrating originality about the City of Man."[3]

This man, whose writings came to mean so much to people in all parts of the world, began his "journey," as he often described his life, on January 31, 1915, in Prades, France, a small village near the Spanish border. He was the son of Owen Heathcote Grierson Merton (1887-1931), a painter–water colorist who was born in New Zealand, and Ruth Calvert (Jenkins) Merton (1887-1921), an artist–designer born in the United States. His only brother, John Paul Merton (1918-1943), who joined the Canadian Royal Air Force during World War II, died when his plane crashed in the North Sea. After his mother's death when he was six, Thomas Merton spent his childhood in several places, sometimes in company with his father, sometimes with his maternal grandparents in New York, and sometimes with "friends"[4] of his father's in odd locations. The younger Merton was exposed early to a literary and artistic milieu best described as Bohemian. He received his elementary education in the United States, Bermuda, France and England. His father died in 1931 when he was sixteen years old and, after a disastrous year at Cambridge University (1933-1934)

---

3. Israel Shenker, "Thomas Merton Is Dead at 53; Monk Wrote of Search for God," *New York Times* (11 December 1968) 1, 42.

4. See Robert E. Daggy, "Birthday Theology: A Reflection on Thomas Merton and the Bermuda Menage," *The Kentucky Review* 7.2 (Summer 1987) 62-89.

in England, his British guardian sent him to the United States to be supervised, financially and otherwise, by his American grandparents. He attended Columbia University in New York City, receiving a bachelor's degree in 1937 and a master's degree in English in 1938. By that time, with both his grandparents also dead, his "journey," particularly after his conversion to Roman Catholicism in 1938, impelled him to secede from conventionality to the margins of society.

This desire for marginality had been, and was to continue to be, a basic thrust in Merton's life. He later remarked: "Even in 1935 the news made me vomit." His Columbia friend, Edward Rice, has stated that at Columbia, Merton and his friends "to a man [were] fighting the Establishment and [were] young, rebellious, alienated misfits and (in their own eyes) downtrodden and poor."[5] Merton dabbled with Communism and peace movements and, apparently, followed a "Bohemian" lifestyle, perhaps because his childhood had left him comfortable only with a lifestyle perceived as marginal (and one must say questionable) by the rest of society. He stood in the vanguard of what was later to be dubbed "the Beat movement"; he and his friends staged "a dry-run of the Beat movement" in the late 1930s.[6]

He converted to Roman Catholicism in 1938 and attempted to join the Franciscan Order, but was rejected. He then secured a job teaching English, but continued to desire greater withdrawal from the world. In 1941, he entered the Order of Cistercians of the Strict Observance (or Trappists) of Gethsemani. The state of Kentucky in the eastern central part of the United States was then sparsely populated and the abbey or monastery was in an area of dense hardwood forest, surrounded by ancient, eroded mountains, called "knobs" in the area. Merton was to live among these trees and knobs for the next twenty-seven years of his life. It was not an easy life for, when he entered, the Order still followed basically a medieval lifestyle, one based on prayer, silence and work. Merton was given the religious name of "Louis" and was ordained priest in 1949.

He aspired to be a writer and had written several novels, mostly autobiographical, before he entered Gethsemani. His search for

---

5. Edward Rice, *The Man in the Sycamore Tree: The Good Times and Hard Life of Thomas Merton* (Garden City, NY: Doubleday, 1970) 30.

6. Wilfred Sheed, "The Beat Movement," *New York Times Book Review* (13 January 1972) 2.

himself and for God caused him to abandon these early aspirations
for a time, though he continued to write poetry. His own inclinations
and requirements of his order, however, led him back to writing as
part of his vocation as a monk. His early productions, aside from
his poetry, consisted of short works on contemplation, pamphlets
about the order, collections of notes on Cistercian saints and blessed,
and two lengthier biographies of Cistercians. In 1948, his autobiography, the story of his conversion to Roman Catholicism and
his entrance into the monastery, was published. Called *The Seven
Storey Mountain* (reference to the levels of Dante's purgatory),
it was an immediate and phenomenal bestseller and brought him
international recognition. Speaking from the margins of society,
Merton touched a nerve in the post-World-War-II world, not just
in the United States, but in war-weary Europe and even in Latin
America. During the next twenty years, he produced an amazing
number of books and articles and increasingly became a voice to
be heard and reckoned with.

His interests and his writings covered a wide range. He was
a poet, biographer, essayist, novelist, diarist, critic, commentator,
synthesizer, sometime satirist, and a letter writer of extraordinary
ability. He was a calligrapher, artist, photographer, educator and
spiritual director. Some forty books were published in his lifetime
and over twenty have been edited and published since his death.

Merton entered Gethsemani to withdraw from the world and to
live on its fringes in silence and solitude. His early writings, those
from the 1940s and into the 1950s, tended to be ascetic, otherworldly, colored by a conviction of the complete separation of God and the
world. Yet, despite this desire for withdrawal and the expression
of it in his early writings, Merton was never quite able to withdraw
totally from the world. Though he continued at Gethsemani in the
1950s to seek greater solitude and though he continued to associate
and identify himself with those whom he perceived as "marginal"
– African Americans, Latin Americans, Native Americans, the
young, and (very early) women – his humanity with the world and
to commentary upon it.[7]

Best known, perhaps, for his writings on spirituality and
contemplation, Merton's concern for cultural integrity and social
justice led him in the 1960s to write and publish on such issues as

7. See Lawrence S. Cunningham, "The Monk as a Critic of Culture," *The
Merton Annual* 3 (1990) 187-99.

ecumenism and spiritual renewal, racial conflict, genocide, war
and peace, the environment, the Third World and other problems
inherent in a technological society. He played an important role in
the development of a cross-cultural consciousness in the 1960s.[8] His
writings and taped lectures on non-Christian traditions helped to
introduce them to U.S. readers – Taoism, Confucianism, Zen Buddhism, Sufism, and Austronesian spirituality. Through his wide
correspondence (he basically never left the monastery), he engaged
in dialogue with scholars and leaders of Hinduism, Islam, Judaism
and other religious traditions. In literature, his translations of Latin
American poets helped to introduce Latin American literature to
the United States.[9] Merton was, however, not a systematic writer
or thinker, and he cannot be considered a "theologian" in the usual
sense of the word. But it has been pointed out that if one thinks of a
"theologian" as "one who speaks of God with the authority of experience . . . in that sense Thomas Merton was probably the greatest theologian that the [United States] produced in the twentieth
century."[10]

In 1965, as part of his search for an even greater solitude, he was
given permission to withdraw from the routine of community life
and to live on the Abbey grounds in a small, concrete-block cabin.
He described his occupation in 1967 as "hermit." In 1968, he was
given permission to travel to Asia on a kind of pilgrimage. There, at
a conference on Buddhist-Christian monasticism outside Bangkok,
he died.

To assess his significance, dead just twenty-five years, with
an active writing career that covered little more than the preceding
twenty years, is a difficult task. We may still be too close to him in
time to judge his ultimate significance in and for our century. That
his popularity continues and increases, that he is for many people
a figure of near cultic proportions, that an academic industry has
already clustered around Merton studies, is true. Those who admire
him feel he is one of the most significant figures of our time. One
estimate stated:

8. See William M. Thompson, "Merton's Contribution to a Transcultural
Consciousness," *Thomas Merton: Pilgrim in Process*, edited by Donald Grayston
& Michael W. Higgins (Toronto: Griffin House, 1983) 147-69.

9. See Stefan Baciu, "Latin America and Spain in the Poetic World of Thomas
Merton," *The Merton Annual* 2 (1989) 13-26.

10. See Lawrence S. Cunningham, "Thomas Merton as Theologian: An
Appreciation," *The Kentucky Review* 7.2 (Summer 1987) 90-97.

Supposing the bets could be collected, which of this century's prophets and sages would a gambler back to show the greatest staying power? Which, that is, will most accurately and comprehensively have conveyed to future generations the experience of being human in the twentieth century, been the surest litmus paper of our problems, sensibilities, hopes and fears, read the signs of the time with the most discerning eye, offered the most effective cure for our diseases and have at least mapped out the best track to follow towards a better world? My own money, however improbable, would be an American monk who lived most of his life in a Kentucky monastery and much of that in a small hermitage, who rarely traveled outside its boundaries and was professionally dedicated to silence and solitude: the Trappist, Thomas Merton. . . . Out of that silence and solitude spoke an authentically twentieth-century voice, articulating with power and grace this century's fevers and frets and, with growing confidence, their relief and remedy.[11]

THOMAS MERTON AND CHINA

Silent Lamp! Silent Lamp!
I only see its radiance
But hear not its voice!
Spring beyond the world!

Dr. John Chin Hsung Wu, friend and correspondent of Merton's, wrote this haiku to him in 1966, gently chiding him for his silence. Wu, convinced that Merton's unusual perceptions and cultural acuity could potentially help bridge the gaps between East and West, had already given him a Chinese name – *Mei Teng* the "Silent Lamp." And there was no doubt that Merton was interested in China and in Chinese thought.

He wrote to Paul Cardinal Yu Pin, one-time Archbishop of Nanking, early in 1961: "I am closer to Confucius and Lao Tzu than I am to my contemporaries in the United States, even, strange to say, many of my Catholic contemporaries."[12] He invited Yu Pin

11. John Francis Xavier Harriot, "A Man for Our Time," *The Tablet* 242.7741 (26 November 1988) 1354.

12. February 11, 1961 letter of Thomas Merton to Paul Cardinal Yu Pin (archives of the Thomas Merton Center [TMC], Bellarmine College, Louisville,

to Gethsemani to aid him in his study of Chinese language, history and philosophy. But Yu Pin never came to Gethsemani and, though Merton read widely in history and philosophy, he did not learn to speak, read or write Chinese. He dealt with Chinese writers in translation and disparaged his attempts at calligraphy as a Westerner's playing with a Eastern art form. Yet there is no doubt that Merton saw this closeness, this empathy which he claimed as something real, not just as something imagined or hoped for. He perceived an affinity with the Chinese, an affinity – an undefinable, even mystical relationship – which his Chinese correspondents, who found Merton's understanding of Chinese thought rare in a non-Chinese person, also thought they perceived and to which they reacted positively.

Merton's interest in Eastern religions and spirituality is well-documented. Though emphasis has been given overwhelmingly to his work on Zen Buddhism, he was interested in all Eastern thought. His earliest reading and work, in fact, was on China, one of the first publications being the essay "Classic Chinese Thought," a study basically of Kung Tzu and Meng Tzu and one work in which he specifically mentioned Mo Tzu. He later examined Lao Tzu in "Two Chinese Classics," an essay re-titled "Love and Tao." His studies inevitably brought him to Buddhism and to Ch'an, the Chinese form of Zen Buddhism, but his interest in other Chinese ways of thought never abated. His bent toward poetry led him, despite his never learning Chinese, to rendering Chinese "parables" and stories from English translations in what he called "interpretations." This interpreting of Chinese classics began when *The Ox-Mountain Parable of Meng Tzu* was privately printed in 1960 and reached its fullest expression in *The Way of Chuang Tzu*, published in 1965.

This inexplicable quality in Merton, this ability to encounter different cultures and interpret them almost as though they were his own, was recognized by several Chinese scholars in the United States. John C. H. Wu, whether tongue-in-cheek or not, concluded that Merton may have been Chinese in a past life. Merton noted in *The Way of Chuang Tzu*:

> John [Wu] has a theory that in "some former life" I was a Chinese monk. I do not know about that, and of course I hasten to assure everyone that I do not believe in reincarna-

Kentucky).

tion (and neither does he). But I have been a Christian monk
for nearly twenty-five years, and inevitably one comes in
time to see life from a viewpoint that has been common
to solitaries and recluses in all ages and in all cultures.[13]

Dr. Paul K. T. Sih, then Director of the Institute of Asian Studies at
St. John's University in New York, shared this opinion of Merton's
acumen in dealing with the East and wrote to him after reading
"Classic Chinese Thought":

Your profound, yet lucid, description of Confucian and
Taoist traditions is both inspiring and thought-provoking.
It reveals that in this twentieth-century we can also see a
St. Thomas in the effective use of a Chinese Aristotle. As
a Chinese, I feel particularly grateful for your presenting
the Oriental culture to the West in such a forceful way.[14]

Some years later Dr. Richard Chi (whose pseudonym is Ernest
Moncrieff), then at Indiana University, praised Merton just as highly
when thanking him for writing an Introduction for his book, *The
Last of the Patriarchs: The Recorded Sayings of Shen Hui*:

Your introduction is really a masterpiece. It will be a classic
in its own right, as soon as it is published. This is the first
time I have seen anything written by a non-Chinese with
such a deep understanding of Ch'an. It will be immortal,
and the work of Shen-hui will also be immortalized by
your introduction.[15]

Dr. Cyrus Lee, part of the delegation at this symposium, was informed of Merton's death on December 11, 1968, right after having delivered a lecture on Merton in his contemporary philosophy
class. In this lecture he said: "There have only been a few, however, American students who went to the East for Oriental studies.
Among these very few Americans, Father Thomas Merton is the
most diligent I have ever known." When told of Merton's death by
one of his students, Lee says that he wept, in part, because "China

---

13. Thomas Merton, *The Way of Chuang Tzu* (New York: New Directions,
1965) 10.

14. April 10, 1961 letter of Paul K. T. Sih to Thomas Merton (TMC archives).

15. April 23, 1968 letter of Richard Hu See-yee Chi to Thomas Merton
(TMC archives).

had lost one of her most Chinese-minded American Scholars."[16]

Merton continued his reading and study of Chinese materials until his death in 1968. There is no doubt that Chinese thought had a great impact on Merton and no doubt that he was accepted as a unique voice by Chinese scholars in the United States. The extent of Merton's influence in helping East and West to better understanding is difficult, indeed impossible, to gauge. It is probably futile at this point in time even to try. Cyrus Lee has perhaps summed it up best: "Merton had enriched himself by studying and experiencing the Oriental traditions – he had revitalized these traditions and tried to transplant them in the soil of Christianity" (Lee 44). In the end he left us with a record of one person's attempt to grasp and understand the cultures of the East, including China, and, through that attempt, to understand all men and women better. He tried, in his own person and encounters, to make the jump which his friend John Wu admonished him to make.

Merton's Reading of Mo Tzu

Even though Thomas Merton was a monk with a vow of poverty (which meant, among other things, that he was not supposed to own books), he gathered together what I would judge to be one of the best collections on Chinese thought in the state of Kentucky. Those books are now housed at the Thomas Merton Studies Center in Louisville, the center over which I preside as director. From these books, in which he made extensive marginal markings and textual underlinings, and from his voluminous "reading notebooks," we gain some idea of what Merton read and what struck him as important and significant.

Did he read about Mo Tzu? Yes, certainly. But his reading of Mo Tzu and some other less well known Chinese figures was not as extensive as his reading of the "bigger figures," i.e. Kung Tzu, Meng Tzu, Lao Tzu, Chuang Tzu, and some Ch'an Buddhist writers. John Wu and his writings exerted great influence on Merton and Merton relied quite a bit on Wu's small text, *Joy in Chinese Philosophy*. In it Wu said: "There are three main currents in Chinese philosophy, namely, Confucianism, Taoism, and Zen Buddhism." Apparently, Merton himself fell into the trap of concentrating most

16. Cyrus Lee, "Thomas Merton and Zen Buddhism," *Chinese Culture Quarterly* 13 (June 1972) 35; subsequent references cited as "Lee" parenthetically in the text.

of his energies in the "Big Three" Chinese traditions despite his warning to others against such ensnarement. In "Classic Chinese Thought," he said:

> One of the most facile generalizations about Chinese thought is that there are "three traditions" corresponding with the "three religions of China": Confucianism, Taoism, and Buddhism. This cliché is all the more tempting to an American because it reminds him of a familiar classification at home: Catholicism, Protestantism, and Judaism in America. Actually there is not the faintest resemblance between the ancient religious situation in China and the present one in America. Oriental religions, while they may differ in philosophy and belief, have a way of interpenetrating quite freely with one another.[17]

It was this "interpenetration" which interested Merton and, since Mohism was little studied even by Chinese at the time, may help to explain why he was less engrossed by Mo Tzu. It is possible, also, that he accepted the usual interpretation of Mo Tzu in the West at the time. One of the texts on which he relied heavily (as did the rest of us students in the United States in the 1960s) was Arthur Waley's *Three Ways of Thought in Ancient China*, originally published in 1939. Let us remind ourselves of what Waley had to say, among other things, about Mo Tzu:

> *Mo Tzu* is feeble, repetitive . . . heavy, unimaginative and unentertaining, devoid of a single passage that could possibly be said to have wit, beauty or force. Of course, part of the obscurity of Mo Tzu in the West is due to the fact that he was till recently very little studied even in China. But he has been accessible in European languages for a considerable time. If Mo Tzu is neglected in Europe it is because he expounds his on the whole rather sympathetic doctrines with a singular lack of aesthetic power. (Waley 121-22)

The "aesthetic" was important to Merton (how important is only now being explored by Merton scholars). Perhaps, it was this lack or supposed lack of an aesthetic in Mo Tzu which prevented his making more of a study of the "sympathetic doctrines" of Mohism

---

17. Thomas Merton, *Mystics and Zen Masters* (New York: Farrar, Straus & Giroux, 1967) 46.

than he apparently did. It is also possible, since Merton was at first much caught up in study of Meng Tzu, that he tended to accept Meng Tzu's rather negative criticisms of Mo Tzu at face value. I suspect, though, that it was more that Merton was not vouchsafed time to explore himself, the "interpenetration" of Mohism with other Chinese traditions. For, as we shall see, there are, in my opinion, several "connections" between Mo Tzu and Thomas Merton – several points at which Merton would have found himself in sympathy with Mo Tzu's thinking.

What did he read? Certainly he read and annotated Waley's section on Mo Tzu in *Three Ways of Thought in Ancient China*. He also read and annotated the section, "Mo Tzu: Universal Love, Utilitarianism, and Uniformity" in *Sources of Chinese Tradition*, edited by Wm. Theodore de Bary, Wang-tsit Chan and Burton Watson. Both are on file at the Thomas Merton Studies Center. From these annotations we can posit some of the "connections" which Merton saw. He also read in E. R. Hughes, *Chinese Philosophy in Classical Times* (1942); Wang Gung-Hsing's *The Chinese Mind* (1946); Fung Yu-Lan's *The Spirit of Chinese Philosophy* (1947); and Augustinus A. Tseu's *The Moral Philosophy of Mo-Tze* (1965). Only the first of these latter books has Merton annotations, but there is (as we shall see) one significant one. These annotations help us to begin to extrapolate something of Merton's thought. I suspect that he may have begun to temper his negativity toward Mo Tzu (as expressed in "Classic Chinese Thought") as his studies deepened and as he became less preoccupied in the mid 1960s with Meng Tzu. Certainly he could have taken no exception to Chuang Tzu's description of Mo Tzu: "Mo Tzu and his followers harm not the weak, rescue people from fights, abhor aggression, advocate disarmament and labor to save the world."[18] These words almost sound like a description of Thomas Merton.

Mo Tzu and Thomas Merton

There are several interesting "connections" between the thought of Mo Tzu and Thomas Merton, several passages in Mo Tzu which he marked which can be said to connect with statements Merton himself made in his writings. To begin, both men led lives of some

---

18. In Gung-Hsing Wang, *The Chinese Mind* (New York: Greenwood Press, 1968) 74.

asceticism and austerity, though Mo Tzu assuredly was less reclu-
sive than Merton wanted to be. Mo Tzu and his followers seem to
have followed a nearly monastic way of life (I am subject to correction here by those more familiar with their lifestyle than I am).
Both Mo Tzu and Merton lived in periods which they perceived as
being in political and cultural upheaval. Merton lamented the "sickness" of American society and wrote to Nobel Laureate Czeslaw
Milosz that the sickness "is terrible and seems to get worse."[19] As
they viewed the "fevers and frets" of their times, they both came to
offer "relief and remedies." Both went beyond being mere cultural
critics. Mo Tzu and Merton were clearly prophets, voices crying
out each in his own wilderness. Like the Biblical Elijah exhorting
before the unreceptive Queen Jezebel, their voices were not always
popular or well received.

Somehow, both finally concluded that the most effective relief
and surest remedy is "love," a universal, all-inclusive love that
pervades not just their society but the whole world. The idea of
"universal love" is undoubtedly the hallmark of Mo Tzu's thinking
– at least to Westerners. And it becomes an overreaching principle
in Merton's thinking. In 1967 he wrote:

> the simple fact that by being attentive, by learning to listen
> (or recovering the natural capacity to listen which cannot
> be learned any more than breathing), we can find ourself
> engulfed in such happiness that is cannot be explained: the
> happiness of being at one with everything in that hidden
> ground of Love for which there can be no explanations. I sup-
> pose what makes me most glad is that we all recognize each
> other in this metaphysical space of silence and happiness,
> and get some sense, for a moment, that we are full of para-
> dise without knowing it.[20]

Merton's paradise here would seem to resonate with Mo Tzu's
"Heaven." Heaven to Mo Tzu was, probably, a more personal entity
than it was to many of his contemporaries and he concluded that
Heaven loved the world and all the people in it. Not only that, but
Heaven, operating through the "cosmic pivot" of the emperor or

19. Thomas Merton, *The Courage for Truth: Letters to Writers*, edited by
Christine M. Bochen (New York: Farrar, Straus & Giroux, 1994) 72.
20. Thomas Merton, *The Hidden Ground of Love: Letters on Religious
Experience and Social Concerns*, edited by William H. Shannon (New York:
Farrar, Straus & Giroux, 1985) 115-16.

ruler, wanted all people to love each other – and from this came the revolutionary idea that all humans (or at least men) are equal before Heaven. One passage which Merton marked, significantly, deals with this concept of Mo Tzu's:

> Hence I say that Heaven is sure to give happiness to those who love and benefit other men, and is sure to bring calamities on those who hate and maltreat other men. I maintain that the man who murders an innocent person will meet with misfortune. What other explanation is there of the fact that when men murder each other, Heaven brings calamity on them? This is the way in which we know that Heaven wants men to love and benefit each other and does not want them to hate and maltreat each other.[21]

Merton also consistently referred to the Love God has for his world and that God wants us all to love one another. In several places, in nearly Chinese fashion, he refers to Adam – the first man in the Judaic-Christian tradition – as a kind of "cosmic pivot" through which the love of God was supposed to be funneled to humans on Earth. Adam failed, of course, but we must try to recover that spirit of "paradise," that primal and universal love which is what God intended. Merton said:

> Love is the soul's bond with God as the source of all reality, and therefore such love is itself the triumph of truth in our lives. Hence it drives out all falsity, all error. To remain in love is to remain in the truth. All that one has to do is to continue loving, in sincerity and truth, and seeking before all else the will of God. Everything else follows. Life is then a perpetual "sabbath" of divine peace.[22]

To that end, both Mo Tzu and Thomas Merton became what we might call "peace activists," discouraging aggressive war (Merton had problems in the 1960s even with the "Just War Theory"), aggression, exploitation, and notions of cultural superiority. And *Love* – though they had very different ideas of how to achieve "universal love" (and Merton didn't much like some of Mo Tzu's methods

---

21. Ernest Richard Hughes, *Chinese Philosophy in Classical Times* (London: J. M. Dent & Sons, 1942) 46.

22. Thomas Merton, "Christian Freedom and Monastic Formation," *American Benedictine Review* 13 (September 1962) 312.

which he saw as "coercive") – *Love* remains for both the underlying principle which they saw leading us toward a better world. In 1967, Merton wrote "A Letter on the Contemplative Life" – a letter formed and informed by his diligent study of other religious and cultural traditions. Without that study, including I think his limited reading of Mo Tzu, he would not have written the following lines in quite the same way:

> If we once began to recognize, humbly but truly, the real value of our own self, we would see that this value was the sign of God in our being, the signature of God upon our being. Fortunately, the love of our fellow man is given us as the way of realizing this. For the love of our brother, our sister, our beloved, our wife, our child, is there to see with the clarity of God Himself that we are good. It is the love of my lover, my brother or my child that sees God in me, makes God credible to myself in me. And it is my love for my lover, my child, my brother, that enables me to show God to him or her in himself or herself. Love is the epiphany of God in our poverty. The contemplative life is then the search for peace not in an abstract exclusion of all outside reality, not in a barren negative closing of the senses upon the world, but in the openness of love.[23]

Robert E, Daggy, Ph.D.
Paper for the Second International Symposium
    in Mohism
Shandong University, Jinan, China
17-21 August 1994

---

23. Thomas Merton, "A Letter on the Contemplative Life," in *The Monastic Journey*, edited by Brother Patrick Hart (Kansas City, MO: Sheed, Andrews & McMeel, 1977) 172-73.

INDEX

abstraction, philosophical: 280
abundance: 136
accretions, accidental: 279; cultural: 279
achievement: 103
Achilles: 169
act(s), evil: 246; existential: 189; mental: 188; of love: 189; of surrender: 189; ritual: 225; selfish: 273
action (*wei*): 101, 106, 148, 150, 159, 196; appropriate: 105; benevolent: 100; creative: 111, 126; intelligent: 287; meaningful: 105; moral: 173; necessity of: 132; of God: 126; of life: 246; of providence: 246; perfect: 152; right: 104, 287; way of: 274; well-considered: 156; well-ordered: 104
activity: 182
Adam: 126, 303
Aeschylus: 165-66, 205; Oresteia trilogy of: 170; *Prometheus Bound* of: 166
affection: 111; degrees of: 111; warmth of: 144
affirmation(s): 183; personal: 207
age, axial: 165; bronze: 168; stone: 168
aggression: 144, 301, 303
aggressiveness: 203
agnostics, intellectuals as: 125
agriculture: 111, 128-29
air, dawn: xxv, 242-45, 247-50, 285
Akazome Emon: 89
alarm: 113
Alexandria, Catechetical School of: 50
alienation: 160, 230; personal: 220; social: 220

altars, ancestral: 156; protection of: 156
alternation, process of: 142
altruism: 99
America, Pre-Columbian cultures of: 92
Amidism: 89-90, 94, 96-97
Amoroso Lima, Alceu: 249
Analects (*Lun Yü*; *Tzu Lu*): xviii, xxi, 33, 81-85, 98-103, 131, 155, 162-63, 172-73, 187, 210, 220-21, 223, 232, 256-57, 261, 265, 269, 271, 276-77
anarchism, practical: 286; Taoist: 273, 286
anarchy: 144
ancestors: 173; cult of: 95-96
ancients, poetry of: 92, 282; wisdom of: 92, 282
angels: 96, 289-90
anger: 84, 102, 104, 143
angst: 230
animals: 168; drawings of: 199; killing of: 168
animism: 95; revival of: 96
Anselm, St.: 187
antelope: 167-68
Antigone: 205
anxiety: 84, 104
aphorisms, moral: 218-19
Apologists: 50
appreciation, power of: 209
approach, contemplative: 194
arbitrariness: 246
archer: 110, 151
archery: 98
Aristotle: 180; Chinese: 3, 298
armies, in paintings: 201
arms race: 240, 248

art(s): xxi, 185, 229; Asian: xxi, 168; Chinese: 193, 201-202; conferences on: 275; European: 198; function of: 201; oriental: xxii; Renaissance: 198; six: 98; spiritual: 89; Taoist influence on: 153
artificial: 144
asceticism: 302
Asia: 215; Central: 177; East: 261, 263-65, 281
Assyria: 92
atheist: 186-87
atmosphere, contemplative: 201
atonement, satisfaction theory of: 187
attentiveness, exercise of: 132, 282
attitude(s), interior: 285; right: 226
Augustine, St.: 188
Auschwitz: 240
austerity: 302
authoritarianism: 129; Legalist: 273
authority, faith in: 228
autonomy, human: 99
awareness: 201; aesthetic: 105; contemplative: 175, 218; sacred: 105; spiritual: 287
awe: 245
axis: 110; of being: 186
Aziz, Abdul: 245-46

Babylonia: 92; exile of Jews in: 166
Babylonian Captivity: 166
Baciu, Stefan: 295
balance, of spirits: 290
Barth, Karl: 241
baseball: 206
beast(s): 249; bite of: 149
Beats: 255, 293
beauty: xxi, 116, 245, 253; love of: 97; of life: 243; secret: 247
behavior, depraved: 114; external: 285; human: 194; wicked: 129
being: 136, 142, 194; as received: 155; center of: 195; direct grasp of: 187; experience of: 194; intuition of: 194; level of: 224; mystery of: 225, 227; pivot of: 194; realization of: 220; wholeness of: 225
beings, spiritual: 82, 283
bell-stand: 151
Benedict, St.: 174, 288
Benedictines, affinity to Confucianism of: 174, 217, 288
benefits: 162
benevolence: 102, 131, 138, 147-48, 163, 171, 217, 224; delight in: 147; path of: 148; spirit of: 234
Bermuda: 292
Bernard, St.: xxi, 158, 162, 171, 209, 277, 285
Berrigan, Daniel, SJ: 44, 249
Berrigan, Philip: 249
Berry, Thomas, CP: 30-31, 44
Bible: 166, 174
Bidlack, Bede: 4
birds: 198-99; waking: 245
birth: 253
block, uncarved: 136-37, 139, 146, 222
body: 206; as gift: 156; respect for: 156; single: 263
bombardments, aerial: 239
Bonaventure, St.: 188
boomerangs: 167
bottle: 207
breakthrough, psychological: 255
breath, dawn: xxv, 116, 242; night: 116; purity of: 145
breathing, techniques of: 114
brigands, packing for: 145
brotherhood: 121; true: 235; universal: 235
Buddha(s): 166, 178; as precursor of Christ: 7; future: 81; past: 81
Buddhism: xiii, 39, 86, 125, 130, 205, 228, 233, 256, 261, 269, 272, 278, 297, 300; as higher religion: 253, 268; combined with Taoism to produce Zen: 153, 278; esoteric: 88; humility of: 35; in China: 90, 92, 94-96; in India: 92; in Ja-

pan: 87-89, 92; Mahayana: 94, 96, 278; Pure Land (Jodo): 88-89, 96; Shingon: 88; T'ang: 88; Tibetan: 177; Zen: 53, 88-89, 91, 94, 216, 258, 261-62, 297, 295, 299
burial, Chinese practices of: 120
business, affairs of: 151
bystander, guilty: 238-39; innocent: 238-39; role of: 240

calamity: 113, 122, 149, 303
calligraphy: 87, 226, 297
camps, concentration: 239
Camus, Albert: 241
capitalism: 134, 254, 269
Cardenal, Ernesto: 53
Carthusians: 182
casuistry, Jesuit: 264
Catholicism: 278, 300
celebration, ritual: 253, 268
center (*chung*): 108-10, 180-83, 185-88, 202-207; as still point: 181-82; contemplative: 194-95; invisible: 191, 201; moral: 208; mystical: 204; of being: 195; of fullness: 195; of silence: 195, 198; religious: 188; spiritual: 203-204
ceremonies: 174; delight in: 147-48
Chan, Wing-tsit: xix, 5-7, 17, 43, 65, 84, 103, 223-24, 227, 281, 301
Chang, Carsun: 7, 34, 37-38
Chang Chien: 53-54
Chang Chung-yuan: 65-67
Chang-Ling: 94, 96
Chang Tsai: 131
Ch'ang-wu Tzu: 142
change, inner: 233; of heart: 233; process of: 143
chaos: 141, 158, 246, 249; political: 232; social: 232; state of: 148; teaching of: 148
character: 100; cultivation of: 84-85, 104, 155-56
characters, Chinese: xx, xxii, 14, 17-18, 28, 86, 108; list of: 105-108
charioteering: 98

charity: 161, 172, 207, 209, 227; deep: 224; order of: 158
Ch'en Tu hsiu: 133
cheng: 109
Ch'eng Hao: 130-31
Ch'eng I: 130-31
Chi, Richard: xxviii, 298
Chiang Kai-shek: 133
chih: 100, 106, 171-72, 177, 288-89
child, heart of: 154, 246
children, education of: 161; of God: 161; parental care for: 161; procreation of: 161
Ch'in Ku-li: 123, 142-43
China: 166, 171, 176; Christianity in: 97-98; emperor(s) of: 90; geography of: 92-93; historic: 115-16; historical periods of: xix, 90-91, 93-95; pre-Confucian: 93; religion in: 90-91; religious spirit of: 95; Republic of: 219; Three Kingdoms period of: 90, 94; unification of: 257; Western influence on: 133
China Institute: 20
Chinese, as moral: 208; as practical: 208
ching: 99; concept of: 153
Ching, Julia: xxiii, 226-28, 232, 235-36
choice(s): 211; capacity for: 171; conflicting: 205; free: 211; heroic: 205; right: 205; selfish: 210; wrong: 205, 210
choir, monastic: 199
Chou Tun I: 130
Chow Tse-tsung: 227
Christ, Jesus: 208-209; as atonement: 179, 289; as brother: 289; as Chinese scholar: xxix, 289; as divine child: 241; as fellow pilgrim: 289; as fulfillment of aspirations: 178; as fulfillment of four-fold pattern: 179, 288-89; as image of God: 191; as justification: 179, 289; as light: 161; as Lord: 191; as perfection: 207; as power of

God: 179; as present in stranger: 289; as sanctification: 179, 289; as sanctifier: 179; as Son of Man: xxix, 289; as source of wholeness: 178; as wisdom of God: 179, 289; as Word of God: xiv, 7-8, 202; coming of: 8; command of: 277; crucified: 178; features of: 191; glory of: 191; gospel of: 191; humility of: 35; illumination of: 191; mission of: xxii; Mystical Body of: 207; passion of: 179; person of: xxix; pleroma of: 95; precursors of: 7; presence of: 195; Real Presence of: 46; sacrifice of: 179; suffering: 166; union with: 46; wholeness in: 178; words of: 162, 195, 253; work of: xxix

Christianity: xiii, 278; as higher religion: 253, 268; official: 230; Orthodox: xv; Protestant: xv; purity of: 97-98; revitalized: 215; structures of: 235

Ch'u, king of: 145

Chu Hsi (*Zhu Xi*): 39, 85, 94, 97, 116, 130-32, 261-65, 271, 281-84; materialistic metaphysics of: 282, 284

Ch'u, king of: 140

Chuang Tzu (Chuang Chou; Chuangtze; Zhuangzi): xiii, xx, 4, 10-12, 14-16, 18, 20, 62-64, 92-93, 123, 134-35, 137, 139-52, 153-54, 160, 166, 168, 285-86, 299, 301; approach of: 140; as precursor of Christ: 7; humor of: 285; principles of: 140; sitting-in-forgetfulness of: 263; teaching of: 275

Ch'ü-ch'iao Tzu: 142

chün tzu: 108, 110, 115, 171, 227

chung: xxii, 99, 109, 146, 180-81, 185, 194, 289

Church: 175, 190, 207, 241; Calvary of: 97; Catholic: 279; Fathers of: 194; history of: 264

Cicero, Marcus Tullius: 264-65

Cistercianism: 209, 293

cities, age of: 169

civility, Roman: 265

civilization(s): 211; Buddhist: 253; Chinese: 259, 280; Christian: 264; city: 168; foundation of: 156; history of: 165; ideal of: 174; Minoan: 92; tomb: 92; Western; 264

Clarke, W. Norris, SJ: 30

class, ruling: 260

classics, Buddhist: 35; commentaries on: 93; Confucian: 85, 99, 236, 256, 260-62, 265, 269, 274, 280; knowledge of: 222; love of: 222; meditation on: 97

Clement of Alexandria: 50-51

cliffs, in paintings: 200

clothing, material for: 114

cloud: 199

cock, fighting: 151

collaboration, interreligious: 279

colonialism: 215

colt, white: 152

comfort: 81

commerce: 128

commiseration: 113, 176

commitment, monastic: 239

communion: 199; holy: 188-89

Communism, Chinese: 133-34, 216, 235, 262; hostility to Confucius: 227

community, social: 277

compassion: 112-13, 156, 218, 236, 240-41, 246-47, 249, 274; Buddhist: 97

complementarity: 142

completeness: 181

complicity: 239

comprehension, integral: 263

computers, age of: 169

concelebration, liturgical: 175-76

conclusions, foregone: 101

condition, human: 247, 272

conflicts: 228; religious: 90

Confucian(s): 93, 128, 143, 232, 234; as poets: 265; individual: 258, 269;

Taoist critique of: 143-44

Confucianism: 3, 39, 93, 95, 115, 153, 169, 173, 208-209, 216, 219, 222-23, 225, 233, 235, 254, 256, 275, 291, 295, 299-300; and aesthetics: 98-99; and civil service exams: 90, 99; and education: xxii, xxiv, 98-99; and ethics: 98, 276; and natural law: xxi, 161-63; and revival of humanism: 227; artificiality in: 95; as complementary to Taoism: 286; as ethical system: 228; as humanist doctrine: 256; as moral system: 276; as non-religious: 276; as personalist doctrine: 256; as philosophy of person: xxiii, 223; as primarily practical and social: 267; as purely philosophical: 276; as religion: xiii-xiv, xxvi-xxix, 254-58, 267-70, 272, 276-77, 290; as sacred philosophy: xxix, 276; as secular teaching: 254, 269, 276; as social ethic: 254, 269, 276; as source of insight: 272; as source of wisdom: 272; as stepchild among religions: xiii; as way of life: 235; as worldly teaching: 254, 268-69, 276; basic virtues of: xxix; catholicity of: xxix, 233, 278-79; classical: 225, 235, 256, 263, 287; coexistence of: 278; contemplative aspects of: xxiii; corrupt: 262, 271; decadent: 257, 262, 271; early: 221; emphasis on social relations in: 277; essence of: 257; essentials of: 284; façade of: 260; false optimism in: 95; favoritism in: 95; formalism in: 95; foundation of: 222, 277; historical development of: 271, 284; humanism of: 99, 222, 228, 236, 256, 269; influence of: xiii; institutionalized forms of: 258, 269, 271; norm of: 131; official: 96; openness to: 290; personalism of: 222, 228, 277; pure: xxvi; reaction against: 133; revival of: 226, 260; schools of: 246; self-conscious virtuousness of: 286; Taoist critique of: 285; timeless view of: 265, 271, 281; triad of: xxii; unhistorical: xxvi; uniform: 96; vitality of: 265; wholeness of: 99

Confucius (Kung Tzu; K'ung Chiu): xx, xxii, 28, 81-84, 90, 92, 95-96, 98-100, 119-20, 142, 145, 162-63, 166, 171-74, 212, 216, 220-21, 225, 227-28, 231-33, 235, 285, 290, 296-97, 299; age of: 144; and previous tradition: 100; as educator: 273, 280; as feudalist: 133; as precursor of Christ: 7; as retrogressive: 133; as wiser than monks: 275; birth of: 84, 93; cult of: 96; death of: 93; deification of: 131, 282; disciple(s) of: 85, 141; doctrine of: 123; ethic of: 162; followers of: 100, 120, 130; fondness for antiquity of: 83; hostility toward: 227; in his village: 83; indignation of: 159; instruction by: 83; mind of: 208; opposition to: 120, 133, 143; philosophy of: 99-100, 109, 171, 177, 217, 233; principles of: 100-101; relationship to heaven of: 276; skepticism of: 122; speaking as Taoist: 146; teachings of: 83, 100; wisdom of: 288

confusion: 142, 186

conscience, arbiter of: 228; moral: 96

consciousness, cross-cultural: 295; paradise: 245

constitution, heavenly: 151

contemplation: 159, 182, 196, 227; life of: 254; of reality: 175; Tibetan Buddhist: 177

contemplative(s): 196, 236

Coomaraswamy, A. K.: 146

Copleston, Frederic, SJ: 180

correction, duty of: 159

correlatives: 184
corruption: 257
cosmology: 130, 181; Chinese: 181, 209; *yin-yang*: 233
cosmos: 223; impersonal: 234; liturgical connection to: 288
courage: 136, 145
courtesy (*li*): 131
covenant, ark of: 138, 247
creation: 111, 126, 143, 245; unity of: 126; work of: 208-10
creativity: 209, 285
creatures: 111, 147
Creel, H. G.: xx, 123, 131-34
Crete: 92
crime(s): 114, 145
criminal(s), dismembered: 145; war: 121
criticism, historical: 132; textual: 133
Cronin, James G. R.: 36
Cronin, Vincent: 289
cross: 289; five as: 180; ten as: 180; symbol of: 185; wisdom of: 178
crow: 148
crucifixion: 253
Cuadra, Pablo Antonio: 220
Cuernavaca: 285
cult(s), of ancestors: 95-96; of family: 235; ritual: 253, 268; social: 224; tribal: 253, 268
cultivation, ethical: 109; moral: 283; of self: 283; spiritual: 266
Cultural Revolution: 262
culture(s): 98, 211, 231, 288; Asian: 4; Chinese: xxvi, 98, 155, 258-59, 290, 299; Christian: 50, 287, 290; classical: 259; Confucian: 93, 270; European: 290; Greco-Roman: 4, 259; individual: 291; Japanese: 258; native: 258-59, 270; oriental: 4, 298; sacred: 276; Western: xxiv
Cummings, Charles, OCSO: 249
Cunningham, Lawrence S.: 294-95
curriculum, core: 261-62, 265
cycle, seasonal: 253, 268

cynicism, official: 257

Daggy, Robert: xxviii-xxix, 291-304
Dahm, Marjorie: 5
dance: 182
dancer: 127; heart of: 199
dancing: 127, 199
Dante: 294
darkness: 152, 191, 247
dawn (*tan*): 106, 244
Dawson, Christopher: 280
day (*ji*): 106, 118
Day, Dorothy: 251-52, 268
death: 137, 206, 253
de Bary, Fanny Brett: 267-68
de Bary, Wm. Theodore: xix, xxv-xxvii, 7, 84, 103, 251-84, 289, 301; reminiscences of: 267-68; WORK: *Great Civilized Conversation*: xxvi, 267-73, 276-77, 279, 281, 283
decisions: 166; for peace: 248
decorum, rules of: 125
Decroix, Francis, OCSO: 236
deference: 224, 227
deliberation, careful: 103
delight(s): 143; eight: 147
delusion(s): 84, 102, 143
Deng Xiaoping: 262
depth, personal: 226-27
Descartes, René: 95, 188, 195
desire(s): 131, 146, 162
despair: 255
desperation: 255
despotism: 133
destiny, human: 166, 171, 176; individual: 169
destruction, global: 239-40
determination: 145
determinism: 223
Deutero-Isaiah: 166
Deuteronomy: 240
development: 208; human: 176
Devine, Richard J., CM: 79
devotions, formalistic: 257
dharma: 146

diagnosis, intelligent: 264
dialectic: 121
dialecticians, Chinese: 183
dialogue, intercultural: 277; interreligious: 39, 277, 279
dignity, human: 227; of person: 277
dilemma, spiritual: 256
dimension, contemplative: 218; ethical: 218; social: 218; spiritual: 218
Di Nobile, Roberto, SJ: 258
disarmament: 144, 301
disciple, monastic: 231
discipline: 198; ascetic:122; insufficiency of: 143
discourse, literate: 260-61
disgrace: 137
disharmony: 102, 124, 144, 220
disinterestedness: 155
disorder: 102, 123, 135, 144
display, external: 144
dissatisfaction: 135
distinctions, relative: 183
distraction: 248
destruction: 205
divination: 95, 99, 160
divinity: 169
doctrine(s), Christian: 283; humanist: 222, 277; personalist: 222, 277; religious: 95, 278
Documents/History, Book of: 33, 93, 95, 99, 114, 271
dogma, religious: 258, 270
doubts, anxious: 149
dragon, symbolism of: 87
drawings, children's: 198-99
dream(s): 142, 149; myth: 249
drum, rhythm of: 199
drunkard: 151
duality: 112
Dumoulin, Heinrich, SJ: 39, 52-53, 58
Dunne, George H., SJ: 258, 274, 282-84
duty: 82, 112, 115, 126, 246; dereliction of: 115; personal: 218; social: 218; to guide superior: 159

dynasty, Ch'in: 93-94, 124, 127, 232; Ch'ing: 132; Chou: 93, 98, 114, 120, 122, 130, 282; Gen (Yuan): 91, 262; Han: 90, 93-94, 96, 98, 132-33, 232, 283; Hsia: 120, 122; Liang: 94; Manchu: 91, 95; Ming: 91, 94, 132, 259; Shang: 120, 122; Shin: 90; Shu: 90; Six: 90; Sung (Song): 90-91, 94, 116, 130, 260, 262, 264, 282; T'ang: 59, 90, 94, 134, 283

earth (*t'u*): xxii, 106, 108-109, 112, 136-37, 141, 149, 152, 154, 157, 181, 208, 211, 222; as feminine: 200; as nourishing creatures: 209, 211; gods of: 96; service of: 159; *Tao* of: 203; work of: 211-12
earth-mother: 95
ease, untroubled: 148
Eckhart, Meister: 246
eclecticism, Chinese: 93
ecology, mental: 290
Eddington, Arthur: 134
education: 110; Chinese: xxvi, 218; classical: 222, 261; Confucian: 212, 262; humane: 273; liberal: 266; literary: 259; of children: 161; of gentleman: 98; right: 246; system of: 280; true: 231
effacement, Taoist: 97
effort(s): 137; human: 138
egoism: 101
Egypt: 92, 187; enslavement in: 240; kings in: 170
Eli, sons of: 138
Elijah: 302
Eliot, T. S.: xxi-xxii, 181-82, 289; WORK: *Four Quartets*: xxii, 181-82, 289
empathy: 162, 172, 217
emperor(s): 84-85, 94, 157, 302; as priest: 96; as son of heaven: 156
employment, of upright: 103
emptiness: xxii, 111, 135, 137, 139, 141

enemy, defeated: 121
energy: 111; northern: 110; southern: 110
England: 292-93
enlightenment: 132; mystical: 284; sudden: 132, 282; way of: 287
Enlightenment: 265
Enomiya-Lassalle, Hugo, SJ: 39
equity: 105
Erasmus, Desiderius: 260, 265
error: 303
escape: 255
espionage, mutual: 129
essences: 126
eternity: 225
ether (c'hi): 130
ethic(s): 83, 98, 130-31, 287; code of: 99; Confucian: 36, 257, 274; highest: 110; Maoist: 228; natural: 276
ethos, Confucian: 285
Etruria: 92
Euclid: 191
eunuchs, imperial: 132
Eurasia: 165
Euripides: 165
evidence, scriptural: 256
evil: 84, 102, 111, 121, 128, 161; human nature as: 124; punishment of: 122
examinations, civil-service: 262
excellence, man of: 144
excess: 123
exercises, physiological: 143
existence, as existing: 187
experience, aesthetic: 285; human: 296; intuitive: 258; monastic: 225; of being: 194; of is-ness: 194; ordinary: 194; religious: 191; spiritual: 284; uncommunicable: 231
exploitation: 303
extravagance: 123
eye (mu): 106
Ezekiel: 166

face-saving: 224-25

failure: 152
faith: 278; abiding: 234; ancient: 122; bad: 231; Christian: 7, 259, 279; good: 149; illumination of: 161; in God: 236; level of: 204; light of: 191; loss of: 124-25
faithfulness: 84
falsity: 303
fame: 149, 151
family: 96, 104, 114, 224, 228, 253; cult of: 235; humanity in: 105; of creatures: 147; regulation of: 104; visiting of: 159
famine: 115-16, 129
Fan Ch'e: 82, 84, 102
farmers: 128
fashions, popular: 144
fatalism: 120
fate: 206
father: 123; love to: 157; loyalty to: 157; reverence to: 157
Faulkner, William: 176
fear: 84, 104; of punishment: 129
feelings, filial: 224; fraternal: 224; paternal: 128
Fénelon, François: 56
Fenollosa, Ernest: 86
fertility, servitude to: 253
fidelity (chung hsin): 99; in service: 159; to parents: 159; to prince: 159; to word: 110, 162
filiality: 156-59; as cultivation of person: 156; as expression of inmost nature: 156; as first principle of heaven: 157; as foundation of civilization: 156; as foundation of virtue: 156; as most important virtue: 158; as proof of humanity: 156; as ultimate standard of earth: 157; beginning of: 156; duties of: 158; end of: 156; government by: 157-58; of common people: 157; of prince: 156; of scholars: 157; practice of: 158; to father: 159; to mother: 159; to prince: 159
figures, mythical: 170

Fingarette, Herbert: 227
fire, discovery of: 169
fittingness: 177
flood(s): 120; autumn: 150
Fons Vitae Merton Series ix-x, xiv-xv, xxiii, xxix
food: 114; taste of: 152
fools: 142
folly: 124; to gentiles: 178
force: 122; external: 257; of littleness: 202; spiritual: 233, 257
Forest, James: 233, 249
form(s) (*li*): 130-32; Christian: 290; elegant: 150
formalism: 154, 285; rigid: 257
formation, monastic: xxii, 174, 192, 202, 212, 288
fortune, winds of: 186
"Four Books": xxiv, xxvi, 33, 92, 99-105, 131, 219, 231, 261-62, 264-65, 269, 271; canonization of: 94, 131, 261-62; translation of: 264
France: 292
Franke, Wolfgang: 259
freedom: 167, 211-12, 226, 228, 243; from passion: 104; of individual: 140, 233; spiritual: 140, 253; surrender of: 121; traditions of: 157; true: 288
Freud, Sigmund: 170
friendship (*chiao*): 106, 156, 264
frugality: 128
frustration: 186
Führer: 228
Fu-hsi: 150
fulfillment: 205; personal: 218; spiritual: 220
fullness, center of: 195
function: 260-61, 275
Fung Yu-lan: xxii, 113, 160, 172-73, 183-84, 196, 202-203, 208, 301

gain, economic: 81
Gandhi, Mohandas: 215, 241, 252
Gang of Four: 262

Gensho: 88
gentiles: 178-79
gentleman: 125-26, 128, 171; Confucian: 220, 227; education of: 98
Gerdy, Robert: 251, 268
Gethsemani, Abbey of: 237, 247, 292-94, 296-97
gifts, mental: 167; physical: 167; spiritual: 167
Gilgamesh: 169
Giroux, Robert: 43, 251
globe: 182
gloom: 142
glory: 137
God: 193, 202; action of: 126; as end: 161; as Father: 161, 245; as giver of life: 236; as justice: 189; as mercy: 189; as protector of human race: 236; as source of all things: 236; as Yahweh: 170, 247; belief in: 236; bond with: 303; children of: 161; Christian notions of: 235; command of: 249; compassion of: 247; Confucian notions of: 235; epiphany of: 236, 304; existence of: 186-87; faith in: 236; goodness of: 190; grace of: 179, 190; greatness of: 190; ignorance of: 161; in Confucianism: 173; judgment of: 190; knowledge of: 8; light of: 161; living: 235-36; love of: xxviii, 179, 303; mercy of: 240, 247, 250; mind of: 126, 190; name of: 187; non-existence of: 186-87; personal: 96, 231; power of: 179; presence of: 179, 243; self-gift of: 189; sign of: 236, 304; spark of: 246; suprapersonal: 231; trust in: 73; union with: 7-8, 202; voice of: 190; way of: 109; will of: 202, 303; wisdom of: 161, 178; work of: 290
god(s), as almighty: 283; Chinese: 96, 156; Greek: 154, 170-71, 206; of earth: 96; of heaven: 96; of this world: 190; of water: 96;

primordial: 283
Gog: 220
good: 111, 150, 161; highest: 103; resting in: 103; training in: 124
goodness: 112, 246; acquired: 125; economic basis of: 114; innate: 112; of God: 190; of good: 166; of human nature: xxiv, 246, 273
goods, moral: 279; spiritual: 279
Goose Lake monastery: 131
gospel: xxii; as mystery: 190; inculturation of: xxvii; preparation for: 97; production of: xxi
governance, human: 265; humane: 266
government: 102-104, 111, 129; bad: 103, 116; benevolence in: 99; best: 135; by filiality: 157-58; by goodness: 115; good: 103-104, 115, 127; humane: 114; of sage: 158; orderly: 128; principles of: 103
grace(s): 35, 161, 188, 227, 296; illumination of: 161; light of: 191; of God: 179, 190; social: 221
grain, gods of: 156
grass: 199
gratitude: 155
Great Learning (Ta Hsio; Ta Hsüeh): 33, 84-85, 93, 99, 101, 103-108, 131, 138, 256, 261, 263, 269, 271, 287; as adult education: 103; as key to classic Chinese thought: 104; audience of: 103; authorship of: 103; commentary on: 263; major points of: 103; theme of: 103
Great Wall: 84, 90, 96
Greece: 4, 92, 259
greed: 209, 246
Greeks: xxi, 166, 208, 220, 223
growth: 208, 253; love for: 111
Guardini, Romano: 7
guidance, supernatural: 129
guilt: 238-39
Gullick, Etta: 170

Hammer, Carolyn: 86, 197, 244
Hammer, Victor: 86, 108, 117, 197, 243-44, 273
Han Fei Tzu: 127-29
Han Learning, School of: 133
Han-Tan walk: 140
happiness: 149, 302
harmony: xxxix, 95-96, 109-10, 126, 233, 291; central: 223-24, 226; cosmic: 111; ideal of: 86; interior: 105; of earth and heaven: 222; of joy: 144; political: xxiii, 216, 236; religious: 97; social: xxiii, 216, 236; spontaneous: 135; universal: 225; with heaven: 287; with Tao: 135
hare: 128
harp: 192
Harriot, John F. X.: 296
Hartzell, Richard W.: 225
hatred: 121, 143
hawk(s): 190; Cooper's: 190; red-shouldered: 190
Hayes, Carleton, J. H.: 252
healing: 247
heart(s): 101, 105, 159, 189-90, 203, 232, 235; attitude of: 226; change of: 233; cunning: 141; depth of: 253; dictates of: 221; geography of: 229; humble: 225; improvement of: 144; integrity of: 145; light of: 191; of child: 155, 246; of dancer: 199; of heaven: 235; of man: 144; of nature: 235; rectifying: 105; sincere: 225; steadfast: 114; stilling of: 197; stillness of: 246; tone of: 105
heaven(s) (tien): xxii, 102, 106, 109-12, 114, 120, 122-25, 136-37, 141, 144, 146, 149, 152, 154, 157-58, 173, 181, 208, 211, 231, 235, 276; as divine creator: 276; as masculine: 200; as personalized god: 283, 302; as producing creatures: 208-209, 211-12; biddings of: 221; cosmocentric: 96; cult of:

95-96, 222; equality before: 303; faith in: 236; first principle of: 157; gods of: 96; harmony with: 222; of person: 235; human relation to: 125; imitation of: 157; light of: 225; love of for world: 302; mandate of: 231; motions of: 145; movements of: 141; personal: 302; reality in: 109, 111; reality of: 287; relationship with: 173, 218, 234, 276; reverential attitude toward: 276; service of: 159; skepticism of: 124; son of: 121, 156, 159; *Tao* of: 202-203; values of: 150; violation of: 122; virtue of: 149; way of: 109, 138, 148; will of: 122, 287; work of: 211-12

heaven-and-earth: 195, 208, 263

Hebrews: 126, 179

herd, commercial: 248; ecclesial: 248; mentality: 248; monastic: 248; political: 248; technological: 248

hermit, Taoist: 139

hero(es): 169; divinization of: 97; Homeric: 169

hiddenness: 145

Hideyoshin: 88

hierarchy: 157; ecclesial: 235; social: 187

hills, pleasure in: 82; purity of: 149

Hinduism: xiii, xvi, 252, 258, 295; as higher religion: 253, 268

Hiroshima: 240

history: 169, 265-66, 272; Chinese: xix, xxiii, 218, 265, 297; Confucian: 284; creatures of: 290; Japanese: xix, 88-90

History/Documents, Book of: 33, 93, 95, 99, 114, 271

Hitler, Adolf: 252

Hobbes, Thomas: 121

Hoguet, Louise: 20

Hoguet, Robert L.: 20

Hoguet, Robert L., Jr.: 20

holiness: 145

Holy Spirit: 178, 190, 279

Homer: 169

Honan, excavations in: 95

honor(s): 101, 148; man of: 162-63

hope: 249; Christian: 250; Jewish: 178; of gentiles: 178; of philosophers: 178

Hopkins, Gerard Manley: xxi

horse, nature of: 147; not a horse: 184; white: 184

house, in paintings: 199-200

Hsiang, King: 113

Hsiao Ching (Xiao jing) (Classic of Filial Piety): xx, 5-6, 8-10, 22, 24, 26, 37, 41, 59, 153-60, 187, 256, 269, 274, 287; helpful for language studies: 154-55

hsin: 100

hsing: 116

Hsüan, King: 113-15

Hsün Tzu: 93, 124-27, 131, 282; as agnostic: 125; rationalism of: 124; skepticism of: 124; students of: 127

Hu Yuan: 260

Hua Tzu: 144

Huang, François: xix, 95-98, 278, 281

Huang Tsung Hsi: 95, 132

Huei Yan: 96

Hughes, E. R.: 162-63, 301, 303

Hui: 146

Hui, King: 113

Hui Neng: 5, 52, 97

Hui Tzu: 141

human-heartedness: xxi, 99, 104, 110, 123, 161-62, 178-79, 209, 217-18, 277

humaneness: 246, 263

humanism, Chinese: 234; Christian: 50; Confucian: 99, 222, 228, 236, 256, 269; democratic: 278; ethical: 278; integral: 50; intellectual: 278; objective: 278; religious: 222, 256, 265, 278; revival of: 227; sacred: 222, 257, 278; social:

278; universal: 278
humanist, Christian: 260
humanities, Asian: 266
humanity: xxii, 85, 102, 104-105, 111-13, 134, 216; aims of: 98; authentic: 171; common: 116; goodness of: 234-35
humiliations: 206, 215
humility: 139, 202-203, 206; Christian: 97; in Taoism: 96
humor, of Chinese: 208
husbands: 161
Hwang-Ti: 150
hymn(s), religious: 168; sapiential: 111-12
hypocrisy: 139

I Ching (Book of Changes): xix, 33, 85, 93, 99, 131, 271, 285; canonization of: 94; modesty hexagram of: 202
id, Freudian: 286
ideal(s): 280; Confucian: 86, 283
idealism, impractical: 103
ideas, religious: 283
identity, human: 166; knowledge of: 220; loss of: 220; religious: 278
ideogram(s), Chinese: 180, 185, 289
idleness: 128, 141
ignorance: 129; apparent: 141; of God: 161; simplicity of: 135
ills, political: 220; social: 219-20
illumination: 97; higher: 161; of faith: 161; of grace: 161
images, typological: 228
immortality, elixir of: 94, 96
impartiality: 143
implements, stone: 168
impulses, moral: 263; natural: 263
inactivity: 141
India: 92, 166, 258
Indians: 168
indifference: 148-49
indifferentism, religious: 95
individual: 140, 277; as foundation: 114; freedom of: 140, 233; rights

of: 233
individualism: 277
individuality: 165
industrialization: 254, 269
inertia: 215
infinite: 137, 143; realm of: 142
influence, spheres of: 162
iniquity: 257
injustices, racial: 239
innocence: 135, 137, 245; decay of: 139; inexpressible: 245; original: 141
innocent, murder of: 122
insight, Confucianism as source of: 272; human: 125; moral: 276; spiritual: 276
instinct(s), Asian: 153; to love: 246
institution(s): 230-31; Confucian: 280; restructuring of: 230
integration: 198; cosmic: 111
integrity, inward: 143; moral: 109; personal: 215; way of: 141
intellect: 140
intellectuals, as agnostics: 125; Chinese: 283; role of: 239
intelligence: 126, 161, 212; moral: 203; tower of: 152
intuition: 132; of being: 194
invisible, presence of: 195
Ionesco, Eugene: 237
irreverence, to king: 158; to sage: 158
Isaiah: 166
Islam: xiii, 295; as higher religion: 253, 268
is-ness, experience of: 194
Israel: 92, 173; kings in: 169

Japan: 258, 262-63; art of: 86-87; historical periods of: xix, 88-90
Jaspers, Karl: 165, 227
jazz: 251, 268
jên: 85, 96-97, 99, 102, 104, 106, 109-10, 112-14, 127, 171-72, 177, 179, 209, 217-18, 223, 246, 288-89; in Great Learning: 104, 107

jen hsing: 157
Jeremiah: 166, 189-90
Jerusalem, fall of: 166
Jesuits: 258-59, 264-65, 270-71, 278-79, 282-83
Jew(s): 161, 178-79; discouragement of: 178; exile of: 166
Jezebel, Queen: 302
Jiang Zemin: 262
Job: 111-12
John the Baptist, St.: 7
John the Evangelist, St.: xxi, 202
Johnston, William, SJ: 39
Jonas (Jonah): 247
journey, interior: 143; magical: 143; of soul: 143
joy: 101, 143; harmony of: 144
Ju: xxiii, 99, 109, 218, 222; as humanist and personalist doctrine: 277; definition of: 278
Judaism: 278, 295, 300; as higher religion: 253, 268
judgment, concrete: 190; dialectical: 194; of Lord: 190
Jung, C. G.: 85, 285
justice: xxix, 110, 156, 163, 172, 177, 179, 188-89, 274, 288; divine: 283; social: 95
justification, supernatural: 179
Justin Martyr, St.: 7, 50

Kabir: 241
Kang Yu Wei: 133
Katz, Jamie: 267
Ke Kang: 103
Kelly, J. N. D.: 7-8
kindness: 159
king(s) (*wang*): 106, 123, 146, 157; ancient: 95, 126, 155, 158; as divine: 169; as standard and example: 154; bad: 120; early: 128; evil: 122, 143; from *Tao*: 144; good: 120; imitation of: 157; irreverence to: 158; legendary: 128; lost: 122; sage: 122; three: 149; true: 113-14; way of: 123; wise: 95

kite: 190
knowing: 263
knowledge: 111, 135, 145, 150, 152; as root of understanding: 131; delight in: 147; discursive: 97; eagerness for: 83; extension of: 104, 132; faculty of: 150; of classics: 222; possession of: 83; style of: 83
Knox, Fort: 237, 248
koans, Zen: xviii, 81, 261
Kogaishi: 86
Komachi, Ono no: 89
Korea: 87-88, 262-63
Kowalski, Frank: 36
Ku Yen-wu: 95
Kubla Khan: 91
Kung-sun Lung: 184
Kuomintang: 133
Kutsugen: 86
Kwan Yin: 94; faith in: 96
Kyoto: 88

labor, organization of: 163
lamp, silent: 226, 296
land: 163; division of: 114; partition of: 132; sufficiency of: 114
landscape, Chinese: 199-200; elements of: 199-201; spirit of: 200
language(s): 129; abuses of: 219-20; Asian: 254; Chinese: 45, 95, 133, 259, 297; classical: 259, 264; destruction of: 219; figurative: 204; uses of: 219; usurpation of: 219; vernacular: 259
Lao Tzu (Lao Tse, Laozi): 4, 92, 95, 134-35, 137, 141, 144, 156, 168, 261, 286, 290, 296-97, 299; as precursor of Christ: 7; funeral of: 143; skepticism of: 122; teaching of: 275
Laughlin, James: 242
law(s): 127, 144, 162, 173; canon: 235; eternal: 161; moral: 210-11; natural: 161-63, 178, 231, 276-77; new: 261; of nature: 211; rule of: 233; sanctions of: 81, 127; school

of: 129; severe: 129; transgression of: 129
Lax, Robert: 251, 265
leadership, educated: 260
learning: 263; acquisition of: 163; classical: 221-22; Greek: 50; humanistic: 266; school of Han: 132-33
Lee, Cyrus: xxviii, 298-99
Lee, Paulinus, OCSO: 32-33, 35
Legalism: xx, 93, 124, 127-30, 228, 231, 233; as antithesis of Confucianism: 127; as force of Chinese unification: 257; exponents of: 127
Legalists: xx, 92-93, 127-30, 233, 285
Legge, James: xvii, xx, 33, 35, 110, 195, 231; WORKS: *Chinese Classics*: 40-41, 81-84, 100-103, 107, 111, 113, 210; *Texts of Taoism*: 138-39, 146-52, 154
letters: 83
level, moral: 204; of being: 224; of faith: 204; of nature: 211
li (ritual): 85, 98-99, 106, 125-26, 131, 171-73, 175, 177, 217, 222, 285, 288-89; as cannibalism: 133; as good form: 171
li (form; truth): 106, 130-31; celestial: 282; of individual objects: 132, 282
li chi: 131
Li Chi-tsao: 283
Li Szu: 127
Liang, Thomas J.: 215
liberation: 255; spiritual: 255, 269, 277
Lieh Tzǔ: 143, 145, 160, 243
life: 137; action of: 246; ascetic: 203; beauty of: 243; Christian: 207, 279; common: 207; contemplative: 194, 196, 254, 304; contemporary: 230; dangerous: 205; genuine: 245; intellectual: 128; liturgical: 288; love of: 143; meaning of: 191; monastic: xxii, 174, 191-93, 201, 205, 212, 252, 290; moral: 154, 203, 224; mystical: 205; natural: 253; nurturing: 143; of prayer: 192; of renunciation: 192; political: 274; principle of: 176; public: 135; respect for: 168; rhythm of: 134; sacredness of: 225; secular: 255; social: 274; spiritual: 168, 205, 274; way of: 155, 290; wholeness of: 221, 234
light (*kuang*): 107, 191, 200; Christ as: 161; divine: 246; of faith: 191; of God: 161; of grace: 191; of heart: 191; pure: 246
limitations, cultural: 279
lions: 168
literature(s): 170, 185; conferences on: 275; existential: 230; oral: 168; religious: 168; rise of: 168; sacred: 221; secular: 221; written: 168
liturgy (*li*): 173-75, 177, 179, 193, 195, 217; as expression of love: 218; Confucian: 173-74; English: 175; purpose of: 201
Liu Wu-Chi: xx, 122-27, 130-33, 276, 278, 281-83
logic: xxii, 121, 183
logicians, Chinese: 183-84
Logos: 202; seeds of: 7-8
logos spermatikos: 7-8
Lord Shang, Book of: 129-30
Loretto, Sisters of: 13, 15
love: xxix, 107, 110, 112-13, 143, 154, 158-59, 162, 171-72, 174-75, 177, 218, 236, 256, 274, 285, 302-303; act of: 189; all-inclusive: 302; as basic force: 153; as epiphany of God: 236, 304; benevolent: xxviii, 96, 291; benign: xxviii, 291; carnal: 162; Christian notion of: 155; compassionate: 172; Confucian: 217; degrees of: 162; empathic: 288; exchange of: 218; filial: 153-54, 256, 274, 287; for all: 102; for parents: 154, 156, 158, 160-61; for people: 103, 179; greedy: 209;

hidden ground of: 302; human: 179; humane: 223, 257; importance of: 144; interior: 154; liturgy as expression of: 218; mental: 121; mutual: 96, 158; natural: 222-23, 257; non-discriminating: xxviii, 291; of beauty: 97; of beloved: 236, 304; of brother: 236, 304; of child: 236, 304; of classics: 222; of father: 157; of fellow man: 236, 304; of God: xxviii, 179, 303; of life: 143; of lover: 236, 304; of sister: 236, 304; of truth: 82; of wife: 236, 304; openness of: 304; partial: 122; power to: 209-10; primal: 303; redemptive: 179; selfish: 210; social: 162; spirit of: 224, 234; universal: 112, 120-22, 157, 291, 301-303; unselfish: 209; utilitarian: 121, 301; way of: 241
loyalty: 115, 157, 162, 187
Lu, Lord of: 141
Lu Hsiang-shan: 94, 132, 284

MacGregor, Robert: 12
Machiavellianism: 231
machines: 141
madman of Khu: 146, 285
magic: 93-94, 97, 124-25; revival of: 96
Magog: 220
Makra, Mary Lelia, MM: xx, 5-6, 154-55, 274
man: 157, 208; as completing all things: 209, 211-12; evil nature of: 125; great: 114; heart of: 144; inferior: 174-75; interiority of: 234; just: 173; low-minded: 173; mean: 81, 110; modern: 255-56; mountain: 139; noble: 212; noble-minded: 172-73; of excellence: 144; of quality: 110; of *Tao*: 151; of *te*: 145; of virtue: 82; perfect: 151; pure: 145; reality in: 109, 111; realness in: 109; sagely: 147, 151; self-sacrificing: 171, 217; small: 81, 110, 147; small-minded: 233; space: 229; superior: 81-82, 84, 100-101, 108, 110, 125, 147, 159, 171-72, 186, 212, 217, 220, 233, 288; *Tao* of: 202-203; true: 139, 145; way of: 109, 148; whole: 230; wise: 143, 289
mandala: 177; four-sided: xxix, 274, 288
mankind: 96
Mao Tse Tung (Mao Zedong): 133, 262
Marcuse, Herbert: 219
Marxism, mystique of: 95
Mary, Blessed Virgin: 46; Annunciation to: 247; Magnificat of: 202
Mason, Herbert: 169
Mass, Sacrifice of: 46
master, monastic: 231
materials, cultural: 229
mathematics: 191
Mathews, R. H.: 18, 20, 107
matter, cultural: 290
maturity: 226
May Fourth Movement: 227
McCarthy, Senator Joseph: 157
McDonnell, Thomas P.: 58
mean, golden: 224; Greek approach to: 180; virtue of: 180
Mean, Doctrine of (*Chung Yung, Zhong yong*): xxii, 33, 99, 108-12, 131, 138, 146, 180, 208, 231, 256, 261, 269, 271, 287, 289; as Confucian response to Taoism: 109; as unwobbling pivot: 109, 289; central concerns of: 109; doctrine of: 224
meats: 116
mechanization: 169
meditation: 132, 248; Neo-Confucian: 263; Taoist: 263; Zen: 263
meekness: 99
Mei, Y. F.: 223
melioration, social: 255, 269, 277
Mencius (Meng Tzu): xx, xxii, xxiv-xxv, xxvii-xxviii, 75-76, 78, 80, 94, 105-106, 112-20, 131-32, 140,

154, 160, 167, 171, 216, 231, 233, 238, 242, 244, 246, 249, 263, 273, 282, 284-85, 290, 297, 299, 301; as precursor of Christ: 7; *Book of*: 33, 99, 131, 232, 256-57, 261, 265, 269, 271; controversy with Hsün Tzu: 124-25; disciple of: 115; followers of: 125; *Ox Mountain Parable* of: xx, xxiv-xxv, 106, 112, 116-20, 156, 238, 242, 273, 285; philosophy of: 233; principles of: 112-15

mentality, Chinese: 95

mercy: 154, 188-89, 241, 247; divine: 241; faith in: 97; of God: 240, 247; of *Tao*: 136; parable of: 246, 273; Taoist: 97

merit: 151

Merton, Agnes: 14

Merton, John Paul: 292

Merton, Owen: 292

Merton, Ruth: 292

Merton, Thomas, and Buddhism: xiii, xvii, xxvi, 272; and China: 296-99; and Chuang Tzu: 4, 10-12, 14-16, 18, 20, 62-64; and Mo Tzu: 299-304; and Taoism: xiii, xvii, xxvi, xxix, 272; and Zen: xiii, xxix, 23, 39, 43, 73; as advocate of interreligious dialogue: 277; as conscience of peace movement: 249; as contemplative: 265; as guilty bystander: 238; as hermit: 237, 295; as historian: 265-66, 272, 281-84; as master of scholastics: 247; as Mei Teng (Silent Lamp): 226, 296; as monk: 215, 218, 229, 238, 245, 252, 292-93, 297-98; as novice master: xxi-xxii, 44, 48-49, 58, 216, 247, 275, 288; as pacifist: 252; as peace activist: 303; as pilgrim: 295; as poet: xxvii, 265-66, 271-72, 281, 294; as prophet: 229, 240, 296, 302; as religious: 221; as sage: 296; as symbol: 292; as theologian: 295; as writer: 293-94; audience of: 284; birth of: 292; bohemianism of: 293; brother of: 292; catholicity of: xxix; censorship of: 240, 248-49; Chinese studies of: xvii, 32, 44, 48, 58; concern for cultural integrity of: 294; concern for social justice of: 294; conversion of: 293; correspondence of: 247-48, 275; death of: 266, 272, 292; difficulty with publishers of: 43, 61; discussions with Protestants of: 63; early writings of: 294; education of: 292-93; engagement with Confucianism: xiii, xvi-xvii, xxvi-xxvii, xxix, 249-90; hermitage of: xvii, xxi, 219, 237, 247, 288, 290, 296; hospitalizations of: 43, 63; interests of: 252, 294; interior world of: 290; interreligious activities of: xiii; journals of: 275; Latin American contacts of: 239, 295; Louisville epiphany of: 239, 247; love for Asia of: 215; marginality of: 293-94; novitiate conferences of: xxi, 161-212, 216, 238, 275, 288-89; parents of: 292; poetic voice of: 249; prophetic voice of: 249; reading notebooks of: xviii, 275-76, 299; salvation of: 290; significance of: 295-96; silence of: 296; translations of: 295; turn toward world of: 277; visitors to: 247; vocation crisis of: 285; vocation of: xxix, 290; writings on Confucianism of: 272-75; writings on contemplation of: 294; writings on ecumenism of: 295; writings on environment of: 295; writings on genocide of: 295; writings on non-Christian traditions of 295; writings on racial conflict of: 295; writings on spiritual renewal of: 295; writings on spirituality of: 294; writings on Third World of: 295; writings on war and peace of 295; WORKS: *Alaskan Journal*: xxviii; *Ascent to Truth*: 254; *Asian Journal*: xi, xviii, 177; *Behavior of Titans*: 15, 238-39; *Breakthrough to Peace*: 248-49; "Christian Action in World Crisis": 26; "Christian Culture Needs Oriental Wisdom": xiv, xvii, 30, 33, 153, 273, 286; "Christian Freedom and Monastic Formation": 303; *Cistercian Fathers and Forefathers*: 187; *Cistercian Fathers and Their Monastic Theology*: 158; "Christian Looks at Zen": 64; "Classic Chinese Thought": xvii, xx, 3, 74, 76-77, 104-105, 117, 125, 129, 137, 166, 174, 180, 186, 216, 272-73, 276, 278, 280-81, 286-88, 297-98, 300-301; *Clement of Alexandria*: 18, 50; "Climate of Mercy": xxv, 247; *Climate of Monastic Prayer*: 43; *Collected Poems*: 13, 199, 244; *Conjectures of a Guilty Bystander*: xxv, xxix, 168, 238-45, 247, 249, 275, 285, 289-90; *Contemplation in a World of Action*: xxv, 240; *Contemplative Prayer*: 43; *Courage for Truth*: 7, 56, 220, 249, 302; *Dancing in the Water of Life*: xxviii, 63, 172, 175, 197-98, 248; *Day of a Stranger*: xxii, xxviii, 290-91; *Disputed Questions*: 277; *Emblems of a Season of Fury*: 53, 199; *Encounter: Thomas Merton and D. T. Suzuki*: xxviii; *Entering the Silence*: 79; "From Pilgrimage to Crusade": 289; *From the Monastery to the World*: 53; "Gloss on Chinese Text": 63; "Grace's House": 199; *Hidden Ground of Love*: xvii-xviii, 9, 14, 18, 22, 25, 35, 39, 43-44, 48, 58, 61, 63, 67-68, 71, 76, 78, 167, 170, 226, 233-34, 236, 246, 275, 287, 302; *"Honorable Reader"*: xxviii, 73, 216, 240, 268; *Introduction to*

Christian Mysticism: 28; *Introductions East and West*: 253-55, 268; "Is the World a Problem": xxv, 240; "Jesuits in China": 46, 258, 264-65, 270, 274, 279-80, 289; "Learning to Live": 232; "Letter on the Contemplative Life": 304; "Letter to an Innocent Bystander": 238-39; *Life and Holiness*: 48, 73; *Life of the Vows*: xxi, 161-63, 275, 277; *Literary Essays*: 176; *Love and Living*: xxv, 232, 247, 268; "Love and Tao": xvii, 30, 153, 202, 273, 297; "Martyr for Peace and Unity": 26; *Merton/Giroux Letters*: 43; *Merton/Hammer Letters*: 86, 108, 244; *Merton/Laughlin Letters*: 242; "Monastic Christianity Encounters the Spirit of Zen": 58; *Monastic Introduction to Sacred Scripture*: 178; *Monastic Journey*: 304; *Monks Pond*: xxviii; "Mystics and Zen Masters": 52, 58, 63, 65-70; *Mystics and Zen Masters*: xiv, xvii, xx, xxix, 3-4, 30, 46, 52, 63, 65, 73, 76-77, 97, 104-105, 108-109, 117, 125, 129, 137, 153-54, 156, 166, 174, 180, 186, 202, 216, 222, 228-29, 244, 246, 256-58, 260, 262, 264-65, 269-71, 273-74, 276-80, 284, 286-90, 300; "Name of the Lord": 126; *New Man*: 39, 126, 252-53, 268, 277; *New Seeds of Contemplation*: 195, 277; *Nonviolent Alternative*: 26, 36; Notebook 52: xviii-xix, 81-85, 276; Notebook 56: xviii-xix, 86-91; Notebook 58A: xviii-xx, 92-160, 276, 278, 281-84, 287; "Nuclear War and Christian Responsibility": 30; "Other Side of Despair": 228; *Ox Mountain Parable*: xx, xxiv-xxv, 117-20, 237-238, 240, 243-47, 249, 273, 297; *Passion for Peace*: 26, 30, 36; *Peace in the Post-*

Christian Era: 249; "Prayer for Peace": 36; *Pre-Benedictine Monasticism*: 48, 167; *Preview of the Asian Journey*: 230-31; *Raids on the Unspeakable*: xxv, 167, 238, 248; "Rain and the Rhinoceros": xxv, 167, 238, 247-48; "Rebirth and the New Man in Christianity": 253, 268; "Reflections on the Character and Genius of Fénelon": 56; *Road to Joy*: xxviii, 215; "Ruler's Examination of Conscience": 56; *Run to the Mountain*: 268; "St. Anselm and His Argument": 187; *School of Charity*: 7, 175; *Search for Solitude*: xix, 36, 85, 166, 285, 289; *Seasons of Celebration*: 126; *Secular Journal*: 268; *Seeds of Contemplation*: 254; *Selected Essays*: xvii, 30, 153, 273, 284-87, 289; *Seven Storey Mountain*: 239, 251-52, 294; *Sign of Jonas*: 247; *Strange Islands*: 13; *Striving towards Being*: 237; *Thomas Merton Reader*: xvii, 30, 48, 58, 153, 273; *Thoughts on the East*: 253-54; *Turning Toward the World*: xxix, 3, 9, 15, 18, 28, 37, 43-44, 46, 86, 166, 171-72, 242, 245, 275, 285, 290; "Two Chinese Classics": xvii, xx, 9, 25, 29-30, 55, 153-54, 273, 297; *Way of Chuang Tzu*: xv, xxii, 4, 63, 93, 140-43, 146-47, 151-52, 160, 166, 172, 225, 274-75, 285-86, 288, 297-98; "Wisdom": 13; "Wisdom in Emptiness": 16; *Wisdom of the Desert*: 16, 20, 22; *Witness to Freedom*: 169, 238; *Zen and the Birds of Appetite*: 16, 64, 195, 289; "Zen Revival": 52

Merton & the Tao: ix-x, xv, xviii, xxiii, 4, 22, 25, 32, 36-37, 39, 53, 63, 66-67, 71, 76-77, 275, 283

metals: 168

metaphysics: 130

Metzger, Max Josef: 26

Miles, Jack: xiii

Miller, Lucien: 4

Milosz, Czeslaw: 7, 237, 239, 302

mind (*hsin*): 105, 120, 195, 201, 263; and universe: 132; calmness of: 103; dislike of: 113; fasting of: 146; geography of: 229; of Adam: 126; of God: 126, 190; openness of: 260; rectification of: 104; right/wrong of: 113; Taoist: 86; unbelieving: 190; yielding of: 113

ministers: 114; loyal: 139

missionaries, Christian: 46, 264; colonialist view of: 264; Jesuit: xxix, 258; Nestorian: 92

misunderstandings: 215

Mo Tzu (Mo Ti): xxvii-xxix, 92, 96, 112, 120-24, 142-43, 276, 291, 297, 299-304; active theism of: 97; age of: 144; asceticism of: xxviii, 96, 122, 302; as advocate of universal love: xxviii, 302; as man of excellence: 124, 144; as peace activist: xxviii, 303; as precursor of Christ: 7; as prophet: 302; austerity of: 123, 302; birth of: 93; characteristic doctrines of: 120-21, 301; critique of by Chuang Tzu: 123-24, 144; critique of by Mencius: xxvii-xxviii, 123; critique of by Waley: xxviii, 124; disciples of: 121; nobility of soul of: 124; opposition to Confucius of: 120; social class of: 122; social philosophy of: 121-22; style of: 124, 300; theocentrism of: 96; utilitarianism of: 113, 121

moderation: 144

modernity, evil of: 254, 269

modesty: 163, 203

Mohism: xx, xxvii-xxix, 233; sympathetic doctrines of: 300-301

Mohists: 112, 128; self-sacrifice of: 123; Taoist critique of: 143-44

monastery: 192-93, 211, 241, 243,

247; as institution: 230; not an escape: 239; Trappist: 207
monasticism: 192, 288; essence of: 231; fathers of: 191; medieval: 232; true: 231; voice of: 237
money, cult of: 220
Mongols: 91, 262
monism: 132
monk(s): 174; community of: 222
monkeys: 142
moon (*yueh*): 108, 111; brightness of: 149
morality: 129, 132, 140, 145; Chinese: 178; Christian: 178; practical: 95
mortality, human: 160
Moses: 187
Moslem (Muslim): 161
mother, love to: 157
Mott, Michael: 240
mountain(s) (*shan*): 106, 111; in paintings: 200-201
mourning: 125, 143; for parents: 159; period of: 115, 160
movement(s): 181-82, 195-96; Confucian reform: 261; mass: 255; peace: 249; political: 234; social: 233
Mozart, Wolfgang: 241, 243, 245
Mu, King: 143
Mu Tsung, Emperor: 94
multiplicity: 150
Mu-Mon: 81
Munro, Donald J.: 218, 227
Murasaki Shikibu: 88-89
murder(s): 145, 303; judicial: 239; of innocent: 122
music (*yueh*): 85, 98, 100, 102, 116, 126-27, 157; as diversion: 121; as harmonizing manners: 158; as maggot: 129; as teaching love: 154; as transforming manners: 158; importance of: 115; sharing: 115
Muste, A. J.: 249
mystery, gospel as: 190; of being: 225, 227; of *Tao*: 140
mysticism: 204, 206; Asian: 210;

252; occidental: 290
myth(s): 97, 204, 229; figure of: 169

name(s), conventional: 126; divine: xxii; in scripture: 126; perpetuating: 159; preservation of good: 159; reason for: 126; rectification of (*cheng ming*): 219-20, 223
natural: 144
nature (*hsing*): 105, 116, 147, 161, 168, 210; awakening of: 244; common: 162; contact with: 157; correcting: 150; course of: 143; divine: xxvii; earthly: xxvii; effect of: 245; heart of: 235; human: xxvii, 102, 111, 116, 119, 125, 127, 141, 144, 161, 176, 208, 225, 231, 242, 246, 257, 273, 282, 285; inborn: 110; inmost: 156; instincts of: 147; laws of: 211; level of: 211; love of: 90; lost: 132; oneness with: 253, 268; original: 131; principle(s) of: 102, 143; realization of: 110; representation of: 87; true: 131, 150, 282; unconscious: 246; understanding of: 245
Nazareth College (Spalding University): 29
necessity, natural: 253-54; social: 223
negations: 183
Neo-Confucianism: xxvi-xxvii, 91-92, 94, 97, 131-32, 260-65, 271-72, 281-82; speculations of: 283
Neo-Ju movement: 130-31, 283
Neo-Taoism: 94
Nestorianism: 90, 92, 94
New Testament: 178, 202
Ngai, Duke: 111
Niebuhr, Reinhold: 252
night (*yeh*): 106, 118, 248
Ning Woo: 102
Nō drama: 87-88
nobility; of great: 166
nominalism: 126
non-action: 136-37, 149, 196

non-being: 136, 142
non-resistance: 134
non-violence: 249
normality (*yung*): 109
norms, artificial: 144
Norton Anthology of World Religions: xiii, xxix
Nostra Aetate: xiv, 279
nothingness: 139, 141
nourishment: 148
novices: 229
numbers: 179-80, 190

obedience: 100, 126, 128; blind: 159; civic: 157; lack of: 133
obligation(s): 113; social: 255, 264, 269
obstinacy: 101
ocean(s): 111; spirit of: 142
O'Connell, Patrick F.: xiv, xxvii, 267-90
Odes, Book of: 33, 85, 93, 95, 99-101, 105, 112, 271
Oedipus: 170
officers, high: 156
officials, virtuous: 286; well-behaved: 286
Okakura, Kakuzo: xix, 86-91
Old Testament: 111, 178
omens, supernatural: 125
opinion, public: 145
Opium War: 98
opposition, transcending of: 184-85
optimism: 170, 230
order, 95, 135; ascetic: 202; Cistercian: 237, 240; moral: 202, 280; natural: 161; of universe: 187; perfect: 124, 144; political: 218, 234; restoration of: 216; sacred: xxiii; social: 218, 222, 234, 280
ordo caritatis: 158
orthography, Pinyin: 282; Wade-Giles: 282
Otto, Walter F.: 92
ox: 141
Oyer, Gordon: 249

pagan: 161
painters: 86, 197-98; Chinese landscape: 200; T'ang: 134
painting, as contemplative: 197; Chinese: xxi, 196-201, 288; invisible elements of: 197-99; Japanese: 86-87, 90, 196-97; landscape: xxi, 196, 199-200, 288; "Lonely Fisherman": 196-97; mountain–water: 200; Paleolithic: 168; visible elements of: 197-200
paradise: 245, 302; condition: 216, 218, 232, 235; return to: 150; spirit of: 303; unspeakable: 245
parents (*fu mu*): 84, 102, 107; burial of: 160; care in sickness for: 158; duty toward: 160; fidelity to: 159; grief at death of: 158-60; honor toward: 161; love for: 154, 156, 158, 160-61; memory of: 160; mourning for: 160; reverence toward: 156-58, 160; sacrifice to: 158; service of: 155-57, 160; support for: 158;
participation, communal: 199
passion(s): 105, 110, 146; freedom from: 104; impetuous: 101; winds of: 186
passivity: xxv, 242; Chinese: 97; complete: 136; pure: 141
path, in paintings: 200
patronage, governmental: 232
pattern(s), cruciform: 180; of wholeness: 180
Paul VI, Pope: 236
Paul, St.: 46, 50, 190-91
peace (*p'ing*): xxix, 106, 121, 130, 223, 240-41, 257, 291; Christian teaching on: 26-27; commitment for: 248-49; cultivation of: 104; decision for: 248-49; devotion to: 144; divine: 303; importance of: 144; of society: 157; prayer for: 36; sabbath of: 303; search for: 304; true: 73

Pearl Harbor: 252
Pearson, Paul M.: xxiv-xxv, 237-50, 272
peasants: 134
penalties, goal of: 129-30
Pentecost, Feast of: 176
people, common: 84-85, 126, 283; diligent: 128; extravagant: 128; frugal: 128; good of: 113; in paintings: 200-201; lazy: 128
perfection, human: 109; moral: 97; physical: 141; supernatural: 179
person: 277; complete: 217; concern with: 160; cultivation of: 84, 104, 156; dignity of: 277; extraordinary: 205; fully developed: 173-74, 288; heart of: 235; human: 222, 231, 256, 277; humane: 288; individual: 169; integral: 220; integrity of: 160; noble-minded: 274; perfectibility of: 218; philosophy of: 216; respect for: 156; superior: xxiii, 115, 171, 217, 274; whole: 177; worth of: 228, 277
personalism: 222, 235, 277; Chinese: 94; Christian: xxiii, 207; Confucian: 222, 228, 277; genuine: 160, 277; in ancient world: 153
personality: 222; cultivation of: 98, 153, 155; fulfillment of: 225; fully-developed: 217; human: 98-99, 222, 224; true: 225
personhood, full: 277
pessimism: 170, 257
Philistines: 138
philosopher(s): 141; Chinese: 155, 174; dissident: 95; Greek: 165; hundred: 84, 93; Sung: 130-32, 282
philosophy: 134, 177, 229; Arabic: 4; Asian: 168, 185; Chinese: 76, 177, 185, 208, 224, 257, 285, 297; Christian: 209-10; Confucian: 278-79; diabolical: 279; divorced from religion: 124; Greek: 165; Ju: 283; native: 259, 270; neo-Ju: 131, 282; non-Christian: 279; of

evasion: 160; of life: 234; of society: 234; oriental: 59, 169; pagan: 177-78, 279; perennial: 226; personal: 235; personalistic: 219, 223; political: 133-34; religious: 233; sacred: 276; social: 235; spiritual: 235; state: 232; yang-yin: 93
Philoxonos: 167, 237-38
Phoenicia: 92
piano: 192
piety, examples of: 110; filial: 96, 100, 112, 129, 153, 234, 256, 274; Judeo-Christian: 259
pity: 113, 117
Pius IX, Pope: 189
Pius X, Pope: 189
pivot, central: 180, 196, 198, 202, 226; cosmic: 302-303; of being: 194; of silence: 198; of Tao: 288
placidity: 149
Platform Scripture (Liu-tsu T'anching): 5-6, 9-10, 16-20, 23, 29, 33, 35, 37, 39, 41, 43, 45, 51-52, 55-56, 58-59, 61
Plato: 165
pleasure: 162, 210; sensual: 160
Po Chü: 145
Po Chü-i: 94, 240
poetry (shih): xxi, 98, 168, 177, 229, 265; Chinese: 201-202; of ancients: 92, 282; purpose of: 201; Taoist influence on: 153
poet(s): 249; T'ang: 134
point, still: 182
politics 98, 130; human dimension of: 234; humanizing: 234; illuminating: 234; purifying: 234
Polonnaruwa: 253
poor: 122, 128
portents, human: 125
Portugal: 88
position(s), broadminded: 184; impractical: 184; mature: 184; mystical: 184; philosophical: 140; true: 184
possessions: 145

post-history: 169

Pound, Ezra: xx, 85-86, 101, 104-
106, 109-12, 180, 242, 281, 287;
nominalism of: 111

poverty: 162, 236, 304; deserved:
128; vow of: 299

power(s): 145, 296; authentic: 143;
centralization of: 127; inborn:
145; military: 237; of littleness:
202; sanctifying: 179; spiritual:
163; three: 154, 157; to love: 209-
10; vital: 143

practices, physiological: 143

praise: 149

praxis, contemplative: 253, 258,
263, 270; meditative: 253; orthodox: 263

prayer, life of: 192

preaching: 178

Precious Blood, Feast of: 189; mystery of: 189

predestination: 188

predeterminations, arbitrary: 101

preferences, private: 163

presence, of Christ: 195; of invisible:
195

president: 229

pressure, political: 233

pride: 206

priests: 126

prince: 105; human-hearted: 104;
fidelity to: 159; filiality of: 156;
loyalty to: 157; reverence to: 157;
service of: 156

principle(s): 112; feminine: 199;
governing: 291; man of: 162; masculine: 199; metaphysical: 231;
of life: 176; passive: 199; strong:
199; underlying: 304

profit: 113, 172-74

progress, moral: 221; spiritual: 221

Prometheus: 150; as suffering
Christ: 166

prophets, Hebrew: 166, 173

propriety (li): 99, 102, 112-13, 159,
171; rules of: 100

Protestantism: 278, 300

proverb, Zen: 243

providence: 122, 124; action of: 246

provincialism: 219

psalmist: 173

psalms: 173

psyche, human: 176

psychiatry: 255

psychoanalysis: 255

psychology: 219

p'u: 145

punishment(s): 96, 114, 122, 127-
28, 147, 152; capital: 103; fear of:
129; five: 158; strict: 129

purity, climax of: 143; of Christianity: 97-98; of Confucian tradition:
257-58; of soul: 233; way of: 145

purpose, fixed: 103; of art: 201; of
liturgy: 201; of monastic life: 201;
of poetry: 201

quiescence: 195-97

quietism: 97

quietness: 141

quiet-sitting (jing zuo): 263-64

quietude: 135, 137, 149

race: 241; human: 236

rain (yü): 106, 237, 247, 247-50

rationalists, Neo-Ju: 283

reading: 264

realism, moral: 159

Realists: xx, 115, 129-30, 285

reality (ch'eng): 109, 111; contemplation of: 175; of heaven: 287; of
universe: 109; principle of: 287;
vision of: 218

realms, sacred: 217; secular: 217

realness: 100

reason: 50; natural: 155

rebirth: 255; spiritual: 253, 268

reciprocity (shu): 223-24

rectitude: 157

red (communist): 161

redemption: 179; satisfaction theory
of: 187

reform, Confucian: 261; social: 232, 255
regard, fond: 104
regimes, totalitarian: 220
rejoicing: 125
relations, of living and dead: 160
relationship(s): 111-12, 154, 160; abstruse: 228; affective: 222; Chinese social: 187; coercive: 224; father–son: 155-56, 158; five basic: xxix, 154, 156; five moral: 233; formal: 174, 228; human: 223, 231; husband–wife: 155; mother–son: 156; personal: 234; prince–ministers: 158; right: 95, 153; son–parents: 156; to universe: 174, 217; to world: 241; with heaven: 173, 218, 234, 276; with others: 173, 218; younger–elder brother: 156
relativity: 142
religion(s): 177, 283; archaic: 95, 168; as devotional worship: 254, 268; Asian: 254-55; charismatic: 270; Chinese: 97, 256, 278; Confucianism as: xiii-xiv, xxvi-xxix, 254-58, 267-70, 272, 276-77, 290; developed: 168; divorced from philosophy: 124; higher: 253-54, 256-58, 267-70, 276-77, 290; Indo-European: 254, 268; institutional: 270; interpenetration of: 300; *Ju* as national: 133; Judeo-Christian: 4; native: 259, 270; non-Christian: 279; organized: 258, 270; oriental: 73, 300; Semitic: 254, 268; simple: 168; stagnation of: 97
religious, bad: 184; good: 184
Renaissance, European: 259
renewal, monastic: 230; of inner self: 230
renunciation: 207; life of: 192
repose, serene: 103
Reps, Paul: xviii-xix, 81
resentment: 115
respect: 156, 167; excessive: 101; for body: 156; for person: 156
respectfulness: 163
responsibility: 107, 167, 228, 249
rest (*chih*): xxv, 103, 107-108, 116, 242
restraints, external: 140
resurrection: 253
retirement, deepest: 152
revelation, Christian: 50; necessity of: 8; of natural law: 163, 277; religious: 278
reverence: 117, 157, 159; acts of: 195; lack of: 110; toward life: 283; virtue of: 276
revolt: 96-97, 255
revulsion: 255, 269
reward(s): 96, 127-28, 147, 173
rhinoceritis: 249
Ricci, Matteo, SJ: xxvi-xxvii, 251, 258-60, 264-65, 267, 270-71, 274, 279-83, 289
rice: 101
Rice, Edward: 57-58, 74, 251, 268, 293
rich: 122, 128
riches: 101
Richards, I. A.: xx, 105-106, 115-16, 171, 243-44, 281, 285
right(s): 142-43, 170; boundaries of: 226; of individual: 233; standards of: 129
righteousness (*yi*): 81, 99, 101, 112-13, 122-23, 125, 131, 135, 138, 146-48, 171-74, 177, 217, 285, 288; delight in: 147
riots, Watts: 240
rite(s) (*li*): 96, 106, 110-11, 124, 127, 173, 175, 222, 232; as teaching love: 154; centrality of: 125; Confucian: xxiii, 85, 99, 257; liturgical: 222, 229; personal: 232; social: 232; splendor of: 105; system of: 223
Rites, Book of (*Li Ki*): 33, 99, 103, 195, 261-62, 271
ritual(s): xxiii, xxix, 98-99, 157, 173-75, 216-18, 221, 225-27, 232, 234,

262, 274; as maggot: 129; Confucian: 105, 223, 226; dance: 121; interpersonal: 223, 227; liturgical: 287; mystique of: 96; religious: 223; social: 218
ritualism: 120; ancient: 99; exterior: 120; sterile: xxiii
rivalry, selfish: 163
rivers: 111
Robeson, Paul: 251
Rome: 4, 259
Roosevelt, Eleanor: 252
Roosevelt, Franklin: 252, 261
root: 84-85, 100; going to: 100; personal: 104; return to: 137-39, 148, 153, 155
rubrics: 176
ruin: 170
rule(s), artificial: 145; golden: 96, 178, 210, 223; of law: 233; silver: 210
Rule, Benedictine: xxi
ruler(s): 103, 129, 135, 138, 303; as sage: 131; as son of heaven: 121; authoritarian: 121; human-hearted: 162; just: 114; power of: 127; relation to ministers of: 114; sage: 135; service of: 159; stupidity of: 128; treatise for: 135; true: 112
Russia: 26, 134

Sabbath, perpetual: 303
sacrament: 189
sacramentality: 217
sacrifice: 125, 130; great: 102
sadness: 143
safety, of society: 157
sage(s) (*sheng jen*): 106, 111, 117, 125, 128, 137-38, 142, 145-46, 149, 181, 217, 234-35; Chinese: 195, 221, 223, 227, 232; Confucian: xxiii, 102; footless: 146; from *Tao*: 144; humility of: 138; irreverence to: 158; rule of: 158; true: 137; writings of: 233
saint(s): 163, 277; Cistercian: 294;

divinization of: 97
St. John, Donald P.: 4
St. Teresa, College of: 27
salvation, moral: 236; of world: xxix, 291; personal: 96; spiritual: 236
Samarkand: 94
samurai: 88
sanctification: 217
sanctions, supernatural: 129
sanctity: 207
Sartre, Jean-Paul: 230
saying, Greek: 154
Schall, Adam, SJ: 258, 274
scholar(s) (*shih*): 108, 125-26, 157; as advisors of prince: 157; as credit to human race: 280; as glory of nation: 280; as retired warriors: 157; Chinese: 259; Christian: 4, 51; Confucian: 257, 260, 264, 270, 279; filiality of: 157; work of: 284
Schwartz, Benjamin I.: 227
science(s): 133; Arabic: 4; European: 259; social: 219
scriptures, Hebrew: 247
scorpions, sting of: 149
seasons: 110; cycle of: 253, 268; four: 102, 149
secrecy: 152
secret, unspeakable: 245
sectarianism: 258, 270
security: 121, 162, 205, 257
self: 109, 142, 145; cultivation of: 283; forgetfulness of: 227; fragmented: 230; inner: 229-30; metaphysics of: 228; redefining of: 227; renewal of: 230; true: xxiii, 224, 229; value of: 236, 304
self-affirmation: 203, 207
self-assertion: 149
self-consciousness: 167
self-cultivation: 103, 265, 277
self-discipline: 105
self-display: 138
self-effacement: 224
self-emptying: 224
self-esteem: 203

self-examination: 100, 159
self-forgetfulness: 134
self-improvement: 255, 269
self-interest: 100
selfishness: 121, 287
selflessness: 138
self-perfection: 283
self-realization: 109, 134
self-seeking: 186
sense, aesthetic: 220; common: 208; contemplative: 186; moral: 220, 233; philosophical: 186; religious: 185-86
Serrán-Pagán, Cristóbal: 4, 275
servants: 191; civil: 271
service, distinguished: 136; fidelity in: 159; of earth: 159; of heaven: 159; of parents: 155-57, 160; of prince: 156; public: 162, 266
Shakaku: 87
shame: 113, 117
Shan Nang: 150
Shannon, William H.: 43, 229
Shao Yung: 130-31
sharecropping: 114
Sheed, Wilfred: 293
Sheerin, John B., CSP: 30
Sheishonagon: 89
Shen-hsiu: 52
Shen Hui: 298
Shen Tao: 141, 144
Sheng: 158
Shenker, Israel: 292
Shi-nan I-liau: 141
Shinto: 89, 258
shogunate: 88-89
shu: 99
Shun, King: 104, 122, 128
sickness, mental: 216; of society: 229; spiritual: 216
signs, supernatural: 125
Sih, Charles J.: 79
Sih, Paul K. T.: xvi-xviii, xx, xxviii, 3-80, 153-55, 232, 274-75, 287, 298; visit to Gethsemani of: xvii, 14-15, 17-19, 22, 25, 27-28, 30;

WORKS: Decision for China: xvi, 13-14; Democracy in East Asia: xvi; Chinese Culture and Christianity: xvi; From Confucius to Christ: xvi, 12-14; "Mind of Asia in the Modern World": 20-21
silence: xxii, xxv, 136, 149, 191, 194-98, 201, 203, 226, 242, 249, 252, 296, 302; center of: 195, 198; interior: 203; pivot of: 198
silk: 198
simplicity: 135-36, 139, 167; natural: 167; of Tao: 138-39; primal: 150; primordial: 167; pure: 147; Taoist: 160
sin: 161
sincerity (ch'eng; hsin): 84, 100-101, 105, 107, 109, 111, 152, 303; acquired: 111; natural: 111
sinfulness: 247
singer(s): 86; teen: 229
skepticism: 120, 122; religious: 95
skill: 135, 145
sky, in paintings: 200
slaughter: 113
Smith, Vincent: 24
snow-goose: 148
socialism: 114
society, capitalist: 219-20; civil: 265; communist: 219; great: 163; human: 140; mass: 219, 228; modern: 248; peace of: 157; safety of: 157; security in: 257; sickness of: 229; technological: 255; traditions of: 157
Socrates: 165, 233; as precursor of Christ: 7
solemnity: 245
solicitude: 101
solidarity: 115
solitude: 152, 159, 242, 247, 249, 296; sense of: 248; taste for: 248
sons, filial: 139
sonship: 247
Sophocles: 165-66, 170, 205; Oedipus trilogy of: 170
sorrow(s): 143, 149

soul: 141, 145, 148-49, 161, 206, 246; Chinese: 95; devotion of: 83; journey of: 143; purity of: 233

Sources of Chinese Tradition: xix, xxvii, 7, 84-85, 103-104, 109, 111-14, 120-29, 135-38, 140-45, 160, 263, 281, 283, 301

space(s), blank: 198-99, 203; outer: 196

speculation: 132; metaphysical: 204

speech: 101, 195-96; perfect: 152; smartnesses of: 101

Spencer, Thomas T.: 36

sphere: 184-85

spirit(s): 96, 126, 137, 148, 198, 226; balance of: 290; creative: 87; dawn: 116-19; existence of: 96; guileless: 149; hearing of: 146; luminous: 282; manifestation of: 159; night: xxv, 106, 116-17, 119, 242-50, 285; of benevolence: 234; of dead: 149; of love: 224, 234; of ocean: 142; pure: 149; relation to: 152; religious: 95, 278; tower of: 152

spirituality, Asian: 185, 272; Austronesian: 295; Chinese: 7, 290; Christian: 290; personal: 258, 270; rooted in history: 290; rooted in tradition: 290

spontaneity: 150; inner: 285

sports: 192; star: 229

Spring and Autumn Annals: 33, 99, 271

stability: 121, 249; vow of: 245

stagnation: 215

Stalin, Josef: 252

standards, moral: 173

stars: 111

state: 96; foundations of: 114; power of: 130

statement(s), philosophical: 186; religious: 186-87, 189; scientific: 186

statesmen, as conformists: 260, 270, 280; as crooks: 260, 270, 280; as pedants: 260, 270, 280; Chinese: 260, 270, 280

station, high: 162; low: 162

stillness: xxii, 141

Stone, Naomi Burton: 238

stork: 190

strata, social: 224

Strategic Air Command (SAC): 237, 248

streams, purity of: 149

strife: 142

strong: 122

structure, four-fold: 177, 179; numerical: 180

struggle, nonviolent: 252

study: 218, 264; need for: 153

stupidity: 102

submission, fraternal: 100

substance (*ch'i*): 130-31, 133, 260-61

success: 82, 84, 102, 114

suffering(s): 112, 210, 246, 249, 261, 277

Sufism: xv, 216, 295

Sui-Jan: 150

Sumer: 92

sun: 111; brightness of: 149

Sun Chu: 53

Sun Yat-sen: 74, 133-34

Sung Hsing: 144

superior(s): 163; identification with: 120-21

superiority: 141; cultural: 303

superstition(s): 94, 124-25, 283

surrender, act of: 189; of preferences: 208

Suzuki, D. T.: xx, 16, 65-66, 138, 167; WORK: *Zen Doctrine of No Mind*: 52

swallow: 190

sword: 89-90

symbol(s): 172, 185; archetypal: 229; Carthusian: 182; Christian: 185; cross as: 185

symmetry: 86

sympathy (*tse-yin*): 113

syncretism, Chinese: 93, 97; danger

of: 97; popular: 97
system, Confucian: 280; new (*Xin fa*): 261
Sze, Mai-Mai: 197-98
Sze-ma New: 83-84

Tai Chen: 132-33
talents, cultivation of: 153; parable of: 155
T'ang, King: 122
tastes, personal: 212
Tao: 96, 106, 110-11, 123, 135-36, 138-41, 143-44, 149-50, 152-53, 162, 202, 231; abandonment of: 139; as all-inclusive: 142; as beyond right and wrong: 142; as bodiless: 136; as creative power: 202; as empty: 136; as eternal non-being: 141; as existent: 136; as formless: 136-37; as humble: 202; as ineffable: 202; as infinite greatness: 202; as infinite littleness: 202; as mother of all things: 136, 275; as mysterious: 136; as non-existent: 136; as self-sufficient: 136; as soundless: 136; as source of all: 136, 286; as supreme unity: 141; as unchanging: 136; as without strife: 136; as Word of God: 202; aspects of: 140-41; axis of: 183; divine: 286; essence of: 142; eternal: 275, 286; ethic of: 144; ethical: 109, 153, 274, 286-87; frugality of: 136; greatness of: 136; harmony with: 135; human: 286; invisible: 286; law of: 202; man of: 151; masters of: 135; mercy of: 136; metaphysical: 109; moral: 208; mystery of: 140; namable: 135, 274-75, 286; nameless: 135, 275, 286; of earth: 203; of events: 131; of heaven: 202; of man: 202-203; of sageliness within and kingliness without: 144; paradoxical nature of: 140; participation in: xxii; pivot of: 288; political implications of: 144; pursuit of: 99; simplicity of: 138-39; social implications of: 144; substance of: 149; unity of: 141; unknowable: 286; without beginning: 141; without duration: 141; without end: 141
Tao Te Ching (*Tao Te King*): xx, 4-6, 8-10, 20, 22, 24, 26, 36, 41, 59, 134-39, 141, 153-54, 274, 286-87; as treatise for rulers: 135; contrast to Confucianism of: 135; main features of: 154; popularity of: 153
Taoism (Daoism): xx, 3, 13, 109, 111, 125, 134-60, 183, 252, 256, 261-62, 269, 276, 278, 291, 295, 299-300; anarchistic tendencies of: 233, 286; and magic: 135; and superstition: 135; as complementary to Confucianism: 285-86; as contemplative: 153; as mystical: 135; as paradoxical: 135; as passive: 153; as poetic: 135; as popular religion: 94; combined with Buddhism to produce Zen: 153, 278; contrast with Confucianism: 274-75; critique of Confucianism: 285; exercises of: 144; Han: 96; in China: 90, 93-97; influence of: 153, 160; not antinomian: 144; perversions of: 160; philosophical: 216; physiological practices of: 144; principles of: 136-37; unworldliness of: 135
Taoist(s): 109-10, 143, 145, 290; quietism of: 97
Tartars: 91
Tashkent: 94
taxes: 129; heavy: 128
te: 107; as genuine virtue: 141; as mystic virtue: 137; as power, virtue: 145; as vast virtue: 136; man of: 145
tea ceremony: 226
teachings, heretical: 128; perverse: 123; three (*san jiao*): 256, 269

technique, brushstroke: 198
technology: 219
Teilhard de Chardin, Pierre, SJ: 30
tension, creative: 286; fruitful: 286
texts, Confucian: 256, 262; Neo-
  Confucian: 262
Thang, Lord of: 150
theft: 145
theology, moral: 235; Orthodox:
  179; scientific: 188
thieves: 145
things, external qualities of: 263; internal qualities of: 263; investigation
  of: 104, 263; recognition of: 263
thinkers, dialogical: 218
Thomas Aquinas, St.: 3-4, 161, 188-
  89, 298
Thomas Merton Encyclopedia: xiv,
  272
Thompson, William M.: 295
Thoreau, Henry David: 242-43
thought(s), Asian: 183; Buddhist:
  285; Chinese: 95-96, 167, 181,
  194, 202, 257, 262, 285, 287, 291,
  297, 299; classical: 256, 269; Confucian: xxiv; depraved: 101; inarticulate: 105; Indian: 194; medieval: 194; modern: 194; Japanese:
  194; oriental: 194, 284; sincerity
  of: 104; Taoist: xxiv, 285; Western: 194
tiger: 87, 101
Tobin, Mary Luke, SL: 13
toes, webbed: 147
toil: 142
tolerance, religious: 90, 97
tongue, readiness of: 101
tortoise, sacred: 140
totalitarianism, Legalist: 286
tradition(s): 155, 193, 233, 278;
  Asian: 207, 215, 272, 278, 284;
  Black Benedictine: 174, 288;
  book: 192; Chinese: xvi, 256,
  260, 269, 281; Christian: 207;
  Confucian: xvi, 3, 257, 290, 298;
  cultural: 4, 277, 304; East Asian:

xiv, xvi, xviii; Eastern: 7; ecclesiastical: 191; literary: 51; liturgical: 191; living: 192; monastic:
  191, 221; mystical: 224; oral: 168;
  oriental: 299; patristic: 191; philosophical: 51, 284; reinforcement
  of: 98; rejection of: 129; religious:
  284, 304; spiritual: 7; Taoist: 3,
  224, 298; theological: 191; Western: 7; Zen Buddhist: 224
traditionalism, stupidity of: 128
traditionalists: 128
tragedy, Greek: xxi-xxii, 165-66,
  169-71, 176, 185, 204-206, 210,
  275
Traherne, Thomas: 241
tranquility: 134; placid: 150
transformation, contemplative: 277;
  inner: 143; personal: 267; religious: 255; spiritual: 255
treasures, three: 154
tree(s): 248; cut: 117-18; in paintings: 200; straight: 151; useless:
  141, 146; value of: 212
trials, political: 239
trinity, Confucian: xxii, 208-12; of
  creation: 208; theological: 208
trust, in God: 73; mutual: 99; virtue
  of: 265
trustworthiness, virtue of: 265
truth (*li*): 83, 241, 290, 303; knowledge of: 82; love of: 82; perversion of: 241-42; pleasure in: 82;
  ray of: 279; segment of: 155;
  speaking: 239
truthfulness: 83
Tseng Tsze (Tseng Tze; Tseng Tzu):
  85, 101, 105
Tseu, Augustinus A.: 301
Tsian, T. F.: 66-67
T'sin Che Huang Ti, Emperor: 96
Tso-k'ew Ming: 101
Tsung Ts'an: 100
Tsze-chang: 84
Tsze-kung: 101
Tsze-loo: 102

Tucci, Giuseppe: 177
Tu Fu: 69, 71, 94, 290
Tung-lin group: 282-83
turtledove: 190
tyranny: 116; economic: 239
tyrants: 145
tzu, concept of: 153, 156
Tzu-kung: 141
Tzu Ssu: 93, 103, 109, 112

unconscious, collective: 176
understanding: 211; clarification of: 197
unfiliality: 158
uniformity: 233, 301
unity: 95, 142, 145; in society: 223; mystic: 109; of creation: 126; of *Tao*: 141; perfect: 150
universe, center of: 234; man in: 208; reality of: 109
universalism, aspiration to: 97
unknowing: 136
Upanishads: 92
upheaval, cultural: 302; political: 302; technological: 249
upright: 103
uselessness: 146

vacancy, absolute: 149
validity, spiritual: 253
Valignano, Alexandro: 258
valley, awakening of: 244; spirit of: 136
value(s): 114; Confucian: 280; ethical: 228; humane: 279; in oriental thought: 284; of culture: 279; of self: 236, 304; of society: 279; religious: 186-87
Van Bruyn, Marcella, OSB: 175
vases, Greek: 86; Shu: 86
Vatican Council, Second: 51, 279
Vedas: 92
Verwilghen, Albert: 75, 78, 244
Vietnam: 237, 240, 262
viewpoint, monastic: 174
village: 96

Vinciguerra, Thomas: 268
violence: 113, 144, 241, 246, 249
virtue(s) *(te)*: 81, 84, 100-102, 107, 145-46, 151, 156, 161, 202; basic: xxix, 99, 274; cardinal: 171; Confucian: xxi, xxix, 97, 99-100, 112, 171-75, 217, 274; constant: 137; cultivation of: 104; deriding: 160; display of: 139; foundation of: 156; haphazard: 150; highest: 159; illustrious: 103; man of: 82; mandala of: 172; monastic: 202; most important: 158; mystic: 137; natural: 147; of heaven: 149; of reality: 218; perfect: 82-83, 102, 147; possession of: 159; practice of: 159; principles of: 110; source of: 100; vast: 136
virtuousness: 102
vision, modes of: 168; power of: 147
vows, monastic: xxi-xxii
vulnerability, ecological: 249

Wagner, Eusebius, OCSO: 32-33
Waley, Arthur: xx, xxviii, 112-15, 120-21, 123-25, 128-30, 140-41, 143-46, 154, 221, 223, 244, 246, 281, 285, 291, 300-301
Wang An Shih: 130
Wang Gung-Hsing: 301
Wang Pi: 195-96
Wang Tai: 146
Wang Wei: 94
Wang Yang-ming: 7, 34-35, 37, 39, 41, 94, 132, 283; closeness to Zen of: 132; latent Buddhism of: 39
war: 26, 129, 240, 246, 248-49, 254, 269; aggressive: 303; Christian attitude to: 26-27; civil: 260-61; cold: 26, 233, 242, 248; righteous: 120; Vietnam: 237
warlords, unscrupulous: 133
wastefulness: 123
water *(shui)*: 96, 101, 106, 136, 138, 197; gods of: 96; in paintings: 200-201; pleasure in: 82; running:

146; source of: 200-201; sweet: 151

waterfalls, in paintings: 200

Watson, Burton: xix, 7, 84, 103, 281, 301

way, nature of: 112; of action: 274; of heaven: 109, 138, 148; of human life: 274; of life: 155, 290; of man: 109, 148; of purity: 145; power of: 141; right: 155, 158-59; vital: 155

weak: 122, 301

weakness, strength of: 134

wealth: 82; American: 237

weariness: 149

Wei, king of: 144

Wei-ming, Tu: 227

well, of sweet water: 151; parable of: 113

well-field system: 114, 127

wen: 98

Wen, Emperor: 93

Wen, King: 93, 122

Wen Hui, cook of: 141, 143

West: 215; activism of: 216; contemporary: 229; violence of: 216

whole, great: 183

wholeness: 138, 180-85, 230; Confucian: 178; human: 176; idea of: 180-81; in Christ: 178; of being: 225; of life: 221, 234; pattern of: 180; perception of: 289; preordained: 218; restoration of: xxiii; search for: 216; seeds of: 218; spiritual: 177; structure of: 177; symbolic: 177; way of: 141, 145

wickedness: 84, 102, 162

willfulness: 246

Wilhelm, Helmut: xix, 98-99, 281

will, free: 188; good: 218; of God: 202, 303; of heaven: 122, 287

wind: 103, 196-97, 247

wisdom (*chih*): xxix, 9, 99, 102, 106, 113, 124, 131, 139, 145-46, 149, 151, 171-72, 174-75, 177, 179, 203, 217, 237, 245, 274, 285,

288; archaic: xxix, 276; Asian: 276; Chinese: xxix, 95; Christian: 50; Confucian: 217; Confucianism as source of: 272; delight in: 147; divine: 111; Eastern: xxiv, 289; higher: 241; increase of: 197; non-Christian: 179; of ancients: 92, 282; of cross: 178; of divine child: 245; of God: 161, 178-79, 289; oriental: xiii; oriented to action: 286; oriented to contemplation: 286; political: 233; presence of: 284; religious: xxix, 276; self-conscious: 135; silent: 216; spiritual: 290; true: 232; Western: 20

witches: 126

wives: 161

Wolff, Helen: 56

women, emancipation of: 133; subjection of: 133

wood, uncarved: 145

woods, effect of: 245; value of: 212

word(s) (*yen*): 106, 226; creative: 126; fidelity to: 110, 162; transparent: 231; true: 231; well-chosen: 156

work(s) (*yung*): 108; detached: 148; good: 96; hard: 122, 128; of earth: 211-12; of heaven: 211-12

world: 181, 301; corrupt: 255; exterior: 195; god of this: 190; human: 245; interior: 195, 290; modern: 254; natural: 245; return to: 243; salvation of xxix, 291; turning: 181, 289

worldview, Christian: 282

worship: 177; ancestor: 234, 257; devotional: 254, 268

worthy, exaltation of: 121; zeal of: 121

writing(s) (*shu*): 98; Legalist: 256; Taoist (Daoist): 256

wrong: 142-43, 170; standards of: 129

Wu, Agnes: 77, 80

Wu, Emperor: 93, 232

Wu, King: 93, 122

Wu, John C. H.: xv, xvii-xviii, xx, xxiii, xxviii, 4, 6, 8-12, 14-16, 18, 20, 22, 25, 30-32, 36-37, 44-45, 53, 59, 63-65, 67, 69, 71-72, 74, 76-80, 202, 216, 226-27, 233, 274-75, 283, 296-97, 299; marriage of: 77-78, 80; visit to Gethsemani of: 37, 39, 41; WORKS: *Beyond East and West*: 216; *Chinese Humanism and Christian Spirituality*: 69, 72, 231-32; *Chinese Mind*: 233; *Four Seasons of T'ang Poetry*: 59, 71-72; *Golden Age of Zen*: 64, 72, 76, 78, 80; *Joy in Chinese Philosophy*: 299; *Sun Yat-sen: The Man and His Ideas*: 74

Wu, John, Jr.: xxiii-xxiv, 4, 76, 215-36, 272

Wu, Teresa: 219

wu wei: 125, 135-36, 141

yang: 85, 136, 199; active: 288

Yang Chu: 112, 123, 160; hedonism of: 160; philosophy of evasion of: 160; sensualism of: 160

yao tao: 155

Yao, King: 104, 122, 128

Yen Yüan: 132

yi: 99, 113, 171-72, 177, 288-89

yin: 85, 136, 199; passive: 288

Yin Wen: 144

Yoder, John Howard: 249

yoga: 92, 114

yü: 143

Yü, King: 120, 122

Yü, Lord of: 150

Yu Pin, Cardinal Paul: 79, 296-97

Yutang, Lin: xx, 134-35, 137-38, 154

zebras: 168

Zen: 6, 23, 43, 53, 96-97, 252, 266, 290; as combining Buddhism and Taoism: 153, 278; as revolt of interior conscience: 96; as school of individualism: 89; Northern School of: 52; Southern School of: 52; study of: 56

About the Editor

Patrick F. O'Connell, a founding member and former president of the International Thomas Merton Society, edits the ITMS quarterly publication *The Merton Seasonal* and is co-author with Christine M. Bochen and William H. Shannon of *The Thomas Merton Encyclopedia* (Orbis, 2002). He has edited thirteen volumes of Thomas Merton's writings, including *Selected Essays* (Orbis, 2012), *Early Essays, 1947-52* (Cistercian, 2015), *Cistercian Fathers and Forefathers* (New City, 2018), nine volumes of the Initiation into the Monastic Tradition series of Merton's monastic conferences (Cistercian, 2005-2019), and most recently *A Monastic Introduction to Sacred Scripture* (Cascade, 2020), the first of three volumes in the series of Merton's Novitiate Conferences on Scripture and Liturgy.